The Power of Power Politics

John A. Vasquez

The Power
of Power Politics

A Critique

Rutgers University Press
New Brunswick, New Jersey

Library of Congress Cataloging in Publication Data

Vasquez, John A., 1945–
  The power of power politics.

  Bibliography: p.
  Includes index.
  1. International relations—Research.
  2. Balance of power—Research. I. Title.
JX1291.V38   327'.072   81–5849
ISBN 0–8135–0919–X   AACR2

For Barbara
Some things, although understood,
still passeth all understanding.

Contents

Chapter 1
The Role of Paradigms in Scientific Inquiry:
A Conceptual Framework and a
Set of Principles for Paradigm Evaluation
Defining the Concept of Paradigm / *Describing Scientific Inquiry /*
Evaluating Scientific Inquiry
1

Chapter 2
The Role of the Realist Paradigm in the Development of a
Scientific Study of International Relations
The Idealist Phase / The Realist Tradition / The Realist Tradition
and the Behavioral Revolt / Conclusion
13

Chapter 3
Research Design:
Defining and Operationalizing the Realist Paradigm
Deriving Propositions / Defining the Realist Paradigm /
Operationalizing the Realist Paradigm
24

Chapter 4
Theory Construction As a Paradigm-Directed Activity
Introduction / Preliminary Empirical Tests / Continuity and Change in the
Intellectual Development of the Field: An Interpretive Review
of the Literature / Conclusion
38

Contents

Figures

Tables

Preface

This book is concerned with two aspects of the power of power politics. The first deals with the ability of power politics perspectives to dominate the field of international relations inquiry; that is, to guide and direct the theory and research of most of the practitioners of the discipline. The second deals with the ability of power politics to explain phenomena adequately. Although power politics can be found as far back as the ancient civilizations of Greece, India, and China, this analysis will deal only with its twentieth-century manifestation, the realist paradigm. This book will seek to demonstrate two controversial claims: that the realist paradigm has dominated the field of international relations since the early fifties, and that this paradigm has not been very successful in explaining behavior.

The analysis has a descriptive and an evaluative component. In its descriptive section it will demonstrate empirically that the realist paradigm has indeed dominated the field. This will be accomplished by showing that the paradigm has guided theory construction, data making, and research. In its evaluative section it will demonstrate that the realist paradigm has been a scientifically inadequate approach for explaining behavior in international relations. This will be accomplished by applying criteria of adequacy for paradigm and theory evaluation developed by various philosophers of science. The major criterion to be employed is that paradigms, in order to be adequate, must produce significant findings after a reasonable period of time and research.

The analysis presented here is important for two reasons. First, the descriptive component, in providing a sketch of the research agenda of the field and a report on how systematically that agenda is being followed, allows practitioners and students of the discipline to form a gestalt out of the welter of events occurring in the field. As the number of scholars and their output increase within a field, communication becomes a problem because of information overload. In order to deal with that problem, part of the scholarly effort of any discipline must be devoted to describing the activities of other scholars. Consequently, in any discipline there can always be found bibliographies, abstracts, book reviews, inventories, and overviews.[1] The descriptive component of this

1. Recent examples of such work are Dougherty and Pfaltzgraff (1971); Jones and Singer (1972); Porter (1972); Alker and Bock (1972); McGowan and Shapiro (1974); Greenstein and Polsby (1975); Zinnes (1976); and Taylor (1978b).

book stems from this tradition. What differentiates the description reported herein from other recent efforts is that it attempts to delineate long-term trends by the use of quantitative analysis. Second, the analysis is important because the evaluative component provides practitioners and students with a review of what hypotheses have been statistically tested, what findings have been produced, and how useful certain fundamental conceptions of international relations are for explaining behavior scientifically. It will be demonstrated in the descriptive component that most scholars in the field share a fundamental view of the world that was promulgated by the realist scholars. If this view is indeed pervasive, then it is extremely important to assess its scientific utility. One of the fundamental principles of the scientific method is that theories should be tested against empirical evidence and in light of that evidence either be rejected, reformulated, or accepted. By reviewing tests of hypotheses that have been made, the evaluative component provides the evidence and analysis required by that scientific principle.

This evaluation is particularly important now because there has been no systematic attempt to evaluate the adequacy of the realist paradigm in light of the extensive quantitative research that has been conducted.[2] It has been over thirty years since the publication of Morgenthau's *Politics Among Nations* (1948), and at least twenty-five since the publication of the first article attempting to test statistically an explanatory hypothesis about international relations (Deutsch 1956).[3] It would appear that this amount of time has been sufficient to produce enough evidence on the adequacy of the realist paradigm to warrant review, but not so much evidence that a review would be unmanageable.

The scope of this analysis is limited by two parameters. First, only empirical and nomothetic work—that is, work concerned with constructing highly general and scientific theories of international relations behavior—will be systematically reviewed. Work that is primarily devoted to normative concerns, such as policy prescriptions, or to idiographic analysis, such as historical descriptions, will not be reviewed unless it bears directly on a nomothetic work. Second, the analysis is intended to apply only to the United States branch of the field of international relations. Scientific work outside the United States is only referred to

2. There have of course been numerous conceptual critiques of Morgenthau's work. Typical of the best of this work are Tucker (1952); Claude (1962); and E. B. Haas (1953). There have also been tests of specific propositions; see J. D. Singer, Bremer, and Stuckey (1972); and J. D. Singer (1980).

3. Jones and Singer (1972:vii) list Deutsch (1956) as the earliest data-based correlational/explanatory article in the field of international relations. They do not include such forerunners of the quantitative movement as Lewis Richardson.

when it has had a major impact on the development of the field within the United States.

In order to substantiate its claims, the analysis will be organized along the following lines. In chapter 1, a conceptual framework that can be used to describe and evaluate scholars' activities will be developed. The concept of a *paradigm* will be defined and its utility demonstrated. An empirical theory of how scientific inquiry is conducted, most notably associated with the work of Thomas Kuhn, will be outlined. Finally, a set of principles that can be used to evaluate the adequacy of paradigms will be presented and justified. Chapter 2 will employ the conceptual framework presented in chapter 1 to interpret the activities of international relations scholars. An historical theory of the role the realist paradigm played in international relations inquiry will be elaborated. In chapter 3, the realist paradigm will be defined and operationalized. The propositions crucial to the claims of the analysis will be specified and a justification of the research design of the book presented. Chapters 4 through 6 will test the proposition that the realist paradigm has dominated international relations inquiry. Chapter 4 will test the proposition that the realist paradigm has guided the theory-construction activities of scholars. Chapter 5 will test the proposition that the realist paradigm has directed the data-making efforts of scholars. Chapter 6 will test the proposition that the realist paradigm has guided the quantitative research of scholars. Chapter 7 will provide a data-based evaluation of the adequacy of the realist paradigm in light of the statistical findings it produced in the fifties and sixties. Chapter 8 will supplement this synoptic analysis with an in-depth review of two of the major areas of research in the 1970s, foreign policy and war, to identify the main anomalies that have emerged to undercut the fundamental assumptions of the paradigm.

Acknowledgments

A scholar's first book often begins as a doctoral dissertation, and that is the case with this work. Of the many people who have aided me a special place must be reserved for Bill Coplin, my dissertation adviser, who inspired the topic and encouraged me to investigate its feasibility. Without his steadfast support and intellectual stimulation, the dissertation, which gave rise to this book, could not have been written. Several other persons have aided me. Michael K. O'Leary, with whom I collaborated in an earlier critique of the realist paradigm, provided important guidance in making this a scholarly work. After the dissertation was completed, J. David Singer and Harold Guetzkow, although they hardly agree with all that is presented here, provided aid and encouragement in getting the work published and offered a number of specific criticisms that saved me from several errors. Marie T. Henehan, both student and friend, proved invaluable in discussing revisions and in preparing the manuscript for publication, often taking more care and showing more concern for the finished product than did I, and working down to the wire at great personal sacrifice. Diane Wallace and Diane Swartz respectively typed the initial and final drafts of the manuscript with care and patience. Finally, the Syracuse University International Relations Program provided financial assistance for the data collection, and the Rutgers University Research Council provided funds for reviewing research published in the 1970s and for typing the manuscript.

A number of other individuals, although they have not directly assisted me in this book, have had such a profound influence on my development that they deserve mention. Fred Frohock first introduced me to the writings of Thomas Kuhn and to philosophy of science. Frank Nevers and Raymond Duncan first introduced me to the realist paradigm. Howard Zinn shattered the hold the realist paradigm had had on my early conception of politics, and in doing so provided me with a critical perspective on both scientific theory and national policy. Finally, a note of thanks to my sister, Margie, who got me through some difficult times in 1976–1977. Although all of the above have influenced me, I have not always heeded their instruction; therefore the final responsibility for this work is my own.

Of all the people who helped me throughout the years of my graduate education, the most important was Barbara Vasquez. She gave as much of her life to this work as I did my own. When I entered graduate school she left a highly rewarding position to come with me. Without her at my side I could never have finished. To her I dedicate this work with love for the time together and sorrow for the time wasted. εὐχαρίστω.

The Power of Power Politics

The Role of Paradigms in Scientific Inquiry: A Conceptual Framework and a Set of Principles for Paradigm Evaluation

The work of Thomas Kuhn (1962; 1970a) has attracted much interest from historians and philosophers of science because it offers a way to describe and evaluate scientific inquiry. For this reason it provides a framework for determining whether the realist paradigm has adequately guided inquiry in international relations. Before the framework can be applied, a number of questions that have been raised by critics of Kuhn must be addressed.[1] The three most important are: how to define *paradigm*; whether Kuhn's description of scientific change is correct; and how paradigms can be evaluated. Each of these will be examined in this chapter.

Defining the Concept of *Paradigm*

Despite its wide use, the paradigm concept remains very difficult to define. The reason for this stems from its original usage by Thomas Kuhn in *The Structure of Scientific Revolutions* (1962). A textual analysis of that work by Margaret Masterman (1970) has shown that the concept, *paradigm*, was used by Kuhn in at least twenty-one different ways. In the postscript to the second edition of the book, Kuhn (1970a: 174–191) recognized this criticism and attempted to clarify the definition. He maintains that most of the varying usage is due to stylistic inconsistencies but concedes that even after these inconsistencies are removed, the concept is used in two distinct ways:

> On the one hand, it stands for the entire constellation of beliefs, values, techniques, and so on shared by the members of a given community. On the other, it denotes one sort of element in that

1. For a criticism of work in political science that has failed to take note of Kuhn's different definitions see J. Stephens (1973).

constellation, the concrete puzzle-solutions which, employed as models or examples, can replace explicit rules as a basis for the solution of the remaining puzzles of normal science [Kuhn 1970a: 175].

The first definition is what Kuhn (1970a:181) has called "the constellation of group commitments." In this first definition, it is the shared constellation which is the basis of classifying an aggregate of scholars as a community (Kuhn 1970a:176–178, 182). Kuhn (1970a:182; 1971:462–463; 1977:xvi–xxiii) has suggested that this use of the concept *paradigm* may be too broad in scope to support the central thesis of his book. He has therefore chosen to call this notion of paradigm a *disciplinary matrix*, the chief components of which are: (1) symbolic or theoretical generalizations, such as $f = ma$; (2) metaphysical beliefs or beliefs in certain models, such as heat is kinetic energy of the constituent parts of bodies; (3) values, such as predictions should be accurate, what constitutes accuracy, what is inconsistency, what is plausibility, what is parsimonious, etc.; (4) an exemplar, which is the element in the disciplinary matrix that by itself forms the second definition of paradigm (Kuhn 1970a:184–186; 1971:464).

The second definition is what Kuhn (1970a:187) has called the *paradigm as exemplar*, or *shared example*. In order to understand what an exemplar is and why it has such force within a scholarly community, it is necessary to examine how future professionals of a discipline are educated. According to Kuhn (1970a:187–189) scientific education involves primarily "problem-solving." Problem solving is a central component of scientific education in two ways. First, the ability to solve new problems is the primary educational objective of scientific training. Second, the basic means of achieving this objective is to have students solve problems to which the correct answers are already known. The assumption behind this philosophy of education is that if students are capable of arriving at the correct solution to old but difficult problems, they will acquire the ability to solve current and new problems. According to Kuhn (1970a:189), these sets of problems function to inculcate the student with a fundamental way of viewing the world (see also Kuhn 1971: 472–482). In addition to providing sets of solved problems, the exemplar is used in scientific education to inform the student about the existing unsolved problems or puzzles in the field. The latter bit of information tells the student what is worth knowing. These sets of problems constitute the concrete manifestation of the exemplar. But the paradigm as exemplar consists not of the problems themselves but of the elements that are used to perceive, define, and solve problems.

Unfortunately, this reformulation of the concept has not satisfied most of Kuhn's critics (see Shapere 1964; 1971; Toulmin 1967; 1970; Watkins 1970). Their original criticisms can be reduced to two points: that the concept is ambiguous in that it refers to so many aspects of the scientific process that his thesis is almost nonfalsifiable; and that it is so vague that it is difficult to identify (in operational terms, for example) the specific paradigm of a discipline (Shapere 1964:385–386). The problem of ambiguity is quite severe. At times it seems that the paradigm concept refers to a set of research questions, the publication of a seminal work that changes inquiry in the field (exemplar), a particular theory, an epistemological viewpoint, or a method of investigation (Masterman 1970: 61–65).

Clearly, focusing on one of these elements while ignoring the others will produce a very different description of a discipline. Kuhn's selection of puzzle solutions attempts both to solve this problem and produce an operational indicator. Yet this notion is not adequate. In any science, there are numerous puzzle solutions, and Kuhn does not provide any criteria for distinguishing among or classifying these solutions. Are puzzle solutions to be defined on the basis of their method, their dependent variables, their independent variables, or their connection to an exemplar? Kuhn does not address these questions adequately, and it is not surprising that, of the original critics (compare Shapere 1964 and 1971; Toulmin 1967 and 1970), none is satisfied with his response.

These conceptual problems have led some of the scholars who have applied Kuhn's concept in describing inquiry within political science to produce very different and sometimes contradictory analyses (cf. Stephens 1973). Lijphart (1974) argues that within international relations behavioralism is a paradigm, whereas Beal (1976) argues that Lijphart places too much emphasis on method and ignores the fact that many quantitative scholars have tested traditional propositions. Lijphart and others such as Wolin (1968), who view behavioralism as a paradigm, see it as the attempt to employ the scientific method to study politics and distinguish this approach from traditional and normative methods. Keohane and Nye (1972) are more concerned with the substantive focus and have argued that international relations is dominated by a state-centric paradigm, whereas Handelman et al. (1973) have argued that a realist paradigm has dominated the field. While Keohane and Nye (1974; 1977) have more recently spoken of the realist rather than the state-centric paradigm, others, for example Ashley (1976), have argued that international relations is in a pre-paradigm stage, and that there are many different conceptual approaches and "theories" in the discipline (see also Alker 1971). Such disagreements are primarily a function of emphasizing different aspects of Kuhn's conception of paradigm.

If Kuhn's concept and his subsequent analysis are to be employed, they must be defined more precisely, and procedures must be established for operationalizing them. Since Kuhn has not adequately resolved these problems, this analysis must provide its own stipulative definition. Stipulative definitions are neither correct nor incorrect, since they are not empirical statements (see Ayer 1946; Wilson 1956); rather, they can be evaluated on the basis of their ability to conceptualize a set of phenomena in a way that clarifies rather than obscures relationships. In this sense, the most useful stipulative definition of *paradigm* is one that can utilize most of Kuhn's insights and provide an adequate account of how science proceeds.

To provide such a definition, it is important to stipulate what is not a paradigm. A paradigm is neither a method nor a theory. In the first instance, the scientific method and its various modes of testing (experimentation, simulation, statistical analysis, comparative case studies) cannot constitute a paradigm in any Kuhnian sense, because all the physical sciences share this method and would be dominated by a single paradigm. Clearly, Kuhn is not interested in the shared elements of the

Figure 1.1. The Analytical Relationship among Paradigms, Concepts, Propositions, and Theories

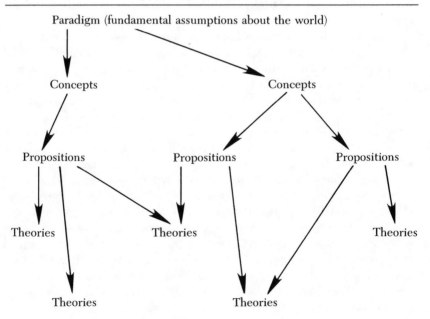

physical sciences, but in what makes them individual and coherent disciplines.

The heart of the paradigm concept must be substantive and not methodological, but a paradigm is not necessarily the same thing as a dominant theory. First, there can often be more than one theory in a field or shifts in accepted theories without producing what Kuhn would call a paradigm shift. Second, a paradigm is in some sense prior to theory. It is what gives rise to theories in the first place. Toulmin (1967) in particular is intrigued by the question of what exists in a field when there is no theory (a question certainly relevant to international relations inquiry), and suggests that Collingwood's (1940) notion of absolute presuppositions serves the same function as Kuhn's notion of paradigm.

The concept of *paradigm*, then, could be stipulatively defined as *the fundamental assumptions scholars make about the world they are studying*. These assumptions provide answers to the questions that must be addressed before theorizing even begins. For Kuhn, as Masterman (1970:62) points out, such questions are: What are the fundamental units of which the world is composed? How do these units interact with each other? What interesting questions may be asked about these units? What kinds of conceptions will provide answers to these inquiries? By responding to these questions, the fundamental assumptions form a picture of the world the scholar is studying and tell the scholar *what is known about the world, what is unknown about it, how one should view the world if one wants to know the unknown, and finally what is worth knowing*.[2]

The preceding definition has been stipulated to distinguish a paradigm from a conceptual framework or theory. To clarify this distinction, figure 1.1 specifies the analytical relationships. A paradigm consists of a set of fundamental assumptions of the world. These assumptions focus the attention of the scholar on certain phenomena and interpret those phenomena via concepts. Propositions, in turn, are developed by specifying relationships between concepts. Finally, theories are developed by specifying relationships between propositions (see Blalock 1969).

2. This stipulative definition differs considerably from the components of a research paradigm that are identified by Alker (1971, reprinted in Ashley 1976: 154). Alker's list is not used here because its requirements are so stringent that only very narrow research efforts, like work on the Richardson arms race model, would be seen as having a paradigm. Ashley (1976:155) is even more restrictive. Such a position comes close to the notion that the paradigm concept should be employed only to distinguish the narrowest scientific community, the invisible college. At times, in his revisions, Kuhn (1971:461–462) comes close to saying

It can also be seen from figure 1.1 that a pyramid effect is in operation. For example, if A, B, C are concepts, the following propositions, among others, can be logically derived:

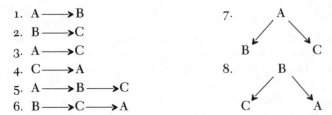

1. A $\longrightarrow$ B
2. B $\longrightarrow$ C
3. A $\longrightarrow$ C
4. C $\longrightarrow$ A
5. A $\longrightarrow$ B $\longrightarrow$ C
6. B $\longrightarrow$ C $\longrightarrow$ A

Likewise, as shown in figure 1.1, a given set of propositions can be linked in different ways to give rise to a variety of theories. Therefore it follows that one paradigm can give rise to more than one theory. On the basis of this analysis, it can be stipulated that a paradigm only changes when its fundamental assumptions or view of the world changes.[3] "New" concepts, propositions, or theories that do not change the assumptions of the paradigm do not constitute new paradigms, but only the elaborations, or what Kuhn (1970a:24, 33–34) calls articulations, of the old one.

One of the main advantages of this stipulative definition is that, by reducing the ambiguity of the term, it does not affect most of Kuhn's propositions about scientific inquiry, yet it specifies clearly the conditions under which paradigms change, thereby permitting Kuhn's thesis to be falsified. Throughout the remainder of this analysis, unless otherwise indicated, whenever the concept *paradigm* is employed, including references to Kuhn's use of the term, it should be thought of in terms of the stipulative definition given here.

---

this, but he recognizes that there are different levels of a scientific community. Each of these in some sense may have its own shared-examples. Clearly, however, classics such as Newton's *Principia* function at the broad disciplinary level and provide an exemplar or paradigm for the disciplinary matrix and not just for the invisible college. As will be seen later, the primary difference between the role of realism in the international relations field and that of other approaches, like decision making or systems, is that some of the fundamental assumptions of realism are shared by most scholars in the discipline, whereas the shared-examples of the other approaches are confined to a narrower group. In this analysis, *paradigm* is defined in a very broad (but not necessarily imprecise) manner. For a recent reconstruction of Kuhn that attempts to delineate how assumptions lead to a picture of the world and then to a research program, see Tornebohm (1976). For an attempt to delineate invisible colleges within international relations, see Russett (1970a).

3. This statement agrees with Kuhn (1970a:chap. 10, "Revolutions as Changes of World View").

Describing Scientific Inquiry

The utility of the paradigm concept can be demonstrated by showing how Kuhn uses the concept to describe scientific inquiry. Kuhn's description is concerned with how paradigms dominate a field and how they are displaced. A dominant paradigm is usually provided by a single work, which is viewed as so unprecedented in its achievement that it becomes an exemplar of scientific analysis in a particular field:

> Aristotle's *Physica*, Ptolemy's *Almagest*, Newton's *Principia* . . . these and many other works served for a time implicitly to define the legitimate problems and method of a research field for succeeding generations of practitioners. They were able to do so because they shared two essential characteristics. Their achievement was sufficiently unprecedented to attract an enduring group of adherents away from competing modes of scientific activity. Simultaneously it was sufficiently open-ended to leave all sorts of problems for the redefined group of practitioners to resolve [Kuhn 1970a:10].

Once a paradigm dominates a field, scholarship enters the stage Kuhn (1970a:10, 23–25) calls *normal science*. Scholarly behavior in this stage is characterized by extensive articulation of the paradigm by a research program that guides the theory construction, fact gathering, and research of scholars (Kuhn 1970a:34). Theory construction in normal science is not haphazard, but highly systematic because the paradigm constrains scholars to the elaboration of theories that do not violate the fundamental assumptions of the paradigm (Kuhn 1970a:24).

In addition to suggesting what are legitimate theories, the paradigm also suggests what, out of the welter of phenomena, are theoretically significant facts (Kuhn 1970a:25). Much of normal science consists of gathering these facts. Before "facts" can be gathered, however, scientists must create tools that will permit the facts to be measured, just as the thermometer had to be invented in order to observe and measure heat. Finally, having gathered the facts, the theory is tested by matching it with the facts. After the tests, the theory is further elaborated and refined.

Theory construction, fact gathering, and research, then, are systematically linked through a feedback process. This does not mean that there will not be drastic changes in theories. There will be, as theories are tested, but any "new" theories will never violate the assumptions of the paradigm (Kuhn 1970a:33–34). When a truly new theory emerges, it signals the existence of a new paradigm(s) and may under certain conditions result in what Kuhn (1970a:52–53) calls *scientific crisis and revolution*.

Normal science begins to come to an end when an anomaly—"the recognition that nature has somehow violated the paradigm-induced expectations"—is unable to be removed by paradigm articulation (Kuhn 1970a:52–53). The persistence of the anomaly(ies) results in a crisis in the field. Crisis is met by devising "numerous articulations and ad hoc modifications of . . . theory in order to eliminate any conflict" between fact and theory (Kuhn 1970a:78). However, if the anomaly can be accounted for only by seeing the world in a new and different way (i.e., by the creation of a new paradigm), then the stage is set for a struggle between the adherents of the competing paradigms (Kuhn 1970a:53, chap. 10). If the struggle results in the displacement of the old paradigm and the dominance of the new paradigm, then this period is viewed with hindsight as a period of scientific discovery and revolution. New textbooks rewrite the history of the field, students are trained to see the world according to the new paradigm, and the process repeats itself.

Some critics (Shapere 1971:706; Toulmin 1970:41) have questioned this description of scientific inquiry by challenging the sharp distinction between normal science and revolutionary science (what might be better termed extraordinary science [see Kuhn 1970a:34]), arguing that the distinction is really a matter of degree and that such discontinuities are not as common as Kuhn implies. This criticism underlines the more general point that within paradigms there can be considerable variation and disagreement, and out of this process there can evolve what Kuhn would call revolutions. For Toulmin, these "revolutions" tend to be a product of many earlier changes; he therefore finds the process of change described by Kuhn incomplete because it does not explain how knowledge evolves through learning (1967:339–346; 1970:46). Blachowicz (1971: 182–183; 186–188) goes further, arguing that Kuhn so underestimates the amount of learning and changes that he must see theories as arising from a random process.

Kuhn has in part responded to the criticism by granting that there might be microrevolutions, but he is unwilling to abandon the more fundamental distinction between normal and revolutionary science and insists that normal science can involve considerable conceptual jettisoning without any rejection of the paradigm (see Kuhn 1970b:249–259; 1970a:250). He thereby rejects the more evolutionary notion of progress implied by Toulmin, maintaining instead that only certain anomalies and conceptual changes are revolutionary. Paradigm shifts, not variation and microrevolutions, bring about fundamental changes in thought.

These criticisms of Kuhn are primarily empirical and can only be answered by further research. It must be remembered that Kuhn's thesis is based on generalizing from his earlier work on the Copernican revolution (Kuhn 1957) and may not in fact apply to all other cases, as some have readily pointed out in the case of theories of matter (Shapere

1964:387; Popper 1970:55; Watkins 1970:34). Yet one exception is hardly a disconfirmation. Kuhn's thesis needs systematic investigation in the physical sciences and should not be seen as having been "confirmed" or refuted by the discussion it has generated (L. P. Williams 1970:50).

Keeping in mind the various qualifications and caveats that have been introduced, it should be clear that Kuhn provides a theoretically interesting and general conceptual framework for describing scientific inquiry. For international relations inquiry it suggests questions such as: Is the field dominated by a single paradigm? What is that paradigm? How did it displace the old one if there was an old paradigm? How does it guide theory construction, data making, and research? How do conceptual variation and change occur yet still remain within the paradigm? More important, Kuhn's framework provides a way of asking the major questions of this analysis—Is the dominant paradigm adequate? Is it producing knowledge? Before these last two questions can be addressed, a set of criteria for evaluating paradigms must be developed. Here Kuhn provides little aid.

Evaluating Scientific Inquiry

Evaluation differs from description in that its purpose is to apply a value criterion to a situation or object, whereas the purpose of description is empirical veracity.[4] Therefore, in order to evaluate scientific inquiry, some acceptable value criteria must be employed. Philosophers of science have spent a great deal of time attempting to delineate and justify such criteria. Although there are many disagreements among these philosophers, there is a certain minimal content on which they all agree. Part of this content includes a set of criteria for evaluating theories. Although there is dispute over the logical status of these criteria, there is not a dispute either among philosophers or practicing scientists about what these criteria actually state (see Braybrooke and Rosenberg 1972). It is upon this basis that criteria for evaluating paradigms can be erected.

The main criteria that these scholars accept rest on the assumption that science can produce knowledge. Part of Kuhn's analysis, however, led to a debate in philosophy of science over whether science is a rational enterprise that can claim to be producing knowledge. The part of Kuhn's analysis that caused the debate was his discussion of paradigm comparability and displacement. Kuhn appeared to argue that para-

---

4. On the differences and similarities of evaluative and empirical analysis see Toulmin (1950); on the relationship between evaluation and value criteria see Urmson (1968:chap. 5) and Frohock (1974:chap. 3); on the purpose of description see R. Brown (1963:chap. 2) and Hempel (1968).

digms were not disproven but discarded on the basis of a struggle for power between the adherents of competing paradigms. Many critics took this argument to mean that Kuhn was maintaining that science was irrational and subjective.[5] In a later work, Kuhn attempted to defend himself by saying that although he maintained that paradigm displacement is a matter of persuasion, he did not mean to suggest "that there are not many good reasons for choosing one theory rather than another. . . . These are, furthermore, reasons of exactly the kind standard in philosophy of science: accuracy, scope, simplicity, fruitfulness, and the like" (Kuhn 1970b:261; see also 1977:320–339). Kuhn (1970a:186) maintained that what makes these reasons good is determined by the value component of the disciplinary matrix. This clarification makes it clear that Kuhn is willing to evaluate paradigms by employing the standard criteria used in science to determine the adequacy of theories. Therefore, the basic criterion that a paradigm must produce knowledge can be employed to evaluate paradigm adequacy. In order to determine exactly how this basic criterion can be applied and to understand what the debate between Kuhn and his critics has been about, it is necessary to review briefly some of the epistemological arguments that have been made about the confirmation of theories.

The earliest respectable view about confirmation was that theories are proven when there are a sufficient number of facts to support them.[6] The basic fallacy of this position is known as *the riddle of induction*. This debate over induction goes back at least to the time of John Stuart Mill. The debate was replayed in the twentieth century when Rudolph Carnap attempted to derive a logical position asserting that hypotheses could be proven.[7] Carnap, however, was unsuccessful in this effort; the consensus of philosophers of science is that such confirmation is impossible to achieve.

Sir Karl Popper (1935) attempted to place confirmation of theories on a firmer logical foundation by introducing the principle of falsification. According to Popper, a theory is a theory only if it specifies in advance what would be accepted as disproof of the theory. Experimentation in Popper's view never proves a theory but simply fails to falsify it. Popper's principle provides a clear, precise, and logically sound rule for evaluating theories. It was not until Kuhn introduced the concept of paradigm that the principle was seriously challenged.

---

5. See Scheffler (1967); Lakatos and Musgrave (1970). Also see Shapere (1964; 1971); Popper (1970); and Shimony (1976).

6. An excellent history of this debate is Lakatos (1970).

7. This is obviously a simplification of Carnap's work. The two books that adequately summarize his early work on this question are Carnap (1952; 1962).

Despite the fact that Kuhn's claim of paradigm incommensurability has been rejected in part because of the work of Scheffler (1967), the challenge to Popper has carried more weight (see Lakatos 1970). Kuhn (1970a:146–148) has attempted to show that Popper's rule is simply not followed in the physical sciences. Theories and the paradigms out of which they arise do not stipulate what will count as falsifying evidence. Furthermore, when falsifying evidence is encountered, it does not lead to a rejection of the paradigm. Finally, according to Kuhn no paradigm has ever been "rejected" unless there is a competing paradigm ready to take its place. Popper's (1970:52–53, 56–58) response is not that this does not occur, but that it need not necessarily occur and will not if scientists are trained properly. What most of the debate has been about, then, is how to confirm competing theories that may emerge from competing paradigms and their research programs.

On what basis can one decide to follow one research program rather than another? Lakatos (1970) has attempted to solve the problem by synthesizing Kuhn's work with the standard view of philosophy of science. He has given a major concession to Kuhn in that he admits that confirmation is a matter of decision and not logic.[8] He comes to this conclusion because he maintains that theories and paradigms can produce an infinite number of plausible ad hoc hypotheses to account for falsifying evidence. Nevertheless, he does think that the decision can be based on rules that are clearly stipulated in advance. Among the most important rules are the following: (1) T' (rival theory) has excess empirical content; that is, it predicts novel experimental outcomes (anomalies) that are improbable or forbidden by T (original theory); (2) T' explains all the unrefuted content of T; and (3) some of the excess content of T' is corroborated (Lakatos 1970:116). Lakatos has thus provided a set of principles that can be used to compare theories. In this scheme, paradigms and their research programs can be evaluated on the basis of the theories they produce.

The philosophical problem over which there is much contention is whether there is some logical foundation for rules that tell scientists when to stop introducing ad hoc explanations or theories, or whether the foundation is merely sociological consensus (see Worrall 1978; Musgrave 1978; Koertge 1978; and Feyerabend 1976). The latter position saves science as a rational enterprise, but whether science can have a more solid logical foundation is a matter of hot debate. At a minimum, the justification of Lakatos's rules could rest on the kind of instrumentalist argument often associated with Toulmin (1953; 1972:478–503).

This justification rests on the acceptance by philosophers of science

8. Some argue that this grants too much to Kuhn; see Musgrave (1976:482).

and scientists of the following type of argument: (1) the purpose of science is to produce knowledge; (2) knowledge itself is a semantic concept; that is, one can determine whether something is known by stipulatively defining what is meant by knowledge and establishing decision-rules on how to employ the word;[9] and (3) what is meant by knowledge (at least in part) is empirical corroboration of hypotheses. A theory or a research program that has the most corroborated hypotheses and the least anomalies is obviously the best or the most promising one to use in order to achieve the purpose of science.

In social science, particularly in international relations inquiry, the problem of evaluating paradigms turns not so much on comparing the corroborated empirical content of rival theories and their research program but on finding any theory with a corroborated content of any significance. Since a paradigm is used to produce theories, it is possible to evaluate the adequacy of a paradigm in terms of the corroborated hypotheses it produces. This is the basic criterion that will be used here to evaluate paradigms. However, as Lakatos suggests, applying this criterion is a matter of decision. How many corroborated hypotheses must there be? How much paradigm-directed research must there be, and for how long must this research continue before a paradigm can be declared inadequate? All of these are unanswered questions in the field of international relations. But it does seem reasonable to assume that if various theories and hypotheses produced by the use of a paradigm fail over time to produce a significant number of findings, the problem may very well be that the picture of the world being used by scholars is simply inadequate. If the science of international relations is to be systematic, it is incumbent upon scholars to examine periodically what paradigm (if any) is dominating the field and to evaluate its usefulness in the terms outlined. In a discipline where there are very few corroborated hypotheses, there will always be disagreements over whether a paradigm and its research program are useful. But attempts at evaluation are important because they provide empirical evidence that scholars can use to come to a rational conclusion. As more research is conducted and more evaluations of it are made, a trend may become clear and the disagreements will probably subside. It is in this spirit that the present evaluation is offered.

9. For a justification for this position in regard to the word *truth* see Tarski (1949).

Chapter 2

The Role of the Realist Paradigm in the Development of a Scientific Study of International Relations

Kuhn's analysis implies that a proper understanding of the historical development of any science involves identifying the rise of a paradigm and how it is displaced. In this chapter, a historical interpretation of how the scientific study of international relations is conducted will be offered by drawing on a number of Kuhn's insights. Although the study of international relations can be said to go back at least to the time of Thucydides, the starting date of this analysis will be the formal creation of international relations inquiry as an institutionalized discipline. This is commonly taken to have occurred in 1919, with the creation of "the world's first Chair in International Politics . . . at the University College of Wales, Aberystwyth" (Porter 1972:ix).[1]

In the interpretation, emphasis will be placed on delineating the role the realist paradigm has played in international relations inquiry, and the relationship between that paradigm and idealism and the behavioral revolt. The resulting analysis shows how the idealist paradigm helped institutionalize the discipline and instill it with purpose, how the anomaly of World War II led to the displacement of the idealist paradigm and to the dominance of the realist paradigm, and how the behavioral revolt did not change the paradigm of the field but provided a conception of scientific methodology. Only historical examples will be given here to demonstrate the plausibility of the interpretation, but systematic evidence will be presented in chapters 4 through 6.

The Idealist Phase

The twentieth-century history of international relations inquiry can be roughly divided into three stages: the idealist phase; the realist tradition; and the "behavioral" revolt (see Bull 1972:33). The first stage of interna-

1. See Morgenthau and Thompson (1950:3); W. Olson (1972:12) and Kirk (1947:2–5) for similar justifications.

tional relations inquiry was dominated by the idealist paradigm.[2] The immediate origins of this paradigm stemmed from the experience of the First World War and the belief that such a conflagration could and must be avoided in the future (Kirk 1947:3–4; Fox 1949:68). Its fundamental belief was that by using reason, humans could overcome such problems as war (Carr 1939 [1964:25–27]; Dunn 1949:81). All humans were seen as having a common interest that formed a "nascent world community" (Wolfers 1951 [1962:86]). Given a basic harmony of interest among all people, a system of peace could be established under the proper conditions. The scholar's purpose was to reveal this fundamental truth and to delineate those conditions so that it would be possible to establish a set of institutions that by their very structure would force nations to act peacefully and thereby cause a revolution in the way international politics was conducted (Carr 1939 [1964:27–31]).

The best-known intellectual force behind this paradigm was, of course, Woodrow Wilson, and his specific theory of democracy as the cause of peace and dictatorship as the cause of war formed the heart of the paradigm.[3] According to this theory, the masses never benefit from war, and with proper enlightenment they will realize this. Through education and contact with others, ignorance and prejudice would be eliminated. Through the spread of democracy, the masses would prevent sinister interests from promulgating wars. Finally, the institutions that prevented violence at the domestic level could be created at the global level to resolve disputes nonviolently.[4] These ideas were embodied in the League of Nations, the Permanent Court of International Justice, and in the emphasis on international law, arbitration, disarmament, collective security, and peaceful change (Fox 1949:74–75). Together, these theory-laden beliefs constituted a research program for idealist scholars.

Wilson's ideas were widely shared by others in the United Kingdom and the United States and adopted by a group of scholars whose conscious purpose was the investigation of the major tenets of the paradigm in order to better promote its normative goals. They attempted to create an analytical model of a system characterized by peace and then to show how the present world system deviated from that model (Fox 1949:77;

2. The terms *idealists* and *utopians* were never used by those scholars who were guided by the paradigm. It was applied to them by the realists, particularly by E. H. Carr (1939).

3. Carr (1939 [1964:8, 14, 27, 32–38]); Wolfers (1962:81–82, 234); Kirk (1947:3); Fox (1949:68–77); Dougherty and Pfaltzgraff (1971:6–7). For a general review of the sources of the paradigm see Carr (1939 [1964:chap. 2]). For Wilson's theory of democracy see Wolfers (1951 [1962:86]); and Waltz (1959:110–123).

4. For documentation on the role of education, contact, democracy, and global institutions in idealist thought see Fox (1949:70) and Bull (1972:34).

Dunn 1949:93). Among the major scholars sharing this paradigm were Alfred Zimmern, S. H. Bailey, Philip Noel-Baker, and David Mitrany of the United Kingdom and James T. Shotwell, Pitman Potter, and Parker T. Moon of the United States (Bull 1972:34).

Inquiry under this paradigm was of two kinds: historical and legal-institutional. The historical aspect at times emphasized the "mistakes" of history in the hope that rational knowledge of these mistakes would prevent their reoccurrence. James Bryce's *International Relations* (1922) was one of the popular texts of the time and reflected this historical emphasis (Fox 1949:75–76; W. Olson 1972:19). Knowledge of the past was only part of the answer to the problem of peace. If history provided a negative example, the study of international organization was to provide the positive example. Since the idealist paradigm guided scholars toward a normative and prescriptive analysis, the study of international organization consisted of the role international institutions should and could play in establishing an era of peace (Kirk 1947:4–5). The best reflection of this view was Alfred Zimmern's *The League of Nations and the Rule of Law* (1936).[5] The dominance of the paradigm is reflected by the fact that the two most popular approaches to teaching international politics in the United States during the interwar period were current events and diplomatic history and international law and organization (Thompson 1952). In addition, there was a strong emphasis on interdisciplinary study, including anthropology, sociology, economics, demography, geography, law, psychology, and even animal behavior (see Kirk 1947:14–21).

The idealist phase was important in terms of institutionalizing the field and creating the emphasis on peace and war. The idealist phase reflects characteristics of many of the early forerunners of a scientific discipline—for example, alchemy. Both idealism and alchemy share the common characteristic of establishing a separate field of inquiry and making the major purpose of that field highly practical and valuable to laymen. In many ways, the purpose of the idealist paradigm was to provide a panacea for the major problem of the early twentieth century —war.

The Realist Tradition

Since the idealists tested their "theories" not in the laboratory but in the real world, by attempting to guide policy, the anomaly that led to a scientific crisis and eventual displacement of the paradigm was the inability of international law and organization to prevent World War II

5. Cited in Bull (1972:35). For a short introduction to the idealist perspective see Alfred Zimmern, "Introductory Report to the Discussions in 1935," in Zimmern (1939:7–13); reprinted in Morgenthau and Thompson (1950:18–24).

(see Kirk 1947:6–7; Fox 1949:67–68). It was the background of the war that made E. H. Carr's *The Twenty Years' Crisis* (1939) a devastating and seminal critique of idealism. He began by calling for a true science of international politics and maintained that in order to have a science, inquiry must take account of how things actually are (i.e., of "reality") and not solely of how things should be (1939 [1964:9]). He stated that it was the idealists' inability to distinguish aspiration from reality that made idealism an inappropriate perspective for either the study or conduct of international politics. Carr maintained that the purpose of realism is to understand and adapt to the forces that guide behavior and warned that such a perspective might lead to a conservative acceptance of the status quo, but that in this stage it was a "necessary corrective to the exuberance of utopianism" (1939 [1964:10; also chap. 6]). He then went on to shatter systematically the "illusions" of the utopians, or idealists, by employing a type of Marxist analysis that became more evident in his later work and by pointing out the need to consider the importance of power in international relations.[6] Carr's work, however, was essentially a critique and offered only the vaguest outline of an alternative picture of the world (see W. Olson 1972:19).

Others besides Carr were reacting to the same events, and it was these other writers along with Carr who began to develop the realist paradigm. These leading writers and their most influential works were: Frederick Schuman, *International Politics* (1933); Harold Nicolson, *Diplomacy* (1939a); E. H. Carr, *The Twenty Years' Crisis* (1939); Reinhold Niebuhr, *Christianity and Power Politics* (1940); Georg Schwarzenberger, *Power Politics* (1941); Nicholas Spykman, *America's Strategy in World Politics* (1942); Martin Wight, *Power Politics* (1946); Hans J. Morgenthau, *Politics Among Nations* (1948); George F. Kennan, *American Diplomacy* (1952); and Herbert Butterfield, *Christianity, Diplomacy and War* (1953).[7]

These writers represent the attempt of an entire generation to understand and express their most fundamental beliefs about international

6. For examples of Marxist influence in Carr's later work see E. H. Carr (1947; 1951); on the importance of power see Carr (1939:chap. 8).

7. This list is taken basically from Bull (1972:38). It agrees fairly closely with the classification of Dougherty and Pfaltzgraff (1971:1–30 and chap. 3). I have taken the liberty of adding Frederick Schuman to the list; W. Olson (1972:19) lists his work as one of the "landmarks" in the field, and Dougherty and Pfaltzgraff (1971:74–75) appropriately classify it as realist. Also, I have substituted Niebuhr's *Christianity and Power Politics* (1940) as the most influential of his realist work for Bull's selection of *The Children of Light and the Children of Darkness* (1945). Because it played a prominent role in debunking utopianism and pacifism in American Protestantism, Niebuhr's early work was more influential. On this

politics. Together they were successful in displacing the idealist paradigm by accounting for the anomaly of World War II in terms of power politics.

Hans J. Morgenthau best expressed, promulgated, and synthesized the work of these writers. Because his *Politics Among Nations* (1948) was so comprehensive, systematic, and theoretical, it became the exemplar of this group. With the advantage of hindsight, there can be no doubt that Morgenthau's work was the single most important vehicle for establishing the dominance of the realist paradigm within the field. Recent historians of the field all agree on this point. Stanley Hoffmann, writing in 1960 (p. 30), maintained that Morgenthau's realist theory had occupied the center of the stage in the United States for the previous ten years.

Dougherty and Pfaltzgraff (1971:12,15) assert that *Politics Among Nations* was the most influential textbook within the field. Finally, William C. Olson, writing in 1972, states that *Politics Among Nations* "was by all odds the most influential textbook of the early post-war period and is thought by many, if indeed not most, *to have transformed the field from idealist advocacy to realist analysis*" (W. Olson 1972:19–20, emphasis added).

In order to account for the anomaly of World War II, Morgenthau attempted to delineate those realistic laws of behavior that Carr claimed the idealists had ignored. He maintained that all politics was a struggle for power, that nations strived to protect their national interests, and that the power of a nation(s) could be most effectively limited by the power of another nation(s) (Morgenthau 1960, 1973:chaps. 1 and 11).[8] In

---

question see Bingham (1961) and Meyer (1960). Finally, I have removed F. A. Voight's *Unto Caesar* (1939) from the list; Bull (1972:38) himself admits this has not stood the test of time. With these three exceptions the list is the same as that of Hedley Bull. Schuman (1933), Carr (1939), Wight (1946), and Morgenthau (1948) were labeled by W. Olson (1972:19) as landmarks in the field. These works can be viewed as the most influential works within the field in both the United Kingdom and the United States in the early post–World War II period.

8. The third edition of *Politics Among Nations* is used throughout this book for purposes of direct quotation. The changes in the various editions are minor, consisting mostly of updating the analysis with current events and analyzing those events in light of the paradigm. For example, Morgenthau writes in the preface to the third edition: "I have felt the need to change the emphasis here or there while leaving assumptions, tenets, and theoretical structure intact." In order to insure that the quotes are central to Morgenthau's analysis, the fifth edition (1973) will also be cited. The most recent edition is the 5th revised edition (1975), which removes a number of minor changes in the 5th edition, thereby making it even more similar to the 3rd (see preface to the 5th revised edition).

delineating these general "laws," Morgenthau provided a view of the world the international relations scholar was investigating and provided answers to what Masterman (1970:62) has said are the major questions of any paradigm: What are the fundamental units of which the world is composed? How do these units interact with each other? What interesting questions can be asked about the units? What conception of the world should be employed to answer these questions? Morgenthau's answers provided a view of the world that made three fundamental assumptions:

1. Nation-states or their decision makers are the most important actors for understanding international relations.
2. There is a sharp distinction between domestic politics and international politics.
3. International relations is the struggle for power and peace. Understanding how and why that struggle occurs and suggesting ways for regulating it is the purpose of the discipline. All research that is not at least indirectly related to this purpose is trivial.

The picture of the world provided by the realist paradigm has been aptly summarized by numerous scholars in the field (see K. W. Thompson 1960; Tucker 1952; T. W. Robinson 1967; Platig 1967; and Taylor 1978a) and will be discussed in chapter 3. What is important at this point is that acceptance of the three assumptions in the World War II period constituted, in Kuhn's terms, a revolution in the way scholars viewed their world. The idealists, for example, did not believe that nations were the most important actors (Wolfers 1951 [1962:86]). To them, the most important actors were individuals and the emerging international organizations that would replace the nation-states as the organizing unit of civilization (Fox 1949:68–71; see Bryce 1922:lectures 7 and 8). Studying these institutions and improving their processes would bring about peace. Nor did the idealists accept the second assumption. Indeed, their entire purpose was to make international politics more like domestic politics, as was emphasized by Wilson's hopes for a League of Nations (Carr 1939:chap. 2). Finally, the assumption that international politics consisted of a struggle for power and peace was not accepted. Although the idealists believed that some selfish persons acted in terms of power politics, they did not believe that the real world worked this way. They did not believe such behavior was in harmony with the real world, because it led to war. What was in harmony with the real world could be determined by using reason to establish a new global order (Wolfers 1951 [1962:86]). This, of course, was the way to achieve the goal of the field—the establishment of peace.

By the early 1950s, however, Morgenthau and the other realists suc-
ceeded in getting their assumptions about the world accepted by other
scholars in the United States and the United Kingdom (Burns 1972:75).
The acceptance of the new paradigm led the field to develop the normal
science characteristics of a discipline. Having settled on a picture of the
world that emphasized certain phenomena and ignored others, scholars
began to develop and test alternative theories and propositions about
international politics that rested on the (untested) validity of the paradigm's three fundamental assumptions. These theoretical explanations,
of which Morgenthau's was only one, were used to explain contemporary
and past events and were periodically revised on the basis of the adequacy of these explanations. As research continued, the field became
more specialized, with fewer attempts at "grand theory" à la Morgenthau and more investigations of the limited topics originally delineated
by Morgenthau and the other early realists as legitimate research areas.
In the fifties and sixties this division of labor, which is often confused
with competing schools of thought, consisted of: the study of foreign
policy; the study of systemic processes such as the balance of power; the
related study of the causes of war; the study of bargaining and strategy
such as deterrence; and the study of supranationalism, including integration and international law and organization. Each of these topics or
subfields, and the way they have been handled, can be interpreted as
attempts to articulate the realist paradigm and make that picture of the
world more detailed.

The contribution of the realist paradigm to the development of a
scientific study of international relations has been, first, to point out that
science must be empirical and theoretical, not normative and narrowly
historical, and second, to provide a picture of the world (i.e., a paradigm) which has permitted the field to develop a common research
agenda and to follow it systematically and somewhat cumulatively. The
power of the realist paradigm to guide the development of the field
toward normal science has been overlooked by scholars because of a
preoccupation with and misunderstanding of the "behavioral" revolt.
The nature of that revolt and the relationship between it and the realist
paradigm will now be examined.

The Realist Tradition and the Behavioral Revolt

The term *behavioral revolt* is somewhat inappropriate to describe the
conflict that arose between the traditionalists and nontraditionalists in
international relations inquiry, since traditionalists also study behavior,
not just legal documents and institutional flow charts. The debate is not
over whether behavior should be the focus of inquiry; nor is it really a

debate over empirical versus normative concerns. Rather, as will be shown, the debate is over scientific methodology. In this light it is often tempting to call the nontraditionalists the scientific-oriented, which is occasionally done (see J. D. Singer 1972). This would be unfair to the traditionalists, however, who long ago claimed the scientific label (see Carr 1939). Since the term *behavioralists* has been widely used in international relations inquiry, and everyone seems to understand who are the behavioralists and who are the traditionalists, the term will be used here despite some of its confusing connotations.[9]

In the late 1950s and early 1960s the behavioral revolt began to make its influence felt.[10] Among the first major scholars reflecting this new emphasis were Morton Kaplan and Karl Deutsch. Their work reflected the three main characteristics of the new approach: a concern with philosophy of science; an attempt to borrow from the physical and more "developed" social sciences; and an attempt to apply mathematical, particularly statistical, analysis to international relations inquiry. Kaplan's *System and Process in International Politics* (1957), for example, reflected the first two characteristics.[11] The concern with philosophy of science led Kaplan to attempt to develop models of the international system. The attempt to achieve the rigor of physical science led him and many others to borrow conceptual frameworks from these other fields and apply them to international relations (Bull 1972:40). Kaplan borrowed the systems language of W. Ross Ashby's *Design for a Brain* (1952).[12] Deutsch also borrowed from the physical sciences, using communications and cybernetics theory.[13] Unlike Kaplan, however, Deutsch (1956) attempted to employ statistical tests as a means of determining whether the evidence supported a hypothesis. The work of Kaplan and Deutsch, taken together, can be seen as setting the pattern for the type of analysis conducted by the adherents of the new behavioral approach.[14]

9. On the use of the term in international relations see J. D. Singer (1966b) and Klaus Knorr and James N. Rosenau (1969a).

10. For example, Knorr and Rosenau (1969b:5) state: "the impact of the behavioral revolution upon the international field was delayed. Not until the 1960's did its vitality and practices become prominent." This occurs despite the call of Guetzkow (1950) for a more scientific approach.

11. It should be noted that some behavioral scholars, although they grant that Kaplan claims to be scientific, maintain that his understanding and application of scientific procedure is faulty. See in particular Levy (1969).

12. Kaplan acknowledges the influence of Ashby in Kaplan (1967:150).

13. See Karl W. Deutsch (1964b; 1953) and Karl Deutsch et al. (1957). The influence of cybernetics on Deutsch came from Norbert Wiener. For an overview of cybernetics theory proper see Wiener (1954).

14. Kaplan's and Deutsch's work is taken as an indicator because it gave rise to a sustained movement that adopted the scientific or behavioral approach to

What the behavioralists wanted was a more systematic way of testing explanations. They believed that if their procedures were followed, truly scientific and cumulative knowledge could be gained. The procedures, which were most controversial, consisted of the use of quantitative analysis to test hypotheses. In addition, many behavioralists were not willing to grant that the traditional method produces scientific knowledge, but at best only untested conjecture. (See J. D. Singer 1969b:70–72).

From the behavioralist perspective, what was in contention was not the three fundamental assumptions of the realist paradigm but how the realists had conceived of science, particularly scientific methodology. The traditionalists agreed; Hedley Bull (1966 [1969:20]), speaking for the traditionalists, characterized the debate as one between "explicit reliance upon the exercise of judgment" and "strict standards of verification and proof"; he maintained that confining the field to the latter would make it impossible to say anything of significance.[15]

If the conclusion that the debate was over method and not substance is accurate, then in Kuhn's terms it would be incorrect to think of the behavioral revolt as a paradigm-displacing event.[16] The picture of international relations provided by the realist paradigm has not been displaced, nor for that matter has it been seriously challenged. Klaus Knorr and James Rosenau provide evidence that the picture has not changed. They state that the scholars engaged in the debate do not challenge each other about the way they identify international phenomena (1969a:4).[17] Knorr and Rosenau (1969a:13) say that while authors have similar con-

---

international relations. Earlier mathematical work such as that of F. W. Lancaster (1916) or Lewis Richardson (1939) did not give rise to a sustained movement (see Burns [1972:73ff.]). Likewise Quincy Wright's A Study of War (1942), while clearly employing the behavioral approach, is better seen as a forerunner of the movement, since the type of analysis he employed was not greatly copied until the 1960s. Guetzkow's (1950) early call clearly stems from his social psychology training, and hence can be seen partly as an outside influence.

15. Morgenthau's position is generally in agreement with Bull. See Morgenthau (1973:vii–viii) and (1967).

16. For the view that behavioralism is a new paradigm see Lijphart (1974). Lijphart (1974:61), however, agrees that behavioralism did not introduce new substance in the field when he asks, "Can we regard behaviorism as a paradigm-based school if it does not possess any substantive content?" Unfortunately, Lijphart never seriously addresses this question. It is necessary to distinguish the world view of a field from its use of the scientific method; otherwise all the physical sciences would have the same paradigm.

17. For additional exchanges in the debate see the other essays in Knorr and Rosenau (1969a), particularly those by Kaplan, Levy, Vital, M. Haas, and Jervis. Also see Wight (1966); O. R. Young (1969); and Russett (1969). For a review of the debate see Finnegan (1972b).

ceptions of the subject matter they do not have at all similar conceptions of scientific methodology. Therefore, Knorr and Rosenau (1969a:12) rightly conclude that "it is the mode of analysis, not its subject matter, that is the central issue." If it is the mode of analysis and not the subject matter that is the central issue, then it cannot be said that the behavioral revolt displaced the realist paradigm. What the behavioralists attempted to displace was not the paradigm but the methods used to determine the adequacy of the paradigm.

The amount of attention the behavioral revolt has received has tended to obfuscate the role the realist paradigm has played and continues to play in international relations inquiry. With the exception of the methodological debate, much of the work in the field since 1948 bears a remarkable resemblance to what Kuhn has called "normal science." In this interpretation international relations inquiry in the last thirty years or so can be viewed as an attempt to articulate the realist paradigm in light of research, while at the same time learning and debating what constitutes scientific research. This view suggests that the field has been far more coherent, systematic, and even cumulative than all the talk about contending approaches and theories implies (see Knorr and Rosenau 1969b; Dougherty and Pfaltzgraff 1971; and Starr 1974:339, 351).

The basis of this coherence stems from the dominance of the realist paradigm. That paradigm provided a picture of the world that scholars in the fifties and sixties used to focus upon certain phenomena out of all possible events and to create a manageable enterprise. Morgenthau provided a particular set of concepts, explanations, and topics of inquiry that articulated the paradigm. Scholarly activity in the fifties and sixties can be interpreted as clarifying and systematizing Morgenthau's concepts and explanations; providing alternative concepts and explanations that, while at times very different from those employed by Morgenthau, are still with few exceptions consistent with the three fundamental assumptions of the realist paradigm; and conducting research in either the traditional or scientific mode that was then used to advance the conceptual and theoretical work. The behavioralists can be interpreted as systematizing realist work according to their own criteria of adequacy and then quantitatively testing the hypotheses they derived from the paradigm.

While the application of Kuhn's analysis contributes to the preceding insights, it should also be clear that Kuhn's own analysis is quite limited when applied to embryonic sciences such as international relations. Of equal importance to paradigm development and displacement, in terms of the energy they command and the debates they generate, are discussions of what it means to be a science. While Kuhn would probably claim that such debates subside once a science matures, one may suspect that he underestimates the impact of methodological and measurement changes in the physical sciences and mathematics.

Conclusion

This survey of the history of the field since 1919 has shown that each of the three stages—the idealist stage, the realist stage, and the behavioral revolt—has had an impact on developing a science of international relations. The idealist phase helped institutionalize the field and established the emphasis of the discipline on questions of peace and war. The realist challenge to idealism was to state that "wishing for peace does not make it occur." The realists pointed out that the development of utopian strategies to end war could not hope to succeed, because they ignored basic laws of human nature and behavior. The implication of the realist critique was that in order to eliminate war it is first necessary to discover the laws that govern human behavior and the idealists were not aware of these laws or had a misconception of what they were. The realists attempted to move the field from purely normative analysis to more empirical analysis. They did this by displacing idealism and providing a paradigm that clearly specified a picture of international politics and a set of topics of inquiry that if properly researched would delineate the laws of international behavior. The most comprehensive list of those laws appeared in Morgenthau's "theory" of power politics. The behavioral revolt challenged not the picture of the world that the realists had provided but the realist conception of what constitutes an adequate scientific theory and the procedures used to "verify" that theory. Borrowing from the more advanced social and natural sciences, the behavioralists attempted to apply the principles of philosophy of science accepted in these other fields to international relations. The behavioralists asserted that explanations should be stated in such form as to be both falsifiable and testable, that evidence should be systematically collected to test them, and that in light of the tests, explanations and the theories from which they were derived should be evaluated and reformulated. The behavioralists' own work was essentially to apply these procedures to the subject matter, but within the confines of the realist paradigm. The behavioralists then attempted to bring the scientific practices of the field more into line with the practices of the physical sciences, and most observers would probably agree that they have been fairly successful in this attempt. Keeping in mind that summaries are always oversimplifications, it can be concluded that the idealists provided the goal of the discipline, the realists provided the paradigm, and the behavioralists provided the scientific principles.

Chapter 3

Research Design:
Defining and Operationalizing
the Realist Paradigm

While the Kuhnian interpretation of the intellectual history of the field, presented in the previous chapter, appears plausible, its accuracy has not been tested in a systematic and falsifiable fashion. This is important because some critics of Kuhn (e.g., Shapere 1964; 1971) have argued that the paradigm concept is so vague and ambiguous that a specific paradigm cannot be easily identified in a discipline. In this chapter these potential problems will be addressed by explicitly deriving testable propositions that must be true if the Kuhnian interpretation of international relations inquiry is true; demonstrating that the definition of the realist paradigm employed in this analysis is valid; and operationalizing that definition so that it is possible to determine which works are guided by the paradigm.

Deriving Propositions

If an interpretation is to be adequately tested, it is necessary to insure that important and not trivial propositions are logically derived from the interpretation and that the research design constitutes a valid test of the proposition. A number of propositions can be found in the interpretation presented in chapter 2. If the more important or controversial propositions in the interpretation are corroborated, there is more confidence in the adequacy of the interpretation than if some less controversial propositions (such as the proposition that the realist paradigm displaced the idealist paradigm) were corroborated. The most controversial and important proposition in the historical interpretation is that the realist paradigm has guided international relations inquiry after the behavioral revolt.

In order to test this claim, it is necessary to define more precisely the time period to which it applies, and what is meant by *international relations inquiry*. To assess the claim that the behavioral revolt was not a paradigm change, the fifties and sixties (the major period of the revolt) will be examined in the data-based tests. To incorporate all of the seventies would make a more comprehensive test but would involve so much data that it would not be feasible to collect it at this time. Nevertheless, the literature reviews in chapters 4, 5, and 8 will deal with the more recent research.

A more precise definition of international relations can be constructed by examining the major activities of scholars. Kuhn (1970a:chap. 3) points out that there are three major activities of any discipline—theory construction, data collection, and research. Therefore, if the major proposition of this analysis is true, one would expect the following three propositions to be true:

1. The realist paradigm guided theory construction in the field of international relations in the fifties and sixties.
2. The realist paradigm guided data making in the field of international relations in the fifties and sixties.
3. The realist paradigm guided research in the field of international relations in the fifties and sixties.

These three propositions specify much more clearly the spatial-temporal domain of the major proposition and what is meant by the realist paradigm "dominating" international relations inquiry. Since the essential activities of any science are theory construction, data making, and research, it can be concluded that if the realist paradigm guides these three activities, then it is dominating international relations inquiry.

A second problem that has to be solved is how to test the three propositions so that it is possible to determine if behavioralists as well as traditionalists have been guided by the realist paradigm. This problem can be solved by sampling. The first proposition on theory construction will be tested in such a manner that both traditional and behavioral work will be included. The second and third propositions on data making and research will be tested only on behavioral work, because there is more doubt that behavioralists have been guided by the realist paradigm. Also, given the method of the traditionalists, it is difficult to distinguish operationally when the traditionalist is engaged in theory construction, data collection, or research (hypothesis testing). This research design reflects the behavioral assertion that traditional work is really just theory construction through the use of argument and impressionistic evidence without the attempt to collect data systematically and test hypotheses (see Singer 1969b:68). Although traditionalists strongly disagree with this assertion, accepting it here is necessary to simplify the testing procedure and does not bias the results of the tests. This is because traditional work is adequately covered in the first proposition, and the findings of the second and third propositions apply only to the work of the behavioralists.

Defining the Realist Paradigm

Since a paradigm involves a set of fundamental assumptions made in the exemplar, the realist paradigm can be defined by delineating the fundamental assumptions in *Politics Among Nations,* as was done in the previous chapter. This is a valid procedure if *Politics Among Nations* was the most influential of all realist writings. A recent survey by Richard Finnegan (1972a) of international relations scholars confirms this assertion.

Finnegan (1972a:8–9) finds that the leading scholarly work cited by more scholars than any other is *Politics Among Nations.* Over one-third of the scholars chose this book. The next ranking book was Kaplan (1957), which received only 14 percent of the choices. Likewise, when asked to choose the single scholar who has contributed more to the field than any other person, more respondents chose Morgenthau (46.7 percent). The scholar who received the second greatest number of choices was Karl Deutsch, but he was chosen by only 25.2 percent of the respondents.

It was also shown in chapter 2 that *Politics Among Nations* had the three characteristics of an exemplar; namely, recognition as an unprecedented work (that displaces a competing paradigm); attraction of an enduring group of followers; and use as a textbook.[1] Since this is the case, it appears reasonable to assume that *Politics Among Nations* is a valid indicator of the realist paradigm.

The realist paradigm can be defined by delineating the fundamental assumptions made in that text. Because Morgenthau's text provides a theoretical explanation of international politics, it makes many assumptions. Not all of these assumptions are *fundamental* assumptions. For example, Morgenthau's (1960:173–223; 1973:172–221) assumption that the balance of power can sometimes be a useful mechanism for maintaining peace is not a fundamental assumption, because it rests on certain prior assumptions—for example, only nations can balance power. A fundamental assumption is one that forms the foundation upon which the entire edifice of a discipline is built. In order to define the fundamental assumptions of the realist paradigm, it is necessary to delineate the phenomena it focuses upon.

Morgenthau focuses on two phenomena: nation-states and the struggle

1. Kuhn (1970a:10). For its "recognition as an unprecedented work" see W. C. Olson (1972:19–20). "Attraction of an enduring group of followers" should be an obvious fact to anyone familiar with the field. For evidence of its "use as a textbook" see Dougherty and Pfaltzgraff (1971:12, 15).

for power and peace. In doing so, he makes three fundamental assumptions delineated in chapter 2.

The first assumption Morgenthau makes is that nation-states are the most important actors for understanding international relations. Why Morgenthau makes this assumption can be demonstrated by a simple syllogism:

1. Politics consists of a struggle for power, and in order to be a political actor a person or group must wield significant political power (true by definition).
2. In international politics, during the modern state system, only nations wield significant power (empirical statement).
3. Therefore, in international politics, during the modern state system, only nations are actors (conclusion).

Given the first two premises, the conclusion follows logically.[2]

Morgenthau's second assumption is that there is a sharp distinction between domestic politics and international politics. The use of the concept *international politics* as a way of demarcating the field assumes by its definition that there is something about politics that occurs outside nations that makes it different from politics that occurs inside nations. Morgenthau makes the distinction throughout *Politics Among Nations* (1960:27, 38–39, 435–440, 501–518; 1973:27, 40, 429–433, 481–497). In *Dilemmas of Politics*, Morgenthau (1958:47) maintains that the distinction "exerts a persuasive influence on the practice of international politics as well as upon its theoretical understanding." Morgenthau points out in the same work that it is specifically the decentralized or anarchic system of international society that makes domestic politics different from international politics. Domestic politics is played in an arena where the government can legitimately and effectively regulate the actions of the actors, but in the world arena no such regulation occurs (Morgenthau 1960:501–509 and chap. 19; 1973:481–489 and chap. 19). In international politics, only nations have power, and their power can only be limited by the power of other nations. The sovereignty of nations, therefore, has an important effect on the way politics is played; hence a theory of international politics cannot be the same as a theory of

2. In order to determine whether Morgenthau actually makes these premises and the conclusion (which is assumption 1), a textual analysis, reported in Vasquez (1974a:70–74), was conducted. That analysis demonstrates that Morgenthau accepts not only the two premises but the conclusion of the syllogism as well. The appropriate quotations can be found for the first premise in Morgenthau (1960, 1973:27); for the second premise, Morgenthau (1960:9–10; 1973:10; 1958: 67–68); and for the conclusion, Morgenthau (1960, 1973:27–28).

domestic politics. It can be concluded that Morgenthau does in fact make what was delineated as the second assumption.

Morgenthau's third assumption is that international relations is the struggle for power and peace. Morgenthau (1960:23; 1973:24) clearly states that the two concepts around which *Politics Among Nations* is planned are power and peace. It is evident from the following quotation that to Morgenthau (1960:38; 1973:40) international relations is a struggle for power and peace: "All history shows that nations active in international politics are continuously preparing for, actively involved in, or recovering from organized violence in the form of war." The fact that Morgenthau defines the purpose of international relations inquiry in these limited terms and excludes other forms of international behavior by definition is evident from the following statement:

> Two conclusions follow from this concept of international politics. First, not every action that a nation performs with respect to another nation is of a political nature. Many such activities are normally undertaken without any consideration of power, nor do they normally affect the power of the nation undertaking them. Many legal, economic, humanitarian, and cultural activities are of this kind. Thus a nation is not normally engaged in international politics when it concludes an extradition treaty with another nation, when it exchanges goods and services with other nations, when it co-operates with other nations in providing relief from natural catastrophes, and when it promotes the distribution of cultural achievements throughout the world. In other words, the involvement of a nation in international politics is but one among many types of activities in which a nation can participate on the international scene (Morgenthau 1960:27–28; 1973:27–28).

By defining the purpose of his work in this manner, Morgenthau is doing what Kuhn has stated is the prerequisite of all scientific inquiry, that is, focusing on and magnifying certain phenomena while allowing other phenomena to disappear from the picture. There is nothing wrong with this procedure, and, as a number of philosophers of science point out (Kuhn 1970a:chap. 5; Hanson 1965:chap. 1; Popper 1970:51–52), it would be logically impossible for science to proceed in any other manner. By providing a definition of international politics, Morgenthau states what he is going to study, what he is not going to study, and by implication what is important and not important (or less important) to study.[3]

3. It should be pointed out that Morgenthau is not simply making the distinction between international relations and international politics. Because his work

Up to this point, the type of evidence presented to support the accuracy of the three fundamental assumptions of the Morgenthau paradigm has been citation from his texts. The problem with this kind of evidence is that it assumes that the author being cited is fairly consistent and that the passages quoted are representative of his work. Furthermore, it does not allow a hypothesis about an author to be easily and openly falsified, since readers who object to the evidence must find their own counterquotations. In order to deal with these three problems, a content analysis of the index and table of contents of *Politics Among Nations*, which is fully reported in Vasquez (1974a:80–95), was conducted.

If Morgenthau accepted the first and second assumptions, it would be expected that he would tend to use concepts that referred primarily to nations or the relationships among nations. A content analysis of all common nouns in the index of the third edition found that 72.3 percent of the common nouns referred primarily to nations (n = 159). When only nouns that have at least fifteen pages devoted to them were included in the sample, then 77.7 percent of the common nouns referred to nations (n = 27). The evidence that Morgenthau accepted the third assumption was that of the ten section titles in the table of contents, eight referred directly to either the struggle for power or the struggle for peace. These eight sections constituted 85.8 percent of the pages in the third edition.

Although the preceding analysis demonstrates that Morgenthau makes the three assumptions, there might be some question as to whether other scholars also made the same assumptions. A review of one of the leading realists of the time, Arnold Wolfers, who did most of his work after the publication of *Politics Among Nations*, should eliminate any doubts. Wolfers provides even better evidence for the three assumptions than does Morgenthau's own work, primarily because Wolfers was very interested in exploring the basic questions. His acceptance and justification of the first assumption is clear and even goes to the extreme of saying that the decision-making approach is irrelevant because all official decision makers will behave in the same manner given the structure of the current nation-state system (Wolfers 1951 [1962:82]). Likewise, he accepts the third assumption on the struggle of power and maintains that the roles of anarchy and power are so great that domestic

---

became an exemplar, his originally stipulative definition is accepted as defining the scope of the entire field. International relations becomes international politics by definition. What is not international politics is simply irrelevant. Whether or not Morgenthau intended this to occur, it is, according to this theory, the result of his procedure. See Kuhn (1970a:chap. 2) for the general process by which the working definitions of a great scholar become the working definitions of an entire field.

politics is fundamentally different from international politics (Wolfers 1949; 1951; [1962:103–116]).

In defining the realist paradigm it is important to distinguish it from the power politics conceptual framework that Morgenthau, Wolfers, and others have employed. For the purposes of this analysis, scholars who employ that conceptual framework will be referred to as adherents of the power politics school or of real*ism*. These last two terms will be employed the way they are commonly understood in the discipline. The term *realist paradigm*, however, is used in a technical sense and refers only to the three delineated fundamental assumptions, which adherents of realism happened to make, but it does not include all their conceptual baggage or their explanations. This analysis does not deny that there are important theoretical differences between realism (narrowly defined) and other schools such as decision making and systems. It does want to say that realism has provided to the discipline as a whole, and thus to these other schools, a critical shared-example which provides the paradigm of the disciplinary matrix.[4]

The three delineated assumptions make the meaning of the realist paradigm much clearer, but the assumptions do not provide an operational definition. An operational definition requires a set of rules that can be used to determine whether a scholar is guided by the three fundamental assumptions.

Operationalizing the Realist Paradigm

This section tests whether a scholar accepts these three assumptions by use of the coding scheme shown in table 3.1. The coding scheme was developed by selecting indicators of each of the three assumptions. The first two assumptions of the realist paradigm are that nation-states are the most important actors for understanding international relations and that the sovereignty of nations makes domestic politics different from international politics. Given this emphasis on the nation, it is reasonable to expect that a scholar who accepted the first two assumptions of the realist paradigm would study primarily nation-states and neglect other actors, since these nonnational actors would be of only minor importance. Therefore, in order to see if a scholar employs the first two assumptions, one simply examines the actors he or she studies.

The first part of the coding scheme lists all the possible actors an international relations scholar could study. If a scholar's work—whether it be a theory, collected data, or a hypothesis—referred primarily to

4. The adjective *realist* is always used as a shorthand for realist paradigm and not for realism in the narrow sense, unless otherwise specified.

Table 3.1. Coding Scheme

Code	Item
	ACTOR
1	Intergovernmental organization (IGO)
2	International nongovernmental organization (NGO)
3[a]	Nation-state
4	Subnational group or individuals
5	No actor
6	Any combination of 1, 2, 4
7	The nation and any other combination of actors
	TOPIC OF INQUIRY
10[a,b]	Conflict-cooperation
11	Non-conflict-cooperation and non–power perceptions of decision makers
12	Non–(war/peace or power issues), issue positions of actors, and issue salience
13[a,b]	Alignment and alliances
14[a]	Integration and regionalism
15	Magnitude of transactions (target specific)
16[a,b]	National power and/or weakness—including social, cultural, economic, political, and geographic characteristics; penetration, dependence, prestige, success, and failure
17[a]	Isolationism-involvement
18	Miscellaneous
19	Sociological characteristics of actors—age, party, education, religion, etc.
20[a]	Propaganda
21[a]	Supranationalism—support and participation in United Nations, League, or International Courts

[a]Indicators of the realist paradigm.
[b]Central topics of the realist paradigm.

nations and not to any other actor, then the work was coded in category 3 and taken as evidence that the scholar employed the first two realist assumptions. If a scholar studied any other actor or the nation in conjunction with nonnational actors, then the work was coded in categories 1, 2, 4–6, or 7 and taken as evidence that the first two assumptions of the realist paradigm had been rejected.

The use of the nation-state as the actor is only an indicator of acceptance of the first two assumptions. In order to determine if a scholar accepts the critical third assumption, it is necessary to determine whether his or her studies follow the research program established by the exemplar. Kuhn argues that the major influence of a paradigm is the establishment of a research program. Even critics of Kuhn who do not employ the concept of paradigm (e.g., Worrall 1978) recognize the importance of alternative or competing research programs within a discipline. If *Politics Among Nations* is an exemplar, then the topics of inquiry discussed within it constitute a set of dependent variables that followers would seek to investigate empirically and explain theoretically. Similarly, the key independent variables would provide a focus of inquiry because they hold the promise of solving existing puzzles. A review of Morgenthau's *Politics Among Nations* revealed that all topics in table 3.1 marked [a] were present.

Some topics are, of course, more central than others. Clearly, Morgenthau's major dependent variable is inter-nation conflict-cooperation. In order to understand this topic more clearly, Morgenthau delineated a set of topics of inquiry that, if researched successfully, would provide a scientific understanding of the international struggle for power and peace. He thought a proper understanding of the role of national power would ultimately explain inter-nation conflict-cooperation. This provided the heart of his own theoretical explanation and conceptual framework. He went to great lengths to identify the elements of national power. The geographical, political, economic, and sociocultural characteristics of a nation were all viewed as important elements (Morgenthau 1960, 1973: chaps. 8 and 9). In addition to explaining inter-nation conflict-cooperation, national power was used to account for general patterns of foreign policy. Morgenthau submitted that weak nations were being best served by isolationism if they were not threatened (1960:36–37, 159, 196; 1973: 37–38, 196); otherwise an alliance with a stronger power would serve their interests (Morgenthau 1960:173–178; 1973:172–178). Conversely, stronger nations were seen as more likely to be active and opt for the policies of the status quo, imperialism, or prestige (Morgenthau 1960, 1973:28;chaps. 4–6). Which of these policies a nation selects, Morgenthau implied, is a function of the historical context and power relationships among the elite.

Closely related to the topic of national power is Morgenthau's concern with the balance of power and alliances. Whereas national power considerations have an impact on all forms of global behavior, alliances and the balance of power are seen as directly related to the maintenance of peace and the outbreak of war (Morgenthau 1960, 1973:chaps. 11–14, 21).

These three topics—national power, alliances, and inter-nation conflict-cooperation—constitute the central core of the realist paradigm. This conclusion is supported by a rank order of the common nouns in the index of *Politics Among Nations*, which showed that the three most frequently used nouns were *balance of power* (86 pages), *national power* (69 pages), and *war* (62 pages). (See Vasquez 1974a:89–90, 92 for the data and evidence.)

Even though these three concepts provide the conceptual framework for Morgenthau's own theoretical explanations, they also provide a research program for other scholars. Any exemplar provides not so much answers as the promise of answers, if scholars work to improve the conceptual frameworks and theoretical explanations given in the exemplar. One would expect considerable attention to be devoted by adherents of the realist paradigm to clarifying major concepts like national power and the balance of power and specifying precise relationships between these concepts and various dependent variables. New definitions, measures, and alternate hypotheses all would constitute part of a systematic investigation into every aspect of the topics and their connection to each other.

A group of scholars that accepted the third assumption would be expected to study more frequently the topics in the research program that Morgenthau saw as more promising, and to study these in the manner he suggested until the research showed that these leads no longer must be followed up, either because they proved fruitless or because they had been fully exhausted.

While inter-nation conflict-cooperation, national power, and alliances provided the central core, Morgenthau saw other topics as important for a complete understanding of the field even if they were not central. Because Morgenthau was writing in opposition to the idealists and at a time when many Americans hoped the United Nations could become, at some point, the foundation for a world government, supranationalism was an interesting topic to him. He had two main concerns with it. The first was to debunk illusions about the United Nations and argue that the United Nations simply reflected existing power relationships and the struggle for power. The second was to stipulate the conditions that create a stable supranational entity. He dwelt on what forces created a nation and how a world community (and from there a world state) might be created (Morgenthau 1960, 1973:chaps. 27, 29, 30). It is because of this last concern that inter-state integration is labeled as part of the realist research program, even though Morgenthau's own purpose was to show that the proper conditions for supranationalism did not exist. Finally, Morgenthau (1960:338–345; 1973:332–339) used the concept of propaganda to explain some of the verbal acts of states, although his concern with it was marginal.

The following topics of inquiry were taken as indicators of work outside the realist paradigm: non–conflict-cooperation and non–power perceptions of decision makers; non–war/peace issues, issue positions of actors, and issue salience; magnitude of transactions; sociological variables of actors—age, size, party, education, etc.; and finally a miscellaneous category to make the classification logically exhaustive. A scholar who studied one of these topics would be said to have rejected the third assumption.

Studying aspects of decision making other than inter-nation power relationships suggests a topic of inquiry that sees decision making itself as the primary dependent variable. Such a perspective implies a rejection of all three assumptions. If individuals other than leaders of nation-states are studied, then the first two assumptions are violated, particularly if the explanations are psychological and/or social psychological, since this implies a single theory at the individual, group, and state level. The third assumption is also violated because the unique nature of global anarchy is not seen as affecting behavior.

Studying issues other than war/peace is seen as a rejection of the second and third assumptions, because Morgenthau (1960, 1973:27) explicitly states that all substantive goals can be reduced to the struggle for power. To study different kinds of issues is to imply that the realist paradigm is applicable only to one aspect of the global system, and hence incomplete.

Studying transactions is a vestige of the idealist paradigm, particularly Mitrany's (1943) functionalism. Finally, sociological characteristics usually violate the second assumption because, by borrowing from other social sciences (not just sociology), they imply that there need not be a special theory of international politics or even a special theory of politics, but perhaps only a theory of various aspects of human behavior (e.g., decision making, conflict, perception, bargaining, etc.).

A scholar's work was coded as realist only if *all* the actor and topic categories were realist. For example, if a scholar studied nation-states but did not study them in the context of a realist topic of inquiry, then the entire work was coded as nonrealist, because the third assumption was rejected. In other words, all three assumptions had to be employed before a work was coded as realist.

A strong case for the validity of this coding scheme can be made. The central validity question is whether the three delineated assumptions of the realist paradigm are indeed the fundamental assumptions made by that paradigm. It has been shown that Morgenthau's *Politics Among Nations* is a valid indicator of the realist paradigm and that it is based on those three assumptions. The second validity question is whether the indicators employed in the coding scheme actually measure a scholar's acceptance of the three realist assumptions. It has been shown that Morgenthau emphasized certain actors and topics of inquiry which have been taken as indicators of the realist assumptions in the coding scheme.

It seems reasonable to expect that scholars who accept the assumptions of the realist paradigm would also tend to employ the same actors as Morgenthau and follow his research agenda. The third validity question deals with the mechanical problem of whether it is easy or difficult to code a work as realist. Because the coding scheme requires that both actor and topic categories must be realist before a work is coded as realist, it is more difficult, mechanically, for a work to be coded realist than nonrealist. Since only one actor category is labeled realist, there are only seven possible ways in which a work could be coded realist. Conversely, there are thirty possible ways a work could be coded as nonrealist. Also, anything with a miscellaneous topic is coded as nonrealist.

A more serious criticism is that the coding scheme is so broad that any work about world politics would be coded as within the realist paradigm. The Marxist paradigm, however, shows that this is not the case, in that class is the most important actor and the distinction between domestic and international politics is not emphasized. Nations are viewed as an artificial creation and inter-nation conflict as bogus; only classes and class conflict are real. Likewise, the Marxist paradigm does not accept the third assumption, in that it considers the most important set of questions to be the evolution of economic production and its effect on behavior whether or not that behavior leads to inter-state war.

Finally, it might be argued that the coding scheme is too imprecise because it might code substantive power politics propositions in the same categories as propositions derived from game theory or systems analysis if they studied only nations and conflict-cooperation. This criticism misconstrues the purpose of the coding scheme, which is not to make distinctions among propositions or theories that share the same fundamental assumptions about the world but to make distinctions among propositions that have very different views of the world. To insist on the former distinctions is to reduce the realist paradigm to Morgenthau's specific power politics conceptual framework. This would be like saying that because Marx, Kautsky, Lenin, Mao, and Marcuse are all different, they cannot share the same paradigm. Since the coding scheme is intended to provide an analysis of the effect of accepting or rejecting realist paradigmatic assumptions, to criticize it for not analyzing the dominance and adequacy of various realist elaborations within the dominant paradigm and research program is to suggest an analysis that is not directly relevant to the thesis being tested here.

Nevertheless, the coding scheme does label certain topics as central, so that it is possible to identify the degree to which a proposition within the paradigm is near the core or at the periphery of the paradigm (see figure 3.1). The most central are those propositions that claim that na-

Figure 3.1. Rank Order of Propositions
within the Realist Paradigm According to Centrality

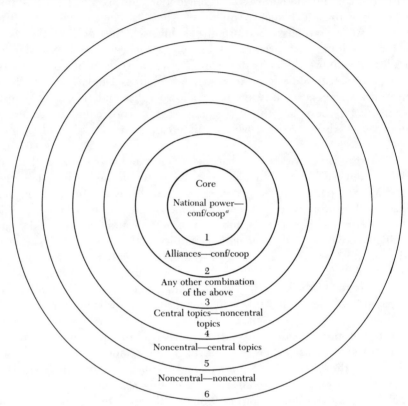

Core

National power—
conf/coop[a]

1

Alliances—conf/coop

2

Any other combination
of the above

3

Central topics—noncentral
topics

4

Noncentral—central topics

5

Noncentral—noncentral

6

Outside Paradigm:
Any central or noncentral topic coupled with a nonrealist topic
Any topic not studied exclusively on nation-states

[a]First topic is an independent variable; second is a dependent variable.

tional power explains inter-nation conflict-cooperation. Next come those
that state that alliances are related to inter-nation conflict-cooperation.
Other interrelationships among these three central concepts would be
farther from the core. They are followed by those propositions that
employ the central topics to explain a noncentral one. Next come the

inverse relationships; finally, propositions that relate noncentral concepts are at the periphery of the paradigm.[5]

The coding scheme has been found to be quite reliable. It has been applied to different documents (books, abstracts, data files, and hypotheses) in a series of tests employing various coders with reliability scores ranging from .86 to .93.[6] Specific reliability scores are reported in chapters 4 through 6.

Because the coding scheme appears to be valid and has been found to be reliable, it will be employed to determine whether the realist paradigm has guided theory construction, data making, and research in the field. This will be done respectively in chapters 4 through 6 by coding the theories that have been articulated in the field, the data that has been collected, and the hypotheses that have been tested. Since each of these chapters has its own research design, there is no need for further methodological discussion here.

5. A more refined treatment of differences within the paradigm is presented in chapter 4. See also Russett (1970a).

6. The formula used to calculate reliability was the number of successes divided by the number of decisions.

Chapter 4

Theory Construction
As a Paradigm-Directed Activity

Introduction

The Proposition

Kuhn's notion that theory construction is a paradigm-directed activity
has both an analytical and an empirical meaning. Analytically, the proposition means that it is logically impossible to construct theories without the prior existence of a paradigm (Kuhn 1970a:15–17). This aspect of
Kuhn's notion is substantiated by definition, since it is impossible to
have a theory that does not make certain fundamental assumptions.
Empirically, the proposition means that a single specific paradigm
guides theory construction (Kuhn 1970a:10–11). It is this empirical aspect that is embodied in the proposition that will be tested in this
chapter: *The realist paradigm guided theory construction in the field of
international relations during the fifties and sixties*.

According to Kuhn, theory construction in normal science involves
clarifying the concepts presented in the dominant paradigm and employing them in light of research to elaborate theories. Kuhn calls theory
construction *paradigm articulation* because the process is conducted by
a division of labor, with different scholars working in specialized problem areas suggested by the research agenda of the paradigm. In a sense,
the paradigm provides an outline, and theory construction articulates
the paradigm by filling in the details. The paradigm provides guidance
in that it focuses scholars' attention on certain problems and provides
them with a set of fundamental assumptions that the new theoretical
work never violates.

The need for paradigm articulation presupposes that the work that
originally presented the paradigm did not provide all the answers. Kuhn
(1970a:23–24) states that a paradigm often does not provide any answers
at all, only the promise of answers. How much and what type of articulation is necessary depends on the specific paradigm and the state of the
science or field. In some fields, very little new conceptual formulation
is needed. In other cases, particularly when the science is in a qualitative stage, conceptual reformulation may dominate efforts at paradigm
articulation (Kuhn 1970a:29, 33).

It is clear to most people that international relations inquiry has been in a qualitative stage. Consequently, it should come as no surprise that a great deal of emphasis has been placed on developing alternative conceptual frameworks. Such an emphasis in the field, however, does not mean in itself that the realist paradigm has not directed theory construction. That would only be the case if the various conceptual frameworks did not employ the three fundamental assumptions of the paradigm. It is claimed in this chapter that most of the conceptual and theoretical work within the field and the research that has given rise to it has accepted those three fundamental assumptions, and, as a result, various aspects of the realist paradigm have been articulated fairly systematically and somewhat cumulatively.

This does not mean, however, that there will be no conceptual change or innovation. Indeed, to the extent to which critics of Kuhn like Toulmin (1967; 1970; 1972) and Shapere (1964; 1971) are correct (and they seem to be, in part), the paradigm should evolve as well as be articulated. Since Kuhn has conceded that microrevolutions can occur in normal science, the debate between Kuhn and his critics is partially semantic. Nevertheless, if Kuhn's emphasis is correct, one would expect innovation to pull back from challenging paradigmatic assumptions, unless anomalies persist. In this sense, the main difference between Kuhn and his critics is over the presence of some sharp discontinuities in the intellectual development of a field.

In terms of the proposition being examined in this chapter, it is important to distinguish Morgenthau's own specific conceptual framework and theoretical explanations (what can be called *power politics* or *realism* in the narrow sense) from the broader set of fundamental assumptions of the realist paradigm itself. The paradigm (see figure 1.1) can be consistent with a number of theories and conceptual frameworks. New conceptual frameworks, even if brought in from sister disciplines, may not necessarily contradict the assumptions of the dominant paradigm and are adapted if they do. Thus, while new frameworks like decision making, systems analysis, game theory, and cybernetics constitute breaks with the power politics framework, they do not necessarily reject the three fundamental assumptions of the realist paradigm. Only if they do can they be said to be outside the paradigm.

Nevertheless, they do constitute real change and evolution, and the further away in time scholars get from the exemplar, the more likely are drastic changes in the original concepts (Kuhn 1970a:28–34). Thus, even among those who saw national power as the key concept and employed a power politics conceptual framework, there were major differences. Morgenthau did not give the same explanation as Schuman (1933), Niebuhr (1940), Spykman (1942), Wight (1946), Kennan (1952), Claude (1956; 1962), Organski (1958), or Wolfers (1962). Yet they all were regarded as working on a power politics theory (see Bull 1972; T. Taylor 1978a).

While early work on the paradigm will tend to follow the theoretical explanations given in the exemplar, later work will be bolder in developing new concepts, particularly if the central ones in the exemplar pose conceptual, theoretical, methodological, or empirical problems. These new concepts will at first appear as radically new approaches, but in fact they evolve out of the concerns of the paradigm, the logic of its own assumptions, and the problems posed by its research program. The more difficulty scholars have in understanding their world, the more drastic the changes they make and the more concepts evolve. If anomalies persist, they may lead to a crisis that may produce a new paradigm.

At what point does the evolution of new conceptual frameworks and theoretical explanations constitute a new paradigm? Only when a theory violates one or more of the fundamental assumptions can a new paradigm be said to exist. Although the latter becomes an operational indicator of a paradigm shift, the discontinuity is clearly not as sharp and surprising as Kuhn implies with his imagery of crisis and revolution. Toulmin's notion of variation and evolution seems a more precise description not only of innovation within normal science, but of the shift from normal science to revolutionary science as well. Kuhn, however, is probably more accurate for describing the transition from revolutionary science to a new normal science. Thus, one can note the collapse of the specific theoretical explanation of the exemplar, then a reconceptualization of a key independent or dependent variable, then the abandonment of the original conceptual framework, then the introduction of new frameworks that get further and further away from the original one, then perhaps the introduction of new metaphors or analogies (maybe from other disciplines or paradigms), then the modification of a fundamental assumption, then calls for a new paradigm, and finally the rejection of all or most of the assumptions and the picture of the world they provide in favor of a new paradigm.

Toulmin's (1967; 1970; 1972) analysis probably best describes all but the last two steps, which, because they are sharp and conscious breaks, are better seen as discontinuities or thresholds rather than just evolutionary products. At any rate, they are certainly perceived by scientists as sharp breaks in retrospect, and for this reason alone Kuhn's analysis should be modified rather than abandoned entirely. Toulmin, however, is certainly justified in pointing out that the activities of most scientists do not differ that much from normal science to revolutionary science.

Research Design

The problem now is how to test the proposition. Testing such a broad proposition requires at least some prediction or statement that would be accepted as clearly falsifying the proposition if the evidence did not agree with it. At the same time, the developmental aspect of the proposition requires that it be able to make sense and coherence out of the intellectual development of the field. These are obviously very difficult tasks to accomplish in a single test or mode of testing. To resolve this problem, two different methods will be employed. The falsifiability requirement will be satisfied by conducting a preliminary empirical test, and the plausibility requirement, (sometimes referred to as *face validity*), will be satisfied by a lengthy but necessarily cursory review of the field's intellectual development since Morgenthau.

The preliminary empirical test makes three predictions. If the realist paradigm indeed dominates the field, then scholars in the discipline should recognize the significance of Morgenthau's contribution and should agree on what work has been the most influential in the field. In addition, other leading works in the field should articulate important problems in the paradigm and should at minimum not challenge the paradigm's assumptions. By making such explicit predictions, problems of nonfalsifiability can be limited.

The problem with such a test, however, is that it loses much of the richness and complexity of the proposition because it looks only at a few predictions, which, while observable, may not be very important or interesting. In particular, a quantitative test cannot adequately assess the development of normal science and the role of conceptual innovation. To resolve these problems, a case study of the intellectual development of the field since the 1948 publication of *Politics Among Nations* will be presented to demonstrate that the literature of the field can be interpreted to show that theory construction has been fairly systematic and somewhat cumulative in articulating the realist paradigm. Such a review will also permit an assessment of the disagreement between Kuhn and Toulmin over the role of change and innovation in normal science.

The works reviewed will include those that have made major theoretical, as opposed to idiographic or policy, contributions to the understanding of international relations. The review will describe how each of the works articulated major aspects of the realist paradigm, how the works embodied the three fundamental assumptions of the paradigm, and how change and innovation were brought about. Finally, the review will discuss works outside the paradigm and indicate why they do not falsify the proposition. There have, of course, been many reviews of the field. This chapter does not represent an attempt to redo this work, but to use it in order to delineate the cumulative nature of work within international relations.

Preliminary Empirical Tests

The most obvious way to test the proposition is to ask scholars in the field what scholarly works and thinkers have been most influential in the study of international politics. If the analysis presented here were correct, then the following two hypotheses would be true:

1a. International relations scholars perceive Hans J. Morgenthau as the most influential scholar in the field.
1b. International relations scholars perceive the exemplar of realist scholarship, *Politics Among Nations*, as the most important theoretical work in the field.[1]

Although a survey was not conducted as part of this analysis, an earlier survey by Richard Finnegan (1972a) provides evidence to support both hypotheses.[2] Finnegan's survey was based on a random sample of international relations scholars in the American Political Science Association. In a question that is relevant to hypothesis 1a, Finnegan asked the respondents "to list the scholars they felt had made a great contribution to the study of international relations" (1972a:9). No specific number of nominations was requested. The findings, which are reported in table 4.1, fail to falsify the hypothesis. The table shows that Morgenthau is the most frequently nominated scholar, receiving almost twice as many nominations (46.7 percent) as the second most frequently nominated scholar (Karl Deutsch, 25.2 percent).

In a question relevant to hypothesis 1b, Finnegan asked respondents to nominate what they considered the three works that had contributed the most to the field. The findings, reported in table 4.2, fail to falsify hypothesis 1b. Finnegan (1972a:9) notes

> . . . the marked domination of the list by one work, *Politics Among Nations*, which is mentioned by one third of the respondents and is mentioned by more than twice as many as the second ranked work.
> In addition, Morgenthau's book is often listed first on the question-

1. These hypotheses are numbered 1a and 1b because they test the first proposition in this analysis.
2. Technically, the use of the Finnegan survey to support hypotheses 1a and 1b does not constitute a valid test because the hypotheses were developed ex post facto. Nevertheless, the findings are reported here because they are highly relevant to the analysis.

Table 4.1. Ranking of Scholars Mentioned by Respondents (Hypothesis 1a)

Scholar	Number[a]	Percentage of total respondents[b]
H. Morgenthau	100	46.7
K. Deutsch	54	25.2
Q. Wright	49	22.9
S. Hoffmann	34	15.8
M. Kaplan	33	15.4
R. Aron	26	12.2
I. Claude	26	12.2
R. Snyder	25	11.7
E. Haas	19	8.9
J. Rosenau	18	8.4
T. Schelling	16	7.5
A. Wolfers	16	7.5
J. D. Singer	16	7.5
H. Lasswell	15	7.0
H. Sprout	13	6.1
C. McClelland	10	4.7
E. H. Carr	9	4.2
W. T. R. Fox	8	3.7
R. Niebuhr	8	3.7
B. Russett	8	3.7
H. Guetzkow	7	3.2
G. Kennan	7	3.2
H. Kissinger	7	3.2
G. Almond	6	2.7
J. Herz	6	2.7
K. Boulding	5	2.2
M. Sprout	5	2.2
K. Waltz	5	2.2

SOURCE: Finnegan (1972a:9). Reprinted with the permission of the publisher.

[a]Scholars mentioned by four or fewer respondents are omitted.

[b]Percentages do not add to 100 percent because of multiple responses.

Table 4.2. Ranking of Scholarly Works Mentioned by Respondents
(Hypothesis 1b)

Work	Number	Percentage of total sample[a]
Politics Among Nations (Morgenthau 1948)	76	35.5
System and Process in International Politics (Kaplan 1957)	30	14.0
Peace and War (Aron 1966)	21	9.8
The Study of International Relations (Wright 1955)	21	9.8
International Politics and Foreign Policy (Rosenau 1961b, 1969b)	19	8.9
The Twenty Years' Crisis 1919–1939 (Carr 1939)	18	8.4
Contemporary Theory in International Relations (Hoffmann 1960)	14	6.5
A Study of War (Wright 1942)	13	6.1
Man, the State, and War (Waltz 1959)	12	5.6
Foreign Policy Decision-Making (Snyder et al. 1962)	12	5.6
Power and International Relations (Claude 1962)	11	5.1
The Strategy of Conflict (Schelling 1960)	10	4.7
Political Community and the North Atlantic Area (Deutsch et al. 1957)	9	4.2
Nationalism and Social Communication (Deutsch 1953)	8	3.7
The Nerves of Government (Deutsch 1964b)	8	3.7
International Behavior (Kelman 1965)	8	3.7
Quantitative International Politics (Singer 1968a)	8	3.7
Swords into Plowshares (Claude 1956)	7	3.3

SOURCE: Finnegan (1972a:8–9). Reprinted with the permission of the publisher.

[a]Percentages do not add to 100 percent because of multiple responses. Works mentioned by six or fewer respondents are omitted.

naires indicating for many of the respondents it is the first book to come to mind.

The findings on hypotheses 1a and 1b lend credence to the proposition on theory construction by demonstrating that Morgenthau and *Politics Among Nations* are regarded as the most influential scholar and book in the field.

A final way to test the proposition is to examine whether other leading theoretical works in the field articulate aspects of the realist paradigm. Since this is a legitimate expectation, the following hypotheses will be tested:

1c. Works that are viewed by scholars in the field as having made a major contribution will tend to employ the conceptual framework of the exemplar, or, failing that, will not violate the three fundamental assumptions of the paradigm.

The works listed in table 4.2 provide evidence to support each of the above hypotheses. Before the evidence can be presented, there must be some way to reliably classify each of the works. This is somewhat problematic, because the coding scheme developed in chapter 3 is not easily applied to an entire book. To resolve this problem, two decisions were made. First, edited books were deleted, since they might employ different approaches in different articles. In addition, there was no easy way of determining which articles prompted a respondent to nominate the book. Second, each book was judgmentally classified into three categories: (1) whether it employed the power politics conceptual framework; (2) whether it accepted the three fundamental assumptions; (3) whether it was outside the paradigm because it rejected one of the assumptions.

The works of Carr (1939), Claude (1956; 1962), Waltz (1959), and Aron (1966) were all classified as employing a power politics conceptual framework. This assessment agrees with that of T. Taylor (1978a:123, 139–140), who classified all of these books, except Claude (1956), which was not reviewed, as part of the power politics tradition. Claude's (1956) work is clearly a power politics critique of international organization. The works of K. Deutsch (1953) and Deutsch et al. (1957), R. C. Snyder, Bruck, and Sapin (1954), Wright (1955), Kaplan (1957), and Schelling (1960) tended to employ other conceptual frameworks but did not violate the three fundamental assumptions of the paradigm. With the exception of Wright (1955), the primary contribution of each of these works was to introduce and apply a new conceptual framework. For Deutsch it was cybernetics or communication theory, for Snyder, Bruck, and Sapin it was decision making, for Kaplan it was systems language, and for Schelling it was game theory. In this manner, conceptual innovation was introduced, but each of these new frameworks, which were consciously borrowed from other disciplines, had to be adapted to fit global politics. In doing so, each scholar, at least subconsciously, employed the picture of the world provided by the realist paradigm. They believed that nation-states were the most important actors, that domestic politics was fundamentally different from international politics, and that international relations consisted of the struggle for power and peace. Each of these authors looked primarily at nation-states as the most important actors; the only possible exceptions are Snyder, Bruck, and Sapin (1954), who looked at decision makers, but they defined a state as its official decision makers. Each of these books embodied the third assumption of the realist paradigm in that it studied, at least indirectly, inter-nation conflict-cooperation. Kaplan studied alliances and their stability, Schelling analyzed deterrence and bargaining. R. C. Snyder and Paige (1958) applied their framework to the decision to intervene militarily in Korea. Deutsch investigated the old idealist propositions that integration and communication could be paths to peace. In this sense, Deutsch's work, although not idealist, reflects nonrealist tendencies and is somewhat on the periphery of the paradigm. However, his strong empirical emphasis and analysis of nation-states saved him from moving too far in a nonrealist direction (see his textbook [Deutsch 1968] for evidence of his agreement with the three fundamental assumptions of the paradigm).[3]

Finally, two books, Wright (1942) and K. Deutsch (1964b), are seen as outside the paradigm. Wright employed both idealist and realist assumptions in his study of war, focusing on individuals as well as states, and attempting to develop a single theory of conflict and violence rather than one unique to the international system. Deutsch presented a general theory of government that violated the second assumption of the paradigm and wrote on a topic not directly relevant to the research agenda of the field. Indeed, most people in the field would probably say that it was a book about comparative politics, not international politics.

On the basis of the above classifications, it can be stated that six of the fourteen leading nonedited books (including Morgenthau 1948) employ a

3. To a certain extent, the edited works of Kelman (1965), J. D. Singer (1968a), and Rosenau (1961b; 1969b) are similar to the books in the second category in that each introduces a new approach. For Kelman it is social psychology, for Singer it is statistical testing of hypotheses, and for Rosenau it is scientific (or "behavioral") theorizing. Hoffmann (1960) is primarily a reader combining power politics approaches and some of the new conceptual frameworks with commentary that is an expanded version of his (1959) essay. The essay is respectful of power politics approaches and does not violate any of the three fundamental assumptions of the paradigm.

power politics conceptual framework and that an additional six do not violate the three basic assumptions and do study a topic of inquiry central in the realist paradigm. The first six can be seen as reflecting realism in the narrow sense as well as being traditional in methodology. The second six are behavioral and attempt to rework power politics propositions in a more scientific manner and to introduce new concepts to aid this task. Since only two books out of fourteen do not reflect work guided by the realist paradigm, it can be tentatively concluded that hypothesis 1c has failed to be falsified.

Although preliminary, the tests in this section have shown that the scholar seen as contributing more to international relations inquiry than any other scholar is Hans J. Morgenthau; the work most frequently nominated by scholars as the leading work in the field is Morgenthau's *Politics Among Nations*; and twelve of the fourteen books nominated by scholars in a sample survey as leading works in the field do not violate the three fundamental assumptions of the realist paradigm. All these findings provide support for the proposition that the realist paradigm guided and directed theory construction in the field in the fifties and sixties.

Continuity and Change in the Intellectual Development of the Field: An Interpretive Review of the Literature

This literature review attempts to demonstrate that theory construction in international relations inquiry has followed a fairly coherent research program that has even built cumulatively on the work of others. This research program can be divided into five subfields, linked to each other by the paradigm's over-all goal of understanding the struggle for power and peace. The articulation of the realist paradigm has centered around five subfields: (1) foreign policy; (2) systemic processes; (3) the causes of war; (4) deterrence and bargaining; and (5) supranationalism. Although each of these five areas introduced major new concepts and explanations to the field that were not found in the writings of early power politics theorists, most of the work in each subfield did not challenge the assumptions of the paradigm.

Foreign Policy

The study of foreign policy has been quite variegated, with different interests and emphases emerging at different times and some not connecting with each other until several years later. Underlying this variation, however, has been a fundamental view of the world which has posed a number of research problems that have been investigated somewhat systematically in a logical if not always chronological sense. The most accurate image to describe foreign policy research is not of a computer following an outline but an amoeba sending out pseudopodia to grasp various pieces of food that surround it. As with an amoeba, foreign policy research does manage to move in a direction eventually, and even link up with other aspects of the research agenda.

The reason for such variation appears to lie with groups of scholars who develop specialized interests and expertise and then form invisible colleges with only episodic and delayed communication among colleges. Research and theorizing seem to require such an intense involvement that concurrent research outside an invisible college has little immediate impact. For example, among the four major research projects in the field—Simulated International Processes (SIP/INS); 1914 Studies; Dimensionality of Nations (DON); and Correlates of War—that were in a position to do so, there were few cases of cross-citation (see Russett 1976b:viii–ix). Nevertheless, there were important links among the various efforts, and a rational reconstruction of their efforts would delineate the following research foci: (1) clarification of the concept of national interest and its prescriptive application to current policy problems; (2) clarification of the concept of national power and its use in explaining foreign policy; and (3) development of a decision-making perspective and a concern with the effect of crisis on the dynamics of decision making, the relationship between stress and decisions leading to war, the role of perception in conflict, and the rationality of foreign policy decisions. A fourth research area, lying outside the purview of the realist paradigm, but influenced by it, has been the examination of how (and whether) open countries make foreign policy democratically.

The National Interest Concept

Among the earliest work of paradigm articulation was the attempt to develop a concept that could not only explain foreign policy but also guide policy makers. In two of his most famous works, Morgenthau (1951; 1952) argued that foreign policy could be explained by realizing that the specific foreign policy of any nation was a function of its national interest. If this were the case, then the present and past actions of a nation could be interpreted, and future actions anticipated by simply putting oneself in the shoes of a decision maker and deducing what a "rational" decision maker would do to secure the interests of the nation. In order for this scheme to work, some definition of the national interest had to be provided, and Morgenthau's conceptual analysis of the definitional problems was seen as one of his major contributions. He offered a precise definition, stating that territorial integrity, national sovereignty, and cultural integrity constituted the heart of the national interest in that only these three elements defined precisely what is essential to the survival of a nation-state (Morgenthau 1951; 1952:971–978). Building on Charles Beard (1934), he asserted that any interest other than survival would either be subnational or supranational and would not be in the interest of everyone within the nation.

The problem with such a narrow set of criteria, as Morgenthau pointed out, was that decision makers do not wait for immediate threats to these three goals in order to protect them. Consequently, decision makers develop specific policy goals that are "logically compatible" with maintaining territorial integrity, national sovereignty, and cultural integrity (Morgenthau 1952:972–978). There is then both a narrow and a broad definition of the national interest, and Morgenthau (1952:971ff.) pointed out the danger of the broad definition swallowing up the narrow so that almost anything could be justified as in the national interest.

Nevertheless, Morgenthau, unlike later critics (e.g., Wolfers) believed that despite the ambiguity of the concept it could still be used for analysis by sophisticated observers. The concept had two uses for him and other early realists. First, it provided a sharp contrast to the idealist notion that foreign policy should be based on moralism and legalism, and second, the narrow definition provided a way of evaluating misapplications stemming from too broad a definition.

Given the historical contingencies of the immediate post–World War II era, the debate on idealism commanded the immediate attention of the leading foreign policy scholars. While Morgenthau provided a synthesis of what an entire generation had been trying to express, his was neither the first nor last word on foreign policy. Reinhold Niebuhr's (1940) early work played an important role in applying realism to advocate American intervention in World War II. After 1945, Niebuhr (1953) applied realism to prescribe American policy toward the United Nations and the Soviet Union. In the same vein, Nicholas Spykman (1942) played a highly influential role in applying realist principles to advocate that the United States play a central role in world politics. George Kennan, who has been called the father of America's containment policy because of his famous "Mr. X" article in *Foreign Affairs* (Kennan 1947), also criticized past American foreign policy for its moralistic foundation and neglect of the national interest (Kennan 1952). His later work attempted to delineate clearly the national interest of the United States (Kennan 1966). In a more systematic historical fashion and in a less polemical manner than Kennan, Robert Osgood (1953) examined the moralistic influence in past American foreign policy by tracing the conflict between ideals and self-interest. Kenneth W. Thompson (1960) provided an overview of the major realist writings and applied their principles to

U.S. foreign policy in his highly influential *Political Realism and the Crisis of World Politics: An American Approach to Foreign Policy*. Finally, John Spanier (1960; 1977) provided a widely read history and assessment of American foreign policy since World War II in terms of power politics principles. These scholars followed Morgenthau both in tone and in the concepts they employed. Their contributions tended to be in application, concept clarification, and theoretical elaboration, with only minor changes in the conceptual framework advanced by Morgenthau.

The onset of the Cold War and the shattered hopes for an effective· United Nations doomed the efforts of the remaining idealists and made the power politics framework, with its promise that it could explain and guide the policy of any nation, even more attractive to analysts and policy makers. At this point, it was the effort to avoid misapplication of the concept of national interest that became the focus of attention. Throughout the fifties, sixties, and seventies, Morgenthau (1970) offered analyses of specific problems in American foreign policy. Often they reflected his concern with the misapplication of the principles associated with the concept of the national interest, as his early opposition to the Vietnam War on the basis of realism made clear (Morgenthau 1965a).

The influence of the concept of national interest is demonstrated by the fact that no other concept could replace it in American foreign policy. It quickly dominated both public and scholarly discussion and remains potent to this day, as a perusal of leading American foreign policy journals (e.g., *Foreign Affairs, Foreign Policy, Orbis*) will demonstrate. Even some who consciously sought to develop an antirealist perspective found that when they had to explain or evaluate a major event, like the Cuban missile crisis, only the power politics framework provided any guide (e.g., Coplin 1980:14–18).

Despite the tremendous attention devoted to actual policy questions, some analytical work on the concept was conducted. The two most important contributors in this vein were John Herz and Arnold Wolfers. Herz's major contribution was to criticize and replace (for most scholars) Morgenthau's underlying philosophical rationale for the motivation of pursuing the national interest. For Morgenthau (1960:27–35; 1973: 27–36), nation-states strove to increase their power because of an inherent craving for power. Herz (1950; 1951) argued that nation-states strove for power because they were insecure, never knowing when they might be attacked. This security dilemma was a product of global anarchy, a point elaborated at length by Waltz (1959:chap. 6). Herz (1957) went on to argue that since the nation-state could no longer provide protection for its security because of atomic weapons, it would disappear. The failure of this bold prediction led him to admit error in the late sixties, an unusual move for an academic (Herz 1968).

Theory Construction

Arnold Wolfers (1952) argued that the concept of national security was so ambiguous that it could include just about anything. Consequently, it would tend to become a political symbol that all sides would claim. This criticism did not seem to carry much weight at the time, but it continued to haunt those who employed the concept, reaching a high point in the Vietnam and Watergate periods, when everything from conducting a secret war to refusing to release the Nixon tapes was justified in terms of the national interest.

If the concept had severe limitations from a policy-making perspective, it was even more problematic as an empirical description. Nation-states, argued Wolfers (1952; 1962), had other goals besides security. Furthermore, having attained a modicum of security, a nation-state may not want to sacrifice other goals or values for additional security. Survival may be the most important goal of states when they are directly threatened, but it may not guide their daily activities as much as other goals.

Other alternatives besides idealism and power politics did exist but for a variety of reasons did not command much influence among policy makers and analysts. The most obvious alternative was the Marxist paradigm. Providing both explanations and prescriptions, it offered a mode of analysis as general and as powerful as the realist paradigm. The coming of the Cold War and the defeat of Henry Wallace, followed by the McCarthy era, successfully eliminated from the American scene those who might have employed the paradigm. Not until the Vietnam War and the emergence of a New Left did ideas derived from a Marxist paradigm have much impact either in the political domain or within the international relations discipline (see Parenti 1971). Nevertheless, prior to Vietnam, sections of other disciplines, particularly the revisionist movement within American history, did employ Marxist assumptions (e.g., W. A. Williams 1959; Kolko 1968). The political environment alone, then, cannot account for the failure to employ Marxist concepts. Once the realist paradigm became dominant, it had its own separate and reinforcing effect.

The second major alternative to a general national interest explanation was the area-expert approach encouraged by funding from the National Defense Education Act. This approach, with its emphasis on total immersion in the politics, culture, history, and language of a specific nation or region, could easily complement the general explanation of the national interest by providing a better understanding of how to put oneself into the shoes of specific foreign decision makers. Academically, however, it undercut Morgenthau's notion that general laws exist that can explain the foreign policy of any country. Consequently, highly idiographic studies of the foreign policies of specific countries continued to be published (e.g., Macridis 1958; 1962; 1967; Northedge 1968; 1974). The theoretical vacuum within which these studies were written did not make them very useful in the field, and they were harshly criticized for this reason.[4] Eventually, the comparative foreign policy movement arose as an explicit attempt to solve this problem.

The final alternative to the power politics approach stemmed from social psychology. Beginning in the late 1950s, a number of social psychologists began to have an impact by providing theoretical analyses of foreign policy. Charles Osgood (1959) provided a clear alternative outside the realist paradigm in his proposal for ending the Cold War arms race. So did Morton Deutsch (1973), Milton Rosenberg (1967), and Ralph White (1966; 1970), who produced trenchant analyses of perception, trust, and war. These explanations were eventually incorporated into the field by the mirror-image hypothesis of the Cold War (Bronfenbrenner 1961; Gamson and Modigliani 1971).

The efforts of these social psychologists, who remained outside the field, were aided by those who sought explicitly to develop a social psychology perspective within international relations. Foremost among these were Harold Guetzkow (1968; Guetzkow et al. 1963), Herbert Kelman (1965), and Dean Pruitt (1965). While their analyses tended to be empirical rather than normative, their studies added weight to the notion that social psychological prescriptions were not simply idealistic or naive recommendations from those who did not understand political power. Nevertheless, not until the Vietnam War and détente did this perspective gain significant influence in policy-making circles and journals. While the policy analyses of social psychologists were limited, the influence of social psychology proved to be greater on empirical questions related to decision making.

Even with the preceding exceptions, policy analysis was dominated by a power politics perspective which employed the national interest concept to analyze substantive foreign policy questions. This is true not only of intellectuals like Morgenthau who have affected policy indirectly, but also of those intellectuals like Kennan, Kissinger, and Brzezinski who have held government positions.

If the concept of national interest has proved influential in explaining specific substantive policies and providing evaluations of existing policies as well as prescriptions, it has been less successful in gaining acceptance

---

4. Politically, area experts found their way into U.S. policy-making positions and often argued with "the grand strategists," who employed a more general power politics approach. Because the secretary of state and national security advisor were often the generalists, local experts usually lost the major disputes that arose within the American foreign policy establishment.

as a general explanation. Specific foreign policy explanations have suffered from two fatal errors—they have usually been post hoc and they have tended to be nonfalsifiable. In addition, as Wolfers (1952 [1962: 158–165]) has pointed out, states seek other values besides security. Many behavioralists believe that the concept cannot be employed in empirical analysis because of its overriding normative aspect, a point made sharply by Rosenau (1968a). Consequently, in recent years it has fallen out of use in the field as an empirical concept (see Frankel 1970:11).

Only two analyses came close to developing new concepts that are functionally equivalent to the empirical aspects of the national interest concept, and neither of them represents conscious attempts to deal with it. These are James Rosenau's (1970) concept of adaptation and William D. Coplin and Michael K. O'Leary's (1971; Coplin, Mills, and O'Leary 1973) concept of issue position. Drawing on a systems framework, Rosenau (1970; 1981) suggested that nation-states in order to survive must adapt to their environment and combat threats from it. One of the goals of any state is to maintain its differentiation from the environment by maintaining its boundary, particularly against other actors seeking to penetrate it (see also Thorson 1974; McGowan 1974b). As O'Leary (1974) pointed out, this theory performs many of the functions that the national interest concept did. It posits a goal for all states that relates to survival and that is assumed to guide behavior. It also has a similar problem—it mixes empirical and normative aspects in that the analysis implies, despite denials, that not only do nations adapt, but if they want to survive they should adapt. Such views give rise to problems of ambiguity similar to those that Wolfers (1952) pointed out about the national interest. Despite these problems, Rosenau and others tried to deal with them by reducing normative considerations and drawing an analogy to systems theory by introducing the notion that foreign policy was a function of needs (see Kean and McGowan 1973).

The work of Coplin and O'Leary (1971; Coplin, Mills, and O'Leary 1973) is potentially much more influential than the notion of adaptation, because in effect it successfully removes all the normative aspects and points to a possible operationalization. The major problem for realists had been determining what was the national interest. As long as there was a normative aspect to this question, it could not be operationalized validly and therefore would not serve as a possible dependent variable. Coplin and O'Leary's notion of issue position solves this problem by stipulating that the issue position of a state's official decision makers is, empirically, the national interest of the country. Whether this issue position is really in the interest of the state or anyone else is a separate normative question. Once the normative element is removed, it becomes possible to develop an empirical theory explaining why a state or any actor has the issue position it does. This new dependent variable empirically conceptualizes what Morgenthau originally meant by foreign policy: its substantive content. In the PRINCE simulation Coplin and O'Leary (1971; Coplin, Mills, and O'Leary 1973) use this new conceptualization to provide a theory of change in foreign policy.

The work of Rosenau and of Coplin and O'Leary demonstrates the extensive conceptual variation that can accompany a normal science research program. These works can be seen as normal science, because the problems that they addressed and helped resolve were problems posed by the realist paradigm. Therefore, solutions to them became a way of elaborating the paradigm by changing its concepts and propositions while preserving its assumptions. Even if an individual scholar should go on to challenge the assumptions, as Coplin and O'Leary did in their issue politics paradigm, other scholars are free to employ the concepts in a less radical fashion. But even if other scholars take the radical leap, the attempt to solve a puzzle posed by the old paradigm with the creation of a new one uncovers the links between the two paradigms and suggests that the discontinuities between normal and revolutionary science may not be as sharp as Kuhn (1970a:chap. 8) believed, although this example does not suggest that the transition from normal to revolutionary science is as placid as Toulmin's (1967) evolutionary image implied.

Even though Rosenau and Coplin and O'Leary work on problems posed by the national interest concept, they are in effect abandoning that concept. Their alternative concepts are not really substitutes for the original concept, because they only refer to one of several of the empirical aspects of the original. This feeling of the concept's empirical inutility has been shared widely, and as a result, those who have been interested primarily in empirical and general explanation have turned to other concepts, in particular, national power.

The National Power Concept

The concept of national power has been at the center of the realist paradigm and has been much more influential than the concept of national interest. The earliest effort, which developed in parallel to the discussion in political science about the meaning of power (see R. Bell, Edwards, and Wagner 1969), was devoted to defining the concept. Morgenthau's (1960, 1973:chaps. 8–10) contribution to resolving the definitional problem was to identify in a precise fashion the sources of power, and then point out the three major errors of evaluating the power of states. The first is failing to remember that power is always relative, a major problem with initial behavioral uses of national attributes. The second is that the power of a state is never permanent, a point related to the fact that what may be a preeminent element of power at one time (e.g., foot soldiers) may not be as important as other factors at a later date (e.g., air power). The third is the fallacy of the single factor, which attributes overriding significance to one element of power like Halford Mackinder's emphasis on geopolitics or Alfred Mahan's emphasis on naval strength.

The major problem area for defining power lay in disentangling the various empirical referents and senses that were contained within this single word. Was the concept of *power* the same as capability, influence, coercion, force, or just another word for *cause*? (See R. Bell, Edwards, and Wagner 1969; and Hopkins and Mansbach 1973:chap. 4 for a review.) This was related to the problem of operationalization, which occupied a great deal of the behavioralists' attention. They tended to settle on the notion of capability or resources as exemplified by the national attributes of states as the proper operationalization, that is, the one that would be the most explanatory and predictive (see Rummel [1971]; Small et al. [forthcoming]; J. D. Singer, Bremer, and Stuckey [1972]; Ferris [1973]; Choucri and North [1975]).

This still leaves the question of which elements of capability are important. The problem with Morgenthau's list was that it contained too many items and failed to specify the relative potency of each element. Although operational concerns made this a pressing issue, it was a theoretical question that both traditional and behavioral scholars treated. Many scholars spent their time on military elements, as exemplified by Knorr (1956; 1970). Obviously, the major change in the immediate post–World War II period was the presence of atomic weapons, and John Herz (1959) and Kenneth Waltz (1964), in different ways, saw this as the single most important and overshadowing element of power.

Other scholars looked at more subtle influences on capability. One of Organski and Organski's (1961) major contributions, for example, was the emphasis on demography as a central element of power. Harold Sprout and Margaret Sprout (1951) maintained that the neglect of geographical and general factors of the physical environment as affected by technology were important omissions in assessing power. For Marshall Singer (1972), the major failure of power politics was its overemphasis on coercive rather than "attractive" (i.e., cooptative) techniques, and its emphasis on objective power rather than psychological feelings of dependence and interdependence. Johan Galtung (1964c), working from a sociological perspective, maintained that status was the main determinant for behavior. For Edward Morse (1976), an emerging economic interdependence in the late sixties was having profound effects on the relative weight of elements of power. For Choucri and North (1975), power was best conceived as an interaction of population, resources, and technology. Meanwhile, borrowing from Dahl (1963), Coplin, Mills, and O'Leary (1973) argued strongly for an issue-specific notion of power in which the key elements of power would differ depending on the issue area.

Operationally, the problem of data availability made for a narrower focus and more consensus, as a review of the major research projects will indicate. For Harold Guetzkow, basic capability (economic resources) and force capability were important attributes of states in INS (see Noel 1963). Rummel (1971 [1977a:213]) saw economic development and military strength as the two determinants of high status in the contemporary period. For J. David Singer, Bremer, and Stuckey (1972), power consisted of three dimensions—demographic, industrial, and military—that have an effect on diplomatic status. Finally, Choucri and North (1975) looked at demographic indicators in combination with resources and technological ability.

The Inter-University Comparative Foreign Policy Project and Comparative Research on the Events of Nations (CREON) have employed Rosenau's size, development, and polity as a definition of capacity (see Rosenau et al. 1973; East 1975). These three variables, of course, had been suggested earlier by Sawyer (1967), among others. Although not part of a larger research project, Ferris (1973:34) attempted to create an index of capability that would emphasize military power by combining six indicators: military personnel, defense expenditure, population, government revenue, trade value, and territorial area. Alcock and Newcombe (1970) found that the perception individuals have of the power of different nations correlates strongly with these countries' GNP and military expenditures.

The major effort on national power was, of course, devoted not to defining power but to determining how the concept could be used to explain international politics. All the main texts of the period—whether traditional like Schuman (1933), Organski (1958), Stoessinger (1961), Hartman (1957), Spanier (1972), and Burton (1967), or more behavioral like Wright (1955), K. W. Deutsch (1968), K. J. Holsti (1972), Hopkins and Mansbach (1973), and Coplin (1974)—devoted large parts of their analyses to explaining world politics using the concept of national power or reconstructed facets of it (like size).[5] Morgenthau's own contribution was to use national power to explain two major aspects of foreign policy—inter-state conflict-cooperation and, to a lesser extent, participation and elite dominance. Conflict-cooperation was seen to be a function of

5. This point is made by Dougherty and Pfaltzgraff (1971:12–13), although the example is my own.

the struggle for power, therefore the degree of conflict-cooperation in any nation's foreign policy was seen to be related to its relative power. Given that this is the case, considerable resources are necessary to play and survive in this game. Major powers account for most behavior and generally run the system.

The works that have been most successful in theoretically elaborating the effect of national power on foreign policy have been Rummel's DON project and the work centered around Rosenau's pre-theory. The initial inspiration for Rummel's early research came from outside the field in the work of Raymond Cattell (1949), whose test relating internal conflict with external conflict Rummel attempted to replicate. Having failed to discover a relationship (Rummel 1963; Tanter 1966), Rummel examined whether there were any relationships between a nation's attributes and its conflict behavior. This phase of Rummel's work provided the most systematic empirical investigation of various indicators of national power, in terms of national attributes, to date, reaching at one point about two hundred variables (Rummel 1968).

Although Rummel drew on psychology to provide the theoretical framework (Kurt Lewin's field theory) and the methodology (factor analysis), his research procedure followed what might be considered classic normal science. Once behavioralists decided to collect and analyze data, the two most obvious and rational things to do would be to collect data on the elements of national power that Morgenthau suggested, and then to relate those indicators to conflictful and cooperative behavior. Rummel's (1972b) descriptive work on the dimensions of nations, then, became important primarily in light of the realist paradigm, and his correlation of attributes with behavior, although often criticized as inductive and too atheoretical, was the most logical step for him to take, given Morgenthau's work.

Rummel's (1968) work on national attributes failed to produce any strong findings, a pattern that other research confirmed (see Vasquez 1976b:200–207). In retrospect, this is not surprising, since Rummel committed what Morgenthau said was one of the three major errors of evaluating power; that is, by looking at national attributes, he treated power as if it were an absolute rather than a relative condition. This he corrected in his elaboration of field theory and later status-field theory, which can be viewed as attempts to make mathematically precise what Morgenthau had verbally suggested about the role of power, in light of Lewin's and later Galtung's theoretical frameworks. Rummel did this by looking at dyads and how differences in attributes led to differences in behavior. In status-field theory, Rummel (1971 [1977a:253]) incorporated Morgenthau's beliefs that international relations is a struggle for power and that nations attempt to balance power (status-field Theorems 4 and 5).

Despite these links with Morgenthau and the realist paradigm, Rummel introduced a number of important conceptual changes and at points challenged one of the assumptions of the paradigm. Most of the more radical changes came from the introduction of the status concept, particularly as used by Johan Galtung. Galtung's work (1964c; 1971) is a mixture of conventional sociological treatments of status and a Marxist approach; indeed, his work on status leads to a theory of imperialism (Galtung 1971). To bring in the status framework the way Rummel does is to pose a conceptual framework fundamentally different from that of power politics; it sometimes makes the same predictions, but for different (explanatory) reasons. At the same time, this framework challenges the second assumption of the paradigm: that a unique theory is needed for international politics. It does this by providing a single theory to account for individual, group, and state behavior, while simultaneously opening the door for a link to the Marxist paradigm. Although Rummel pursued some of the implications of the sociological sources of the status framework, he tended to disregard the Marxist links of Galtung's later work (see in particular Rummel 1979).

If reconceptualizing the dynamics of national power in terms of status theory was Rummel's main theoretical contribution to the independent variable, his work on the dependent variable was even more profound. Through his empirical work, Rummel (1972a:97–100) showed that conflict and cooperation were not unidimensional, but rather at least two unrelated dimensions of behavior. Since they were unrelated, different independent variables would be needed to predict each. Morgenthau's and Rummel's work suggested that different national attributes would explain different types of foreign policy behavior. Thus, in order to explain foreign policy, a typology more precise than conflict and cooperation was needed. Rummel (1972a) solved this problem, in part inductively, by factor analyzing American foreign policy behavior. This resulted in six distinct patterns, which can be seen as certain types of conflict behavior (e.g., deterrence, Cold War, negative sanctions) and cooperative behavior (aid, Western European versus Anglo-American kinds of cooperation). Choi (1977) extended this analysis to see whether the patterns of American and Soviet foreign policy have been stable over time. Relating these new dependent variables to the newly constructed status-field independent variables proved very successful in predicting American foreign relations, producing some of the highest correlations ever published in the field. However, these findings raise questions about whether international politics is as unidimensional as the third assumption of the realist paradigm implies; this question will be addressed systematically in chapter 8. Suffice it to say for now that Rummel, working painstakingly for over fifteen years, managed to develop a theoretical explanation based on national power that could successfully pass empirical tests. Although the answers he gave were very different and perhaps revolutionary in their implications, Rummel began to provide solutions to a puzzle initially posed by the realist paradigm. If Morgenthau taught that understanding the role of national power would provide an understanding of inter-state conflict-cooperation, Rummel showed how to reconstruct that statement to see what was accurate and what was inaccurate in it.

The other major effort to specify the relationship between national power and foreign policy has been associated with Rosenau's pre-theory. Although Rosenau (1968b) has been highly critical of most of Morgenthau's concepts for their lack of scientific rigor, he has shared the belief that general explanations of foreign policy can be provided by looking at a state's attributes. It was not an accident that the three major independent variables Rosenau selected—size, economic development, and polity—constituted not only a reduction of Morgenthau's list of the elements of power but a precise and testable ordering of their relative potency. In this manner, Rosenau transformed, as had Rummel, some of Morgenthau's verbal suggestions into explicit and specific propositions that conformed to behavioral conceptions of scientific explanation.

While Rosenau employed national attributes as the foundation for his pre-theory, the more immediate source of his work was R. C. Snyder, Bruck, and Sapin's (1954) decision-making approach (see Rosenau 1967a). In fact, one of the pre-theory's major contributions was to combine the decision-making approach with Morgenthau's more general explanation. Rosenau did this by first reducing the checklist of variables provided by R. C. Snyder, Bruck, and Sapin to five variable clusters: idiographic (later relabeled *individual*); role; governmental; societal; and systemic. In order to move toward a theoretical explanation, Rosenau (1966) saw the need to specify when individual as opposed to role effects, for instance, would be more important in the decision-making process. To do this, he developed eight genotypes of nations based on size, development, and polity, suggesting that whether one cluster was more potent than another would depend on the type of nation. The theoretical rationale for this ordering was given almost as an afterthought in what became the most famous footnote in the field, footnote 45. Rosenau (1966 [1968b: 112]) argued that size affected the potency of systemic influences; development determined the order of individual and role factors; and polity affected the relative potency of governmental and societal factors.

Before concluding the pre-theory, Rosenau introduced two more independent variables that made him deviate even more from Morgenthau's notion of national power. The two new variables were *penetration* and *issue area*. When examined carefully, the first was a very sophisticated critique of what was an idealist vestige in Morgenthau's conception of national power: namely, that nations were powerful because they were sovereign. Morgenthau assumed that if a nation-state was sovereign it was in complete control of its people, resources, and territory. This assumption, along with the realist notion that nations should not interfere in the domestic affairs of other nations, was more of a legal reality than an empirical one. Penetration became a way of describing some of the recently recognized techniques like covert intervention (see Scott 1965; Agee 1975), economic investment, or dependency (see Magdoff 1969) that made one nation able to influence another by participating in its internal economic or political process.

The idea of penetration was potentially radical because it linked domestic and global politics in a manner that challenged the sharp separation of the two implied by the realist paradigm's second assumption. Rosenau pursued this line of thought in his later studies on linkage politics (Rosenau 1969b). Penetration also implied that the billiard-ball model of international politics, which conceived of states as holistic, impenetrable units, might be incorrect. Although Rosenau himself did not pursue this line of thought, others such as Kaiser (1971) and Galtung (1971) were pursuing it from perspectives outside the realist paradigm. For them, subnational, transnational, and/or even supranational actors could be important agencies of penetration that were not under the control of any other nation-state. For Kaiser, and others like Keohane and Nye (1971; 1977), this led to the development of an alternative paradigm; for those like Galtung, it led to a more Marxist orientation. For Rosenau, the more radical implications were cut short by the development of adaptation theory, which postulated the blocking of penetrations as one of the purposes of foreign policy (Rosenau 1970).

The issue-area concept also had radical implications for the realist paradigm. This concept attacked the third assumption of the realist paradigm, which maintained that all issues could be reduced to one issue, the struggle for power (see Morgenthau 1960, 1973:27). Rosenau implied that issue areas could be so different that not only the internal decision-making processes but also inter-nation behavior would vary depending on the issue area. As with the concept of penetration, Rosenau did not pursue some of the more radical implications of his own thought; others, however, did, in their efforts to develop an issue politics paradigm (see Keohane and Nye 1971; Handelman et al. 1973; Coplin 1974). As for Rosenau, he investigated the extent to which foreign policy making was a unique domestic issue area, as Lowi (1964) had suggested, and developed a hypothesis that specified when it would be unique and when it would not (Rosenau 1967b:49–50).

Rosenau's pre-theory had immense influence within the foreign policy subfield, and among behavioralists was probably even more influential than Morgenthau. This was primarily because Rosenau provided an easy way of testing the effects of national power on foreign policy behavior, whereas Morgenthau did not provide explicit, testable propositions on foreign policy. With few exceptions, most of the research centered on size, development, and polity as a way of explaining foreign policy behavior, which in effect was operationalized as either inter-state conflict-cooperation or participation. The exceptions to this trend generally looked at the five variable clusters. These studies consisted primarily of Rosenau's (1968c) study, which tested the hypothesis that U.S. senators would be more influenced by role variables than by individual variables because the United States was a developed nation; Stassen's (1972) critique of it; and Moore's (1974a; 1974b) examination of the relative influence of governmental and societal factors in open and closed nations.

The work on the genotypes, although very systematic, has had a problem in conceptualizing precisely what is supposed to be explained. Conceptualization of foreign policy had varied considerably from Morgenthau's (1951) notion of a substantive policy embodying goals, means, and a rationale. Instead, the focus was placed on more measurable aspects of particular behavior. On the most general level, Moore (1974b) operationalized foreign policy in three distinct ways. First he looked at a state's voting record on three United Nations issue areas (Cold War, Africa, and supranationalism); next he examined their interactions as recorded by Rummel (conflict, participation, and alignment); finally he looked at the amount of their defense expenditures. Using these measures, he attempted to discover whether different types of nations (large versus small; developed versus nondeveloped; open versus closed) had different foreign policies. He found that there were significant differences among the states, but aside from that conclusion, it is difficult to draw many other useful insights from the analysis because the dependent variables are so broad and defined in a somewhat atheoretical fashion.

Rosenau himself recognized that one of the major problems of the pre-theory was that he never defined foreign policy behavior. He tried to correct that omission in a later study (Rosenau and Hoggard 1974:120) by seeing how well the pre-theory could predict conflict-cooperation. In a test that was later replicated by Rosenau and Ramsey (1975), Rosenau and Hoggard examined whether the internal attributes of size, development, and political accountability (the former polity variable) are more potent than external variables like distance, homogeneity, and military balance for explaining inter-nation conflict-cooperation. They found that the eight genotypes more strongly predict conflict (.928) and cooperation ($-.952$) than do the external variables (.357 and .214 respectively) (Rosenau and Hoggard 1974:134). More extensive controls did not change this conclusion, indicating that the genotypes are predictive of foreign policy behavior. The negative correlation, however, made it clear that the genotypes did not adequately predict conflict and cooperation, but rather that large, developed, closed (etc.) nations engage not only in more conflict, but also more cooperation. What this implied was that size, development, and accountability predict participation rather than conflict-cooperation.

Charles Powell et al. (1974) pursued this line of inquiry. They developed a causal model by looking at the separate effects of size, development, accountability, distance, homogeneity, and military balance rather than by combining them into two typologies. When this was done they found that only size and sociocultural homogeneity were related to conflict-cooperation (which is probably really participation given the way it was measured). If this is true, it means that the typologies are not necessary to explain foreign policy behavior; only the specific variables (size or economic development or accountability) are needed. In addition, only one internal variable—size—can be said to be more important than other external variables.

East and Hermann (1974) investigated the original genotypes in more detail by examining whether the separate or various interaction effects of size, development, and accountability were more potent with regard to nine dependent variables that separated aspects of participation, resource use, and conflict-cooperation from each other. Their major finding was that there is no statistical interaction among the three independent variables and that the genotypes are not necessary to explain behavior; it is better to look at the separate effects of the independent variables, which differ with the dependent variable.

The single most potent variable is size, which is related moderately (.45 to .61) to various aspects of participation (such as the frequency of interaction, who is involved, and the use of certain kinds of resources) (East and Hermann 1974:290–299). This finding is supported by a number of studies (S. A. Salmore and C. F. Hermann 1969; East 1975), and it prompted Kean and McGowan (1973) to develop a theoretical explanation of it employing elements of Rosenau's (1970; 1981) theory of adaptation.

After size, accountability and accountability interacting with development were found to be the most potent variables. Here the significant finding is that accountability is somewhat moderately related to conflict and cooperation in the way Rosenau had hypothesized: namely, the more open, the more cooperative (−.433 and .401) (East and Hermann 1974:296–297). However, East and Hermann (1974:282) suggested that the reason for this may lie in part with the fact that the present global system is less compatible with the goals of closed (especially communist) states. If this is the case, it is not so much accountability in the classic Wilsonian tradition that explains conflict, but whether a state is status quo- or revisionist-oriented. These findings suggest that national power, at least in terms of size, may be more important for explaining participation rather than conflict-cooperation.

Additional research by members of the CREON project elucidated this question. Reconceptualizing foreign policy behavior into six variables—professed orientation to change; independent or joint action; commitment; affect (intensity and direction); acceptance/rejection of proposals; and external consequentiality—they have attempted to systematically investigate the three independent variables and the five intervening variable clusters to see what patterns can be delineated (see Brady 1975; Callahan, Brady, and M. Hermann 1982). The highest correlations (.45 to .62) were found by Maurice East (1975) who, while utilizing Rosenau, returned explicitly to Morgenthau's use of national attributes as indicators of the capacity to act (see also East 1978). He operationalized capacity as size and social organization, employing economic, military, political, and social indicators. He found that larger nations tend to act alone, express more negative affect than smaller nations, have more of their acts rejected, and have more external consequentiality (i.e., other nations respond to their acts). Size accounts for a good deal of foreign policy behavior, including not only aspects of participation, but certain kinds of conflict (e.g., expressing hostility and having one's proposals rejected). Social organization is primarily related to the level of commitment. Professed orientation to change and intensity of affect remained unpredicted by East. Linda Brady (1975) found a fairly moderate relationship between situational characteristics and professed orientation to change. Meanwhile Barbara Salmore and Stephen Salmore (1975) showed that there are only weak relationships at best between regime constraints (including accountability) and the six dependent variables. Finally, in later research, M. G. Hermann, C. F. Hermann, and Dixon (1979) showed that personal characteristics in certain decision-making structures can affect all six variables, including affect intensity (the only variable that no one previously had much success in predicting).

The research on the pre-theory has filled in many gaps and helped make the picture of the world posed by the paradigm more like a photograph, as would be predicted if Kuhn's analysis of normal science were correct. In the process, these findings, even when supportive, called for further theoretical elaborations that would give more detailed explanations that could integrate the sometimes complex findings. The CREON project is now in the midst of such theory construction, moving far beyond Rosenau's pre-theory and trying to integrate some of the insights from the decision-making approach (see East, Salmore, and C. F. Hermann 1978; C. F. Hermann and M. G. Hermann 1979).

The Decision-Making Framework

Decision making has provided the third major focus of paradigm articulation in the field. Among foreign policy scholars, the decision-making approach of R. C. Snyder, Bruck, and Sapin, first published in 1954, was heralded as a new and innovative approach that provided an alternative to the prevalent power politics approach (Rosenau 1967a:254–256). The conceptual framework was, of course, very different from that of power politics, but since its utility stemmed from solving conceptual problems posed by the realist paradigm itself, it can be seen as an articulation of the paradigm through an extension of its research program.

The framework's major contribution was to elaborate upon what Morgenthau and other early realists meant by a nation-state. Although Morgenthau had maintained that the nation-state was really individual decision makers, the use of the shorthand term *nation-state* had often given an anthropomorphic tone to his work as well as that of others. R. C. Snyder, Bruck, and Sapin (1954) served a demythologizing function, and in doing so they clarified what specific variables would be useful for providing data. They did not, however, challenge the paradigm's fundamental assumptions. They were still concerned with nation-states, and the first application of their approach to the Korean War (R. C. Snyder and Paige 1958) indicated that they still were concerned with the struggle for power and peace.

Some would reject this conclusion and argue that decision making and other conceptual frameworks like systems analysis, communications, theory, and game theory are alternatives to the realist paradigm. Obviously, the frameworks are radically different in the concepts they introduce, and they share certain characteristics with paradigms, in that they tend to give rise to their own specialized research programs with peculiar modes of analysis like decision making's penchant for group dynamics and game theory's fascination with payoff matrices. Because they reflect more a division of labor within a field or even subfield rather than a set of assumptions that could provide a coherent focus to unite the various divisions of labor into a single discipline, the frameworks are not called paradigms here. More important, conceptual frameworks cannot be said to be outside the paradigm unless they reject the paradigm's assumptions and provide an alternative world view.

None of the major frameworks within the field have posed a different picture of all of world politics. What they have done is to try to illuminate one aspect of it, usually an aspect that has been posing a puzzle for a subfield, by borrowing language from another discipline. For R. C. Snyder, economics and public administration provided the framework, and later social psychological concerns greatly informed research directions. But as with the other frameworks, decision making was applied by R. C. Snyder to international politics. In this manner, the concepts were made to fit and clarify an already existing view of the world. Only in rare instances did these applications result in changing all the fundamental assumptions; usually they did not change any. Scholars tend to be conservative, changing only what is necessary to solve the immediate puzzle. This is what Kuhn assumed when he argued that only persistent anomalies leading to a prolonged crisis result in a paradigm shift. If this is the case, it can be seen that the transition from normal science to revolutionary science is one of degree. Normal science becomes more like revolutionary science the extent to which small changes are unable to solve puzzles.

An analysis of the sources and consequences of the introduction of new conceptual frameworks like decision making provides some insights into the process of innovation, change, paradigm articulation, and paradigm displacement. For Kuhn, all change is a product of problem solving. In international relations, one method of problem solving and hence a source of innovation has been borrowing conceptual frameworks from other disciplines. The new frameworks become criteria by which to evaluate old concepts and explanations. The scientific method itself was borrowed; it became a major source of conceptual innovation by providing criteria like operationalization, falsifiability, and hypothesis formulation that the concepts and explanations of the power politics framework had difficulty in satisfying. In addition, new conceptual frameworks like decision making provided new ways of testing (e.g., comparative case studies, simulation, and experiments) that introduced new dependent variables. In turn, this research posed new puzzles for older explanations and even challenged certain paradigm assumptions. But new developments brought counterefforts to integrate them with the old explanations as well as with research in the other subfields. This helped refine the picture of the world that was being studied. A review of the various research efforts with a decision-making focus will illustrate how these complex processes unfolded.

A rational reconstruction of the research program associated with foreign policy decision making suggests that the initial promise of the framework was to replace or at least supplement the national interest emphasis on a rational actor pursuing its interest with a detailed empirical (usually case study) investigation of the various possible factors that might influence a decision. In this way, a decision could be predicted and explained. This approach made the actual decision-making process (its group dynamics) a topic of inquiry for the field, especially with regard to crisis decision making. This concern raised one of the major questions in public administration: How rational is the decision-making process, and is it less rational during periods of crisis? This sort of focus linked nicely with other research programs in international relations, particularly bargaining and causes of war. It was only natural that a theory of war based on misperception should flow out of a focus of inquiry on foreign policy decision making. In addition, the theory of misperception fitted in nicely with the concern about irrationality in the decision-making process. The introduction of a new framework, the bureaucratic politics "paradigm," raised further questions about rationality that directly challenged some of the rational actor assumptions made by the early realists. By the late seventies, these attacks were buttressed by a wealth of evidence on perception from psychology and social psychology. These insights were employed to explain not only internal foreign policy decision making but inter-state interactions as well.

The initial publication of R. C. Snyder, Bruck, and Sapin (1954) met with a mixed reception. Although early realists like Morgenthau accepted the caveat that nation-states should be conceived as official decision makers, they were not as quick to abandon the notion that the actions of these decision makers could be understood by deducing their behavior from a rational-actor model. Arnold Wolfers (1962:12–13) in particular argued that it was not necessary to investigate in any detail the specific characteristics of decision makers, because it could be assumed that under the conditions of most interest to international politics theorists (Wolfers's [1951] famous pole of power and pole of indifference), all decision makers would tend to conform to the behavior of a rational actor. Despite the authoritative tones in which it was couched, Wolfers's point was only an untested hypothesis.

The limitation and contribution of the R. C. Snyder, Bruck, Sapin framework are best assessed by looking at the research it produced. The framework was clearly case oriented, and access to data proved a major problem. The only major application of the framework was Glenn Paige's (1968) extended study of the Korean decision (see also R. C. Snyder and Paige 1958). The most interesting aspects of Paige's work and of those that studied crisis decision making were the hypotheses related to group dynamics. While interesting, these hardly fulfilled the promise of explaining why nation-states had the foreign policy they did; instead they seem simply to explain how decisions came about. Little further specific use of the framework was made, but it contributed to a variety of new trends. Those who were more interested in the "why" questions tended to follow Rosenau who, as discussed earlier, integrated the decision-making framework into a more general pre-theory that combined R. C. Snyder's insights with some of the more general explanations based on national attributes.

The attempt to find a general explanation of foreign policy decision making was continued by Harold Guetzkow through studies and elaborations of the Inter-Nation Simulation (part of the larger Simulated Inter-National Processes project) (Guetzkow and Valadez 1981a:7). Beginning in 1957, Guetzkow applied a number of insights from social psychology, including small-group experimentation and simulation, to develop a model of international politics (Guetzkow 1963b; 1976). Much broader in his concerns than R. C. Snyder, Guetzkow developed a simulation that related internal decision making, including decisions about domestic problems, to inter-nation interactions and even systemic processes like the outbreak of war. Through the observation of players of the simulation, who acted as surrogates for actual decision makers but were free to develop their own relations (Guetzkow 1963b:148–149), and by conducting independent validation studies, the Inter-Nation Simulation (INS) became a way of building a theory of world politics.

INS itself provided its own research program and generated considerable attention and effort.[6] One line of inquiry pursued theory construction through revising INS. This was followed by creating entirely new simulations; Paul Smoker's (1972) International Process Simulation (IPS) and Stuart Bremer's (1977) Simulated International Processer (SIPER) are the best-known. A second line of inquiry was to use simulation to test hypotheses. Charles Hermann's work on crisis decision making and various studies about the spread or use of nuclear weapons (Brody 1963; Crow 1963; Raser and Crow 1963; 1969; Zinnes 1966; C. F. Hermann, M. G. Hermann, and Cantor 1974) are examples of these. A third and very prolific line of inquiry was to conduct a number of validation studies which attempted to test the assumptions employed in the simulation. Guetzkow commissioned several studies that investigated the validity of using human surrogates (see Guetzkow 1959; Driver 1965; Druckman 1968), while Richard Chadwick (1969) employed independent data to test assumptions employed in the model. Finally, although not a validation study, the effort to simulate the outbreak of World War I (C. F. Hermann and M. G. Hermann 1967) became a way of testing assump-

6. Although the uses of INS for undergraduate education have been noted in the field (see Alger 1963; J. A. Robinson et al. 1966; Cherryholmes 1966), one of the main by-products of the project must be seen in terms of the graduate and professional training it provided. The project left its mark on a number of graduate students and young scholars who went on to make significant contributions of their own.

tions, since a simulation that could replicate past behavior would be better than one that could not (see Guetzkow and Hollist 1976:334; C. F. Hermann 1967; Thorson 1976).

The studies that contributed most to understanding foreign policy decision making were those on human surrogates and crisis decision making. The studies on human surrogates were important primarily because they brought with them a number of insights from social psychology that later undermined power politics assumptions about the rational-actor model. Guetzkow (1968:211–225) reported much of this research before it was published (see also Guetzkow and Valadez 1981b); he will be relied on here. Driver (1965) found that surrogates with simple (as opposed to complex) cognitive structures tended to involve their nations in more aggressive behavior. Michael Shapiro (1966) found that students high in rigidity tended, like Woodrow Wilson and John Foster Dulles, to evaluate outside stimuli in moral terms. Wayman Crow and Robert Noel (1965:8, 20) found that surrogates who had a militaristic world view were more apt to escalate, as were those who were more nationalistic. These findings and others were important because they suggested that Wolfers was incorrect and that individual characteristics could be of importance.

Later research by Margaret Hermann (1974; 1976; 1978; 1980), a former student of Guetzkow with a Ph.D. in psychology, attempted to specify the conditions under which personal characteristics would affect foreign policy decision making. This research also linked up with Rosenau's pre-theory. She hypothesized that personal characteristics of decision makers will affect foreign policy making under the following conditions: the greater the decision makers' interest in foreign affairs, the less their training, and the less sensitive they are to the environment. Personal influences are also accentuated if the situation encourages wide decision latitude and permits decision makers to define the situation themselves. Using content analysis to delineate personality characteristics, she found that more nationalistic leaders are generally more conflictful and less willing to commit resources, while the more cognitively complex are more cooperative and tend to engage in deed rather than verbal behavior (an indicator of commitment) (M. G. Hermann 1974:220–223). Also, leaders high in nationalism, low in cognitive complexity, closed-minded, and not having great belief in their ability to control events tend to be conflictful and more willing to try to influence unilaterally other states. In other research, M. G. Hermann, C. F. Hermann, and Dixon (1979) found that personal characteristics have a significant and at times strong effect on foreign policy output when controlling for decision-making structure.

Recent research not related to INS has added support to the thesis that personality can have important influences on foreign policy. In a study of U.S. State Department personnel, Lloyd Etheredge found that advocacy of force was correlated negatively with self-esteem, political transcendence (which was defined as not feeling emotionally subordinate to one's nation), and trust, and positively related to idealization of American foreign policy, neuroticism, competitiveness, and hostility (Etheredge 1978:chap. 4:127). In a related analysis of disagreements among high-level foreign policy makers (U.S. presidents and their advisers), Etheredge hypothesized that those scoring high on dominance would advocate the use of force and would oppose conciliatory moves. A review of forty-one cases supported his hypothesis in thirty-eight instances (77.5 percent) (Etheredge 1978:85, 79). In a second hypothesis, he postulated that, in disagreements about policy toward the Soviet Union, those who were more extroverted would advocate more cooperative, inclusive policies (e.g., more trade and contact); he found that eleven of thirteen cases (84.6 percent) supported his hypothesis (Etheredge 1978:83).

In a much broader research effort Michael Haas (1974:110–125) examined thirty-two different major decisions (including domestic as well as global decisions) to try to find the conditions associated with the use of violent threats, the suggestion of violence as a policy option, and the decision for violence. He found that high need for power, perceptions of hostility, propensity to take risks, and cultural dissimilarity are associated at the $\pm .40$ level or higher with each of the three dependent variables. In addition, distrust is associated with violent threats and consideration of violent policy options, but not with the actual decision for violence. Haas's research is interesting because it elucidates how personal characteristics interact with other characteristics. He finds violent decisions are also associated with substantive rather than procedural outcomes; cruciality of the decision; the ability of outcomes to create destabilization; the cumulative impact of the decision; outcomes that are viewed as turning points in history; decisions that are recorded unofficially; prior concern with the issue; foreign policy (as opposed to domestic) decisions; information underload; and choosing maximizing rather than satisficing outcomes. Haas's research, however, must be seen as suggestive, since his sample was neither random nor representative. Nevertheless, it represented a useful beginning.

Other important research that came out of INS was Charles Hermann's work on crisis, which ultimately melded together the work on decision makers' perceptions with R. C. Snyder's and Paige's hypotheses on group dynamics in crises and linked them to the 1914 studies on crisis and the onset of war (C. F. Hermann and Brady 1972). Charles Hermann's (1969a) main contribution was his perceptual definition of crisis as high threat, short time, and surprise. The INS was then employed to test the effects of these variables on decision-making variables like the number of alternatives considered, amount of internal and external communication, and contraction in authority (Hermann 1969b; 1972a). This research followed suggestions made by J. A. Robinson and Snyder (1965) and complemented the research of Paige (1968), who looked at the effect on crisis decision making on organizational, informational, and normative variables. Because simulation permitted Hermann to separate the effects of the elements of crisis (threat, time, and surprise), he was able to suggest that there was no statistical interaction of threat, time, and surprise but that time and threat had separate effects while surprise was of little utility (C. F. Hermann 1972a). Paige's (1972) comparison of the relatively short Korean decision with that of the longer Cuban missile crisis permitted the effects of time to be disentangled. Paige also maintained that the two crises pointed out that there were two kinds of surprises. Korea was a surprise to decision makers because, although a threatening act was anticipated somewhere, it was not expected in Korea. He called this AGUS (Anticipated Generally but Unanticipated Specifically). In contrast, missiles in Cuba were a surprise because the USSR had denied their presence. Paige (1972:53) called this BATO (Betrayed Assurances to the Opposite).

This sort of research inaugurated a concern with group dynamics that brought in the contributions of those outside the field. Since the focus on group dynamics could only indicate how decisions were made and not why, research of this sort was seen as more relevant to questions of rational decision making. Once this became a topic, then the work of Simon (1957), Lindblom (1959), and Braybrook and Lindblom (1963) became more influential within the field. Social psychologists like Irving Janis (1972) suggested that certain organizational processes could encourage "groupthink," which could result in poor policy. The negative effects of other characteristics of group decision making were explored from both empirical and normative angles (see Janis and Mann 1977; George 1972; Destler 1972; C. F. Hermann 1979).

Despite the interest in rationality, the main concern of Charles Hermann and others in the subfield was to explain foreign policy. J. A. Robinson and Snyder (1965) and Dean Pruitt (1965) had maintained that the key to explaining action lies with how decision makers define the situation. C. F. Hermann (1969b) expanded his definition of crisis to a typology of situations and offered a number of propositions that related the situations to general internal reactions like *innovation, inertia, reflexive, deliberative, routine, administrative*. He then suggested that these might produce certain kinds of foreign policy behaviors.

Hermann's situation typology produced some important research.

Thomas Brewer (1973) empirically investigated the extent to which Hermann's situation typology might predict internal and external behavior and found it more potent than James Rosenau's or Theodore Lowi's issue-area typology. Linda Brady (1975; 1978) was instrumental not only in investigating the utility of the typology but also in introducing a number of theoretical changes so that the typology itself was replaced by a set of variables characterizing the situations decision makers face. Along with other members of the CREON project, Brady widened the range of foreign policy behaviors that situational variables would be able to explain. C. F. Hermann (1978) himself extended his concerns to developing a classification of the kinds of decision structures that exist (e.g., leader-staff group, autonomous assembly), linking these to the internal decision process (positive reinforcement, bargaining, group maintenance), and then trying to delineate the impact these two factors might have on the group's behavioral tendency. All these efforts were integrated with Rosenau's pre-theory in the CREON project's attempt to develop a comparative theory of foreign policy (S. A. Salmore et al. 1978; C. F. Hermann and M. G. Hermann 1979).

Linkages such as these among various research approaches are important because they give a coherence to the research program of the entire field. In this regard, the integration of the decision-making research with the national-attribute approach of the Rosenau genotypes links this research to Morgenthau's national power approach, indicating not only how national power may affect definitions of the situation but how decision makers, perceptions, and processes may affect the use of national power in foreign policy. Of equal importance in establishing the research coherence of the field is the link between crisis decision making and the attempts of other subfields to explain general international politics and war.

Crises were, of course, being studied by others, and in 1967 Charles Hermann was instrumental in bringing together many of these researchers so that they could integrate their research (see C. F. Hermann 1972b:ix). There were four other research efforts on this topic. The earliest and most pathbreaking was that of Charles McClelland, who studied crisis from a systemic and interaction approach (McClelland 1961; 1968; 1972a). Because his definition of crisis looked at drastic changes in the external behavior of a nation-state, it provided a way of linking the internal processes of the decision-making approach with the actual interaction of states. McClelland (1968; 1972a) found that in a crisis the frequency and type of interactions of states deviate considerably from their pre- and postcrisis interactions. In addition, he found patterns of interactions in both the escalatory and abatement phases. This kind of research was extended by Edward Azar (1972), who introduced the concept of "normal relations range" to explain crisis behavior and was able to confirm many of the tendencies McClelland had found and suggest how they might be related to war. The latter was of particular interest to Michael Brecher (1974; 1975; 1977), who attempted to relate crisis decision making to the outbreak of war. Research like that of McClelland and Azar was of obvious policy relevance and led to a concern with crisis management, particularly in governmental circles (see R. Young 1977; Hazlewood, Hayes, and Brownell 1977; Andriole and Young 1977; Milburn 1972). From a more academic perspective, crisis was also a focus for those interested in bargaining.

Crisis management involves an understanding of bargaining, which, as will be examined later, was a major focus of inquiry (see G. H. Snyder 1972 and G. H. Snyder and P. Diesing 1977). All these efforts are important for the realist paradigm, because ultimately all of them say something about the conditions in crises that would lead to or avoid war. The most important research efforts on decision making that spoke to this question were, of course, the 1914 studies.

Under the direction of Robert North, a series of empirical studies attempted to elaborate and test a theory of the onset of war that had the following elements.[7] (1) In a crisis, decision makers are under severe stress that (2) increases the probability that they will misperceive the intentions and level of threat posed by others. (3) Under certain conditions, this tendency to misperceive will lead to an overreaction, which can fuel a hostile escalating spiral which, if unabated, leads to war. Of the three statements, the first garnered the least support; the relationship between stress and misperception was never firmly established in the 1914 studies. For example, O. R. Holsti, North, and Brody (1968:152–155) argued that nation-states that were more involved in the 1914 crisis (Dual Alliance) would have a lower correlation between the incoming stimulus and their response than the nations less involved, presumably because the latter would be under less stress. In fact, the opposite was found to be the case. In addition, low involvement made for underreaction, and high involvement made for overreaction. Misperception was present, but its relationship to stress and involvement was unclear. These findings are consistent with the research of Paige (1968) and C. F. Hermann (1972a), which showed that, in crises, stress often increases attention and improves performance. In later research, Ole Holsti and Alexander George (1975) attempted to disentangle the

---

7. These studies include O. R. Holsti (1965a; 1972); Holsti, Brody, and North (1965); Holsti, North, and Brody (1968); Zinnes (1968); Zinnes, North, and Koch (1961); Zinnes, J. Zinnes, and McClure (1972). See North (1976); and North, O. R. Holsti, and Choucri (1976).

positive and negative effects of stress and integrated the findings on decision-making rationality in order to reestablish the first statement (see also George 1974).

Considerably more evidence exists for the misperception proposition. O. R. Holsti (1972) and O. R. Holsti, North, and Brody (1968) found that in a crisis, decision makers tend to perceive incoming acts as more threatening than they are, to perceive their policy as less hostile than their opponent's, to react more conflictfully than they think they are reacting, and to see the other side as having more options and flexibility than they do. The problem with a single case, of course, is that there must be some attempt to show that accurate perception can prevent war. This attempt was made in studying the Cuban missile crisis, where O. R. Holsti, Brody, and North (1965) argued that accurate perception was indeed present.

This research did not explain why there was accurate perception. If crises always produce stress, then why did the stress in 1962 not affect perception and behavior? This kind of question led back naturally to problems of escalation and crisis management, a third area of inquiry, which the project did not pursue. One implication, however, is that crisis itself may not be as important as particular dynamics of hostile perception and expression. Using the project data, D. Zinnes, J. Zinnes, and McClure (1972:160) attempted to make this point, maintaining that "decision-makers do not perceive hostility when none exists" and do "react in proportion to incoming stimuli." While this statement does not deny that behavior is escalatory (i.e., nonreciprocal), it does deny the implication that misperception rather than a real conflict of interest is the foundation of disputes. In this sense, the 1972 study is more supportive of power politics approaches than those of cognitive psychology.

The approaches drawing on cognitive psychology have grown since the 1914 studies, with their heydey coming in the late 1970s. The roots, however, go back much further. Among the first works to use psychology to study politics was Harold Lasswell's (1930; 1948) pathbreaking application of psychoanalytical theory. Later studies included the psychoanalytical biography of Woodrow Wilson by Alexander and Juliette George (1956) (see also Rogow 1963). More influential than the studies drawing on psychoanalytical theory were those drawing on cognitive and/or social psychology research. Kenneth Boulding's *The Image* (1956) drew on studies of perception and argued that only images of reality, not reality itself, determined policy. These studies were followed by Harold Guetzkow's use of social psychology in INS to provide a general interpretation of decision making (Guetzkow 1963a; 1963b; Collins and Guetzkow 1964). Next came Herbert Kelman's (1965) explicit attempt to introduce international relations scholars to social psychological applications. Finally came deRivera's (1968) effort to construct a psychological theory of foreign policy making.

Two main trends can be delineated in the more recent work. The first is an attempt to use psychological insights to reconstruct how a decision maker sees the world. The first significant attempt at this was O. R. Holsti's (1962; 1967) very early analysis of Dulles's belief system, which found that Dulles's cognitive structure was such that regardless of the nature of Soviet behavior he would give it a negative evaluation; if the Soviets were cooperative, this was a sign of weakness or a trick. But Holsti only looked at one aspect of Dulles's belief system; if foreign policy was to be explained, the entire system had to be analyzed. Building on the earlier work of Leites (1951; 1953), Alexander George (1969) argued that foreign policy decisions could be explained by delineating the operational code of a leader. This led to a number of attempts to reconstruct operational codes (O. R. Holsti 1970; McLellan 1971; see O. R. Holsti 1976 for a review) or cognitive maps (Axelrod 1976a; Bonham and Shapiro 1976; M. J. Shapiro and Bonham 1973). But as O. R. Holsti (1976) admitted, many of these were too descriptive. Even if the hope that an accurate portrayal of a cognitive map will permit prediction comes to fruition, this is hardly an explanation of foreign policy (see Bonham and Shapiro 1973; 1976; and Bonham, Shapiro, and Trumble 1979 for attempts to predict with simulation).

A more useful aspect of cognitive psychology research came from the attempts to delineate the inaccuracies of the rational-actor model employed by early power politics analysts. The earliest intrusion of this perspective occurred with the mirror-image hypothesis of the Cold War (see Bronfenbrenner 1961; Eckhardt and White 1967; also Rosenberg 1967). The implication of these studies was that a rational deductive prediction of the other side's behavior would be incorrect, and although they did not directly compare cognitive models with a rational-actor model, William Gamson and Andre Modigliani (1971) did show that the American image of the USSR predicted Soviet behavior in the Cold War very poorly. In a more traditional analysis, John Stoessinger (1971) explained Chinese, Soviet, and American relations in terms of misperception. Stoessinger (e.g., in 1961:chap. 14) was one of the few traditional political scientists who long ago argued for the need to analyze world politics in terms of misperception and delineate the role misperception played in the struggle for power.

The inaccuracy of images as a form of misperception also provided the focus of Ralph White's (1966) critique of the Vietnam War and his later, more general, account of war (1970). For White (1966:4–5), the onset of war was characterized by six forms of misperception: "a diabolical enemy image, a virile self-image, a moral self-image, selective inattention, absence of empathy, and military overconfidence." More recently, White (1977) looked at the Arab-Israeli dispute in terms of misperception. Daniel Heradstveit (1979) tested several of the hypotheses on misperception and war using the Middle East as his data base. Although most scholars looked to psychology for the sources of decision making, some turned to the biological characteristics of decision makers (see Wiegele 1973; 1978; see also Corning 1973).

Perhaps the recent work most devoted to the analysis of images has been that of Robert Jervis (1970; 1976). He attempted to show how images affect and are affected by communication and to analyze where they come from and what changes them. Throughout his analysis, he drew directly from findings in social psychology, which he employed to give new interpretations to a plethora of historical cases (1976). For Jervis, learning was an important process that explained the development of images, an insight that also underlined the work of May (1973). One of the problems with the use of learning theory is that it has tended in the foreign policy context to be descriptive. M. J. Shapiro and Bonham (1973), however, have attempted to develop a general model of decision makers' thinking, and Vasquez (1976a) has offered explicit propositions based on learning theory to explain the behavior of mass influencers of American foreign policy.

The impact of social psychology in the late seventies began to undercut the realist paradigm's hold on at least part of the field. Although the paradigm could easily accommodate itself to the focus on decision makers and crisis decision making, the increasing incorporation of social psychological findings and perspectives challenged the second assumption of the paradigm by suggesting that it may be possible to have a single theory of interpersonal, intergroup, and inter-state behavior. It also implied that the third assumption of the paradigm, that international relations is a struggle for power, may be incorrect. From a social psychological view, the third assumption is simply an image of reality, not reality itself. What must be explained are the conditions under which such an image arises, the conditions under which it is most accurate, and the conditions under which it will change. This sort of perspective implies that at best, power politics and the realist paradigm as a whole can only fit certain periods of history or issue areas. Only after the seventies, however, were there explicit calls for a new paradigm based on social psychological insights (Mansbach and Vasquez 1981b). The main reason for this seems to be that most of the scholars who felt comfortable with a social psychological approach were psychologists who, rather than trying to change another field, were content to make interdisciplinary contributions (e.g., C. E. Osgood, White, Rosenberg, M. Deutsch, Kelman and Pruitt).

The other major criticism of the assumptions of the rational-actor model that grew out of the emphasis on decision making was the bureaucratic politics approach. While the work of Allison (1969; 1971) and Halperin (1972; 1974) (see also Allison and Halperin 1972) has been associated with this effort, it is clear that they built on the work of others (e.g., Neustadt 1960; 1970; Hammond 1965; and Rourke 1969). Their major contribution was to point out that foreign policy is not made through a rational calculus of the national interest, but through the tugging and pulling of conflicting bureaucratic and even personal interests. These interests affect policy not only directly when issues are being discussed but also beforehand through informational and organizational variables and afterward by the way the bureaucracy implements the decision. While there is much case evidence to support the plausibility of this claim (see Halperin and Kanter 1973), it is necessary to specify the conditions under which bureaucratic factors will override other determinants of policy (C. F. Hermann 1978:74). The only major significant theoretical work after that of Allison and Halperin that has emerged in this area is that of Steinbruner (1974), who attempted to explain how the bureaucracy itself makes decisions.

While theoretically interesting and policy relevant, the bureaucratic politics explanation has been very difficult to test empirically. The major means of doing this has been to assume that a foreign policy determined by bureaucratic pressures would be incremental and highly correlated with its own previous actions, whereas a foreign policy geared to the environment would be correlated with the output of other nations. By making such assumptions, Raymond Tanter (1974) and James McCormick (1975) attempted to examine respectively the effect of bureaucratic politics in the Berlin and Middle East crises. This research ties in with the earlier work on crisis interaction (McClelland 1968; 1972a; Azar 1972) and that of Allison and Halperin by posing the former as counter-theories to the latter (McCormick 1975:17). Although the findings of Tanter and McCormick were somewhat mixed, it was clear that the models apply under different conditions; in particular, Tanter (1974:26–38) and McCormick (1975:24) argued that the models apply to different phases in the crisis and to different nation-types. Tanter (1974:178) found that McClelland's model fits best in the conflict-intensification phase and that the organizational model fits best in the conflict-reduction phases, but that these general findings may be distorted for specific blocs. McCormick (1975:42) found that McClelland's model fits better in the intense phases, but that the organizational model does not fit the less intense phase as had been hypothesized.

On a broader level, Warren Phillips attempted to integrate the research of Tanter and McCormick with the earlier research on reciprocity, developing a set of hypotheses meant to apply to general foreign policy behavior. Much work in the field was concerned with the degree to which states reciprocate behavior (O. R. Holsti, North, and Brody 1968; Milstein 1972; Phillips 1973; Wilkenfeld 1975; Wilkenfeld et al. 1980). Empirically, Warren Phillips and Robert Crain (1974) found moderate support for the hypothesis that inter-state communication, which reflects highly patterned behavior (low uncertainty in terms of McClelland's [1972a] measure of uncertainty), does not result in inter-state reciprocity, but communication that reflects high uncertainty does produce reciprocity. This relationship held for both cooperation and conflict for states that interact fairly frequently, but held only for co-operation for states that interact on a less routine basis (Phillips and Crain 1974:251). Phillips (1978) then developed a theoretical model linking these findings with the tendency to overreact or underreact, which he argued might be a product of domestic politics, in particular a reaction to internal conflict (see Phillips 1973). In making this argument, Phillips linked the bureaucratic approach with the crisis studies of McClelland and Azar, the 1914 studies on overreaction, and the research on internal conflict leading to external conflict. Furthermore, all this was done in the context of the CREON project's attempt to develop a comparative theory of foreign policy.

The contribution of the bureaucratic politics approach to the articulation of the realist paradigm is twofold. First, it examines the role of bureaucracies, something early realists overlooked. It maintains that by examining bureaucratic positions it is possible to explain why a foreign policy position was taken and how the decision to take it was made. In this sense, the bureaucratic approach is more explanatory than is the group dynamics emphasis of R. C. Snyder, Paige, and C. F. Hermann. Second, it makes policy analysis more critical. There is a real concern with the rationality of foreign policy. Halperin (1974) shows that many decisions are taken not for reasons of state but for internal bureaucratic as well as domestic political reasons. This means that not only must actors be aware of overrationalizing each others' actions but that if they interpret foreign policy from a rational actor perspective, like that of power politics, they may be prone to misperception and to taking actions that will not result in the anticipated consequences.

Democracy and Foreign Policy

The final area of research on foreign policy was that least informed by the realist paradigm. It was instead directed by the concerns of the American politics field to evaluate political behavior in terms of its conformity to a democratic model. In this area, rather than seeing another discipline intrude on international relations inquiry, it is more accurate to see power politics intruding into another field.

The earliest concerns of the power politics theorists in this subfield centered on the dangers of public involvement in foreign policy making. Morgenthau (1960, 1973:chap. 32) and Kennan (1952), reflecting opinions most notably associated with Lippmann (1922), argued that the public was too easily swayed by moralistic passion to be permitted to guide foreign policy. The public did not see the need for flexibility and compromise but instead viewed the world in terms of good and evil and oscillated between isolationist withdrawal and violent intervention to cleanse the world of evil. For these theorists, foreign policy had to be made by experts in terms of the national interest and should not be affected by domestic political considerations. For Morgenthau (1960:567; 1973:547), "The government is the leader of public opinion, not its slave."

This concern gave rise to two research orientations. The first attempted to describe whether the American public did in fact oscillate between involvement and isolation. The main proponent of this view has been Klingberg (1952; 1970; 1979), who elaborated the thesis in theoretical terms and illustrated it with data. The main critic was Caspary (1970), whose empirical test failed to support Klingberg's thesis. The impact of public opposition to the Vietnam War renewed interest in the thesis, with various attempts to measure changes in the opinion structure that may have been brought about by the Vietnam War. Bruce Russett (1972) measured the decline of public support for military spending during the late stages of the Vietnam War, and O. R. Holsti and Rosenau (1979a; 1979b) attempted to delineate empirically two conflicting and potentially polarizing belief systems that emerged after Vietnam within the mass and the elite. Underlying much of this research was the early power politics concern that democracies would have ineffective foreign policies. This question was investigated directly by Kenneth Waltz (1967), who argued that American and British foreign policy was not hampered by democratic processes.

The second research orientation that emerged on public opinion attempted to delineate the ways public opinion could potentially influence foreign policy and then to see if indeed it had any impact. Much of this research stemmed from the public opinion-public policy linkage tradition in American politics. The research showed that public beliefs about foreign policy do not affect legislators or voting behavior (see Miller and Stokes 1963; Pomper 1972). Nevertheless, several scholars attempted to delineate how the concerns of the attentive public and interest groups might affect foreign policy (Almond 1950; Rosenau 1961a; 1962; Bauer, Pool, and Dexter 1963; Lowi 1964; 1967; Milbrath 1967; Coplin 1974: chap. 3). The most systematic research in this area was that of Benjamin

Cohen, who looked at the various domestic factors influencing the Japanese peace settlement (1957), the role of the press (1963), and the attitudes within the State Department about the public's influence (1973).

Both these research orientations were seen as important from the perspective of American politics because they spoke to the question of accountability. Most of the explanations and findings in this area took the view that the public and Congress generally follow the president's lead. Kenneth Waltz (1967) argued that the public has tended to follow the president. In a very informative empirical test, Martin Abravanel and Barry Hughes (1975) showed that the public develops attitudes toward foreign nations consistent with the behavior of their own nations toward other nations. Theodore Lowi (1967), James Rosenau (1967b), and William Zimmerman (1973) argued that Congress is only apt to have a significant impact to the extent that an issue is a noncrisis and involves considerable expenditure of resources. Samuel Huntington (1961) argued that defense policy is also a special issue area. James Robinson (1962) showed that when Congress participates, the major issues are dominated by the Executive.

More recently, this traditional view has come under attack, particularly in light of Vietnam. John Mueller (1971) showed that the public's support for war, although it will rally around specific tactical changes of a president, will systematically decline in direct proportion to the number of casualties (as casualties rise by a factor of 10, support for the war declines by about 15 percentage points). Benjamin Page and Richard Brody (1972) attempted to see if these attitudes have affected voting behavior, while Paul Burstein and William Freudenburg (1976) looked at their impact on Congress. On a more general level, Ronald Moe and Steven Teel (1970) argued that Congress has not been the handmaiden of the president. In a similar vein, Craig Liske (1975) marshaled data to show that Huntington (1961) was incorrect in claiming that defense policy is a special issue area different from most other domestic issues. All this research, along with congressional actions—prohibiting U.S. intervention in Cambodia or Angola, passing the War Powers Act, and controlling (at least for a time) the CIA (see Franck and Weisband 1979)—suggests that many of the earlier findings may be time-bound, and that the role of Congress and public opinion can vary under certain conditions. What these conditions are is a future avenue of inquiry.

Systemic Processes

After foreign policy, the second major area of inquiry and paradigm articulation was systemic processes and the related study of the causes of war. Although systems language did not appear until the late 1950s, about half of Morgenthau's *Politics Among Nations* (1948) dealt with systemic mechanisms—like the balance of power, collective security, and the world state—that were supposed to prevent war and regulate or at least mitigate the struggle for power.

Since much of this attention was a reaction to the idealist attempt to transform the system, Morgenthau tried to show why various peace solutions had failed by demonstrating that their empirical assumptions were faulty or that the conditions necessary for them to work were not present. Thus, disarmament would not work because the assumption that people fight because they have weapons is untrue; people have weapons because they seek to fight (Morgenthau 1960:408; 1973:398). Likewise, a world government will not emerge, and even if it did, it would not work, because in order for governments to prevent violence, they must have authority, and authority requires a preexisting community. Since there is no world community, there can be no effective world government (Morgenthau 1960, 1973:chap. 29). By providing analyses like these, Morgenthau was able to account for the anomalies that led to the demise of the idealist paradigm—the failure of the League of Nations and the coming of World War II.

Morgenthau's evaluation of various mechanisms that claimed to bring peace gave rise to an entire genre of inquiry that persists to this day. More often than not, the scholars involved wrote competing textbooks covering much of the same material as Morgenthau in the same manner, but offering new insights on one or two of the mechanisms as well as disagreeing with Morgenthau on particular theoretical points. The best and most influential works of this type were Claude (1956; 1962), Sprout and Sprout (1951), Organski (1958), Stoessinger (1961), Hartmann (1957), and Bull (1977). Providing a more complete alternative "grand theory" of world politics, yet still within this genre, was Aron's *Peace and War* (1966).

The mechanism which Morgenthau and the other scholars of the fifties spent most of their time on was the balance of power. Much of the analysis dealt with the concept's ambiguity and imprecision and the conditions necessary for the balance of power to work. Morgenthau led the way on this problem as he had on the concepts of national interest and national power. He pointed out the difficulty of balancing power with only two nations, the need for a balancer, and the problem that a state's interest might not always require it to help maintain a balance. Later, when conceptual confusions on bipolarity and multipolarity abounded, he reminded people that there was a difference between a bipolar world where two states had a preponderance of power between them and a two-bloc system (Morgenthau 1960:349–351; 1973:340–342).

As with other major concepts, Morgenthau's did not provide the first or last word. Martin Wight (1946:45) had pointed out that the balance of power meant different things to different historians and scholars. Ernest Haas (1953) provided a very early critique on the various meanings of the concept, showing how this inconsistency limited its scientific utility. Gulick (1955) provided an influential historical assessment of the balance of power in Europe, thereby helping to delineate its empirical components. Arthur Lee Burns (1957; 1961) attempted to develop around the concept a pure theory of power politics that would link the dynamics of Renaissance diplomacy with the nuclear deterrence of the post–World War II period. John Herz's (1957; 1959) work was very important in delineating the effect of atomic weapons on traditional balance of power processes (see also Burns 1957). These effects were viewed as so profound that most strategic analyses shifted from the balance of power to nuclear deterrence as a special case of the balance of power.

Much attention was also focused on the dynamics of the balance of power that would prevent war. In a widely read book, Liska (1957) looked at the limits of the balance of power and attempted to develop a system of peace around the notion of an international equilibrium. A. F. K. Organski (1958:chaps. 11 and 12) provided a powerful critique of the balance concept, arguing that nation-states do not seek to balance power but to gain a preponderance of power, since only that will make them secure. The problem, then, becomes whether war is more likely under conditions of certainty (the power distribution makes it clear who will win or lose) or uncertainty (the power distribution gives each side a chance of winning). Organski's (1958:chap. 12) main contribution was to offer the power transition proposition, which maintained that conflict and war are most likely to occur when one side is gaining on the other. A more recent attempt along these lines has been made by Blainey (1973:chap. 8).

Inis Claude (1962) clarified the concept further by pointing out its limitation as an empirical generalization and also tried to delineate the changes in uncertainty and certainty that would be most associated with war. Zinnes, North, and Koch (1961) attempted to systematize many of these propositions so they could be tested, and Zinnes (1967) criticized other behavioralists for employing research designs that did not test the exact propositions that traditionalists had formulated. Nevertheless, only as testing began did the various possible positions and combinations become clear (see J. D. Singer, Bremer, and Stuckey 1972).

The concern with balance of power focused scholarly interest on a related topic, behavior within alliances. Although Morgenthau showed how it was in the mutual interest of great powers and weak ones to ally, he said little beyond that. The earliest works to attract major attention were that of George Liska (1962), which reflected traditional approaches, and that of William H. Riker (1962), which developed a general deductive theory of coalitions. Employing Riker's size principle, Bruce Russett (1968b) attempted to elaborate the conditions that generate alliances. He also employed notions of collective goods to explain problems of shared payments among allies (Russett 1970b:chap. 4). Through factor analyzing the various characteristics of alliances, including prealliance bonds, integration, duration, commitment, and war participation, Russett (1971) developed an empirical typology of military alliances.

Dina Zinnes (1970) was also concerned with alliance membership, contrasting Riker's (1962) logic with the traditional balance of power logic. Meanwhile, Ole Holsti and John A. Sullivan (1969) investigated what makes allies, such as France and China, deviate. Holsti, Hopmann, and J. Sullivan (1973) developed a proposition that argued that intrabloc cohesion increases with interbloc conflict, a hypothesis that each had investigated earlier (see Holsti 1965c and Hopmann 1967). Michael Sullivan (1976:241–245), however, questioned some of their data analysis and placed greater stress on Healy and Stein (1973), whose study on the nineteenth century does not support the hypothesis. Related to this sort of research are the effects on an alliance of a balanced triangle (where two allies have opposite attitudes toward a third party), an area of research investigated initially by Arthur Lee Burns (1957) and tested by Healy and Stein (1973). Finally, Harvey Starr (1972) was interested in how coalitions divide spoils after war, and Sabrosky (1980) was interested in whether allies keep their commitments to go to war.

Despite this research, the internal dynamics of alliances was a somewhat peripheral topic in the field, in part because while the subject has links to foreign policy, systemic processes, war, and bargaining, it really belongs to none of these categories and has been overshadowed by other work.

After the work of early power politics theorists on peace mechanisms and the balance of power, the next major development in this subfield was the introduction of systems language. Morton Kaplan (1957) introduced the systems framework to study the balance of power. By creating a model for each of six systems, including some hypothetical ones, like the unit-veto system, Kaplan was able to clarify and posit competing explanations about the balance of power so that they could be examined empirically. The rules of each system served as propositions that could be investigated. In addition, theory in the field was advanced by stipulating the conditions under which systems and hence behavior would change.

As with other new conceptual frameworks, this was borrowed from another field and then applied to international relations. Ross Ashby's *Design for the Brain* (1952) provided the source for Kaplan (1967:150).

Others who employed the systems approach were more influenced by Bertalanffy (1956), Parsons (1961), and by the example set by Easton's (1965a; 1965b) and Almond's (1960) structural-functionalism in general political science (see Dougherty and Pfaltzgraff 1971:102–114).

Unlike the decision-making framework, the systems framework introduced little that was innovative other than nomenclature. Perhaps the reason for this was that, unlike social psychologists, those who originally employed systems theory did not come into the field bringing their own propositions, theories, and paradigm. Kaplan, for example, in applying the systems framework, did not challenge the assumptions of the realist paradigm. His concern was with how the balance of power would be affected by changes in the system and the implication of those changes for the struggle for power and peace (see Kaplan 1957:chap. 2; and Dougherty and Pfaltzgraff 1971:125–130). Except for his fifth model, the hierarchical international system, Kaplan always employed the nation-state or blocs of states as the sole actors. Nevertheless, Kaplan made a major contribution to the paradigm by specifying clearly alternative models and hypotheses that in the rest of the literature were either nonexistent or underidentified and ambiguous.

After the publication of *System and Process* (1957), Kaplan collaborated with Arthur Lee Burns and Richard Quandt to employ game theory to test different aspects of Kaplan's and Burns's hypotheses on the balance of power (see Kaplan, Burns, and Quandt 1960; see also Burns 1961; Quandt 1961). The major research that evolved out of Kaplan's (1957) effort was the attempt to identify different systems in history, account for the behavior within them, and delineate the conditions that led to their transformation. The earliest research, by Kaplan (1968) and his students (Chi 1968; Franke 1968; Reinken 1968), used historical case studies and computer modelling.

The work that attempted to cover systematically the major systems in the history of western civilization was Rosecrance's *Action and Reaction in World Politics* (1963) (see also Rosecrance 1973). Yet it was difficult to see what Rosecrance added to generally accepted historical accounts except systems nomenclature. The real contribution is at the end of the book, where Rosecrance tried to stipulate conditions of change and stability, particularly his suggestion of a correlation between global instability and the domestic insecurity of elites (Rosecrance 1963:304).

Closer to Kaplan's (1957) model building was Fred Riggs's (1961) attempt to employ functional analysis to suggest that the current international system was "prismatic," that is, halfway between a totally fused society (*Agraria*) and a completely refracted one (*Industria*) (see F. Riggs 1957 for the definitions of these ideal types). These assumptions were then used to account for different behavioral tendencies. Meanwhile, Modelski (1961) further explored the original distinction between *Agraria* and *Industria*.

The most recent effort in this area is that of Luard (1976), who abandoned systems language and wrote of types of international societies. Drawing primarily on sociology and anthropology, he described differences and similarities of seven historical global societies on nine dimensions: ideology, elites, motives, means, stratification, structure, roles, norms, and institutions. The most interesting aspect of his work, as with Kaplan's, is the positing of possible future systems, in his case three: the transnational society, the international (organization) society, and the spheres of influence society (Luard 1976:chap. 14).

The other recent research of theoretical and policy interest on systems was that which identified new trends and fundamental changes that may lead to the breakdown of the traditional nation-state power politics system (Keohane and Nye 1977; Coplin 1974:chap. 13; Morse 1976; McClelland 1977). This tendency to view the traditional system as waning was also evinced by the more idealistic schemes that have sought to create new global systems of order on the basis of "current fundamental changes in the system." Clearly, this work is very antirealist in character. The foremost example was the World Order Models Project (Mendlovitz 1977; Kothari 1975; Falk 1975; Mazrui 1976; Galtung 1980).

Others in a more realist vein looked at past systems to see how peace might be preserved. The most influential work of this kind, primarily because of the author's subsequent political position, was Kissinger's (1957b) review of the Concert of Europe and of the Metternich system. Illustrative of other significant attempts along traditional and historical lines were Bull (1977) and Elrod (1976), and, along more theoretical and quantitative lines, Choucri (1972).

Despite some interesting insights, particularly about hypothetical future systems, the identification of systems and the problem of system stability proved too descriptive and atheoretical (probably because of the long time span) to give rise to significant research. As a consequence, the most important work on systemic processes came not from studies of historical systems but from the development of propositions at the systemic level of analysis. Before this could be done, however, a number of conceptual confusions about the systems framework had to be corrected. J. David Singer and Charles McClelland were of critical importance in bringing about these changes and thereby changing the field's thinking about systems analysis.

For J. David Singer (1961), what was important about systems language was not the nomenclature but the idea of a systems level of analysis—the macroperspective (see also Hopkins and Mansbach 1973:

chap. 6). For Singer the creation of an international relations theory would come from either a foreign policy perspective which took the internal view of states and then looked outward or from a systemic perspective that emphasized primarily the relations among nations and their environment. Singer, like early power politics theorists, saw the systemic level as more useful. He believed that nation-states behaved the way they did because of the environment, not because of internal characteristics. Foreign policy was basically a reaction to other states and the environmental conditions under which each must operate (J. D. Singer 1963). If one could understand the characteristics of the system —the distribution of power, the kinds of alliances, the level of institutionalization provided by intergovernmental organizations—then one could explain important processes within the system, like the frequency and severity of war. These factors then could be related to individual perceptions (see J. D. Singer 1979b:27; 1958). For Singer the path to scientific knowledge did not lie with developing complete models of a system but with identifying specific systemic characteristics that could be related as independent and dependent variables.

If Singer's major contribution was to show the utility of the system perspective in comparison to the foreign policy perspective, Charles McClelland's (1966) contribution was to show how the systems level could be linked with the foreign policy level and operationalized, an essential process if any empirical research was to be conducted. Beginning with his own work on the acute international crisis, McClelland (1961) conceived of reactions among states as a series of interactions forming specific patterns of communication in terms of both frequency and content (see also McClelland 1968). The acute crisis changed that pattern. In principle, a system consisted of all the interaction links among the actors and their pattern of interaction. McClelland's work on crisis led to the creation of the World Event Interaction Survey (WEIS), one of the earliest event–data sets (see McClelland 1976). Because this work (McClelland 1961; 1968; 1972a) and that which followed it (Azar 1972; Tanter 1974) was dyadic, some commentators argued that it created an interaction level of analysis that linked the foreign policy and system levels (see Coplin 1971:183–184). The work on crisis pointed the way to the dyad as a unit of analysis, an important contribution since dyadic research was much more successful than research on a single actor, the so-called monad (see Kegley and Skinner 1976).

A considerable amount of research, including some of the best findings on conflict-cooperation, was done at the interaction level. Rummel's work in the DON project, for example, was ultimately an interaction analysis, with the examination of U.S. foreign policy (Rummel 1972a; Schwerin 1977) and later China's foreign policy (Rhee 1977a; 1977b) merely a device to test status-field theory (see also Choi 1977). In addition, status-field theory, to the extent it relied on a status pecking order and looked at distances between attributes, provided a systemic perspective. Rummel's work, then, although starting at the actor level with an internal attribute, crossed all three levels of analysis. In this sense, status-field theory provided a way of linking important research in different subfields.

As systems language was being elaborated, the discussion of the meaning of the balance of power concept, its relationship to war, and the effect of nuclear weapons combined in the famous debate over the relationship between polarity and stability. The debate began when Kenneth Waltz (1964) argued that a bipolar system was the most stable, and Karl Deutsch and J. David Singer (1964) argued that a multipolar system was the most stable. While the use of the word *stability* implied an association with system change, the debate was really about the likelihood of conflict and war. This ambiguity in the dependent variable added to the disagreements.

Inevitably, others were drawn into the debate. Morton Kaplan (1957) had argued earlier that a multipolar system was more stable. His position was important because he offered the traditional power-balance rationale, whereas Deutsch and Singer offered an explanation with more of a social psychology emphasis. They maintained that the more interaction opportunities among nations, the less attention devoted to any potential opponent, and the less attention devoted, the less conflict.

Richard Rosecrance (1966) disagreed with all contenders and argued that each system had destabilizing features and that a system of "bi-multipolarity" (one in which two superpowers would be held in check by lesser powers) would be the most stable. Rosecrance believed that bipolar systems would produce few but severe wars, whereas multipolar systems would produce frequent but less severe wars.

Wolfram Hanrieder (1965) doubted that the entire system could be characterized as either bipolar or multipolar and suggested that some issue areas had aspects of one system and other issues areas aspects of the other. P. Dale Dean, Jr., and John Vasquez (1976) maintained that both sides of the debate were incorrect in terms of the relationship between polarity and war/peace. They argued that there was no relationship between the number of actors in the system and the presence of peace, and that the number of issues was critical. Building on Deutsch and Singer, they suggested that the greater the number of issues in the system the more moderate conflict-cooperation would be, and the fewer the number of issues in the system the more intense conflict and cooperation would be.

The debate generated several empirical studies. J. David Singer and

Melvin Small (1968) provided the initial test and found different relationships for the nineteenth and twentieth centuries. A careful review of their findings by Dean and Vasquez (1976:15), however, showed that of sixty correlations only one explained more than 10 percent of the variance (11.56 percent) and was statistically significant. A second test by Michael Haas (1970) found that only unipolar systems were peaceful; all others had different amounts of war, suggesting some support for Rosecrance's thesis (see also M. Haas 1974:chap. 10). A third test by Rosecrance et al. (1974) for the 1870–1881 period supported the findings by concluding that there is not much of a relationship between the balance of power and conflict.

By the early seventies, the tests became more sophisticated in their measurement and data analysis. Michael Wallace (1973b) found a curvilinear relationship between polarity and the severity and magnitude of war. When there was very high and very low polarity, there were severe wars. When there was only moderate polarity, wars were considerably less severe. Bruce Bueno de Mesquita (1978) separated the occurrence of war from its severity, and, while finding no relationship between these dependent variables and the number of poles or their tightness and discreteness, he did find a relationship between war and increases in systemic tightness (see also Bueno de Mesquita 1975). The latter finding, however, was only for the twentieth century. Increasing tightness tended to lead to war, while declining tightness did not. In addition, increasing tightness tended to produce longer wars in the twentieth century.

Finally, Charles Ostrom and Francis Hoole (1978) redid Singer and Small (1968), looking at the number of dyads of inter-state war and the number of dyads having defense alliances. They found no relationship unless they controlled for time; then the relationship varied and only explained eleven percent of the variance. For time lags of 0 to 3 years there were some significant positive relationships. For lags of 4 to 12 years the relationship was more frequently significant but negative; that is, as alliance commitments increased the probability of war declined. In the long term (time lags greater than 12 years) there was no effect. What these findings may mean is that at the time defense commitments are made, there is a danger of war, but 4 to 12 years later there is not.

The polarity debate and the extensive testing it has generated indicate that the field's major interest in systemic processes has been with war. This was certainly true of the early power politics literature and the extensive discussions of the balance of power. The contribution of the systems framework in this process has been fairly limited, providing a perspective and a level of analysis rather than any real theoretical insights. An examination of other work on the causes of war will support this assessment and will show that because of ecological fallacies (see Wallace 1973a:86), propositions had to be tested at the interaction level, as well as the systemic, before any valid inferences could be made.

Causes of War

Ironic as it may seem, Morgenthau did not have a formal theory of the causes of war, nor did he write much about it. His concern was much broader; he saw the outbreak of violence as simply the natural culmination of unrestrained and mismanaged struggles for power. He believed that the only realistic road to peace was to use diplomacy to regulate the power struggle. He regarded other solutions and their latent theories of war as illusions. He saw even those to which he devoted the most attention, like the balance of power, as fraught with problems. All this reflects Morgenthau's underlying pessimism about making fundamental changes in world politics. For him the purpose of inquiry was describing realistically the regularities of behavior and then uncovering the laws that explained its dynamics. The purpose of inquiry was not to uncover the conditions or causes of behavior so that behavior could be changed through social engineering. This Morgenthau regarded not only as idealistic but as too mechanistic to account for the intricate texture of reality (see Morgenthau 1946; 1973:vii–x).

Despite the realist paradigm's tremendous impact, the goal had been set by the idealist paradigm; and although Morgenthau may have been resigned to rely only on diplomacy, others, including the early power politics theorists who analyzed the causal assumptions of the balance of power, were not. They searched for causes of war.

The earliest were concerned with debunking the idealist explanation. Of the works coming out of the early power politics tradition, the most important attack on idealist explanations of war was Kenneth Waltz's *Man, the State, and War* (1959). Waltz attempted to lay out the various explanations of war found in the Western political tradition and assess their relative merit. To this end he distilled most of the explanations of war and classified them into three images: as a function of human nature; as a function of the characteristics of states; and as a function of the anarchic nature of the global system. Waltz's study represented the high point of the traditional analysis of war. The reliance on trenchant logical argument supplemented by anecdotal but informed historical evidence took the traditional approach as far as it could go. What was needed was systematic scientific research to provide the evidence for rejecting inadequate explanations and reformulating more promising ones. This was not to appear until the late sixties; in the meantime analyses of war were conducted by elaborating the traditional wisdom in the context of research on systemic processes and the balance of power.

The onslaught of the behavioral revolt and its use of scientific criteria caused some scholars to become frustrated with the imprecision and contradiction inherent in so much of the traditional approach (see J. D. Singer 1969b:70–71; 1980:xxxv). Although the behavioralists began by converting various realist propositions into testable hypotheses, their view of inquiry was much more causal and their belief in ending war less pessimistic than that of early traditionalists like Morgenthau. In the mid-sixties these perspectives led to a systematic effort to search for the causes of war, with the hope that in the distant future a truly empirical and scientific understanding of war (not like the normative, uncorroborated theory of the idealists) would make a world at peace possible.

Given the emphasis on mathematics, causal analysis, and the use of knowledge to change behavior, it was not surprising that the mentors of this peace research movement were two prerealist scholars—Lewis Richardson and Quincy Wright (see J. D. Singer 1970:527–528). Lewis Richardson, a British Quaker, was a physicist who devoted his retired life to mathematically analyzing conditions that led to war. His work, originally published in 1939, did not gain widespread recognition in his lifetime but received more attention after a summary by Rapoport (1957) and its posthumous publication in two books—*Arms and Insecurity* and *Statistics of Deadly Quarrels* (1960a; 1960b). The first was a mathematical model of arms races, the second a statistical analysis of conditions of violence. Underlying both works was a psychological paradigm that saw war as simply one manifestation of human aggression.

Quincy Wright was an American political scientist who, reacting, like Richardson, to the First World War, attempted to delineate the causes of war. Unlike Richardson, who worked essentially alone and outside his trained specialty, Wright's project at the University of Chicago was massive in scope and received institutional assistance and recognition. Wright (1942) summarized most of the theories of war in the various social sciences and attempted to apply their insights to account for war. The most significant contribution of the two-volume *Study of War* (1942), however, was that it was the first to research the causes of war by systematically collecting data on war, going back to the fifteenth century. Beginning the project in the 1920s, Wright was influenced by the idealists during the early stages of the project, although he was much more empirically oriented than they or later realists. Behavioralists were attracted to Richardson's use of mathematics and Wright's use of systematically collected data.

The main behavioral research effort on war has centered around the Correlates of War project, primarily because it has been the major data source even for those not directly connected with it. This group's initial efforts have focused on collecting data and analyzing it to determine exactly what the correlates of war are. Once this "brush-clearing" phase is completed, attention can shift from correlates to causal explanation. The brush-clearing phase has consisted of reformulating and testing many imprecise realist propositions on alliances and power, elaborating and testing alternatives to realist explanations based on status inconsistency, and testing and rejecting propositions on crowding and war, and on democracy and war.

Testing the realist propositions first made the most sense given the dominance of the realist paradigm and the previous literature on systems and the balance of power. The examination of the role of alliances was conducted in studies by J. D. Singer and Small (1966a; 1968), Wallace (1972), Bueno de Mesquita (1978), and Ostrom and Hoole (1978). These studies naturally gave rise to an assessment of propositions related to the role of power in the onset of war. The most definitive study to date has been that of J. D. Singer, Bremer, and Stuckey (1972), who examined the relationship between the distribution of power, changes in that distribution, and the onset of war. They found that in the nineteenth century, peace was associated with systemic parity of power and change toward parity ($R^2 = .65$), but in the twentieth century, systemic preponderance of power and the absence of power shifts were found to be moderately associated with peace ($R^2 = .30$). On the actor level, Bremer (1980) found that states ranking high on capability are involved in more wars (including more initiations of war) than states that have a lower rank.

The relationship between power and war was also investigated by some outside the project. Of these studies, the most important were those by Ferris (1973), Garnham (1976), and Weede (1976). Ferris (1973:115–116), whose study is the most carefully done and hence the most reliable, found no relationship between disparity of power or change in disparity and the probability that conflict will escalate to war. He did find, however, that: (1) there is some relationship between the change in the distribution of power in the system and the amount of war in the system; (2) the greater the disparity of power between states or the greater the change in power capabilities of states, the greater the probability the states will become involved in intense conflicts. Garnham (1976) found some support for the relationship between capability and war, but his finding was so narrow that it loses most of its explanatory power. In effect, Garnham (1976:384, 390) found that *if* a country has a violent confrontation with a neighbor (from 1969–1973), it will probably be the neighbor that is most equal in power to it. This hardly supports the proposition that parity is associated with war, nor does it refute Ferris's contradictory findings, which Garnham ignored.

Weede (1976:402–404) found that when there is an overwhelming (ten to one) preponderance of power in Asian (including Middle Eastern) dyads, there is no war (1950–1969). This conclusion must be tempered by the fact that Weede's data set contains few cases of war. Consequently, there are not many wars in the absence of preponderance (phi = .31). When Weede (1976:407–409) looked at dyads that had a history of either latent territorial or Cold War conflict, he found a moderate association (phi = .40 to .50) between the absence of overwhelming preponderance and war. The Weede study is important because it suggests that the contradictions between the Ferris finding that disparity of power is associated with conflict and Garnham's finding that parity is associated with war (as well as the Singer, Bremer, and Stuckey 1972 findings that parity in the nineteenth century but preponderance in the twentieth are associated with peace) can be resolved by more precise measurement of different aspects of parity, greater specification of the dependent variable, and controlling for the nature or presence of serious disputes.[8]

These studies have provided important evidence that some aspects of realist explanations could be correct, but they also raise questions about what causes this power politics behavior in the first place. When this kind of question is asked, power politics becomes a model that only holds under certain conditions, and it becomes necessary to have a more encompassing theory that can explain when power politics will occur, when it will not, and what will bring about the transition. Several of the researchers in the Correlates of War project searched for such an explanation in the literature on status inconsistency.

The earliest studies in this vein were those of Michael Wallace (1971; 1973a), who attempted to see if a power explanation would be more potent than a status-inconsistency explanation. After a series of tests, he concluded that status inconsistency was a more potent correlate of war than changes in capability. Wallace (1972) then went on to provide the most complete working model to date on the paths to war and peace. He argued that changes in capability are related to changes in the amount of

8. Also relevant to this question are two other studies, one by Naroll, Bullough, and Naroll (1974) and one by Blainey (1973). Naroll et al. (1974) examined (for selected periods from 225 B.C. to 1785 A.D.) the proposition that military strength will prevent war under certain conditions. They found that military strength variables were not related to the amount of war experienced by certain "conspicuous dyads." Severe methodological criticisms of this study warrant caution in its use, however (see Gochman 1976:41–44). Blainey (1973), in a sweeping review of the modern history of war, concluded that war occurs when each side disagrees over who would win the war if it were fought. Obviously such disagreements over relative power are more likely to occur in conditions of parity. While Blainey's work is reminiscent of Waltz's (1959), he ignored much of the extensive quantitative literature that emerged in the late sixties.

status inconsistency in the system; his earlier study (1971; 1973) had shown that after a considerable time lag, systemic inconsistency is related to war. This status inconsistency can make a system war-prone in the presence of certain intervening variables (Wallace 1972). High status inconsistency tends to give rise to alliance polarization, which promotes arms races, which in turn are highly correlated with the onset of war. This path to war, which Wallace (1972) delineated, is complemented by a path to peace in which low status inconsistency is related to the creation (and presumably the effective use) of international intergovernmental organization. The presence of many IGOs is negatively related to arms races, which are positively correlated with the onset of war. This last path is related to Waltz's (1959) third image, which assumes that war will only become less frequent to the extent that there are alternative ways of making authoritative decisions. In his later research, Wallace (1979a) investigated the linkage between arms races and war by showing that of the 28 cases where there were arms races *and* serious disputes (between 1816 and 1965), 23 erupted in war; in the 71 cases in which there were serious disputes but no arms races, only 3 erupted in war (Yule's Q = .96). Further investigation of this finding, after a criticism by Weede (1980), reconfirms it (see Wallace 1981).

The main limitation of Wallace's research was the possibility that it might be subject to an ecological fallacy because it investigated the proposition only at the systemic level and not the actor level. The work of Manus Midlarsky (1975), James Lee Ray (1974; 1978), and Charles Gochman (1975; 1980) all helped resolve this problem. Using Correlates of War data, Midlarsky (1975) found that status-inconsistent states were more likely to resort to violence (see also East 1972). James Lee Ray, also employing Correlates of War data, found no relationship between status inconsistency and participation or initiation of war by European nation-states. This contradiction is explained, in part, by Gochman (1980), who found that in predicting the threat or use of military force, a capability model best fits major European powers, but a status-inconsistency model best fits non-European and newer powers like the United States, China, and Japan.

The research associated with the Correlates of War project has been successful in delineating some theoretically significant correlations of war by examining variables measuring capability, status inconsistency, alliance polarization, intergovernmental organization, and arms races. In addition, the project found that other correlates that had been suggested in the literature did not emerge in preliminary investigations. The propositions that crowded states would be more aggressive and democratic states more peaceful were rejected when tested (see Bremer, Singer, and Luterbacher 1973; Small and Singer 1976). On each of these questions, however, research has been continued by some scholars outside the project (see Choucri 1974; Choucri and North 1975; Russett and Monsen 1975).

As the 1980s approached, the Correlates of War project began work on a new research design that attempted to look at the causes of war by focusing on serious disputes (see J. D. Singer 1979a; 1980). The more recent research of the project reflects an interest in five questions. (1) What generates serious disputes?[9] (2) Why do some serious disputes give rise to threats of violence and when does the threat of violence escalate to war (Gochman 1980; Leng and Goodsell 1974; Leng and Wheeler 1979; Leng 1980; Sabrosky 1975)?[10] (3) When do wars expand (Siverson and King 1979; Sabrosky 1980; Yamamoto and Bremer 1980)? (4) When do wars terminate (Cannizzo 1980)? (5) What are the consequences of war (Wheeler 1980)?

Others outside the project have also addressed these questions, and some, of course, had initially raised them. Two of the other major projects in the field, the 1914 studies and the DON project, devoted part of their attention to the causes of war, providing links between this research and the research on foreign policy conflict and on bargaining. The work of Nazli Choucri and Robert North (1975) sought to delineate the systemic conditions under which serious disputes arise. They argued, along almost Marxist lines, that growth in population, need for resources, and technological capability lead nation-states to expand. As states expand, their interests intersect and serious disputes erupt. These disputes in turn give rise to perceptions of threat that fuel military expenditures and alliances. The earlier work on the 1914 crisis and misperception can then be used to suggest what factors send a serious dispute out of control.

The convergence of the 1914 studies and the Correlates of War project toward a common theoretical framework is made even more evident by an examination of Rummel's (1979) explanation of war derived from the DON project studies on inter-nation conflict. Rummel employed his earlier work on field theory (Rummel 1977a) to construct a theory that would explain the emergence of disputes in light of a general theory of conflict (Rummel 1976c; 1977b). The potential for what Rummel (1979: chap. 10) calls *latent conflict* is a function of the sociocultural distance between two actors, the distance between their capability (including

9. This relates nicely to the work on status inconsistency by assuming that systems with high status inconsistency would give rise to more serious disputes.
10. The question of escalation is also treated in the context of bargaining and deterrence in the next section of this chapter. One of the major studies is Smoke (1977).

military power, wealth, and size [resource base]), and the difference in their polity (democratic, authoritarian). These factors form a structure of conflict and shape actors' goals and attitudes. How these tendencies affect behavior depends on: the situation of conflict, which for Rummel (1979:160, 163–164) involved the perceived nature of the situation (whether there is a threat or opportunity); the existence of opposing interests; the relative capability of the actors; and the actors' expectations. Structural and situational characteristics determine the likelihood of conflict. Once a confrontation is set off by some trigger action, the interaction of states enters a situation of uncertainty, where each actor tests the other and behavior is a function of will and preparedness (Rummel 1979:186). Rummel (1979:chap. 12) analyzed conflict interaction in terms of status quo testing, which can take coercive and/or non-coercive paths. Which paths are taken is, in part, a function and reinforcement of hostility patterns. Nevertheless, interaction is reciprocal until crises emerge that signal escalatory changes in behavior (Rummel 1979:22). Rummel (1979:chap. 13) then attempts to delineate the factors that make a crisis escalate to war. Clearly, this framework is not so different from the new research design offered in the Correlates of War, although each project seems to have developed independently of the other (at least, the researchers do not cite each other's recent work [see Rummel 1979; J. D. Singer 1980]). In addition, Rummel's work is obviously influenced by much of the work in comparative foreign policy and reflects a conscious attempt to embrace most of the quantitative research in international politics and a good deal of conflict theory outside international relations inquiry (see Rummel 1979; 1977b).

What distinguishes Rummel's work from other efforts to date is that he attempts to construct a unified theory of war, not just a framework. Through a systematic search of the scientific literature on wars, he marshals evidence for each of his propositions (1979:parts V and VI). He concludes (Rummel 1979:241–242) that international conflict is caused by opposing interests and opposing capabilities (which are a function of specific sociocultural differences and similarities [field theory]); contact with and the salience of other actors; significant change in the balance of powers (sic); individual perceptions and expectations; a disrupted structure of expectations; and a will-to-conflict. Conflict is encouraged by sociocultural dissimilarity, cognitive imbalance, status difference, and the presence of coercive state power. It is inhibited by sociocultural similarity and weak coercive power. It is triggered by the perception of opportunity, threat, or injustice, and by surprise. Conflict of this sort often results in violence or war in the presence of authoritarian or totalitarian states, status quo disruption, and confidence of success. The tendency toward violence is aggravated by system polarity (centralization of coercive power), big power intervention, weakness of the status quo power, and a challenge to an actor's credibility or honor. War is inhibited by cross-pressures, the presence of democratic states, strong status quo powers, and world opinion. In addition, war is uniquely aggravated by power parity and class conflict and uniquely inhibited by power disparity. Finally, nonviolent conflict behavior and low-level violence are encouraged by cross-pressures and inhibited by system polarity (centralization) and a stable status quo.[11]

While listing these factors cannot do justice to Rummel's specific propositions and their theoretical rationale, it should be emphasized that Rummel has not, like others (e.g., Blainey 1973), simply reviewed every factor ever mentioned as a correlate of war. Instead, he has attempted to piece together carefully many of the different findings in order to solve the puzzle of war. In the process, it should be clear that field theory and status-field theory (Rummel 1977a:chaps. 2 and 9) have become subsumed within a more general power politics framework. The adoption of a more traditional emphasis seems, in part, to be associated with Rummel's abandonment of logical positivism; at least that is what he associates with his de-emphasis on field theory (Rummel 1979:215, note 2; see also the very candid Rummel 1976a). He now places more emphasis on coercion and the balancing of powers, although his use of the latter is much broader than anything referred to by the early realists under that concept (see Rummel 1979:chap. 12).

In his most recent work, Rummel has moved away from the direction of the more status-oriented theorists like Galtung and Wallace and back toward the early power politics theorists. Nevertheless, there remain within his work latent tensions that challenge aspects of the realist paradigm. Foremost among these is the belief that a single theory of conflict can account for individual, group, and state behavior (a rejection of the second assumption) (Rummel 1976c; 1979:190). Next is the strong emphasis, throughout, on psychology and perceptions as opposed to actual physical capacity and actions (see, for example, Rummel 1979:191, where he goes so far as to refer to military actions as simply "epiphenomena of shifts in the psychological field"). Finally, the tests in *Field Theory Evolving* (Rummel 1977a) still stand on their own, subject to interpretations more radical than and less tied to the realist paradigm.[12]

11. Except for some stylistic changes and the order of presentation, this list of factors is taken almost verbatim from Rummel (1979:241–242).

12. At this writing, J. D. Singer and his associates in the Correlates of War project are just beginning to integrate their findings into a preliminary theory of war (see K. W. Deutsch 1980:293). It will be interesting to see to what extent they challenge power politics explanations and the assumptions of the realist paradigm.

Somewhat surprisingly, there has emerged among the three major projects in the field a consensus that the best way to study the causes of war is to look at the factors that generate serious disputes or crises and then to examine what causes these confrontations to escalate to violence. In light of this research program, several studies on escalation take on new theoretical significance. Two of the earliest studies, those of Wright (1965b) and Kahn (1968), have been the object of renewed interest (see Rummel 1979:193–200). Wright (1965) attempted to delineate the stages by which a crisis escalated to war, while Kahn (1968) was more concerned with the escalation of limited war to nuclear war (see also Bloomfield and Leiss 1969). Both, however, were concerned with the causal processes underlying conflict spirals. In the 1970s these theoretical questions were investigated in three empirical studies. Northedge and Donelan (1971) examined fifty disputes from 1945 to 1970 and attempted to describe the stages of escalation (see also Donelan and Grieve 1973). More quantitative was the work of Richard Barringer (1972), who developed a phase model of the transformation of disputes into war. Barringer believed that definite thresholds were crossed in the escalation of disputes, and he analyzed statistically some 300 factors (including the structure, resources, capabilities, objectives, and performances of each actor in 18 confrontations) to determine where these thresholds might lie (Barringer 1972:49–50). The result is one of the most detailed statistical descriptions of factors associated with moving from one stage to another in transforming disputes into wars (see Barringer 1972:chap. 6 for the findings). Finally, Richard Smoke (1977) employed a more in-depth comparative case study method to determine the factors common to the escalation of limited war to wider wars. He examined three wars that did not escalate—the Spanish Civil War, the Austro-Prussian War of 1866, and the Franco-Prussian War of 1870–1871—and two wars that did—the Crimean War (1854–1856) and the Seven Years' War (1756–1763).

Although the causes of war occupied the center stage of inquiry, several scholars were interested in the termination phases of war. The earliest studies were on how and why wars end. Lewis Richardson (1960b:299) believed that a certain level of population loss would result in the termination of war, and he found that for less populous states this level was somewhere between .05 percent and 5.0 percent of its population. Frank Klingberg (1966) suggested that a 3.0 percent or 4.0 percent loss of population or two significant military reversals would result in surrender. The most comprehensive study, however, was that of Steven Rosen (1972:181–182), who found that wars are won by governments with more revenue and a lower percentage of population loss (population loss can vary from .004 percent to 4.1 percent [Rosen 1972:179]). Other studies have shown that public support for war declines as casualties increase (Mueller 1971; see also Modigliani 1972; Mueller 1976). The intriguing question is whether wars end because of public pressure on governments. This proposition is only beginning to be investigated empirically for open societies (see Burstein and Freudenburg 1976), not to mention closed ones.

By examining payoffs and costs, other research in this area has focused on the logic of how wars end. The most obvious explanation is a rational cost-benefit analysis, and this approach can be significant when deductive mathematical analysis is employed (see Wittman 1979). More empirical was Paul Kecskemeti's (1958) study of surrender in World War II. Fred Ikle (1971) discussed some of the problems of ending war from a broader negotiation perspective. Finally, Harvey Starr (1972) looked at the termination of war from the perspective of dividing spoils among the victors.

The consequences of war have been explored only in the most preliminary fashion. Michael Stohl (1975) looked at the effect of war on domestic stability and on repression in polyarchies. Arthur Stein (1980) looked at America's involvement in recent wars to delineate the effects of war on internal cohesion, concentration of production, and inequality. In a very interesting study, A. F. K. Organski and Jack Kugler (1977; 1978) examined how long it takes defeated states to recover their capability. They found that after World War I and World War II, in the short run, all belligerents declined in GNP, but losers experienced more severe declines. After fifteen to twenty years, however, losers' GNP equaled and sometimes exceeded that of winners. Charles Doran (1971) attempted to determine what policies and power factors make for successful assimilation of a defeated "hegemony-seeking power" by examining the Peace of Westphalia, the Treaty of Utrecht, and the Congress of Vienna.

Clearly, the research on the causes and termination of war have elaborated a research area of central importance to the realist paradigm. In addition, the research program has focused on the two central concepts of the realist paradigm—national power and the balance of power. Much of the work in the area has made explicit or implicit propositions in the power politics literature much more precise and has subjected these propositions to statistical analysis. In this sense the research agenda of this area has been dominated by the realist paradigm and has not challenged the paradigm's three fundamental assumptions. This does not mean that there has not been important change and growth. The introduction of status propositions and conceptualization, as well as the Marxist implications of Choucri and North's (1975) model, raise tensions in the paradigm that may begin to challenge the three fundamental assumptions.

Deterrence and Bargaining

A fourth major development of the paradigm came out of the work on deterrence and bargaining. The primary academic concern in this area was to discern the effect of nuclear weapons on the power structure of the system and/or bargaining processes and to employ these insights to amend traditional power politics theory. This research focus was made even more policy relevant by the interest of the U.S. government in developing a strategic doctrine that would rationalize the various aspects of its military program. This led in the early phases to the financing of individual scholars and groups of scholars in so-called "think tanks" such as the RAND Corporation and Project Michelson of the U.S. Navy. Among the notable scholars associated with RAND at various times were Bernard Brodie, Herman Kahn, Albert Wohlstetter, Thomas Schelling, and Daniel Ellsberg.[13]

Although governmental concerns intervene more in this area than anywhere else, the research program of this subfield has evolved according to a logic of its own. The effort can be divided into four categories, each interrelated but with identifiable topics and approaches: (1) early work on the effect of nuclear power on traditional balance of power theory and its implications for practical strategic doctrine; (2) the use of game theory to explain and apply nuclear deterrence and bargaining, and to examine the limits of rationality; (3) the empirical examination of the assumptions of deterrence theory and general coercive diplomacy; (4) the elucidation of general bargaining theory. These four efforts can be seen as elaborating what Morgenthau saw as a central component of international politics—the struggle for power—in light of changing systemic conditions brought about by the development of nuclear weapons.

Nuclear Weapons and the Balance of Power

Arthur Lee Burns (1957) and John Herz (1959) were among the most influential scholars who saw the need to reformulate traditional balance of power theory because of atomic weapons. The rapid technological changes of the post–World War II period kept this research alive and well funded. Brodie (1945) first raised the possibility that atomic weapons could be used to prevent war (see also Brodie 1959). Burns (1957) related this notion to traditional balance of power conceptions and

13. On RAND, see Burns (1972:77) and B. L. R. Smith (1966); on Project Michelson see Milburn (1969). For general reviews of deterrence scholarship, see Burns (1972); Jervis (1979); Brodie (1973:chap. 9); Licklider (1971); Dougherty and Pfaltzgraff (1971:chap. 9).

power politics generally. In a very influential article in *Foreign Affairs*, Albert Wohlstetter (1959) raised the possibility of surprise attack on the Strategic Air Command, highlighting the vulnerability of this delicate balance of terror. This fear has fueled American insecurity and the arms race down through the current period, even though many strategic thinkers believed that a surprise attack was highly unlikely (Brodie 1966).

Thomas Milburn, directing Project Michelson, coordinated an interdisciplinary attempt to examine some of the fundamental questions associated with deterrence (see Milburn 1969) and contributed some of the basic conceptual work in this area (Milburn 1959). From a broader perspective, Boulding's (1962) use of systems analysis showed how rapid changes in technology had eliminated many of the obstacles to long-range attack.

The work that had the most impact, however, was that of Herman Kahn (1960; 1962). Kahn not only was responsible for introducing some of the basic concepts, like second-strike capability, into the logic of deterrence, but also discussed in detail how nuclear weapons had to be used to win or at least survive a nuclear war. Kahn's work was the culmination of much of the previous work in strategic studies and also inaugurated a new concern with fighting total and limited wars.

Deterrence and nuclear weapons were now seen in the broader context of coercive diplomacy and Clausewitzian conceptions of war. Several analysts, including Secretary of Defense Robert McNamara (1968), investigated what options would be available to the United States in the event of a nuclear war. From this perspective, nuclear weapons were seen as weapons of strategy rather than total annihilation (see the earlier discussions in Knorr and Read 1952). Others, in particular Henry Kissinger (1957a; 1961), felt that the increasing reliance on the threat of massive retaliation limited the United States to a choice of destroying the world or surrendering. He argued that the United States should rebuild its conventional forces and also learn how to combat guerrilla wars. The concern with the limitation of nuclear deterrence for defense was also pursued by Glenn Snyder (1961; 1965) in a more theoretical fashion. The most extreme attack on the utility of deterrence came from William W. Kaufmann (1964), who argued that deterrence had failed to inhibit the Russians; this position brought a sharp rebuke in 1965 from Brodie (1973:410–412). Nevertheless, these concerns reflected a renewed interest in the doctrine of limited war (see R. Osgood 1957). As Vietnam increased in salience, this renewed interest gave rise to a series of studies on counterinsurgency warfare (Licklider 1971:157; see Mitchell 1968; Russo 1972).

Since one of the major problems with limited war is preventing its escalation to total war, RAND sponsored studies on this question, the most significant of which were Kahn (1968), Brodie (1966), and Sallagar (1975, originally produced in 1969). With the Vietnam experience coming to an end, Brodie (1973) provided a fairly comprehensive statement on the problem of strategy and war from a Clausewitzian perspective, reviewing World War I, World War II, Korea, Vietnam, and nuclear strategy. By the time of the Reagan administration, attention was focused on fighting and winning a limited nuclear war (see Sigal 1979; Gray and Payne 1980; Pipes 1981).

While some of the research in this area was concerned with coercive diplomacy and fighting war, other research was devoted to arms control and nuclear proliferation. Most of the work on arms control throughout the period from the height of the Cold War (Schelling and Halperin 1961) through the end of the seventies (e.g., Blechman 1980; Lodal 1978–1979; Burt 1978; Rummel 1976b) remained very policy oriented even though it occasionally made theoretical insights. Nevertheless, some scholars moved beyond these questions to more general ones, such as the conditions that might bring about arms control or under which it might work (C. E. Osgood 1959; Rapoport 1964). The work on nuclear proliferation followed a similar pattern, with early work devoted to specific policy concerns (e.g., Buchan 1966; Quester 1972), and later work being supplemented by a more general theoretical concern with the causes of proliferation and the dynamics of a multi-nuclear world (Kegley, Raymond, and Skinner 1980; Kaplan 1957; Brody 1963; Rosecrance 1973: chap. 20; C. F. Hermann, M. G. Hermann, and Cantor 1974; Rosen 1977). These more general concerns easily spilled over into the second major effort in this area—the use of game theory to elaborate deterrence theory.

Game Theory

Game theory was the major conceptual innovation provided by this subfield in articulating the realist paradigm. In the early sixties, game theory in the work of von Neuman and Morgenstern (1944), Nash (1950), and Luce and Raiffa (1957) began to have an impact on political science, particularly through the more social-science-oriented applications of Harsanyi (1961) and Shubik (1959; 1967). In international relations, game theory became the basis of some of the most important work on deterrence and coercive diplomacy.

The work of Arthur Lee Burns (1957; 1961; 1968a; 1968b) stands out as a forerunner in the use of game theory to elaborate a doctrine of deterrence. Although Burns is influenced by the theory of games, he does not employ formal game theory, but a rational deductive mode of analysis characteristic of much economic theory. This approach, which

Riker (1962) made famous in political science, was very useful because a number of hypothetical and anticipated military technological changes could be assessed in a theoretical format. Burns's use of rationality provided almost a "micro-exemplar" for much of the work in this subfield, even though the subsequent work of Kahn and Schelling somewhat overshadowed his contribution. Nevertheless, many of his analyses of future events—like the effect of a guided missile defense system, the logic of nuclear proliferation, and the defection of allies—were prescient (Burns 1957:511–515, 517–519, 520–524). In his later work, Burns (1961; 1968a) attempted to elaborate a game theory of inter-nation conflict and cooperation building upon Riker's (1962) size principle and coalition theory and developed with Kaplan and Quandt (Kaplan et al. 1960) a game to explore some of these hypotheses. However, Burns (1968a: 175–179; 1968b:200–224; 1972:71–72) felt that formal game theory was very limiting, because its assumptions were too rigid for international politics. Throughout his analyses, the purpose was to adapt the game-theory approach to build, in Burns's words, "a theory of pure power politics" (Burns 1961:26; see also 1968a:175).

The seminal work in this area was that of Schelling (1960; 1966), parts of which had been published earlier, 1956, 1957, and 1958. Schelling (1960) began by pointing out the severe limitations of formal game theory in understanding international politics caused by the inapplicability of its assumptions; he went on to explore a game-theoretic rationality that permitted the observer to deduce an opponent's moves as well as the consequences of one's own policy. Through this technique, Schelling provided important insights about limited war, surprise attack, and disarmament. In addition, he converted much of deterrence theory into a more general coercive bargaining approach by distinguishing deterrence from compellence and specifying the conditions necessary for each to work (Schelling 1966:79–80). Many of Schelling's ideas, it should be noted, came from his experience at RAND and were influenced by other analysts at RAND (like Daniel Ellsberg, Bernard Brodie, Herman Kahn, William Kaufmann, and Albert Wohlstetter) (see Schelling 1960:vi; cf. Ellsberg 1959). In fact, Schelling's main influence can be interpreted as giving a broader theoretical foundation to the emerging deterrence doctrine.

After Schelling, the other major use of game theory to elaborate deterrence theory appeared in Glenn Snyder's (1961; 1972) work. In his early writings he attempted to revamp the concept of balance of power in terms of the effect of nuclear weapons and the advent of long-range missiles, and then explore the implications for defense. In his later work he made more direct use of game theory, particularly the chicken game analogy for certain crisis situations. Like Schelling, G. Snyder found formal game theory too restrictive, and he employed game theory matrices primarily to suggest how perceptions of payoffs and game structure (e.g., chicken game) could be used to explain the bargaining sequences and final outcomes. Unlike Schelling, G. Snyder was more concerned with the relationship between crisis and the onset of war. In his major work on crisis bargaining, coauthored with Paul Diesing (G. Snyder and Diesing 1977), game theory is elaborated to permit for different perceptions of the contenders so that the traditional chicken and prisoner's dilemma games give way to new game models like "Deadlock, Called Bluff, Bully, Protector, Critical Risk, and Expanded Chicken."

Although Schelling and others avoided using formal game theory, the entire effort, particularly when linked with the strategic studies, was throughout the sixties a highly deductive, rationalistic enterprise that relied heavily on argumentation and rarely on empirical analysis (see Jervis 1979:301–314). While numerous critics continued to question rational assumptions in deterrence theory (e.g., Morgan 1977; J. Snyder 1978), the major undercutting of deterrence assumptions and propositions came from the attempt to investigate empirically, either through systematic case studies or statistical analysis, the way in which deterrence actually works.

The Empirical Examination of Deterrence

Bruce Russett made the first major attempt to investigate empirically some of the problems with deterrence. As early as 1963, Russett collected data on pre- and post-1945 cases in an effort to delineate the conditions under which deterrence would work. He found that a formal, unambiguous commitment and strategic superiority were not factors in successful deterrence. The following, however, were factors: military cooperation and/or economic interdependence between the defender and pawn; the presence of nuclear weapons; and the insignificance of the pawn (low ratio to the defender in population and GNP) (Russett 1963b; see also Fink 1965). This statistical study supplemented two other studies on the breakdown of deterrence—one on the escalation of the 1914 crisis (Russett 1962b) and another on Pearl Harbor (Russett 1967b; see also Quester 1966 and Hosoya 1968)—that explicitly examined the assumptions of deterrence theory. For Russett, deterrence was not a solution but a part of the problem.

While Russett raised a number of questions about the validity of deterrence, most of the work at the end of the sixties and early seventies did not follow his lead. In the theoretical work examining cases involving deterrence, the emphasis was on the broader focus of crisis bargaining and coercive diplomacy. The work that led the way in this area was that of Oran Young (1968). Beginning with a concern with conflict resolution through the use of intermediaries (O. Young 1967), he turned to reviewing several post–World War II crises in an attempt to derive testable hypotheses. In his systematic review of four cases in which deterrence was employed—Berlin (1948–1949), Taiwan Straits (1958), Berlin (1961), and Cuba (1962)—Young (1968) provided the first major instance in which the effect of the deterrence logic was compared with other factors operating in the crisis. When seen in this broader context, the logical arguments of Schelling, Kahn, and others appeared less impressive.

The empirical examination of coercive diplomacy was continued by Alexander George, David Hall, and William Simons (1971). They attempted to delineate the conditions of failure and success of coercive diplomacy by reviewing its uses in Laos (1960–1961), Cuba (1962), and Vietnam (1964–1965). They suggested that American use of coercive diplomacy would succeed given eight conditions: "strength of United States motivation, asymmetry of motivation favoring the United States, clarity of American objectives, sense of urgency to achieve the American objective, adequate domestic political support, usable military options, opponent's fear of unacceptable escalation, and clarity concerning the precise terms of settlement" (George, Hall, and Simons 1971:216). In conducting this review, they were assessing empirically some of the limitations on deterring moderate provocations, what Kahn (1960:chap. 4) had called type three deterrence. It was this type three deterrence that Kissinger (1957a; 1961), G. Snyder (1961), and Kaufmann (1964) had found deficient for more rationalistic-deductive reasons.

While the work of Russett, O. Young, and George, Hall, and Simons was highly suggestive, it was not until the publication of George and Smoke (1974) that serious questions about the validity of the deterrence theory began to be raised within the field (see Jervis 1979:301). George and Smoke (1974:503–508) found that deterrence theory was incomplete and could not account for the complexities of given situations, and therefore provided insufficient guidance to policy makers. In addition, George and Smoke maintain that the way American policy makers applied deterrence hardly followed the strategists' dictates. More important, assumptions about an opponent's rationality failed to predict the opponent's behavior, leaving American policy makers not only surprised but unaware of the dangerous consequences of their own policies. This was because, to the opponent, "rationality" was different. Finally, George and Smoke pointed out that deterrence theory was altogether too narrow; they tried to reformulate it as a subset of a general theory of influence, looking specifically at the questions of initiation, commitment, response, and failure.

The search for deficiencies in deterrence theory was further advanced by the work of Glenn Snyder and Paul Diesing (1977). In the tradition of Oran Young (1968), they examined existing and reformulated game-theoretic interpretations of bargaining by systematically reviewing thirteen crisis cases from Fashoda (1898) to Cuba (1962) and looking at five others (G. Snyder and Diesing 1977:xii). One of their major findings was that rational utility models did not work very well in explaining bargaining behavior (1977:66–79, 180–182). They then went on to account for this by incorporating insights from work on cognitive psychology and decision making, particularly that of Jervis (1976) (see G. Snyder and Diesing 1977:chaps. 4 and 5).

Snyder and Diesing's work can be seen as the culmination of what was a progressive rejection in this subfield of various aspects of the rational-actor model, which early power politics theorists like Morgenthau and Burns had promulgated and early strategic thinkers like Brodie, Wohlstetter, Kahn, and Schelling, had seized upon. The rational-deductive mode of theorizing tended to make deterrence more of a doctrine than an empirical theory. This was in part because the arguments were so persuasive in light of power politics assumptions about reality (Jervis 1979:289–291). Empirical analysis, however, saved the subfield from becoming the captive of dogma. In demonstrating the invalidity of viewing nation-states as rational actors, George and Smoke and G. Snyder and Diesing raised serious questions about the adequacy of the major theoretical explanations within this subfield.

From another perspective, the three research efforts reflect a certain coherence and unity typical of normal science. Topics of central concern to the realist paradigm (i.e., the effect of nuclear weapons on the struggle for power and on the prospects for peace and war) were investigated systematically, with significant ties to research in other subfields. In addition, the point that new conceptual approaches were used to analyze problems related to the realist paradigm and did not in themselves constitute new theories or paradigms is underlined by the use of traditional power politics by Brodie and Kahn; "game theory" by Burns, Schelling, and G. Snyder; systems analysis by Wohlstetter and Boulding; statistical analysis by Russett; and simulation by Brody and in Project Michelson. Nevertheless, these scholars provided conceptual innovation that was dramatically different from the traditional balance of power literature and served to convey influences from economics, mathematics, public administration, and sociology.

Social Psychology and Bargaining

While work on deterrence and coercive bargaining dominated this subfield, other work on bargaining continued. The recent empirical criticisms of deterrence rationality have brought renewed attention to the more general questions of bargaining. Bargaining research was distinguished from the research on deterrence and coercive diplomacy primarily in being much more influenced by social psychological theories, with a considerable amount of work being done by social psychologists; it was also more general, in that it looked at a variety of bargaining situations, not just coercive diplomacy.

In this area, the work most relevant to the work on deterrence has been that of Anatol Rapoport. His *Fights, Games, and Debates* (1960) was important for delineating types of bargaining situations by showing that in a debate one tries to persuade an opponent, in a game one tries to outwit an opponent, and in a fight one tries to destroy an opponent. The type of situation governs not only what strategies are used but which succeed. Rapoport went on to suggest how one could move from fights to games and games to debates, underlining the importance of communication and understanding.

Rapoport's work was also significant because he worked with game theory proper; long before George and Smoke, he saw the need to test how people played games and developed strategies after repeated plays. His work on prisoner's dilemma with Albert Chammah (1965) proved to be a model for many future experimental analyses. Unlike most of the strategic theorists, Rapoport was highly distrustful of deductive rationality, arguing that, in the end, more would be learned by the psychological deviations from rational game playing than from game theory itself (Rapoport and Chammah 1965:11).

Trained as a mathematician and conversant in psychology and social psychology, Rapoport was appalled on both moral and academic grounds by the power politics approach of the strategic thinkers. Interrupting his experiments on prisoner's dilemma, he wrote a blistering attack on deterrence theory (Rapoport 1964), pointing out the strategists' misunderstanding of game theory, their unscientific reliance on rationality, their neglect of psychological factors, and their myopic (and immoral) concentration on coercion. What had to be done was to delineate the conditions that would make it possible to escape from the deterrence game into a more fundamentally peaceful order. While this was a normative goal, he believed that game theory, if properly researched, could provide valuable insights about how to change situations so that one could move from zero-sum games to more cooperative games (Rapoport 1964:chaps. 11 and 12). In addition, he believed that studying the repeated plays of prisoner's dilemma would provide insights about how to build a foundation of trust.

Unfortunately, the 1964 book was not taken seriously by strategic thinkers, mostly because of its political and normative tone, rather than its basic scholarly points. Later, however, Rapoport's analysis proved

more correct than the views of Schelling, Kahn, etc.[14] The overreliance on rationality, the power politics emphasis on toughness, and the
disparagement of anything even hinting of idealist naiveté tended to
make the strategic thinkers disregard the social psychological work,
which placed as much emphasis on cooperation and conflict resolution
as the realists had on coercion and war.

This broader social psychological perspective encouraged researchers
in this area to explore what conditions might make it possible to switch
from zero-sum games and dangerous chicken games to more positive-
sum games. These questions were addressed by Charles Osgood (1959)
in his criticism of strategic thinking. Osgood's famous GRIT (graduated
reduction in tension) strategy, which was later to have an impact on
SALT negotiations and the general establishment of détente, discussed
in nongame theory terms how trust could be built to enable escape
from the prisoner's dilemma (see also C. Osgood 1962). As the Cold
War began to thaw, Osgood's "suggestions for winning the real war
against communism" became a way of explaining the onset of détente,
with the most famous example probably being Etzioni's (1967) analysis of
Kennedy's post–Cuban missile crisis diplomacy toward the Soviet Union
(see also Dean and Vasquez 1976:24–28).

The social psychological perspective also produced a number of studies
devoted to improving inter-nation relations by improving communication and cultural understanding. Many of these involved experiments
that brought different nationals from enemy states together in a controlled environment to see how to promote conflict resolution. Political
science research of this sort was exemplified by the work of John Burton
(1969), who invited government-selected individuals to discuss problems
between two states that had engaged in a violent conflict. The purpose
was to analyze the participants' perceptions and discover ways to resolve
conflict through controlled communication. Burton tried to incorporate
some of these insights into his more theoretical work on world politics
(Burton 1967; see Burton 1969:xvi). In another study, Leonard Doob,
William Foltz, and Robert Stevens (Doob 1970) used T-group methods
with Africans whose governments were involved in a territorial dispute
(Somalia, Kenya, and Ethopia). Since these studies, a number of other
attempts have been made along these lines, the most recent being between Israelis and Palestinians (Cohen et al. 1977).

More influential work related general conflict resolution to bargaining

14. Others in political science did build on Rapoport (1964). See Green (1966)
and the more recent Beres (1980). See Licklider (1971:135–152) for the limited
data available on scholars' attitudes toward some moral questions that can be
raised about strategic research.

and negotiation. The earliest input from social psychologists came with the publication of some of the leading research in this area by the *Journal of Conflict Resolution,* a consciously interdisciplinary journal widely read by behavioralists in international relations. Among the important articles on bargaining, negotiation, and conflict from a social psychological perspective were those of M. Deutsch (1958), M. Deutsch and Krauss (1962), McNeil (1962), Pruitt (1962), and, from game theory, Harsanyi (1961) and Rapoport (1960). Jack Sawyer and Harold Guetzkow (1965) brought together much of this research, including an extensive review of the experimental literature with the more traditional political science analysis of diplomacy, forming a comprehensive framework for further research on international negotiations. The lengthy Sawyer and Guetzkow article was important because it not only set the stage for future research but also summarized existing knowledge in two disciplines.

By the late sixties and throughout the seventies, important theoretical work on negotiations and bargaining from a social psychological perspective were made by Alan Coddington (1968) on strategy and bidding, Morton Deutsch (1973) on conflict resolution, and Otomar Bartos (1974) and I. William Zartman (1977) on outcomes. Meanwhile, other scholars continued empirical research on personal and cultural factors (M. G. Hermann and Kogan 1977; Druckman 1977c; Druckman et al. 1976); strategy and bidding (Hamner and Yukl 1977; Esser and Komorita 1975; Tedeschi and Bonoma 1977; Linkskold, McElwain, and Wanner 1977); and successful resolution (B. R. Brown 1977; Pruitt and Lewis 1977). Rubin and Brown (1975) have provided an excellent comprehensive overview of all research and theory in this area, while Druckman (1977b) has attempted to develop a framework for integrating the findings and extending research.

The work in political science proper has been less empirical, primarily because of lack of access to many negotiations. Harold Nicolson's (1939a) essay was considered a classic and has been read widely since. Morgenthau (1948) himself had placed great emphasis on the rules of diplomacy but did little work on negotiations. On a more general level, J. D. Singer (1963) provided a model of inter-nation influence. The major works in the field have been Fred Ikle (1964), which provided an overall analysis of the subject, and Arthur Lall (1966), which incorporated power considerations in a new theoretical manner (see also Ikle and Leites 1962). John Raser (1965) introduced and applied learning theory to account for general interaction behavior. Patchen (1970) attempted to classify much of the variegated research and theory into three types of models—cognitive, learning, and reaction processes.

Somewhat removed from the bargaining perspective per se, but clearly relevant to nonviolent conflict resolution, is the work of Charles

McClelland (1968; 1972a), who attempted to delineate the factors associated with the abatement of the various Berlin and Taiwan crises. Although specific findings for each situation differed, he found that in the abatement phase of a crisis the following sequence occurs: conflict declines sharply to below noncrisis levels; confrontation (verbal abuse) increases; (and sometimes) attempts to settle increase and comments decrease slightly (McClelland 1972a:97–101). This work reflected a different mode of analysis from the strategic studies and was not to come into vogue in policy-making circles until the mid-seventies, at which point it took the form of crisis management (see McClelland 1977; R. Young 1977; Hazlewood, Hayes, and Brownell 1977; Abolfathi, Hayes, and Hayes 1979). Nevertheless, it pointed beyond deterrence thinking to other logical connections to the broader work on bargaining.

As the burdens and tensions of the Cold War lessened, research on negotiations and bargaining, particularly East-West arms talks, received more attention. Lloyd Jensen (1963) provided an early discussion of U.S.-Soviet disarmament negotiation. P. Terrence Hopmann (1972; see also Hopmann and King 1976) tested various models of negotiations, using the partial test ban treaty as well as the Conference on Security and Cooperation in Europe as a data base (Hopmann 1978). Paul Lauren (1972) focused on the use of ultimata. Johan Galtung (1964b) and W. R. Thompson and Modelski (1976) attempted to discern the conditions under which summits are most likely to be held. Russell Leng (Leng and Goodsell 1974; Leng and Wheeler 1979; Leng 1980), working with the Correlates of War project, examined various realist prescriptions on the use of force, finding some support for the proposition that a reciprocating strategy is the most effective means of avoiding defeat without going to war (Leng and Wheeler 1979). Peter Wallensteen (1968) and Richard Olson (1979) assessed the efficacy of economic sanctions. Finally, David Baldwin (1974) looked at inducements as opposed to coercion as tools of influence.

The final aspect of research in this subfield is that on arms races. Although highly specialized and somewhat isolated, this research has followed many of the suggestions, both theoretical and methodological, of Lewis Richardson (1960b), and it can be included in this area because it is a form of tacit bargaining and is relevant to strategic research. Lewis Richardson's (1960b) explanation of arms races in terms of a differential function minus a submissive factor generated much research not only on arms races (e.g., Smoker 1963; 1964a; 1965b) but also on the escalation of violent conflict (Alcock and Lowe 1969) and on negotiations (Bartos 1974). Considerable research was also devoted to comparing Richardson models with organizational models of arms races (Rattinger 1976; Hollist 1977; Ostrom 1977; 1978; Gillespie et al. 1977; see also the studies in

Gillespie and Zinnes 1976). Neither approach, however, has met with spectacular success (Wallace 1980:282). In recent years, much of the work on arms races has taken a highly deductive character, particularly that of Gillespie and Zinnes (see Gillespie et al. 1977; 1980; Gillespie and Zinnes 1976). Wallace (1980:259–260) has criticized this work as insufficiently concerned with empirical investigation. More recent work, however, has begun to relate arms races with war. Wallace (1979a; 1981) linked serious disputes and arms races with the onset of war. William Thompson, Duval, and Dia (1979) retested Norman Alcock's (1972) thesis that change in defense expenditures leads to the initiation of war.

While the research in this subfield, like the work on deterrence, has been concerned with the struggle for power, it has generally been outside the realist paradigm. First, research on negotiations has been more concerned with conflict resolution and cooperative processes than with coercion, although coercion has received attention. This, of course, stems from a social psychological perspective and paradigm. Second, the research on arms races has reflected a fascination, perhaps excessive, with the Richardson and organizational models, both of which have strong "war is irrational" assumptions underlying them. The contrast with strategic studies is sharp and reflects the differences in the underlying paradigms of the two approaches.

Supranationalism: International Organization/Law and Integration

The fourth major development of the paradigm came out of the work on supranationalism, which itself can be divided into two areas of research —work on international organization and law and work on inter-nation integration. Since both these areas were the central focus of the idealist paradigm and peripheral to the realist paradigm, the realist impact has been weaker than in the other subfields, and there are identifiable idealist vestiges. Whereas the other subfields are best regarded as directed by the realist paradigm with other influences coming from the outside, here the realist paradigm is the outside influence, with much of the inquiry still stemming from basic topics raised by idealism. In this subfield, the realist paradigm can be seen as amending and criticizing an already existing research program rather than creating its own.

The most influential realist work in this subfield was that of Hans J. Morgenthau and of Reinhold Niebuhr, both of whom attempted to demonstrate the limitations of supranational solutions to the problem of war. Morgenthau (1960, 1973:chaps. 29 and 30) noted that although a world state would solve the problem of war, such a solution was not feasible because the world community necessary to bring about an effective world government was unlikely to exist in the foreseeable future. Niebuhr (1941; 1946) applied the principles of realism against the idealists to demonstrate the naiveté of making world government a goal of American foreign policy. He attempted to debunk this notion by developing a theory about how a nation comes into existence. He maintained that a nation presupposes a community, then went on to delineate the conditions of a community (see Niebuhr 1965), and concluded that, since the conditions for a world community did not exist, it would be unrealistic to expect that the United Nations or some other institution could become a world government. On the basis of this analysis, Niebuhr asserted that American policy toward the United Nations should rest on a realistic assessment of U.S. interests rather than a moralistic and unrealistic expectation of forming a world government (see also Niebuhr 1952 and John Herz 1942).

The study of international organization can be divided into three areas: nontheoretical case studies; examination of international organizations to delineate the struggle for power and peace among nations; and the use of international organizations as a data source to test hypotheses derived from the realist paradigm. Many studies can be classified into the category of nontheoretical case studies. Chadwick Alger's (1970) survey of quantitative studies on international organization in the sixties found that almost half of all studies had no theoretical focus at all but were intended to describe the various activities of international organizations (see also Riggs et al. 1970). These studies might be said to provide a current-events function for the field and/or reflect the old idealist concern with historical description and prescription rather than scientific explanation.

Most of the studies with a theoretical focus—and the best work on international organization—fall into the area of the use of international organization to delineate the struggle for power and peace among nations. The actual creation and use of the United Nations naturally spurred a great deal of interest and research. A tremendous emphasis was placed on saying that politics in the United Nations would reflect the struggle for power and that the United States must use the United Nations as a weapon in the struggle for power. Although somewhat contradictory, these two views guided much of the research. Typical of the better studies was that of Daniel Cheever (1949), who argued that events in the United Nations showed that it was part of the struggle for power, and that the United States must not rely solely on it. The fear that the United States would tie its foreign policy too closely to the United Nations was aggravated when the United Nations was used to fight the Korean War. Warnings were raised against the illusion of collective security (Wolfers 1962:chap. 11). Some, however, saw the Korean War as an opportunity to make the United Nations less of a neutral instrument in the world and more of a Western ally in the Cold War. Frederick Dunn (1950) in particular, argued that UNESCO should use social psychological techniques of persuasion and propaganda to eliminate war from people's minds and to point out the aggressive nature of global communism.

One of the problems with much of this work was that it was too narrow and policy oriented and did not offer a complete explanation of the history of international organization, although Morgenthau (1960, 1973:chaps. 23–30) had suggested one in his review of organizations from the Holy Alliance through the United Nations. The work that filled this gap and gave perhaps the best power politics interpretation of the history of international organization and its future prospects was Inis Claude's *Swords into Plowshares* (1956 [1964]). In addition to a theoretical historical interpretation, Claude (1956 [1964:chaps. 5–10]) provided an analysis of various structural problems like voting mechanisms and membership criteria. Finally, reflecting the realist concern with assessing idealist solutions to war, he systematically reviewed the major peace proposals associated with international organization from peaceful settlement of disputes to world government (Claude 1956 [1964:chaps. 11–19]).

Work reflecting the impact of the realist paradigm on the study of international organization was not limited to Claude. All the major theoretically oriented textbooks on international organizations viewed international organization in the context of a global struggle for power. The work of Bloomfield (1960), Stoessinger (1965), Plano and Riggs (1967), and Jacobson (1979) reflected this concern. Each author devoted a section of the text to historical development, but the major theoretical emphasis was on how particular nations or blocs of nations employ organizations, particularly the United Nations, to pursue their own goals or national interests.[15] Furthermore, the assumptions of the realist paradigm were used to explain that international organizations are only successful when powerful nations want the organization to be successful, and that a world government or strong United Nations can only emerge when an authentic world community exists.[16]

By the 1970s, assessments of the success of international organizations in resolving disputes were less hostile. E. B. Haas, Butterworth, and Nye (1972) employed quantitative data to show that such organizations

15. See for example Bloomfield (1960:chap. 3); Stoessinger (1965:vi–vii; chap. 10; et passim); Plano and Riggs (1967:chaps. 6 and 7); Jacobson (1979:chaps. 5, 6, and 12).

16. See for example Bloomfield (1960:chaps. 4 and 5); Stoessinger (1965: Part 2); Plano and Riggs (1967:chaps. 10, 15, and 16); Jacobson (1979:chaps. 8, 9, and 13–16).

can be useful; a more theoretical analysis of this data by Butterworth (1978) attempted to identify the variables associated with success. Work of this sort was related to that on conflict resolution in crises (see O. R. Young 1967).

Despite the work of E. B. Haas et al., most of the quantitative studies attempted to delineate the struggle for power that occurred in the United Nations between the Western, communist, and Third World blocs. Among the notable attempts to analyze this struggle in terms of voting behavior were the studies of Ball (1951), Hovet (1960), R. Riggs (1958), Alker (1964; 1965b), Alker and Russett (1965), Russett (1966), Rowe (1964; 1969; 1971), and Clark, O'Leary, and Wittkopf (1971). The interest in bloc voting provided a major contribution to the paradigm in terms of advancement of measuring the voting agreement of nations. In addition to these studies, the work of Rieselbach (1960b), Lijphart (1963), Brams and O'Leary (1970), and Willetts (1972) was noteworthy in terms of index construction. Other studies went beyond the easily quantified voting patterns to study influence in more depth. The most significant examples of this type were certainly Cox, Jacobson et al. (1973) and the earlier studies by Chadwick Alger (1965; 1968).

By the end of the seventies, the growth of a Third World or southern anti-American bloc in the United Nations focused the attention of scholars and policy makers on the view that the UN was a weapon in the struggle for power that could be used against the West. The work of Yeselson and Gaglione (1977) best captured this emphasis by interpreting the UN's entire history as first a Cold War weapon of the United States and then a weapon of the Third World. Their work's major contribution was its attempt to delineate four different ways the UN could be used as a weapon: to embarrass an opponent; to gain status; to gain legitimacy; and to socialize the conflict (i.e., expand the audience before whom the conflict is conducted).

Finally, several outstanding articles were published using international organization to test specific hypotheses derived from the realist paradigm. Chadwick Alger (1961; 1965; 1968), for example, by systematically observing delegate behavior in the United Nations, attempted to discover the nonresolution consequences of the United Nations for the struggle for power and peace (see also Siverson 1973). Jack Vincent (1968; 1971) has used the attribute indicators of nations (which are often the elements of national power that Morgenthau delineated) to explain the attitudes and votes of UN delegates.

The realist concern with power naturally led to an attack on the idealist conception of international law. The major work in this area was undoubtedly that of Hans Kelsen (1942; 1950; 1952), who combined the realist focus on power politics with the positivistic critique of natural law to destroy many of the idealist assumptions about international law. Nevertheless, some power politics thinkers, for example, Charles deVisscher (1957), considered Kelsen too idealistic. deVisscher (1957), along with Morgenthau (1958) and Schwarzenberger (1962), made an even sharper attack than Kelsen on international law by emphasizing that the reality of power placed extreme limitations on international law in the current nation-state system. As a consequence, international relations scholars within political science did not deal with international law very extensively. The subject tended to fall more within the purview of lawyers, who had their own separate professional association (the American Society of International Law) and journals. Many of the best studies, even if not legalistic, were conducted by those with legal training. Most law schools gave courses on international law, and undergraduate courses in the subject were often taught as prelaw courses.

Where international law was treated by international relations scholars, it had a strong world order focus, reflecting a sophisticated new idealism that was trying to develop a set of institutions to deal with global problems. The Institute of World Order sponsored a cross-cultural project to develop alternative models of a future global system that would enhance certain values—peace, social and economic justice, human rights, and ecological quality (see Mendlovitz 1977; Kothari 1975; Falk 1975; Mazrui 1976; Galtung 1980).

This sort of work never ceased, despite the realist critique, and many of its advocates hoped to convert the United Nations into some form of world government; the most famous of these advocates were the world federalists. On a more academic level, the Clark-Sohn (1958; 1960) model received wide attention throughout the fifties and sixties. Many environmental problems, particularly the issue of law of the sea, were seen as demanding a supranational decision-making structure (Falk 1971; Logue 1972; Borgese 1968). The emergence of international regimes for specific issue areas like economics, food, pollution, and the sea (see Keohane and Nye 1977; E. B. Haas 1975; Ruggie 1975; Coplin 1980: chaps. 4 and 12), however, made normative work in this area less tied to a world federalist structure (see Beitz 1980).

Idealist model building was supplemented throughout the seventies by normative work with a more Marxist perspective. This became centered in a European peace research movement when Johan Galtung in 1971 shifted the editorial policies of the *Journal of Peace Research* to encourage more normative and radical work (see also the *Proceedings of the International Peace Research Association* 1971; Olsen and Jarvad 1970). With the founding in the mid-1970s of a new international journal, *Alternatives*, the normative work combining idealist and Marxist perspectives can be expected to proliferate.

While much of the work on international law moved outside international relations or became part of a normative idealist perspective, some still treated it in a more social science fashion (see Coplin 1970 for a review). Among the most significant approaches of this type were the studies of Myres McDougal (McDougal and Lasswell 1959; McDougal and Felsciano 1961; McDougal, Lasswell, and Vlasic 1963), who viewed international law as an emerging system of global public order and applied this perspective to analyze international law on war, the sea, outer space, and treaties (Coplin 1970:155). Less influential at the time, but of importance in the seventies, was Philip Jessup's (1956) study on transnational law. More within the political science tradition were the studies of William Coplin (1965; 1966a), which employed a functionalist approach to determine why international law exists in its present form; he saw it as reflecting the realities of the present state system. Finally, Michael Barkun (1968) looked at international law as an informal system of law, comparing some of its characteristics to law in primitive societies.

Several studies investigated the role of national power in the International Court of Justice. Coplin (1968) examined bargaining in the world court to see how it reflected national power considerations. Coplin and Rochester (1972) conducted one of the few quantitative studies comparing the League of Nations, the UN, and the two world courts, finding among other things that Third World countries learn not to use the court because they often lose cases. Thomas Hensley (1968) conducted a quantitative study on the court to see if there was national bias in voting among judges.

The other major concern with supranationalism that guided research in this subfield was the focus on inter-nation integration. This research was related to both the idealist and the realist paradigms in that both paradigms saw the formation of a world community as important to the establishment of any world government. The research on integration was relevant to this question, since it was devoted to uncovering the conditions that could give rise to a sense of community beyond the nation-state level and then see how these might be related to some form of integration.

With the call for a European common market as a solution to European war, research gained a new impetus. Scholars were concerned with four research problems: delineating the conditions of community; measuring and describing intra- and inter-state community formation; testing the relationship between inter-nation community formation and inter-state institutional formation; and testing the relationship between inter-nation community formation and inter-state conflict-cooperation. The first two topics stemmed from the realist work on prerequisites for communities. The third stemmed from the argument that community formation is a prerequisite to integration. And the fourth reflected the realist proposition that war more frequently occurs between communities than within them (see Morgenthau 1960:502–509; 1973:480–487), as well as the idealist functionalism of Mitrany (1943).

The earliest work on integration and perhaps the most significant in terms of elaboration of this topic was that of Karl Deutsch and Ernst Haas. Both these scholars were instrumental in outlining the four research problems of the integration approach, and their students carried on their early work. However, since they used different conceptual frameworks, they tended to give rise to two different schools.

K. W. Deutsch (1953; 1964a; Deutsch et al. 1957) attempted to explain the integration process in the North Atlantic region and Western Europe by the use of communications and cybernetic theory. In these works, he elaborated in detail upon the distinction between community and governmental formation suggested by Niebuhr. Deutsch labeled the formation of a supranational government from two or more national governments *amalgamation* and attempted to uncover the relationship between amalgamation and community formation (Deutsch et al. 1957: 5–8, 79–83). In addition to this theoretical work, Deutsch (1954; 1956; 1964c; Deutsch and Savage 1960) wrote a number of studies showing how the two concepts could be measured so that the integration process in Europe could be monitored quantitatively. Clearly, Deutsch made significant contributions to the theory construction, data making, and research of integration.

The work of Ernst Haas differed from Deutsch's primarily in its conceptual framework. Haas employed a functionalist framework originally suggested by the idealist David Mitrany (1943 [1966]) (see also Sewell 1966). Mitrany was concerned with how supranational institutions might arise. Unlike Niebuhr, Mitrany was sympathetic to world government and did not believe it to be utopian. Ernst Haas built on this functionalist tradition without falling captive to its idealist tendencies. He used it to develop testable hypotheses about integration, the most famous of which was the spillover hypothesis. This hypothesis maintains that cooperation in one area will lead to cooperation (spillover) in other areas. Haas examined the plausibility of the hypothesis in a number of case studies employing elaborate theoretical frameworks.[17] As with Deutsch, Haas's work covered the major areas of scientific inquiry: theory construction, data making, and research. On the whole, Haas, like Deutsch, conducted this work within the context of the realist paradigm; that is, he accepted the three fundamental assumptions of the paradigm and built upon the realist work on supranationalism. There was a major exception

17. E. B. Haas (1958a:5–16; 1961; 1964:48ff.; 1967:324–329).

to this conclusion—Haas's (1964) case study on the International Labor Organization, *Beyond the Nation-State*—which challenged all three of the realist paradigm's assumptions. But as will be seen later, this work did not give rise to a movement that seriously challenged the realist paradigm until the 1970s.

A number of scholars were influenced directly by Deutsch and Haas in their work on the first research problem of integration, the delineation of the conditions of community. Bruce Russett (1963a), for example, in his early work attempted to build on Deutsch's work by examining community ties between the United States and Great Britain. Richard Merritt (1966) showed that such ties in themselves do not always prevent severe conflict. In his later work, Russett (1967) delineated regional communities by factor analyzing a variety of indicators. Meanwhile, Haas (1956; 1958b) influenced Joseph Nye, Jr. (1968; 1971), who conducted several outstanding studies on regionalism.

Work on the second and third research problems of integration consisted of development of measures of integration and research on the relationship between inter-state community formation and amalgamation. The attempt to measure integration focused on transaction flows between nations. Steven Brams (1966a; 1968; Alger and Brams 1967) was particularly notable in defining and measuring these transactions. A number of scholars used various measures of integration, the chief one consisting of some type of transaction flow, to describe the amount of integration that had been taking place in Europe and the world as a whole. Significant in this area was the work of Brams (1966b), K. W. Deutsch et al. (1957), Inglehart (1967), Lindberg (1963), and Lindberg and Scheingold (1970). Nevertheless, the relationship between transactions and integration caused a persistent debate in this group and led to a number of attempts at concept clarification and reformulation (see Lindberg and Scheingold 1971). Schmitter (1969a; 1969b; 1970), for example, attempted to revise his earlier work with Haas (Haas and Schmitter 1964).

Work on the fourth research problem, testing the relationship between inter-nation community formation and inter-state conflict-cooperation, provided the theoretical rationale for work in the other three research problems. As noted earlier, it was this area that the early realists such as Niebuhr were interested in debunking and analyzing. Much of the work discussed previously, although it did not specifically test this relationship, was a necessary prerequisite to testing. Consequently, throughout the sixties various scholars used what work was available to assess the validity of the stipulated relationship between supranationalism, peace, and integration. For example, this broader focus was present at the beginning of the decade in the work of Amitai

Etzioni (1962; 1963; 1965) and at the end of the decade in the work of Nye (1971) and the empirical studies of Cobb and Elder (1970).

Up to this point, most of the literature that has been reviewed has been seen as articulating various aspects of the realist paradigm. It is now necessary to examine those groups of scholars who have worked with alternative paradigms and to assess the implications of this for the validity of the claim that the realist paradigm dominated theory construction. Two groups will be examined—those who have worked on transnational relations and issue politics and those who have worked on Marxism.

Beyond Realism: Transnational Relations and Issue Politics

By the early seventies, several scholars who had been interested in the integrationist approach began to break out of the realist paradigm. This new development outside the realist paradigm is only beginning, however, and the picture provided by the alternative paradigm is hardly complete. Ernst Haas's (1964) *Beyond the Nation-State* was clearly a forerunner of this development, since it challenged the assumption that only nation-states were actors in international politics, but Haas's work remained an isolated example for several years. Robert C. Angell's (1967; 1969) work can be seen as a transition from the realist paradigm to the new and yet unnamed paradigm. Angell had a great interest in recording the growth of nonnational actors and in what he called *transnational participation*. Although his research on nonnational actors clearly broke with the early inter-nation transaction flow approach and challenged the first assumption of the realist paradigm, Angell (1969) still attempted to delineate the impact of transnational participation on the reduction of conflict among nations, a concern of both idealism and realism.

The sharpest break came in 1971 with Keohane and Nye's editing of *Transnational Relations and World Politics*, a special issue of *International Organization*. This work clearly represented a conscious attempt on the part of the editors to create a new paradigm that would challenge the dominant "state-centric" paradigm by focusing on two elements—the emergence of independent transnational actors and the presence of different issue areas that did not conform to power politics behavior. The emphasis on transnational politics suggested that the first two assumptions of the realist paradigm were inadequate guides for the study of international relations. The emergence of multinational corporations helped focus interest on the question of nonstate actors and the first assumption of the paradigm, as evinced by the use of the phrase *state-*

centric rather than *realist* paradigm.[18] The emphasis on issue areas and the little attention devoted to characterizing the system as a struggle for power challenged the third assumption.

The initial efforts of those advocating a transnational perspective demonstrated the differences between their approach and the dominant paradigm. The most elaborate theoretical work on the new paradigm, reminiscent of Martin Wight's early essay on power politics, was the work of Karl Kaiser (1971). Writing just before Keohane and Nye, Kaiser looked at some of the radical implications of integration, seeing some forms of interdependence and integration as forms of penetration, which undercut the entire notion of separate unitary nation-states and replaced it with various transnational coalitions. Kaiser (1971) outlined the research implications of this view, juxtaposing his paradigm with the dominant one in the field. In a more restricted fashion, Keohane and Nye (1974) demonstrated how the study of international organization would be fundamentally different in a transnational paradigm as compared to the realist paradigm.

The work of Keohane and Nye received considerable attention and criticism (see McClelland 1977; M. Sullivan 1978; 1979b; Luard 1976; Michalak 1979). Several critics (e.g., McClelland 1977; Michalak 1979; and to a certain extent Luard 1976) attempted to characterize Keohane and Nye's argument as idealist, reducing their claims to a possible future global society in which transnational actors will dominate relations and nation-states will wane. The critics then go on to show that this is unlikely to occur. This criticism seems to be based on a straw man, since Keohane and Nye's (1971; 1974) work was primarily empirical. It pointed out the neglect of transnational actors and delineated their role in different issue areas, finding that sometimes they were more important than nation-states; Keohane and Nye did not say states were unimportant. The second criticism was that Keohane and Nye had only produced a framework for researching a new force in world politics and did not really provide a new paradigm because they had no theory of world politics, let alone a new and nonrealist theory. This criticism had considerably more merit; the attempt to move from a framework to a set of alternative assumptions and to a nonrealist explanation or theory never came to fruition. The second major publication of Keohane and Nye (1977) never gave a theory but simply juxtaposed power politics and

18. Keohane and Nye have apparently accepted the claim, presented here and by Handelman et al. (1973), that the dominant paradigm in the field is the realist paradigm and not a state-centric paradigm. After 1973, they no longer wrote of the state-centric paradigm, only of the realist paradigm (see Keohane and Nye 1974; 1977).

transnational relations as two almost ideal types, neither one of which was always accurate. They still need to develop a new theory that can explain not only all that the old one could, but also the anomalies.

Keohane and Nye, although the first, were not alone in their call for a new paradigm. The most significant criticism of the dominant paradigm after them was made by John Burton (1972; Burton et al. 1974). Throughout the late sixties, Burton, working independently of Keohane and Nye, had been moving away from what he called the *dominant billiard ball model* of international politics (Burton 1968). He did not believe that states were the sole actors or that nation-states were unitary actors (Burton et al. 1974:5–6). He maintained that the geographical nation-state map of the world did not adequately capture the linkages and transactions that shape world society and are unaffected by state boundaries or notions of sovereignty. Burton (1968) combined this perspective with social psychological approaches toward conflict and cooperation to develop a very different non–power politics view of the world which served as a basis for advocating a new paradigm for studying world society (Burton 1972; Burton et al. 1974).

A number of other scholars, all at best only tangentially connected or familiar with each other's work, made similar claims. Harold Sprout and Margaret Sprout (1971) found problems with the dominant paradigm stemming from the growing interdependence promoted and reflected by transnational trends. Donald Puchala and Stuart Fagen (1974) challenged the third assumption of the realist paradigm by arguing that security was not the motivating factor for much of world political behavior and that it would become even less important in the 1970s. Edward Morse (1976) suggested that the spread of industrialization and the process of modernization were producing a more pluralistic world that would make power politics an inadequate guide to inquiry. Even James Rosenau (1972), who never called for a new paradigm and was often critical of some of its advocates, spoke of the implications of growing interdependence for a "postnational order" (see also Rosenau 1980). By the end of the seventies, the transnational relations approach had even produced a major textbook (Feld 1979).

The work of Keohane and Nye (1971) encouraged research on non–state actors. Keohane and Nye made two claims: the first was that transnational actors were important and could not be ignored, and the second was that growing interdependence was breaking down the independence of nation-states and their unitary quality. Keohane and Nye (1971) attempted to research these claims by encouraging several scholars to produce a number of case studies on specific transnational actors. Others attempted to broaden this work by focusing on non–state actors. Multinational corporations received considerable attention, having the entire September 1972 (403) issue of *The Annals of the American Academy Political and Social Sciences* and the December 1972 (vol. 16) issue of the *International Studies Quarterly* devoted to them. Werner Feld's (1972) work on nongovernmental actors and Bertelsen's (1976) work on Palestinian Arabs were very significant works on other kinds of non–state actors.

The most extensive work and the only quantitative analysis of non–state actors was done by Mansbach, Lampert, and Ferguson (1976). Examining three regions—Western Europe, the Middle East, and Latin America—they attempted to demonstrate the importance of non–state actors in each of these regions in terms of both the frequency of their behavior and their responsibility for directly or indirectly promoting conflict. This evidence was used to challenge the dominant state-centric paradigm and to propose a complex conglomerate system as an alternative perspective for world politics (see also Hopkins and Mansbach 1973:chap. 6; Lampert, Falkowski, and Mansbach 1978; and Lampert 1975).

While the research on transnational relations and non–state actors was being conducted, William D. Coplin and Michael K. O'Leary launched an attack on the realist paradigm on a different basis—that it ignored the importance of issues. Coplin and O'Leary accepted the transnational criticism of the state-centric paradigm, but for them non–state actors could be easily incorporated within the dominant paradigm because their inclusion did not really require the abandonment of power politics explanations. Coplin and O'Leary argued that the state-centric paradigm was not an authentic paradigm in the Kuhnian sense, but simply the first assumption of the realist paradigm (Handelman et al. 1973). The real flaw of the paradigm lay in the second and especially the third assumption. By maintaining that international politics was the struggle for power and peace, Morgenthau assumed that the world was unidimensional and consisted of a single issue. Coplin and O'Leary, however, maintained that behavior varied by issue area, with some issues, like the Cold War, reflecting power politics behavior at some points, and other issues, like law of the sea, consisting of behavior not easily explained by power politics (see Handelman et al. 1973; Coplin 1974:chap. 13; 1980:chap. 12; O'Leary 1976; Vasquez 1974b).

Building on the assumptions of their PRINCE simulation, Coplin and O'Leary (see Coplin, Mills, and O'Leary 1973; and O'Leary 1976) attempted to develop a paradigm that would analyze world politics as a process of raising and resolving issues rather than a struggle for power and peace. They called this paradigm the issue politics (or world policy process) paradigm. The first assumption of the realist paradigm is contradicted in the new paradigm in that nations are not the only actors.

Significant actors in the issue politics paradigm are determined by focusing on particular issue areas and examining which groups participate in raising and resolving issues. The second assumption of the realist paradigm is also contradicted in that the issue politics paradigm maintains that the process by which issues are raised and resolved is the same in the domestic and global environments and that "domestic" issues are not raised and resolved solely by "domestic" actors. For these reasons, the issue politics paradigm maintains that the distinction between domestic and international politics confuses rather than clarifies relationships. The third assumption of the realist paradigm is also contradicted, in that the structure and process of the system are not pictured in terms of national struggle for power and peace but in terms of raising and resolving issues. Issues, then, are the primary focus of this new paradigm.

One of the advantages of the issue approach over the transnational approach was that it offered alternative explanations to power politics. Coplin, Mills, and O'Leary (1973) provided an issue explanation of foreign policy (see also Coplin and O'Leary 1971), and Dean and Vasquez (1976) provided a new interpretation of the polarity debate based on the characteristics of issues in the system.

The emergence of attempts to create a new paradigm does not invalidate the proposition on theory construction for two reasons: (1) the proposition is a probabilistic explanation and not a universal explanation; that is, it is meant to hold in a statistically significant number of cases, not in all cases (see Hempel 1966:54–67); and (2) the paradigm did not clearly emerge until after the time frame stipulated in the proposition; that is, after the end of the sixties. This latter point is not just a technicality. It is simply too early to tell how much of an impact the new paradigm will have on the field.

It is interesting from the perspective of this analysis to speculate on what generated the calls for a new paradigm. The paradigm appears to have emerged from a number of anomalies. With the ending of the Cold War, American scholars were beginning to realize that perhaps world politics is not always a struggle for power and peace but only takes on this characteristic under certain specific conditions. This posed the first anomaly. The second anomaly appeared to be the increasing recognition that non–state or transnational actors, particularly multinational corporations, were not being controlled by nations and were having a major impact on the conduct of global politics. The final anomaly was that the increasing penetration and interdependence of nations is making it more difficult to interpret world politics in terms of the first two assumptions of the realist paradigm. Whether these anomalies will force a crisis in the field or whether they can be explained in terms of the realist paradigm through further articulation remains to be seen. However, the force of the realist paradigm in the field is emphasized by the fact that only recently have transnational actors received much attention, even though they have existed for centuries (Nye and Keohane 1971:724–728).

Beyond Realism: The Marxist Paradigm

In the world beyond the United States, the major alternative to realism has been Marxism. The Marxist paradigm rejects all three of the assumptions of the realist paradigm. It does not see the nation as the most important unit of analysis, but focuses instead on the class as the key actor (Thorndike 1978:68, 74, 76–78). The nation is viewed as a concept developed by the ruling class to confuse and distort the perception of the other classes (Lenin 1917; 1914 [1967:658–659]). Finally, the Marxist paradigm does not share the realist concern with the struggle for power among states. Rather, the important questions are those that relate to the mode and means of production and the relationship of the classes to them (Selsam and Martel 1963:182–224). All research that is not at least indirectly related to this question is, in the Marxist paradigm, trivial.

Most of the new developments in the Marxist paradigm have not taken a world politics focus, but have developed different aspects of Marxist analysis of general behavior (e.g., Marcuse 1964; Baran and Sweezy 1968; and Mandel 1969). This occurs in part because world politics was not a primary focus of Marx and Engels, nor was it treated systematically until Lenin (1917), who gave Hobson's (1902) work a more Marxist flavor. Since then, imperialism as both an independent and dependent variable has occupied a central place in any Marxist attempt to account for world politics. A great deal of this work in the United States has been associated with the *Monthly Review* (see Magdoff 1969 and Frank 1969) and is clearly outside the field.

A second area that has been influenced by the Marxist paradigm is the work of revisionist American historians. These historians can be divided into two groups: "hard revisionists," who tend toward a stricter economic interpretation of American foreign policy, and "soft revisionists," who place greater emphasis on noneconomic factors (see Maddox 1973). Among the first group are William Appleman Williams (1959) and Gabriel Kolko (1968; 1969; Kolko and Kolko 1972). In the second category are Fleming (1961), LaFeber (1967), and, to a limited extent, the "post-revisionist" John Lewis Gaddis (1972).

With the possible exception of Kolko and Kolko, none of these historians used Marxist language. The distinction should be made here between those who work within the original Marxian conceptual framework (like Baran and Sweezy 1968), and those who accept the assumptions of the paradigm but may abandon the original conceptual framework and much of the language. While all those who accept the assumptions of the Marxist paradigm might be called Marxists, only those who accept the original conceptual framework would be called Marxian (see Garson 1976:18). Marxian scholars can be seen as working in the center or core of the Marxist paradigm, just as power politics scholars are working at the center or core of the realist paradigm. In this sense, most revisionist historians are Marxist but not Marxian.

A third area guided by Marxist concerns has focused on imperialism from a comparative politics perspective. Major contributions to this work from political science have in recent times come from André Gunder Frank (1969), Fernando Cardoso and Enzo Faletto (1979), and Immanuel Wallerstein (1974; 1976), all of whom reformulated much of Marxist theory by creating a *dependencia* framework; and Johan Galtung (1971), who employed his early ideas on status to explain imperialism and the structure of the current dominant system. With the exception of Galtung (1971), this work has been outside the field of international relations.[19] Until recently, the major function of Marxism in the field has been that of whipping boy, a phenomenon probably attributable to the impact of the Cold War, particularly the McCarthy era, on American scholars (see Garson 1971:9).[20]

The fact that the Marxist paradigm has had an influence in American diplomatic history but not in international relations underscores the potency of the realist paradigm within the field to guide inquiry and push competing paradigms aside.[21] This point is further substantiated by the fact that the Marxist paradigm has had a much greater impact on

19. Such work can be considered outside the field because it has not been published in any of the major journals of political science such as *American Political Science Review, World Politics, The Journal of Conflict Resolution, International Organization, International Studies Quarterly, Journal of Peace Research, Peace Research Society (International) Papers,* and the various regional journals of the political science associations.

20. For examples of treating Marxism as a theory which is so obviously incorrect it need not be examined systematically, see Aron (1955:chap. 3), Morgenthau (1960:48–53; 1973:48–54), and particularly the essays in Part 2 of Hahn and Neff (1960).

21. There is, of course, an intriguing sociology-of-knowledge question here in terms of the extent to which the academic reward-and-punishment system prevented or discouraged international relations specialists from using the Marxist paradigm as a guide, or even treating it seriously. Clearly, the Cold War and the rise of the United States to superpower status made Morgenthau's *realpolitik* a natural ideology for the United States in its struggle for power with both foes and friendly competitors like Britain and France. In addition, the Cold War

comparative politics than it has had on international relations inquiry. Within comparative politics, the influence has been through dependency theory. Part of the reason for this may be that comparative politics has been less parochial than international relations inquiry in that it has been exposed to non-American and non-British scholars, particularly those from the Third World (e.g., Frank 1969 and Cardoso and Faletto 1979).

Nevertheless, the Marxist paradigm has managed to guide some important work in international relations. The strongest and earliest movement in this direction occurred through the International Peace Research Institute in Olso, Norway. Galtung (1971) led the way with his very important and highly influential reformulation of imperialism. Peter Wallensteen (1973) elaborated this even further, producing one of the major studies on system structure and war from a Marxist perspective. Other articles followed in quick succession, covering such diverse topics as equality (Hoivik 1971), structural and direct violence (Galtung and Hoivik 1971), and the effect of structural violence on life expectancy (Alcock and Kohler 1979). All this work was clearly inspired by the Marxist paradigm, but much of it was beyond the original Marxian conceptual framework. It is also significant that this movement, although within the field, was started in Europe and by non-Americans, and it split the Peace Research movement (see Olsen and Jarvad 1970), leading the behavioral branch to change the name of the Peace Research Society (International) to the Peace Science Society (International).

In the United States, while there had always been a few international relations scholars interested in Marxist analysis, the Vietnam War in-

---

and the McCarthy era literally purged or intimidated many adherents to Marxist analysis from many centers of influence, including the universities.

While both these factors are probably very influential, there must be another factor which made international relations more resistent to a Marxist resurgence than fields like history or even comparative politics. The major reason may be that international relations, at least in the United States, has had much stronger and extensive ties with the State Department, Foreign Service, AID, CIA, Pentagon, and Council on Foreign Relations than other fields in political science have had with other governmental or powerful institutions (like Congress, the Democratic Party, or the AFL-CIO). Coupled with the absence of any countervailing influences, like those that emerged in comparative politics through exposure to Marxist scholars, and the fact that the foreign policy elite is a natural constituency for international relations scholarship, these ties to government have created a subtle (and sometimes not so subtle) system of reward and punishment that probably weakened the Marxist resurgence. Even those sympathetic to Marxist ideas often have been prone to "translate" them into non-Marxist language in the hope of having "influence" with the elite.

creased that interest. The initial work stemmed from critics of the Vietnam War (see the essays in Parenti 1971). These were followed by more theoretical and empirical work on testing theories of imperialism (Rosen and Kurth 1974) and of the military-industrial complex (Rosen 1973). Increasingly, more behavioral scholars, who were not Marxists, became interested in testing certain Marxist explanations. Russett and Hanson (1975) led the way in a very important quantitative study that tried to assess the support of big business for war, as well as examining the general relationship between business, the military, and foreign policy.

Most of the interest in the field has been on Marxist explanations of dependency. Robert Kaufman, Chernotsky, and Geller (1975) attempted to falsify, through quantitative testing, some of the dependency propositions, especially those suggested by Frank (1969). This study was "replicated" by McGowan and Smith (1978) for black Africa and by Ray and Webster (1978) for Latin America. Gochman and Ray (1979) examined the dependency structure of United States-Latin American relationships and USSR-East European relationships. A number of studies, both empirical and conceptual, treated dependency as well as interdependence (see the essays in Caporaso 1978; Chase-Dunn 1978; Walleri 1978; and Caporaso and Ward 1979). By the end of the seventies, this led to a recognition that Marxist explanations were, if not being treated sympathically, at least being subjected to analysis (see Lynch 1980:314). This is important because it links this research with the work in comparative politics on dependency, the work of Galtung (1964c; 1971) on system structure, the work on interdependence (e.g., Rosecrance and Stein 1973 and Keohane and Nye 1977), and the more realist concern with power (M. Singer 1972) and penetration (Rosenau 1966).

This neglect among American scholars of the major alternative to realism in the fifties and sixties supports rather than invalidates the proposition. Indeed, Kuhn (1970a:37) states that the existence of a major alternative paradigm and scholars working in the paradigm will be ignored by members of a field on the basis that those other scholars are not within the field. The new interest in Marxism within the field does not invalidate the proposition and can be treated in the same manner as was the transnational/issue politics paradigm. In this case, the anomaly that seems to have increased the interest with Marxism is not the ending of the Cold War but the impact of the Vietnam War upon intellectuals in the United States. That war seems to have caused a number of scholars to rethink their most basic assumptions about international politics. This tendency has been reinforced by emerging North-South problems and the general failure of American foreign policy in the Third World. How much of an impact this rethinking will have on the field remains an open question.

Conclusion

The preceding survey seems to support several general points. First, there is a basic agreement within the field about the nature of international politics and how it should be studied. Second, this agreement has provided a general underlying coherence to work in the field by providing a research program for each subfield that has linked them together. Third, this division of labor has allowed five areas within the realist paradigm to be articulated systematically and somewhat cumulatively. Fourth, articulation of the paradigm has consisted of four types of activities: conceptual clarification in the traditional mode; conceptual clarification in the behavioral mode (i.e., the attempt to operationalize and measure concepts); tests of explanations in either the traditional or behavioral mode; and the reformulation of explanations in light of these tests and the work on conceptual clarification. Fifth, the various approaches and conceptual frameworks that have become popular in the field at different times do not constitute different paradigms but are better interpreted as elaborations of different aspects of the realist paradigm, since they do not reject the three fundamental assumptions of the paradigm. Finally, prior to the seventies no attempt was made within the field to seriously challenge the assumptions of the realist paradigm, and those who used the major alternative paradigm available, Marxism, were viewed as being outside the field. Since the literature review supports these points, the proposition that the Realist paradigm has guided theory construction within the field during the fifties and sixties is given a certain amount of credence. It can be concluded therefore that the findings of the "face validity test" do not falsify the proposition.

From the review of the field several insights can also be derived about the nature of change in normal science. While these are not directly relevant to the proposition, they are interesting in terms of the larger question raised in the debate between Kuhn (1970b:249–259) and Toulmin (1967; 1970; 1972) over normal science. One of the major sources of innovation in the field has been the application of scientific criteria of assessment to traditional explanations. The attempt to apply rigorous scientific analysis made scholars more sensitive to the ambiguity, lack of operational criteria, nonfalsifiability, and absence of explicit propositions in much of the traditional wisdom. As a result, many scholars consciously searched for new concepts by borrowing from other disciplines. This became an established way of attempting to solve puzzles generated through the use of the new methodological criteria. The decision-making approach solved the problem of anthropomorphizing the nation-state. Game theory, because of its deductive quality, gave strategic analysis more explanatory power. Systems analysis helped reformulate discussions of the balance of power and global structure into explicit, testable propositions. Cybernetics elucidated part of the mystery of community formation by pointing to the importance of communication and transaction flows for building ties. While each of these frameworks introduced new rigor and pointed to propositions that were not easily grasped by the power politics framework, the methodological concerns must be seen as the ultimate source of innovation within the field. This is something that Kuhn entirely overlooked in his work.[22]

Of all the frameworks, the one that introduced the most innovation was that of decision making. This was primarily because with the emphasis on decision making came an interest in social psychology, and then cognitive psychology, that began to challenge the assumptions of the paradigm. The introduction of social and cognitive psychology appeared to have a more radical impact because those who introduced these approaches were not political scientists borrowing from other fields, but social psychologists who either remained within psychology or came into international relations but still adhered to a psychological paradigm. Because of this coherence and professional identity, social psychology was the least changed by the realist paradigm in the process of being "adapted" to explain world politics. Throughout, it has undercut more than the other frameworks the emphasis of power politics on rational actors, the use of coercion, and the need to balance power as the only way to live with the security dilemma.

This review of the field has shown that, despite the introduction of conceptual change, there is a remarkable degree to which propositions or conceptual frameworks will not be given up. Rare is the instance in which someone who has actually employed a framework has given it up because of someone else's criticism. Change seems to occur not so much from conversion or changing another scholar's perspective but from adding new approaches or propositions to old ones, which, rather than being refuted, simply seem to run out of new and interesting things to say. From Morgenthau on, every scholar who introduced a new approach never gave it up. He just kept writing until people stopped reading. Cumulative "knowledge" developed not so much from rejection and real advancement but from seeing things from a new perspective. Because

22. This is probably because basic methodological questions are much more easily settled in the physical sciences. Kuhn (1970a:27–28) does, however, discuss the importance of innovation in measurement for bringing about theoretical change.

there is no real rejection based on testing, the emergence of a consensus on any framework could make the field highly susceptible to dogma and ideology. This was particularly the case with deterrence theory, which, because it enhanced the explanatory power of power politics, was never really questioned or even tested by any of its proponents. Often the policy relevance of an explanation seemed to be a more important criterion for its acceptance than its accuracy. For example, when deterrence theory was questioned by Rapoport (1964), the criticism was rejected as too moralistic. Eventually, empirical investigations in the seventies began to have an impact, and the accuracy of deterrence theory was finally doubted.

The main contribution of the behavioral revolt has been to save the field from this dogmatic tendency (see Vasquez 1976b:200–203). If anything, quantitative tests have shown that the field knows considerably less than most of its members think. Theorists' unwillingness to specify what will count as falsifying their explanation or demonstrating the inutility of their approach is the main potential source of ideological rigidity, and only insistence on testing provides any guard against it. If any real cumulative knowledge results from rejection of "false" or inadequate explanations, it will be because quantitative tests have rejected incorrect and imprecise hypotheses.

The danger of ideology is particularly important in international relations because it seems that one of the major sources of fundamental (paradigm-producing) change in the field comes not from laboratory anomalies but from current events. Idealism was rejected because of the failure of the League of Nations and the coming of World War II. Realism was accepted not only because it could explain the anomaly that the idealist paradigm could not but also because it provided a guide to the United States as it emerged as the world's most powerful state. Marxism was rejected primarily because the United States was capitalist and its opponent happened to be communist. The realist paradigm itself began to be questioned because of the Vietnam War, and because, while it seemed able to explain the struggles for power in the two world wars and in the Cold War, it appeared at a loss to explain détente. This is similar to major climatic changes or earthquakes bringing about paradigm shifts in physics.

The intrusion of such events makes decisions about the adequacy of explanations, theories, and paradigms difficult for several reasons. First, it is more difficult to be dispassionate about the evidence, and second, even though the truth value of an explanation is separate from its normative value, explanations may be accepted because of their political consequences or policy relevance rather than the evidence. This will be particularly the case when testing is not rigorous, or the evidence is mixed. When such tendencies occur, it is difficult to separate science from ideology. One of the ways to avoid this problem is to be more laboratory oriented. In the rush to be policy-relevant, the field has overlooked the fact that most physical sciences and even advanced social sciences do not directly predict or explain real world events, only indicators or experimental outcomes. Once these "artificial" phenomena can be predicted and explained, then it may be possible to deal with their more complex (because they are less pure) counterparts in the "real world." At any rate, decisions about data can be more rigorous and based primarily on scientific criteria. In terms of these issues, it must be concluded that an application of Kuhn to the social sciences is limited because he does not provide much role for nonlaboratory evidence and does not speak directly about ideological considerations.

Finally, the literature review provides some clues about the relationship between normal science and the process by which old paradigms are rejected and new ones accepted (i.e., the debate between Kuhn [1970b:249–259] and Toulmin [1967; 1970; 1972]). Paradigm change and articulation seem to be incremental, even though considerable innovation may occur. This change does not evolve into a new paradigm, because when innovation challenges an assumption in the paradigm, the author either pulls back or others reject or ignore the suggestion. Rosenau (1966) and Rummel (1977a) are two major examples of scholars who introduced changes that they later abandoned because they challenged the paradigm. After Rosenau's (1966) use of penetration broke down the notion of unitary and sovereign states, he returned to the realist assumptions by introducing the theory of adaptation. Rummel (1979) moved away from status explanations that challenged the second and third assumptions of the paradigm and moved back to balance of power notions. Others, who were outside the field, like Kolko (1969) or Galtung (1971), or on the periphery, like Nye and Keohane (1971), saw no need to reject the implications of new concepts.

Kuhn, then, is partially correct about discontinuities being present in a field. Paradigm shifts are seen as radical. There is much debate and argument about them. They do not simply evolve, as Toulmin implies. The reason for this is that every possible alternative—conceptual changes, ad hoc explanations, new testing procedures—is tried before fundamental questioning occurs.

Kuhn also seems to be correct in arguing that younger scholars or those on the periphery are responsible for bringing about paradigm shifts. Those who called for paradigm change in international relations often were younger, more junior members of the discipline (Keohane and Nye 1971; Coplin and O'Leary 1971; Handelman et al. 1973; Mansbach, Ferguson, and Lampert 1976). They also tended to work at the periphery of the field and/or had experience outside it. Those who called for a transnational paradigm (Nye and Keohane 1971; Burton 1972; Kaiser 1971) were working in an area, international organization and integration, that had been most influenced by the idealist paradigm. Others, like Coplin (1974), had done work in international law (Coplin 1966a), an area of little concern to the realists, and had worked on social and cognitive psychological approaches (Coplin 1964; 1966b). Likewise, O'Leary (Davidson, Kovenock, and O'Leary 1966) had worked outside the field in analyzing American politics.

Such individuals seemed to have a hostile attitude toward the realist paradigm that made them look for things that would refute its tenets. For this reason, they could see things that others could not. But others ignored them (see McClelland 1977) because they were aware of the hostility and suspected the critics of being latent idealists. Such biases are not necessarily irrational, since they make paradigm critics prove their case beyond a shadow of a doubt. Due compensation is provided, however, because fame and accolade come to the critics if they are successful. This in itself may provide a nonacademic incentive for criticizing paradigms. Within the field, then, the rewards and punishments for fundamental change are fairly well balanced, but they tend to make discontinuities inevitable, if a paradigm shift is to occur.

Toulmin appears to be more relevant for explaining nonparadigmatic change within normal science. Normal science is much more innovative and diverse than Kuhn implied. In addition, Toulmin made an important point by suggesting that conceptual innovation can lead to discoveries that may be anomalous and thereby help bring about a paradigm shift. The use of social and cognitive psychology in the field may be having this effect. This use of a theory from another field's paradigm has had a devastating effect on the rational-actor model in explanations of global state behavior. In addition, as the Cold War waned, social psychological models seemed more relevant for explaining processes to which scholars had not paid much attention because they were so concerned with power struggles. In the presence of anomalies, outside conceptual frameworks can make a subfield more susceptible to a paradigm shift.

These points on normal science are inductive conclusions that have been derived from the review of the field and can be used to make more precise some of the general points Kuhn and Toulmin make about intellectual change. They are, however, somewhat tangential to the main purpose of this chapter, which is to assess the extent to which the realist paradigm has guided theory construction in the field. In that regard, the evidence presented in the preliminary tests and the literature review is very consistent with the proposition, and it can be concluded that not only has the proposition passed a preliminary test, but it also is able to offer a plausible interpretation of normal activity within the field to account for change, continuity, and overall coherence. The next chapter will examine the extent to which the realist paradigm guided data making in the field.

Chapter 5

Data Making As a
Paradigm-Directed Activity

The Proposition

Kuhn's Analysis

Kuhn (1970a:chap. 3) explicitly states that fact gathering (i.e., data making) in normal science is guided by the dominant paradigm in the field; such guidance is necessary because the world consists of numerous phenomena, and phenomena only take on meaning to the extent that they are conceptualized. Conceptualization, as pointed out earlier, is a function of theory construction or paradigm articulation. Facts, then, presuppose a paradigm that sifts through the welter of phenomena to focus on what is important. In the pre-paradigm stage of science, fact gathering tends to be random because there is no single paradigm to distinguish the chaff from the wheat (Kuhn 1970a:16–17). In normal science, however, fact gathering becomes highly directed, not only because the paradigm focuses on certain phenomena, but because fact gathering usually "consumes much time, equipment, and money" (Kuhn 1970a:25). Consequently, the gathering of facts becomes a highly selective activity.

According to Kuhn (1970a:25–27), three types of facts are gathered. The first consists of those that the paradigm has shown to be of great importance for revealing the nature of things. The second, which is much smaller, consists of those facts that, although they are not intrinsically important, can be used to test certain predictions from paradigm theory. Finally, the third class of facts, which Kuhn considers most important, consists of those facts that were not originally central to the paradigm but subsequently become important because of paradigm articulation. Before applying this analysis to international relations inquiry, it is important to specify just what is meant by data making in the field and indicate why it occurred.

Data Making: What It Is and Why It Occurs

Data making is the process by which facts are measured and quantified so that they can be used for hypothesis testing (see J. D. Singer 1965; 1968a:2). This definition is similar to that of Kuhn (1970a:25–28), who defines fact gathering as not only the observation and recording of facts, but their transformation by measurement techniques into a form that allows them to be used to test hypotheses.

Data making is a central activity of any science not only because it provides the evidence for evaluating propositions but also because it is conducted by following specified rules and procedures. Part of the methodology of any discipline is devoted to the rules that should be followed and the techniques employed in converting facts into data. One of the primary rules is that the process should be replicable and reliable; that is, the procedures employed should be clear and precise enough so that another scholar can independently follow those procedures and obtain the same results (J. D. Singer 1968a:2). The term *data* is usually applied only to the product of an activity that has followed this rule.

It is clear from this analysis that it would be possible to predict attempts at data making on the basis of knowing the amount of concern with hypothesis testing in a given field. This conclusion seems to be supported by the fact that it has only been on the two occasions when hypothesis testing became a concern to international relations scholars that data-making projects were initiated. The first occasion occurred with the independent studies of war initiated by Lewis Richardson and Quincy Wright just after World War I, the second with the behavioral revolt of the sixties.

To say that data making arose out of a concern for hypothesis testing does not explain why the latter suddenly became a matter of concern. Lewis Richardson, who was a physicist, aptly summarized why he became concerned with hypothesis testing and data making in two letters to Wright:

> There is in the world a great deal of brilliant, witty political discussion which leads to no settled convictions. My aim has been different: namely to examine a few notions by quantitative techniques in the hope of reaching a reliable answer. . . .
>
> I notice that many of those who are considered to be experts on foreign affairs do not base their opinions on historical facts, but on some sort of instinctive reasoning [cited in Richardson 1960b:v].

Wright expressed a similar concern (1942:chap. 16 and Appendix 25). Other scholars in the field, however, did not share this concern and were occupied instead with the debate over idealism and realism. As a result, Richardson's work was never recognized within the field until the sixties, and, although Wright's work was lauded, it was not imitated. Data making died as suddenly as it had been born.

It was not until the beginning of the behavioral revolt of the sixties that the concern with data making and hypothesis testing was resurrected. Indeed, one of the chief characteristics of the revolt was the initiation of data-making projects. This time, data making did not die out; it grew for over a decade and shows no signs of disappearing. What transpired in the interval between the late thirties and the sixties were two decades of intense theoretical activity. It may have been the existence of this theoretical analysis that allowed data making to become a concern in the field. Charles McClelland provides some hints as to why this may have happened:

> So many interesting concepts applicable to international relations were brought to attention in the 1950's and 1960's that the most urgent problem often seemed to be coordinating the concepts rather than testing them against data. . . . Theory has tended to become doctrine and the facts have been expected to conform to the doctrine. . . .
>
> A new research movement has arisen very recently apparently in reaction to the long preceding period. . . . The movement centers on the collection of international event data and the analysis of that data [McClelland 1972b:16–17].

If McClelland is correct, and there is much impressionistic evidence to suggest that he is, then the second data movement in the field, along with the general concern with scientific method, arose out of the conviction that the kind of theorizing that had been conducted after World War II had gone about as far as it could and it was now time to collect data systematically and test some of the explanations suggested by the theorizing.

Data Making in International Relations during the Pre-realist and Behavioral Periods

The appearance of two distinct periods of international relations data making, before the fifties and during the sixties, provides an opportunity to examine the validity of the proposition that data making in the field has been guided by the realist paradigm in the fifties and sixties. It would be expected that data making in the sixties would be guided by the realist paradigm while data making prior to the fifties would not. In addition, since the two pre-fifties projects are both on wars and Wright's was conducted in the field and Richardson's outside the field, an opportunity is provided to assess Kuhn's idea that different fields will employ different paradigms to study the same phenomena. Since Wright collected his data during the idealist-realist debate he would be expected to

Data Making

incorporate assumptions of both paradigms in his project. Conversely, Richardson, who was outside the field and had a certain disdain for its analysis, would be expected to employ a totally different paradigm. A review of the major data-making projects in the field will demonstrate that the expectations about Wright, Richardson, and data making in the sixties support Kuhn's analysis.

Wright's project reflected the idealist-realist debate by taking assumptions from both idealism and realism. Idealism is apparent in his emphasis on the interdisciplinary approach and on legalism. His use of an interdisciplinary approach was evident in his devotion of large sections of his work to nonnational war (e.g., animal and primitive warfare) and to reviewing the relevant literature in biology, psychology, sociology, and anthropology.[1] His emphasis on legalism was illustrated by the fact that he defined contemporary war in part as a "legal condition" (Wright 1965a:chap. 2, p. 8). However, Wright also reflected the realist emphasis on nation-states, power, and empirical analysis. He stated that the legal definition given at the beginning of the study is not scientific, but derived from the literature (Wright 1965a:685), and a scientific definition would have to emerge from an examination of war itself. Finally, when he came to defining war operationally so he could collect data, Wright combined assumptions of both the realists and idealists by limiting his data to:

all hostilities involving members of the family of nations, whether international, civil, colonial or imperial, which were recognized as states of war in the legal sense or which involved over 50,000 troops. . . . The legal recognition of the warlike action, the scale of such action, and the importance of its legal and political consequences have, therefore, all been taken into consideration in deciding whether a given incident was sufficiently important to include in a list of wars [Wright 1965a:636].

Other uses of armed force, such as revolutions and interventions, were not included (Wright 1965a:636), and participants in a war were only included if they were actually independent (*sovereign* in the realist paradigm) before or after the war. Participants with only de facto status in the war itself were not included (Wright 1965a:637). Thus, Wright employed assumptions of the two paradigms to decide how to collect data on war.

Given the struggle between the idealist and realist paradigms, Wright's procedure seemed legitimate and obvious. To Richardson, who was out-

1. Compare Wright (1965:chaps. 5, 6, and 15) with the idealist approaches of Zimmern (1939).

The Power of Power Politics

side the field, it did not appear at all obvious, and he opted for a very different operational definition. Richardson wanted a definition that would allow him to compare and measure specific wars. Taking assumptions from astronomy and psychology, he replaced the notion of *war* with the concept of a *deadly quarrel* and measured it as one would measure the magnitude of a star. His reasoning is worth quoting at length:

CRITIC: . . . And how have you counted wars? . . . Are all to be counted alike?

ASTRONOMER: Fortunately the logical problem of how to count unequal things has been solved. We should count wars as astronomers count stars, by first arranging them in order of magnitude. To ask whether "civil wars have been rarer than international wars" is indeed about as crude as to ask whether "red stars are rarer than blue stars." You can take another hint from the astronomers: as they have replaced red and blue by "spectral type," so you will probably have to reconsider the meanings of civil and international. Before the counting can begin we need to form a collection or list of wars of all kinds. The less conspicuous incidents are the more numerous —as among stars—so that it is impossible to make a list of them all. Some rule is therefore necessary for excluding the smaller incidents.

Wright's selection rule . . . is however hardly satisfactory for statistical purposes. . . .[2]

An essential characteristic of a war may be said to be casualties. . . . From a psychological point of view a war, a riot, and a murder, though differing in many important aspects . . . have at least this in common, that they are all manifestations of the instinct of aggressiveness. . . . By a deadly quarrel is meant any quarrel which caused death to humans. The term thus includes murders, banditries, mutinies, insurrections, and wars small and large; but it excludes accidents, and calamities [Richardson 1960b:1, 4–6].

Thus, Richardson rejected the dominant notions about war within the field of international relations inquiry, whereas Wright reflected the emphases in the field. The first occasion of data making, then, tends to support Kuhn's analysis of fact gathering as a paradigm-directed activity.

The second occasion of data making in the field occurred in the early sixties and continues through the present. In the sixties, data making

2. For specific criticisms of Wright, which include an attack on the idealist emphasis on legality and the realist emphasis on the importance of wars, see Richardson (1960b:5).

Data Making

was centered on three areas—national attributes, foreign policy behavior, and war. As a result of the articulation of the realist paradigm that had been conducted in the fifties, these three areas were the most obvious ones in which to collect data to test hypotheses related to the realist paradigm. The plausibility of this conclusion can be seen by examining how each area was relevant to the realist paradigm.

National attributes, the first area, was highly relevant because Morgenthau and the other power politics theorists had maintained that knowledge of national power was a particularly revealing aspect of the conduct of international relations. Furthermore, Morgenthau (1960, 1973:chap. 9) had attempted to demonstrate in detail that the elements (or indicators) of national power were what in the sixties would have been called national attributes. Given the paradigm, data on national attributes would not only be of intrinsic value but would also provide a series of key independent variables.

The second and third areas, foreign policy behavior and war, were relevant to the paradigm because they provided the major dependent variables. They were the topics that the paradigm wanted to explain. If the proposition being examined in this chapter is accurate, then it would be expected that data collected in these two areas would reflect the characterizations of foreign policy behavior and wars made by the paradigm; that is, foreign policy behavior would be viewed in terms of a struggle for power and peace (in other words, conflict and cooperation among nations), and war would be viewed as something occurring among nations and related to the balance of power. Since it was demonstrated in chapter 3 that these three areas were of central concern to the realist paradigm, it is only necessary to show that data were collected in these areas.

The initial data published and made available to scholars in the sixties were products more of comparative politics than international relations (see J. D. Singer 1968a:11–12).[3] The collections consisted basically of attribute data on nations, and although not collected specifically with theories of international relations in mind, they provided a set of relevant variables on what Morgenthau had called the elements of national power. The major collections were A Cross Polity Survey (1963) by Banks and Textor and the World Handbook of Political and Social Indicators (1964) by Russett, Alker, Deutsch, and Lasswell of Yale.[4] These

3. Also see the introductions to Arthur Banks and R. B. Textor, A Cross Polity Survey (1963), and Bruce Russett et al., World Handbook of Political and Social Indicators (1964).

4. The book by Banks and Textor did not contain the actual data but did provide a list of the variables available from the Inter-University Consortium for Political Research.

two projects were initiated not only to collect data for specific research projects but to provide general data sets that could be used by scholars working on a variety of projects. Consequently, not only was the data published, it also was made available on computer tapes stored at the Inter-University Consortium for Political Research, which has become the data library for the entire field of political science. A *Cross Polity Survey* provided data from widely scattered sources on demographic, economic, cultural, and social characteristics of 115 nations. In addition, the authors provided new data on political characteristics through the use of content analysis. The *World Handbook* also provided data on the demographic, economic, cultural, social, and political characteristics of nations; however, none of the data was derived by coding. The *World Handbook* differed from the *A Cross Polity Survey* in that it provided more variables (75 versus 57), but most of these were not as "political" as the coded data of Banks and Textor.

By the end of the decade, both these projects had produced more data. Banks provided similar attribute data going back as far as 1815, as well as data on internal conflict (Banks 1971; 1973). These data permitted hypotheses to be tested longitudinally. Charles Lewis Taylor and Michael Hudson published a second edition of the *World Handbook* (1972) containing a great amount of new data. In addition to including longitudinal data on attribute variables similar to the ones in the first edition, data on political institutions, internal conflict, interventions, and 57,268 daily coded events were provided. Both these projects, however, were initiated to collect data for testing comparative politics hypotheses dealing with the prerequisites of democracy, modernization, social change, and internal conflict (e.g., Hudson 1977:405–411).

The earliest data-making project that was directly concerned with international relations was the Dimensionality of Nations (DON) project begun in 1962 by Harold Guetzkow, Jack Sawyer, and R. J. Rummel (see Rummel 1976a:19–21). Rummel has been the guiding force in the project and its director since 1963 (see Hilton 1973:13). As with the two preceding projects, a large number of variables (over 200) on national attributes were collected for various times in the fifties and sixties.[5] Data on internal and external conflict were also collected. The DON project, in addition to providing much more data on what Morgenthau had called the elements of national power, also provided the first extensive data on a dependent variable of interest to the realist paradigm: conflict and cooperation among nations.

The concern in the sixties with collecting data on more of the depen-

5. There was not much duplication among Banks and Textor (1963), Russett et al. (1964), and DON, because different measures were employed.

dent variables of interest to the field led to data projects on foreign policy behavior. One of the most readily available sources of data on the foreign policies of nations was their votes in the United Nations.[6] UN votes were first collected early in the sixties, and this project remained one of the ongoing activities of the Inter-University Consortium for Political Research throughout the sixties and seventies. Votes, however, were not really the kind of behavior that followers of the realist paradigm saw as most important; they were more interested in inter-state interactions.

One of the most imaginative and perhaps most influential projects to collect data on inter-state interactions was the World Event Interaction Survey (WEIS) initiated by Charles McClelland (1967; 1976). This project coded the interactions of nations reported daily in sentences in the *New York Times* into sixty-three categories of behavior. These categories could be collapsed into two types—cooperation and conflict. The actual distribution in the categories, however, suggested that perhaps three types might be more appropriate—cooperation, conflict, and participation (McClelland and Hoggard 1969:714).[7] The excitement generated by the WEIS project is indicated by the fact that it led to an event data movement that resulted in several similar projects and one of the most extensive and lengthy discussions in the field on data making.[8]

War was the third major area in which data were collected in the sixties. The most extensive project in this area and the successor to the efforts of Richardson and Wright was the Correlates of War project of J. David Singer and Melvin Small (1972). They collected data on wars and

6. These were really a substitute for more desirable data, which were not readily available; see Russett (1967:59–60).

7. For other attempts to find underlying dimensions in WEIS data see S. A. Salmore (1972); Kegley (1973); S. A. Salmore and Munton (1974); and Wilkenfeld, Hopple, and Rossa (1979:127–130).

8. The two main topics of discussion were the validity of sources (whether a single source, like the *New York Times*, would bias data either through selection of events or through the journalist's interpretation of the events and whether multiple sources might solve this problem); and how to code behavior (whether cooperation and conflict should be scaled or classified into discrete categories). Both these questions were addressed through empirical research. On source validity, see the studies of Azar (1970); Gamson and Modigliani (1971: Appendix C); Sigler (1972a; 1972b); Doran, Pendley, and Antunes (1973); Hoggard (1974); Burrowes (1974); McGowan (1974a); Bobrow, Chan, and Kringen (1977). On the question of scaling see Moses et al. (1967); McClelland and Hoggard (1969); C. F. Hermann (1971); Brody (1972); Kegley (1973); Kegley, Salmore, and Rosen (1974); S. Salmore and Munton (1974); Azar (1970); Azar and Havener (1976). For general reviews of the event data movement see Burgess and Lawton (1972); Peterson (1975); and Azar and Ben-Dak (1975).

alliances among states from 1816 to 1965. Unlike Richardson, they concentrated only on wars that had at least one nation on each side; unlike Wright, they did not reflect the emphasis on legalism (Singer and Small 1972:18, 30–35). Instead, they took Wright's and Richardson's lists of wars plus any other wars they found record of, and then removed those wars whose participants' political status did not meet their membership criteria or who failed to meet their minimum threshold of battle-connected casualties (J. D. Singer and Small 1972:18–19). The first criterion stems directly from the concerns of the realist paradigm, since political status is determined by the extent to which a participant is a sovereign nation, and nations in turn are divided into two categories ("total system" and "central system") depending on their power (see J. D. Singer and Small 1972:19–24).

In addition to collecting data on war, the Correlates of War project collected data on several important independent variables. The first effort was focused on alliance data, which clearly reflects the realist concern with the balance of power and with the polarity debate (see J. D. Singer and Small 1966a; 1968). The alliance data were collected first for the period 1815–1940 (J. D. Singer and Small 1966b) and then updated to 1965 (Small and Singer 1969). The second major area of data making for the project was on diplomatic ties from 1815 on (J. D. Singer and Small 1966b; see also Small and Singer 1973). This data initially served as a way of determining membership in the central system (see J. D. Singer and Small 1968) and was used by the end of the sixties to test propositions on status inconsistency (Wallace 1970; 1971). Data were also collected on the number of intergovernmental organizations in the system from 1815 to 1964 (J. D. Singer and Wallace 1970). Each of these data sets was updated periodically. Finally, data on national capability began to be collected in the mid-sixties (J. D. Singer 1976:27) and occupied much attention throughout the seventies (see J. D. Singer, Bremer, and Stuckey 1972; Ray and Singer 1979; Bremer 1980).

The selection of these three independent variables and the order in which they received priority reflect the strong influence of the realist paradigm and its priorities. Alliances and national capability were thought by the early power politics theorists to be the two most important determinants of peace and war. The status-ordering data were taken as an indirect indicator of power, and the data on IGOs were employed to test realist propositions (see J. D. Singer and Wallace 1970; Wallace 1972).

The other major data set on wars was that collected for the 1914 studies on the outbreak of World War I. Unlike the other data sets, this one was not placed on file with the consortium for general use. Nevertheless, it played an important role in data making because it was the first data set produced in the field by content analyzing previously secret government documents from various states in order to delineate decision makers' perceptions just prior to the outbreak of a major war.

Each of these data sets is large and comprehensive enough in its own area so that it can be used by many scholars to test a variety of hypotheses of interest to the realist paradigm, but they were all collected with specific propositions in mind. A brief overview of the initial use of the data by their collectors will underline the association between data making in the field and the realist paradigm.

As was seen in chapter 4, the Dimensionality of Nations project mathematically elaborated and then tested verbal suggestions made by Morgenthau and other power politics theorists about the relationship between national power and states' foreign policy behavior and interaction (see Rummel 1963; 1972a; 1979). UN voting data were used to test hypotheses about bloc allegiances, the struggle for power between blocs, and national power (see Ball 1951; Alker and Russett 1965; Rowe 1969). The initial purpose of WEIS was to map inter-state interactions in two arenas of the Cold War, the Berlin and Taiwan Straits crises (McClelland 1968; 1972a). The Correlates of War data was initially employed to test hypotheses on the balance of power, polarity, and war (J. D. Singer and Small 1968). Finally, the 1914 studies related decision makers' perceptions and the outbreak of war (O. R. Holsti, North, and Brody 1968).[9]

Each of the major data sets, then, reflects the realist paradigm's fundamental assumptions that nations are the most important actors and research should be focused on the struggle for power and peace. In addition, each data set was used to test specific hypotheses relevant to the realist paradigm. Consequently, it is not surprising that most of the data consists of national attributes and inter-state conflict and cooperation. The proposition being examined in this chapter maintains that such a result is not an accident but the product of the power of the realist paradigm to guide and direct scholarly activity within the field. Now that the proposition has been elaborated and its plausibility demonstrated, it is necessary to specify how it will be empirically tested.

Research Design

Operationalization and Measurement

In order to test the proposition that the realist paradigm guided data making in the field of international relations in the fifties and sixties, it is

9. All the claims in this paragraph have been substantiated at length and with extensive citation from the literature in chapter 4.

necessary to operationalize *data making* and the *realist paradigm*. Since data making is the transformation of facts into variables for the purpose of hypothesis testing, data making can be operationalized as *variables available to international relations scholars in a form that permits hypothesis testing*. According to this definition, whether an activity is data making is determined by its product, that is, whether it produces variables. In addition, these variables must be in a form suitable for testing and available to international relations scholars. The first criterion means that the variables must be on computer tape or cards, in recognition of the fact that one of the major costs in data making is transforming published data into computerized data. The second criterion allows data that may have been collected by scholars outside the field (e.g., by people in the United Nations or in comparative politics) to be included if the data are available to international relations scholars.

The term *realist paradigm* was operationalized in chapter 3. The coding scheme assumes that if the actors and topics labeled as realist in the coding scheme are indicators of the assumptions of the realist paradigm, variables employing those actors and topics can be used as indicators of realist concepts.

The problem with this measure is that a variable is not necessarily an indicator of only one concept. For example, the variable GNP may be taken as an indicator of wealth, industrialization, and/or national power. In the coding scheme, GNP would be coded as an indicator of national power. A scholar in comparative politics or economics, however, might not view it as such an indicator, and to classify such a variable as reflecting the assumptions of the realist paradigm might be viewed as highly invalid. Since variables do not inherently serve as indicators of a single concept, it is perfectly legitimate to code them as indicators of one concept if that variable is one of the common ways a group of scholars operationalize the concept.[10] This is a valid procedure because within the field, GNP is widely taken and can be used as an indicator of national economic power (see East and Hermann 1974:284). Although the same measures may be taken as indicators of other concepts outside the field, this is not relevant to the analysis. The validity of the coding scheme rests on a consensus within the field about the use of indicators and cannot be validly applied outside the field of international relations.

The only way systematic measurement error could occur would be if the competing paradigms in the field used indicators that were labeled realist in the coding scheme to measure nonrealist concepts. This type of error cannot occur because the major alternative paradigms—transna-

10. Meaning is not inherent in a word or variable; it is determined by use; see Austin (1962).

tional relations, issue politics, and Marxism—do not employ the nation-state as the sole actor, and they emphasize different topics of inquiry. This use of the coding scheme assumes that if most of the variables for which data has been collected have actors and topics of inquiry that are labeled realist in the coding scheme, this finding would not be an accident. Rather, it would indicate that the realist paradigm has guided data making in the field. This seems to be a reasonable assumption to make. Given these validity arguments and the fact that reliability was established at .90, it can be concluded that the dominance of the realist paradigm has been adequately measured for the purpose of this test.[11]

Deriving Hypotheses

Two hypotheses can be derived from the proposition to test its adequacy:

2a. Variables available for use by international relations scholars will tend to provide information on nation-states and topics of inquiry that are labeled realist in the coding scheme.

2b. More variables will be available for use by international relations scholars on the two most central concepts in the realist paradigm —national power and inter-nation conflict-cooperation—than on other concepts.[12]

Hypothesis 2a is the most obvious way to test the proposition. It makes the assumption that if data making was guided by the realist paradigm in the fifties and sixties, then it is reasonable to expect that, out of all the variables produced, a statistically significant number should provide information on nation-states and on topics of inquiry that were deemed important by the realist paradigm; that is, the distribution should not be random. If this were not the case, then it would make no sense to say that the realist paradigm had guided data making, and the hypothesis would be justifiably falsified.

Hypothesis 2b makes a more specific prediction. It not only assumes the accuracy of hypothesis 2a but goes on to say that of all the concepts for which data could be collected, more data will be collected on the two most central concepts of the realist paradigm: national power and inter-nation conflict-cooperation. Since the realist paradigm focused on national power as the chief independent variable and on inter-nation

11. For the reliability formula, see chapter 3, note 6.
12. These hypotheses are numbered 2a and 2b because they test the second proposition in this book.

conflict-cooperation as the chief dependent variable, it is reasonable to expect that more data would be collected on these two concepts.

The Sample

Given the above analysis, it is clear that an important criterion in selecting a sample is to insure that it include only data that is either produced or generally available within the field. A second criterion is that this data be within the time span of the proposition. The major problem in selecting a sample is to find a list of variables produced or available in the field.

Since the Inter-University Consortium for Political Research classifies and lists variables it has on file, the consortium's list of all the variables in its international relations archive was taken as the sample.[13] This provides a nonbiased sample of data available in the field. It also includes the universe of data readily and routinely available to all scholars by the end of the 1960s. It does not, however, include the universe of data produced in the field, since all data may not have been placed on file by that date, either because it was not complete or because the scholars who collected the data may have wanted to analyze it first. While the present analysis might have been more complete if these other cases were included, sufficiently accurate information about them did not exist to make their inclusion feasible.[14] The selection of this sample, however, has the advantage of making the present analysis easily replicable in the future.

This sample provided a list of 1,650 variables, a number more than sufficient for statistical analysis. These variables are presented in the consortium's *Variable Index* as the product of 31 data sets. Since some of the projects produced more than one data set, however, only 20 projects account for all the data on file. With the exception of Richardson's *Statistics of Deadly Quarrels*, all of the data sets were completed in the sixties, and even Richardson's data were not made available in computerized form until Rummel transferred the information to tape in the sixties.[15]

---

13. See Inter-University Consortium for Political Research, *Variable Index for Studies Available from the International Relations Archive* (May 1971).

14. For a review of some of the major data projects not on file by 1971, see Burgess and Lawton (1972).

15. Richardson's data, of course, do not support the proposition.

Figure 5.1. Percentage of Realist Indicators
in the Field (Hypothesis 2a)

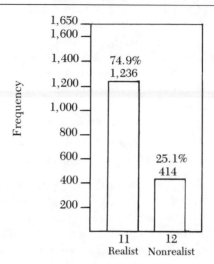

The Findings

Hypothesis 2a predicted that variables produced and available in the field would tend to provide information on nation-states and on topics of inquiry that were labeled realist in the coding scheme. In order to test this hypothesis, the 1,650 variables were classified into two categories—realist indicators or nonrealist indicators. In order to be classified as a realist indicator, a variable had to have the nation as its actor and a realist topic; any mixed cases (nation as actor with a nonrealist topic or vice versa) were classified as nonrealist. If the hypothesis were true, it would be expected that a large proportion of the variables would be usable as realist indicators. The findings are presented in figure 5.1. The figure clearly shows that just about three-fourths (74.9 percent) of the variables can be used as realist indicators. This would hardly appear to be a random distribution, and the calculation of a binomial distribution (p<.01) for interpretive purposes supports this assumption.[16] On the basis of the finding, it can be concluded that hypothesis 2a has failed to be falsified.

Hypothesis 2b predicted that variables produced and available in the field would tend to provide more indicators of national power and inter-

16. For a discussion of the use of the binomial distribution, see chapter 6, note 7.

state conflict-cooperation than of any other concept. Table 5.1 tests this hypothesis by rank-ordering the concepts. It can be seen from this table that the concepts of national power and inter-nation conflict-cooperation compose 66.4 percent of the total variables produced (49.9 percent and 16.5 percent respectively). In addition, none of the other concepts constitute more than 9.1 percent of the data available. On the basis of these findings, it can be concluded that hypothesis 2b has failed to be falsified. These findings provide considerable support for the proposition. The next section will examine data making in the 1970s to see the extent to which it has continued to be guided by the realist paradigm.

Data Making in the 1970s

The major data-making projects of the 1970s can be divided into three categories: national attributes; event data; and, for lack of a better term, reconstructed historical interaction data. The data on national attributes reflect the efforts of two groups to collect independent variables. Both are noteworthy for advancements in measurement rather than for new collecting procedures or new types of data. The first group is that associated with attempts to test Rosenau's pre-theory. Various indicators of size, wealth, and polity were collected by Burgess and Harf (1975) as part of the Inter-University Comparative Foreign Policy project (see also Burgess 1970). Additional data on these concepts were collected as part of the CREON project, with new indicators of regime constraint, capacity to act, and decision makers' personal characteristics and perceptions of the situation (see B. G. Salmore and S. A. Salmore 1975; East 1975; M. G. Hermann 1974; M. G. Hermann, C. F. Hermann, and Dixon 1979; and Brady 1975). With the exception of the perceptual variables of decision makers, these data are all undoubtedly indicators of a reformulated concept of national power.

Even more explicitly tied to the national power concept has been the effort of the Correlates of War project to collect indicators of national capability from 1815 to 1965. Researchers in this project defined capability as containing demographic, industrial, and military dimensions (see J. D. Singer, Bremer, and Stuckey 1972). The primary contribution of this effort, which involves at least two indicators for each dimension, is the care that has been taken to obtain reliable indicators from historical sources. As with the data on war (J. D. Singer and Small 1972), these will eventually be published as a handbook (Small et al. forthcoming, cited in Singer, Bremer, and Stuckey 1972). Of even greater significance than the collection of the raw indicators has been the attempt to develop sophisticated measures of national capability by combining the three dimensions (see especially Ray and Singer 1973 and Ray 1980).

Table 5.1. Rank Order of Indicators According to Amount of Data (Hypothesis 2b)

Actor	Topic	Frequency (number of variables)	Percentage	Rank
NATION	NATIONAL POWER[a]	824	49.9	1
NATION	CONFLICT-COOPERATION[a]	273	16.5	2
Nations and other actors	Conflict-cooperation	150	9.1	3
Nation	Transactions	85	5.2	4
NATION	SUPRANATIONALISM[a]	56	3.4	5
NATION	ALLIANCES[a]	46	2.8	6
NATION	ISOLATIONISM[a]	39	2.4	7
Nation	Issues	37	2.2	8
Nations and other actors	Sociological characteristics	35	2.1	9
Subnational	Conflict-cooperation	16	1.0	10
IGO	Supranationalism	15	0.9	11
IGO	Conflict-cooperation	14	0.8	12.5
Nation	Miscellaneous	14	0.8	12.5
IGO	Issues	11	0.7	14
Nations and other actors	National power	9	0.5	15
IGO	Miscellaneous	5	0.3	16.5
Nations and other actors	Miscellaneous	5	0.3	16.5
Nations and other actors	Alliances	3	0.2	18
Subnational	Issues	2	0.1	21
Subnational	Alliances	2	0.1	21
None	Miscellaneous	2	0.1	21
Nations and other actors	Integration	2	0.1	21
Nations and other actors	Propaganda	2	0.1	21
NGO	Miscellaneous	1	0.1	25
Non-national	Conflict-cooperation	1	0.1	25
Nations and other actors	Transactions	1	0.1	25
		1,650	99.9	

[a]Realist concept.

Attempts to improve measures have also taken place on data collected earlier on alliances (Wallace 1973b; Bueno de Mesquita 1975) and on intergovernmental organizations (Wallace 1975). The collection of data on national capability marks a transition of the Correlates of War project from testing propositions related to alliances to testing propositions on the distribution of power (see Singer, Bremer, and Stuckey 1972; Bremer 1980; Gochman 1980). The connection between these data and the power politics tradition should be obvious, but, as if to eliminate any doubt, Singer (1980) gave the following subtitle to the second volume of the Correlates of War—*Testing Some Realpolitik Models*.

While the Correlates of War project tested some central realist propositions during the 1960s (see Singer 1976:26), data collection toward the end of the 1970s indicated that it was moving toward a more general study of violence that might challenge the second assumption of the realist paradigm. This tendency is best evidenced by the publication of data on civil wars from 1816 through 1977 (see Small and Singer 1979). Whether this will give rise to a body of work that challenges the realist paradigm, as some of the work on status inconsistency did, remains to be seen. Nevertheless, the collection of civil war data is certainly something that would not be expected given the first two assumptions of the realist paradigm.

While the efforts to collect more national attribute data are important, particularly in terms of measurement, the real explosion in data making in the 1970s was with event data. The two major event data projects, the heirs to WEIS, have been CREON (Comparative Research on the Events of Nations) and COPDAB (Conflict and Peace Data Bank). The CREON data set has foreign policy data for thirty-six nations for randomly selected periods between 1959 and 1968. The specific nations were selected for theoretical reasons and can be thought of as a representative sample to test propositions related to the Rosenau pre-theory on political accountability and on size (see C. F. Hermann et al. 1973:23). The project has made two major contributions, one methodological and the other theoretical. Methodologically, CREON reflects several advances over WEIS, the two most important being the conceptualization of a foreign policy event (C. F. Hermann 1971; C. F. Hermann et al. 1973) to include an indirect target, and the development of a coding scheme that could tap a variety of behavior, not just cooperation and conflict. The last development is intimately related to CREON's major theoretical contribution, which is to reconceptualize the notion of foreign policy behavior inherited from Rosenau. Based on the empirical work of S. A. Salmore (1972), CREON attempted to collect data on several different aspects of foreign policy behavior, with major attention being devoted to foreign policy position change, independence/interdependence of action, commitment, affect intensity and direction, acceptance/rejection ratios, external consequentiality, the number and salience of substantive problem (issue) areas receiving attention, and the instrumentalities (resources) employed (see Brady 1975; M. G. Hermann, C. F. Hermann, and Dixon 1979; East, Salmore, and Hermann 1978). As with other data efforts in the seventies, the CREON group has made important contributions to measurement (see Callahan et al., eds., 1982).

The main criticism of CREON has been that it has only one data source, *Deadline Data*. This has raised serious questions among a few scholars about the data's validity. The response of the members of the project is that they have employed not the summaries but the uncollapsed set of *Deadline Data* obtained from the publishers; they argue that, while this base is not sufficient as a complete record of behavior, it is sufficient for the specific propositions they wish to test (C. F. Hermann et al. 1973:17–21).

Data that rely on a single source can never be as good as data derived from multiple sources, but the tone and character of some of this criticism, especially that given verbally at professional meetings (but see also Bobrow, Chan, and Kringen 1977), suggests a misunderstanding of the nature of the scientific enterprise. Science does not progress with the sudden birth of perfect research designs, data collections, and statistical analyses. Every design and measure is flawed to a certain extent. The scientist's task is not to replicate reality in the laboratory but to establish a set of conditions under which hypotheses are tested; as long as these conditions are not biased in favor of a particular hypothesis, certain inferences can tentatively be made, keeping in mind any potential validity problems. As others, employing different research designs and data, test the same propositions, more evidence can be brought to bear to determine the utility of any specific proposition. To be too perfectionistic at early stages of inquiry will reduce what little real evidence there is.[17] This is an important point, because collecting data on foreign policy behavior has been the major area of difficulty in the field, and event data provide one of the few hopes for establishing a reliable base for testing hypotheses on inter-state behavior.

17. It is interesting to note that Bobrow, Chan, and Kringen (1979) (see also Chan, Kringen, and Bobrow 1979), after criticizing CREON, have severe problems of their own in collecting event data. This is because instead of going directly to the *People's Daily* of China, they use a data set derived from that source by Katz (1972) and Katz, Lent, and Novotny (1973) for the U.S. army. By their own admission, this data set is incomplete (December 1972 is missing), and the validity of some of the topics in the coding schemes is questionable (see Chan, Kringen, and Bobrow 1979:277).

The most ambitious event–data set is Azar's COPDAB. Initially a multiple source data set that attempted to collect regional event data on all the Middle Eastern nations and the major powers from 1945 through 1969 (Azar 1970:13), it has expanded to global coverage of about 135 nations, based on over 70 data sources, for the period from 1948 through 1980 (Azar 1980:146). Clearly, this is a conscious attempt to fulfill the dream of the WEIS project to become the main data bank for the field for inter-state interactions. The data itself is highly reliable and its source validity should be unquestioned, at least in terms of public sources. In this regard, COPDAB has overcome the major problem of WEIS and CREON. COPDAB's main problems are that there are too few dependent variables, and that the way they are measured, particularly the thirteen-point cooperation-conflict scale, may be too limiting for the data set to serve as the major data bank for inter-state interactions. Nevertheless, a significant number of propositions could and no doubt will be tested with the existing variables. In addition, the mere abstraction of the raw events could prove invaluable to researchers, who could then code their own variables.

While COPDAB has attempted to provide a data set for the entire field, most event–data sets in the seventies had more limited ambitions. It was the problems with the global WEIS set that initially led Azar (1970) to collect multiple-source regional data on the Middle East. This effort to collect regional data was supplemented by Patrick McGowan's AFRICA project on sub-Saharan foreign policy interactions (see McGowan and Johnson 1979). McGowan collected event data on participation and cooperation-conflict. This was then supplemented by a variety of national attributes, including data on leadership style, dependence, and penetration, as well as more conventional indicators. Additional African data has been provided by William Copson (1973), who collected event data focusing primarily on conflict. Comparable regional data for Latin America and Asia were not forthcoming, although Doran, Pendley, and Antunes (1973) did explore regional Latin American sources. The hope that global data sets might be supplemented by more in-depth regional sets was eventually fulfilled at the end of the decade by the expansion of Azar's (1980) COPDAB, which includes the best multiple sources for each region.

The most influential effect of the event data movement, which accounts for the myriad of data-making efforts, was the use of event data by individual researchers to test specific hypotheses. Among the best work in this area was Gamson and Modigliani's (1971) highly imaginative use of the front page of the *New York Times*, including interesting scaling techniques for determining salience and weighting measures to reduce bias, to test alternative explanations of the Cold War. Bobrow, Chan, and Kringen (1979) used event data to produce the first major quantitative analysis of the People's Republic of China's foreign policy (see also Chan 1978; 1979). A final example is that of Michael Sullivan (1972; 1979a) who coded American presidential speeches to determine how they correlated with escalation in the Vietnam War.

A number of event–data sets were also collected to study inter-state interactions in the Middle East. The most extensive data sets were those of Wilkenfeld, who borrowed from Rummel's DON coding scheme (see Wilkenfeld 1975). Burrowes (1974; Burrowes and Spector 1973) collected data from several sources to test the hypotheses that internal conflict leads to external conflict. Blechman (1972) used event data to provide a detailed account of Israeli reprisals toward the Arabs. Milstein (1972) looked at the role of big-power intervention through the use of event data.

While these studies are only illustrative, it should be clear that the overwhelming focus of event data has been on the major dependent variable stipulated by the realist paradigm—cooperation and conflict. In addition, many of these studies employed national attributes to predict the patterns of inter-state interactions; this was certainly the case with some of the CREON tests (see East 1975; B. G. Salmore and S. A. Salmore 1975). Even those who moved to the periphery of the paradigm by looking at decision makers' perceptions or personalities still focused largely on nation-state conflict-cooperation (see M. G. Hermann 1974; Brady 1975; M. G. Hermann et al. 1979; see also Brewer 1973).

By the mid-1970s, however, some of those who were calling for a new paradigm tried to collect data, usually event data, to support their case. O'Leary (1976) recoded WEIS data to show the difference controlling for issues made in analyzing event data and to attempt to test aspects of the PRINCE simulation model. Mansbach, Ferguson, and Lampert (1976) collected data on non–state actors to delineate empirically the role that such actors play in world politics (see also Lampert 1975). Mansbach and Vasquez (1981a) attempted to bring these two trends together by delineating the distortions that could result from analyzing event data without including non–state actors and controlling for issues. Analyzing the same data, Henehan (1981) began to test specific issue area typologies to see which would be the most potent. Since both CREON and COPDAB contain an issue-area variable, more work in this last area may be expected.

Toward the end of the seventies, a new type of data, attempting to overcome some of the problems inherent in event data, began to be collected in several quarters. These various efforts constitute the third area of data making in the 1970s, and in many ways are the most exciting. They differ from event data primarily in that specific cases are preselected and the data about them is usually collected from a variety of sources, not just newspapers. Since this often involves reconstructing a case, these data might be called *reconstructed historical interaction data*.

Although not completed, the most important data set in this area will probably be the collection of serious disputes by the Correlates of War project (see Wallace 1979b; J. D. Singer 1979; Gochman 1980). The effort began with an attempt to locate all serious disputes between 1815 and 1965 in which one or more major power threatened or used military force (see Gochman 1980; A. Levy 1977). Including intervention in a civil war, Gochman found 171 serious disputes (1980:92–93). Various data were then collected around or about these disputes. J. D. Singer (1979a), with an updated version of the data (1815–1975; 225 disputes), attempted to analyze what makes a dispute escalate to war with data about the disputants' geographical contiguity, alliance pattern, military capability, and defense expenditures. Singer's preliminary analyses were very encouraging.

A more limited analysis of the relationship between serious disputes and the presence of arms races was made by Wallace (1979a; 1981; see also Wallace and Wilson 1978). Methodologically related to this effort is the work of Russell Leng (Leng and Goodsell 1974; Leng 1980; Leng and Wheeler 1979) on the relationship between bargaining tactics and the escalation of a crisis to war. He analyzed this set of propositions by comparing crises that preceded war with crises that did not lead to war. This effort on serious disputes, no doubt, will be greatly aided by the work of the Stockholm International Peace Research Institute (SIPRI), which has been systematically collecting data on international conflicts (see SIPRI 1968/1969 and Thompson, Duval, and Dia 1979).

Some attempts to collect data on specific cases predated the data-making work in the Correlates of War project. Two works—those of Barringer (1972) and Butterworth (1976)—are of particular interest. Trying to answer some of the same questions about war, escalation, and conflict resolution that are of concern to the researchers in the Correlates of War project, both these scholars, working independently of each other and of the project, collected similar data. Richard Barringer (1972) took eighteen disputes and collected data on 300 variables associated with the cases. He then analyzed the data inductively to determine what variables are associated with conflict patterns. Robert Butterworth (1976; 1978; see also E. B. Haas, Butterworth, and Nye 1972) collected data on 310 instances of conflict management from 1945 to 1974 in an attempt to discern the elements that promote successful conflict management and resolution. Although less successful than Barringer (1972) or the Correlates of War studies in producing strong findings, the published summaries of each instance and the variables associated with them provide valuable sources for future studies. More comprehensive and theoretical than these two efforts is the planned project of Michael Brecher (1977) to collect a variety of data on numerous crises. Once completed, this will be an important addition to the comparative study of crises.

The final major effort that can be included in this group is a very large data set collected for the U.S. Defense Department on instances of crisis management (defined very broadly as any instance requiring a rapid response from the Pentagon which will affect the national interest; see Hazlewood, Hayes, and Brownell 1977:79). These data were collected by CACI, Inc., under contract from ARPA (Advanced Research Projects Agency of the Department of Defense), and include 289 instances of domestic and international "crisis" from 1945 to 1975 (see CACI 1975). These data have been supplemented with more detailed information on 101 global crises from 1956 to 1976 from data supplied by Blechman and Kaplan (1978), and by Mahoney (1976) (see Abolfathi, Hayes, and Hayes 1979). Forty-one of the crises were investigated further, being coded for 70 different management problems that might arise (Hazlewood, Hayes, and Brownell 1977:90). More recently, data on perceptions of the U.S. Department of State, the CIA, and the Department of Defense for 36 crises from 1966 to 1975 were analyzed by Phillips and Rimkunas (1979). This project is related to Chinese perceptions during crises (Chan 1978; Bobrow, Chan, and Kringen 1979) and Soviet perceptions of crises (Mahoney and Clayberg 1980), the latter containing data on 386 "crises" from 1946 to 1975.[18]

Clearly, the work on reconstructed historical interaction data has produced much material that can be used to test propositions important to the realist paradigm generally and to power politics explanations specifically. The work on serious disputes, although it may ultimately support social psychological models (see Wallace 1979b), has tested a number of explicit realist propositions (see Leng 1980). The studies of Barringer (1972) and Brecher (1977) focus on nation-states or their official decision makers and on inter-nation conflict-cooperation. Finally, Butterworth's (1976) data seem to have been gathered to test propositions on the periphery of the paradigm, that is, on the success of IGOs. Thus, while much of the data can and will be used to test realist hypotheses, preliminary use suggests that they may also give rise to findings that may undercut some of the paradigm's fundamental assumptions.

While three major efforts—national attributes, event data, and reconstructed data—reflect the type of data making that has predominated in the 1970s, they have been supplemented by data making on two other

18. Less relevant theoretically or methodologically, but of political interest, is CACI's related project on the attitudes of the American public toward military spending from 1930 to 1978 (see Abolfathi 1980).

topics, arms races and economic dependency. Like some of the work on national attributes, most of this data making involves employing statistics gathered by other agencies; the main contribution tends to be measurement, rather than data making per se. Nevertheless, the collection of new data by those outside the field can have a significant impact on research within the field. No other research program better exemplifies this than the arms race studies. Somewhat data-poor at the beginning of the decade, the work on arms races by the end of the seventies had gathered such a large amount of data that much went unanalyzed, leading two reviewers to claim that there was now a "surfeit of data" (Moll and Luebbert 1980:178).

The major data sources have been the annual publications of the Stockholm International Peace Research Institute (SIPRI) and the U.S. Arms Control and Disarmament Agency (ACDA) on defense expenditures and armaments. These data have then been used to make very sophisticated measures and models of arms building. In terms of this chapter, it is these measures that can be seen as the data contribution, since the actual data is already available. This point is less true of the more historical data on arms expenditures that have been retrieved by the Correlates of War project, since these were not made available by outside sources. Nevertheless, even here there has been significant measurement innovation (see Wallace and Wilson 1978:177–179; Wallace 1979a).

Although most of the efforts of the 1970s have produced additional or new indicators for the realist paradigm, by the end of the decade data relevant to several Marxist propositions began to be collected. The earliest came from comparative politics with the Kaufman, Chernotsky, and Geller (1975) test of some dependency propositions (see also Ray and Webster 1978). In addition, McGowan collected economic dependency data for Africa in an effort to replicate the Kaufman et al. (1975) study (see McGowan and Smith 1978). Economic data of this type have also been employed by Gochman and Ray (1979) to delineate structural disparities in Latin America and Eastern Europe from 1950 to 1970. Clearly, since most of this economic data has been collected by outside agencies, the data-making contribution is primarily in measurement, particularly measurement of Marxist concepts. In this regard, major advances in this area can be expected from major quantitative national study on dependency directed by Bruce Russett and funded by the National Science Foundation.

Not all measures of economic data related to dependency took their lead from Marxist concepts. A number relied on power politics concepts related to coercion and influence. This was particularly the case after the 1973–1974 Arab oil embargo. Interesting measures of dependence and interdependence have been developed by Caporaso (1978) and Caporaso and Ward (1979). From a broader comparative foreign policy perspective, Wilkenfeld, Hopple, and Rossa (1979) have developed a set of measures to tap energy, food, and trade dependency. In contrast to the more Marxist measures, these measures attempt to tap aspects of what used to be regarded as national power. The development of alternate measures will make for interesting future comparisons between realist and Marxist concepts of power, dependency, interdependence, imperialism, and dominance.

This review of the major data-making efforts in the seventies suggests that, although the realist paradigm was not as total in its dominance as it was in the sixties, it still provided the focus for most of the data making in the field. Only by the end of the decade were seriously funded projects on nonrealist indicators beginning to emerge. Since in many ways control of data projects determines future research, it can be expected that research in the eighties will revolve largely around evaluating aspects of the realist research program and be more concerned with assessing elements of the Marxist, issue politics, and transnational paradigm research programs. In addition, if this latter research remains within the field, serious and conscious attempts will be made to compare the explanations and performances of the alternative paradigms.

Conclusion

The findings of this chapter provide considerable evidence to support the proposition that data making in international relations was guided by the realist paradigm in the fifties and sixties. A review of the major data projects conducted during this time period shows that they have collected data primarily on nations and realist topics of inquiry. It has also been found that the initial use of this data has been to test realist hypotheses. Conversely, it was found that data collected outside the field (Richardson) or inside the field prior to the fifties (Wright) was not guided by the realist paradigm.

The quantitative tests reported in the second section of the chapter also support the proposition. Of the data on file in the International Relations Archive of the Inter-University Consortium for Political Research, 74.9 percent consisted of realist indicators. The two concepts for which most data were collected—national power and inter-nation conflict-cooperation—were also the most central concepts in the realist paradigm. On the basis of the above findings, it can be concluded that the realist paradigm guided data making in the field during the fifties and sixties.

Finally, the review of data making in the seventies suggests that the proposition still held for most of the projects, but that elements in the field were beginning to investigate new measures for tapping Marxist concepts and to collect data on issue politics and non–state actors. If these efforts continue in the 1980s, authentic paradigm debates (as opposed to debates over competing conceptual frameworks) would be expected to emerge. This prediction specifies a future event which, if it did not occur, could be taken as evidence that would falsify the proposition.

The collection of a large number of realist indicators in the 1960s only demonstrates that a large amount of data has been collected that can be used to test realist hypotheses. It is logically possible, however, that scholars would concentrate their attention on the few nonrealist indicators, or use the realist indicators to test nonrealist hypotheses. To investigate this possibility, chapter 6 will examine the hypotheses that have actually been tested in the field in the fifties and sixties.

Research As a
Paradigm-Directed Activity

The Proposition

Kuhn maintains that the chief characteristics of normal science are that research is guided by the dominant paradigm and that research is seen as a puzzle-solving activity (Kuhn 1970a:chap. 4). In normal science, the scientist's primary role is to develop hypotheses to explain puzzles that the paradigm has focused upon. One of the significant characteristics of this research, according to Kuhn (1970a:146–148) is that the paradigm's failure to resolve puzzles does not lead to the falsification of the entire paradigm but to incremental changes known as paradigm articulation. Persistent failure to resolve puzzles is not seen as a flaw in the paradigm but as a flaw in the individual scientist (Kuhn 1970a:35–36). Thus, while Karl Popper's (1959) notion of falsification may be applied to individual hypotheses and even to theories, it is never applied to the most fundamental assumptions of the field, that is, the paradigm (Kuhn 1970a:146–148). Hypothesis testing in normal science tends to be a process of testing competing hypotheses "derived" from the same paradigm rather than testing hypotheses derived from competing paradigms (Kuhn 1970a: 24). The latter, if it occurs at all in science, occurs during periods of scientific revolution and is then viewed as more of a change of world view than of testing hypotheses from competing paradigms (Kuhn 1970a:chap. 10). The notion of a crucial experiment is only established with the aid of historical hindsight and is an indicator that the new paradigm has gained dominance in the field (Kuhn 1970a:chap. 11).

Normal science research, then, is quite narrow. It consists of three types of research, which correspond to Kuhn's three classes of facts (1970a:25–26). The first consists of descriptive research, which attempts to describe and often measure phenomena in terms of those concepts and variables that the paradigm has seen as particularly revealing of the nature of things and hence of intrinsic value (Kuhn 1970a:30–31). This type of research does not test hypotheses, but assumes their validity (Kuhn 1970a:25–26). The second type of research is explanatory in nature and involves testing hypotheses that are not central to the paradigm or of intrinsic importance but do allow for the testing of specific predictions of the paradigm (Kuhn 1970a:26–27). The third type of research differs from the second only in that the hypotheses being tested are viewed as being of intrinsic importance and central to the paradigm either initially or through the process of paradigm articulation (Kuhn 1970a:27–29).

In order to apply Kuhn's analysis to the field of international relations, it is necessary to have some criteria by which to demarcate research activity from theory construction and data making. As was seen in chapter 2, the behavioral revolt resulted in two distinct notions of what constitutes adequate research in the field. Because the proposition that "behavioral" research has been guided by the realist paradigm is more controversial than the proposition that traditional research has been guided by the realist paradigm, and because behavioral research is more similar to the type of scientific research Kuhn analyzes, only behavioral research, that is, research defined as descriptive, or correlational/explanatory analysis that employs data, will be examined in this chapter.

Research Design

Operationalization and Measurement

The two key terms in the proposition that must be operationalized are *research* and the *realist paradigm*. Since the proposition will be limited to behavioral research, which has been defined as descriptive or correlational/explanatory analysis that employs data, then *research* can be operationalized in terms of the use of measured variables to describe or predict phenomena.[1] The operational definition of the realist paradigm has been adequately discussed in chapters 3 and 5 and will be defined here as the actors and topics of inquiry employed in variables and hypotheses. Reliability for the data in this chapter was calculated at .87 for the first sample and .90 for the second sample.[2] As in the previous tests, this measure's validity rests on the assumption (which appears reasonable) that research guided by the realist paradigm would tend to employ in its variables, actors, and topics that are viewed as important by the realist paradigm.

Deriving Hypotheses

Seven hypotheses can be derived from the proposition to test its adequacy:

1. This criterion is similar to that of Jones and Singer (1972:3–6).
2. See chapter 3, note 6 for the method used to check reliability. The two samples are discussed on pp. 160–162.

3a. Variables used in descriptive research will tend to have actors and topics of inquiry that are labeled realist in the coding scheme.[3]

3b. Independent variables used in correlational/explanatory research will tend to have actors and topics of inquiry that are labeled realist in the coding scheme.

3c. Dependent variables used in correlational/explanatory research will tend to have actors and topics of inquiry that are labeled realist in the coding scheme.

3d. Correlational/explanatory hypotheses tested will tend to relate independent and dependent variables whose actors and topics of inquiry are labeled realist in the coding scheme.

3e. National power will tend to be the most frequently used independent variable.

3f. Inter-nation conflict-cooperation will tend to be the most frequently used dependent variable.

3g. The most frequently tested proposition will be the one that employs national power to predict or explain inter-nation conflict-cooperation.

Hypothesis 3a tests the aspect of the proposition that relates to descriptive research. If Kuhn is correct in stating that descriptive research will focus on those facts that the paradigm suggests are the most revealing of the nature of things, it is reasonable to assume that variables used in descriptive research will emphasize realist actors and topics. If this were not the case, that is, if the distribution were random, then it would not be accurate to claim that the realist paradigm guided descriptive research.

Hypotheses 3b and 3c attempt to test the aspect of the proposition that refers to correlational/explanatory research. If Kuhn's analysis is correct, it is reasonable to expect that the independent and dependent variables employed in correlational/explanatory research will be realist.

Hypothesis 3d is the most important of the seven hypotheses being tested. It examines the way independent and dependent variables are related to form hypotheses. It is important to examine hypotheses and not just variables, because individual variables can be related in numerous ways.[4] Hypothesis 3d therefore serves as a validity check on hypotheses 3b and 3c.

3. These hypotheses are numbered 3a, etc., because they test the third proposition presented in this analysis.

4. In the coding scheme, a realist hypothesis is defined as a hypothesis in which every variable is a realist indicator. If a hypothesis consists of four variables and only one is nonrealist, then the entire hypothesis would be coded as nonrealist. Hypotheses 3b and 3c, however, provide a much less stringent test,

Hypotheses 3e, 3f, and 3g test another aspect of the proposition. It was seen in chapter 3 that, while the realist paradigm employed several topics of inquiry, it emphasized national power as the independent variable and inter-nation conflict-cooperation as the dependent variable. If the realist paradigm guided research in the field, it would be reasonable to expect that, while not all independent and dependent variables would be limited to these two topics, they would probably be the modal categories. Likewise, it would be expected that the most frequently tested proposition would be the one that employed national power to explain inter-nation conflict-cooperation.

The Samples

The primary problem in choosing a sample is to determine what is international relations research as opposed to comparative politics or social psychological research, and to obtain a list of that research. Such a definition must, of course, be based on the perceptions of scholars in the field. In order to avoid possible bias it would be best, as in chapter 5, if someone other than the author provided the definition and the list of research. Fortunately, this is the case. In *Beyond Conjecture in International Politics: Abstracts of Data-Based Research*, Susan Jones and J. David Singer (1972) provide a definition as well as a list, which they claim represents the universe of data-based research published as articles prior to 1970 (Jones and Singer 1972:4–12). They define international politics research as "the political interaction of national, sub-national, and extra-national units in the context of the international system" (Jones and Singer 1972:8). On the basis of this definition, they delete articles that deal solely with the distribution of public opinion within nations (Jones and Singer 1970:8–9).

The question arises whether such a list would provide an adequate sample for this analysis. First, since the Jones-Singer definition of research is similar to the operational definition employed in this chapter, that aspect poses no problem. Likewise, their definition of international relations research in terms of international politics appears broad enough to include research employing non–state actors, but limited enough to reflect the perceptions of most scholars in the field. Third, their exclusion of books and nonpublished research makes the list less than complete. However, since many books give rise to at least one related article, the omission of books is not as serious as it would first

---

since they would find three realist variables and only one nonrealist variable. To insure that mixed cases falsify rather than support the proposition, hypothesis 3d has been included.

Research As a Paradigm-Directed Activity

appear. What is important is that these omissions are not likely to bias the sample; that is, any measurement error in the analysis conducted here resulting from the omission of books or unpublished articles can be regarded as random. This can also be said of any published articles Jones and Singer may have missed.[5] Finally, Jones and Singer's classification of articles into descriptive and correlational/explanatory research, and their listing of variables employed in that research, make it easy to test the hypotheses derived in this chapter. Therefore, the abstracts provided in Jones and Singer were selected as one sample.

These abstracts were converted into data by the following procedure. In each abstract a list of variables employed in the article is provided. In addition, information on the purpose of the research, the spatial-temporal domain of the variables, the data sources and operations, and how the data were manipulated and analyzed were provided in the abstract. This information was used along with special instructions for the use of the coding scheme to determine the actor and topic of inquiry of each variable, thereby providing the data base for this chapter (see Vasquez 1974a:Appendix I).

Although the Jones and Singer volume has many virtues for use as a sample in this study, it has one major flaw that led to a decision to use a second sample—not all hypotheses tested in correlational/explanatory articles are fully reported. Instead, only the major findings are reported. While this device is certainly appropriate for the purpose of providing abstracts, it is less than adequate for testing hypothesis 3d, which is the most important hypothesis being tested in this chapter. It was therefore decided to return to the original articles that Jones and Singer classified as correlational/explanatory and collect a list of hypotheses. A total of 7,827 hypotheses that related one or more independent variables with a dependent variable to determine statistical significance and/or strength of association were collected from 51 of the original 76 articles classified as correlational/explanatory by Jones and Singer.[6] The variables in these

5. A random sample of journals showed that no articles were missed. However, this author knows of at least one anthology article that was missed: Coplin (1968). See Alger (1970) for other possible omissions.

6. Hypotheses from the other 25 articles were not included because neither inductive statistics nor measures of association were employed in the data analysis. This criterion was adopted essentially to reduce the high costs involved in data making. Since support for the project was based on the use of the data in chapter 7 to examine statistical significance and strength of association, collection of data outside that realm could not be justified. Exclusion of these articles does not appear to affect the study in any significant manner. First, these articles are included in tests based on the first sample. Second, a comparison of tests using the two samples reveals that the second sample gives much greater support to

hypotheses were then coded into actor and topic categories. On the basis of this coding, each hypothesis was coded as realist only if every variable employed in it had both a realist actor and a realist topic code. This coded data provided the second sample for the study. The descriptive and correlational/explanatory articles included in the samples are listed in tables 6.1 and 6.2, respectively.

The Findings

Hypothesis 3a predicted that variables used in descriptive research would tend to employ the nation-state as the actor and have a realist topic of inquiry. In order to test this hypothesis, the variables listed in the 82 descriptive articles abstracted in Jones and Singer (sample 1) were examined. These articles employed 377 variables. Of these, 74.3 percent (280) were found to be realist indicators according to the coding scheme, and 25.7 percent (97) were found to be nonrealist indicators. This finding is remarkably similar to the finding in chapter 5 (hypothesis 2a) that 74.9 percent of the data produced consisted of realist indicators. This distribution would hardly appear to be random, and the calculation of a binomial distribution (p<.01) for interpretive purposes supports this assumption.[7] On the basis of this test, it can be concluded that hypothesis 3a has failed to be falsified.

Hypothesis 3b predicted that independent variables used in correlational/explanatory research would tend to employ the nation-state as the actor and have a realist topic of inquiry. In order to test this hypothesis, the two samples were employed. Sample 1 consisted of the independent variables listed in the 76 articles abstracted in Jones and Singer. These articles employed 385 independent variables. Of these, 68.1 percent (262) were found to be realist indicators according to the coding scheme, and 31.9 percent (123) were found to be nonrealist indicators. The cal-

---

the proposition than the first sample; that is, scholars relate realist variables to each other much more often than they relate nonrealist variables with each other or with realist variables. Three of the excluded articles were randomly selected to see if this tendency held among them, and it did. Thus any measurement error resulting from the exclusion would falsify the proposition rather than support it. Third, most of these articles test relatively few hypotheses, compared to those that use measures of association, often with large correlation matrices.

7. The calculation of the binomial distribution is only reported to offer a guideline for interpretation, not as evidence, since its use is mathematically inappropriate when the universe rather than a sample is employed. See Blalock (1960:chap. 10) for the application of the binomial distribution in social science. A table for significance can be found in Harvard University Computation Laboratory, *Tables of the Cumulative Binomial Probability Distribution* (1955).

Table 6.1. Descriptive Research Included in Sample 1
(Jones and Singer's Classifications)

ATTRIBUTES OF THE SYSTEM

Alger and Brams (1967)
Alker and Puchala (1968)
Angell (1965)
Barrera and E. Haas (1969)
Bernstein and Weldon (1968)
Brams (1966a)
Brams (1966b)
Brams (1968)
Brams (1969a)
Brams (1969b)
Caplow and Finsterbusch (1968)
Feldstein (1967)
Fisher (1969)
Lamb and Russett (1969)

Lijphart (1963)
Lijphart (1964)
Naroll (1968)
Rieselbach (1960b)
Russett (1966)
Russett (1968a)
Russett (1968b)
Russett (1968d)
Russett and Lamb (1969)
Schmitter (1969a)
Small and Singer (1969)
Smoker (1965a)
Taggepera (1968)
Teune and Synnestvedt (1965)

ATTRIBUTES OF NATIONS

Brecher, Steinberg, and Stein (1969)
Choucri (1969a)
Cimbala (1969)
Coddington (1965)
B. Cohen (1967)
Deutsch (1966)
Deutsch and Eckstein (1961)
Eckhardt (1965)
W. Fleming (1969)
Galtung and Ruge (1965a)
Graber (1969)
Jensen (1969)
Laulicht (1965b)

Lerner and Kramer (1963)
Namenwirth and Brewer (1966)
Rosenau (1962)
Sawyer (1967)
Sigler (1969)
J. D. Singer (1964)
Singer and Small (1966b)
Weissberg (1969)
White (1949)
Wright and Nelson (1939)
Zaninovich (1962)
Zinnes, North, and Koch (1961)

NATIONAL BEHAVIOR

Alcock and Lowe (1969)
Alger (1965)
Angell (1967)
Ball (1951)
Choucri (1969b)
Denton (1966)
Denton and Phillips (1968)
E. B. Haas (1962)
O. Holsti and Sullivan (1969)
Horvath (1968)
Horvath and Foster (1963)
Jacobsen (1969)
Jensen (1968)
Kay (1969)
Keohane (1969)

Klingberg (1952)
McClelland (1968)
McClelland and Hoggard (1969)
Manno (1966)
Meyers (1966)
Rowe (1964)
Rowe (1969)
Rummel (1963)
Rummel (1966b)
Rummel (1967a)
Rummel (1967b)
Rummel (1969)
Voevodsky (1969)
Weiss (1963)

Table 6.2. Correlational/Explanatory Research Included in Sample 1
(Jones and Singer's Classifications)

ATTRIBUTES OF THE SYSTEM
None found

ATTRIBUTES OF NATIONS

Armor et al. (1967)
Bell (1960)
Brickman, Shaver, and Archibald
    (1968)
Campbell and Cain (1965)
[a]Cobb (1969)
[a]Deutsch (1956)
[a]Galtung and Ruge (1965b)
Gregg (1965)
F. Hoffman (1967)
[a]O. R. Holsti (1967)
Jensen (1966)
[a]Kato (1968)
[a]Laulicht (1965a)

Moskos and Bell (1964)
[a]North and Choucri (1968)
Ohlstrom (1966)
[a]Rieselbach (1960a)
Rieselbach (1964)
Ruge (1964)
[a]Russett (1962a)
[a]Russett (1964)
[a]M. Singer and Sensenig (1963)
[a]R. Smith (1969)
[a]Vincent (1968)
[a]Vincent (1969)
[a]Weigert and Riggs (1969)

NATIONAL BEHAVIOR

[a]Alger (1966)
[a]Alger (1968)
[a]Alker (1964)
[a]Alker (1965b)
[a]Chadwick (1969)
[a]Choucri and North (1969)
[a]East and P. Gregg (1967)
[a]Ellis and Salzberg (1965)
[a]Fink (1965)
[a]Galtung (1964b)
Galtung (1966)
Gamson and Modigliani (1968)
Gleditsch (1967)
[a]Gleditsch (1969)
[a]M. Haas (1965)
[a]M. Haas (1968)
[a]M. Haas (1969)
K. Holsti (1966)
[a]O. R. Holsti (1965b)
O. R. Holsti (1966)
[a]O. R. Holsti, Brody, and North (1965)
[a]O. R. Holsti, North, and Brody (1968)
[a]Hopmann (1967)
Jensen (1965)
Klingberg (1966)

[a]McGowan (1968)
[a]McGowan (1969)
[a]Midlarsky and Tanter (1967)
[a]Milstein and Mitchell (1968)
Milstein and Mitchell (1969)
[a]O'Leary (1969)
Reinton (1967)
[a]Rummel (1964)
[a]Rummel (1966a)
[a]Rummel (1968)
Russett (1963b)
[a]J. D. Singer and Small (1966a)
[a]J. D. Singer and Small (1968)
Smoker (1963)
[a]Smoker (1964a)
Smoker (1964b)
[a]Smoker (1965b)
[a]Smoker (1966)
[a]Smoker (1967)
Smoker (1969)
[a]Tanter (1966)
[a]Wilkenfeld (1968)
Wright (1965b)
[a]Zinnes (1966)
[a]Zinnes (1968)

[a]These articles constitute sample 2.

culation of a binomial distribution (p<.01) shows that this is not a random distribution. The test on this sample, then, fails to falsify hypothesis 3b.

The second sample used to test hypothesis 3b consisted of the independent variables actually employed in hypotheses in the 51 articles that employed inductive statistics or measures of association. In this sample, rather than analyzing each independent variable separately, all the independent variables employed in one hypothesis were coded as a unit. Therefore, if a multivariate relationship were being tested with five independent variables, all five variables would receive one code—realist or nonrealist. A realist code was given only if every independent variable in the hypothesis had a realist actor and topic code. A total of 7,827 independent variable units were found in the articles included in the sample. Figure 6.1 reports the findings. From figure 6.1 it can be seen that 94.0 percent, or 7,356 independent variable units, were realist indicators and only 6.0 percent (471) were nonrealist. This figure supports the conclusion that, although on occasion nonrealist independent variables may be produced and employed in research, the emphasis in hypothesis testing in the field is on realist independent variables. On the basis of these two tests, it can be concluded that hypothesis 3b has failed to be falsified.

Figure 6.1. Percentage of Realist Independent Variables
Employed in Hypotheses (Hypothesis 3b)

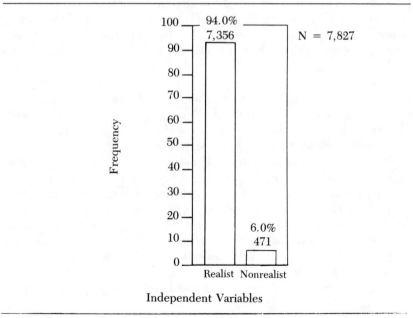

Figure 6.2. Percentage of Realist Dependent Variables
Employed in Hypotheses (Hypothesis 3c)

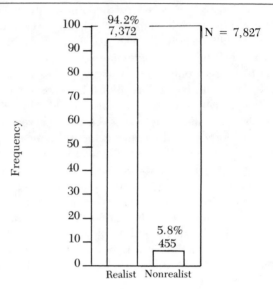

Hypothesis 3c predicted that dependent variables used in correlational/explanatory research would tend to employ the nation-state as the sole actor and have a realist topic of inquiry. This hypothesis is slightly more important than the previous two, because one of the major functions of a paradigm is to establish a research agenda on what phenomena are to be explained. Samples 1 and 2 were used in this test. The abstracts employed in sample 1 listed 233 dependent variables. Of these, 78.9 percent (184) were found by the coding scheme to be realist indicators, and only 21.4 percent (49) were found to be nonrealist indicators. This would not appear to be a random distribution, and the calculation of a binomial distribution (p<.01) supports this assumption.

The second sample used to test hypothesis 3c consisted of the actual dependent variables employed in the 7,827 hypotheses collected from the original articles. Figure 6.2 reports these findings. From the figure it can be seen that 94.2 percent (7,372) of the dependent variables are realist indicators and only 5.8 percent (455) are nonrealist. This finding supports the conclusion of the previous test that, although nonrealist variables may occasionally be produced and employed in research, the emphasis in hypothesis testing is on realist indicators. On the basis of these two tests it can be concluded that hypothesis 3c has failed to be falsified.

Figure 6.3. Percentage of Realist Hypotheses
Tested in the Field (Hypothesis 3d)

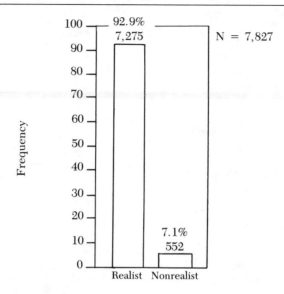

Hypothesis 3d predicted that hypotheses actually tested in research would tend to relate independent and dependent variables that were realist indicators. This hypothesis is the most important for testing the proposition's adequacy. If the actual hypotheses tested are not realist then it cannot be said that the realist paradigm has guided research. Sample 2 was employed to test hypothesis 3d. In order for a hypothesis in the sample to be coded as realist, every variable in that hypothesis had to have a realist actor and topic code. Given these strict requirements, the findings reported in figure 6.3 are quite remarkable. This figure shows that 92.9 percent (7,275) of the hypotheses tested in the field were realist and only 7.1 percent (552) were nonrealist. On the basis of this test, it can be concluded that the critical hypothesis 3d has failed to be falsified.

Hypothesis 3e predicted that national power would be the most frequently employed independent variable in correlational/explanatory research. The independent variable units of sample 2 were employed to test this hypothesis. Independent variable units were given a topic code only if all the variables in the unit had the same topic; otherwise, they were classified as having a mixed topic. The findings are reported in table 6.3, which was produced by cross-tabulating the actor and topic codes of the variables and then rank ordering the independent variables.

Table 6.3. Independent Variable Units Employed in Research
(Hypothesis 3e)

Independent variables	Frequency/percentage		Rank
National power[a]	4,650	(59.4)	1
Inter-nation alliances[a]	1,050	(13.4)	2
Inter-nation conflict-cooperation[a]	604	(7.7)	3
Nation (mixed topic)	544	(6.9)	4
Nation and supranationalism[a]	247	(3.2)	5
National isolationism[a]	209	(2.7)	6
Nation and sociological characteristics	123	(1.6)	7
Nations and other actors and power	116	(1.5)	8
Inter-nation integration[a]	59	(0.8)	9
Nations and other actors and decision makers	56	(0.7)	10
Subnational actors and sociological characteristics	42	(0.5)	11
Nations and other actors and sociological characteristics	32	(0.4)	12
Subnational conflict-cooperation	25	(0.3)	13
Nations and other actors conflict-cooperation	24	(0.3)	14.5
Nations and other actors issues	24	(0.3)	14.5
Nations and other actors (miscellaneous topic)	8	(0.1)	16
Subnational alignments	6	(0.1)	17
Nations and other actors alliances	4	(0.1)	18
Nation (miscellaneous topic)	3	(0.0)	19
IGO and NGO conflict-cooperation	1	(0.0)	20
	7,827	100.0	

[a]Realist independent variables.

Table 6.4. Dependent Variables Employed in Research
(Hypothesis 3f)

Dependent variables	Frequency/percentage		Rank
[a]Inter-nation conflict-cooperation	4,734	(60.5)	1
[a]National power	1,193	(15.2)	2
[a]Nation and supranationalism	970	(12.4)	3
[a]Inter-nation integration	281	(3.6)	4
Nations and other actors and conflict-cooperation	260	(3.3)	5
[a]National isolationism	99	(1.3)	6
[a]Inter-nation alliances	95	(1.2)	7
Nations and issues	70	(0.9)	8
Subnational conflict-cooperation	55	(0.7)	9
Nation and (miscellaneous topics)	34	(0.4)	10
Subnational supranationalism	21	(0.3)	11
Nations and sociological characteristics	10	(0.1)	12
Nations and other actors and supranationalism	5	(0.1)	13
	7,827	100.0	

[a]Realist dependent variables.

It can be seen from the table that national power is the modal or most frequently used independent variable unit, constituting 59.4 percent (4,650) of the independent variables. The second ranked independent variable unit, inter-nation alliances, only constituted 13.4 percent (1,050) of the independent variables.[8] On the basis of this test, it can be concluded that hypothesis 3e has failed to be falsified.

Hypothesis 3f predicted that inter-nation conflict-cooperation would tend to be the most frequently used dependent variable in correlational/explanatory research. Sample 2 was also used in this test. From the findings reported in table 6.4, it can be seen that inter-nation conflict-cooperation is the modal, or most frequently employed, dependent variable, constituting 60.5 percent (4,734) of the dependent variables. The

8. It is significant that inter-nation alliances, which rank second, is also the second most important independent variable in *Politics Among Nations*, as noted in chapter 3.

second ranked dependent variable, national power, included only 15.2 percent (1,193) of the dependent variables. On the basis of this test, it can be concluded that hypothesis 3f has failed to be falsified.

Hypothesis 3g predicted that the most frequently tested proposition in the field would be the one that used national power to predict or explain inter-nation conflict-cooperation. Sample 2 was used to test this hypothesis. Each proposition was rank-ordered in table 6.5 on the basis of the number of hypotheses that tested it. It can be seen that national power related to inter-nation conflict-cooperation was the most frequently tested proposition in the field, having been tested by 3,018 hypotheses (41.7 percent of 7,241 hypotheses). The second-ranked proposition used inter-nation alliances to predict inter-nation conflict-cooperation, which was tested by only 651 hypotheses (9.0 percent of 7,241 hypotheses).[9] On the basis of this test, it is clear that hypothesis 3g has failed to be falsified.

Conclusion

The findings of the nine tests conducted in this chapter provide considerable evidence to support the proposition. Employing the Jones and Singer (1972) abstracts, it was found that: (1) about three-fourths (74.3 percent) of the variables employed in descriptive research were realist; and (2) 68.1 percent of the independent variables and 78.9 percent of the dependent variables employed in correlational/explanatory research articles were realist. An examination of how these variables were combined to form hypotheses, using the second sample, revealed that the realist variables are used much more frequently than is suggested by the abstracts in Jones and Singer. It was found, for example, that 94.0 percent of the independent variable units and 94.2 percent of the dependent variables employed in actual hypotheses were realist. A review of how these independent and dependent variables were combined showed that 92.9 percent of the 7,827 hypotheses tested in the field were realist.

In addition to these tests, a number of predictions were made about the specific variables and propositions used in research. Employing the second sample, it was found that the chief independent variable of the realist paradigm, national power, was the most frequently employed independent variable in research (59.4 percent of all independent variables). It was also found that the chief dependent variable of the realist

9. It is noteworthy that the second-ranked proposition, inter-nation alliances predicts inter-nation conflict-cooperation, is also the second most important proposition in *Politics Among Nations*, as shown in chapter 3.

Table 6.5. Rank Order of Propositions Tested in the Field
(Hypothesis 3g)

Proposition[a]	Number of hypotheses	Percentage	Rank
316—310	3,018	41.7	1
313—310	651	9.0	2
316—316	626	8.6	3
316—321	539	7.4	4
310—310	433	6.0	5
313—321	347	4.8	6
316—314	281	3.9	7
317—310	208	2.9	8
310—316	162	2.2	9
321—316	153	2.1	10
716—710	116	1.6	11
316—317	93	1.3	12
314—310	57	0.8	14
711—710	56	0.8	14
321—321	55	0.8	14
710—710	49	0.7	16
719—710	48	0.7	17
319—310	47	0.6	18
313—312	40	0.6	19
321—310	39	0.5	20
316—313	33	0.5	21
316—312	30	0.4	22
319—321	29	0.4	23
319—318	28	0.4	24
719—721	26	0.4	25
712—710	24	0.3	26
319—319	10	0.1	27
718—710	8	0.1	28.5
713—710	8	0.1	28.5
316—710	6	0.1	30
319—317	5	0.1	31
310—318	4	0.1	32
313—316	3	0.0	33
310—313	2	0.0	34
313—313	1	0.0	38
313—317	1	0.0	38
316—318	1	0.0	38
317—316	1	0.0	38
318—310	1	0.0	38
318—318	1	0.0	38
710—316	1	0.0	38
	7,241	100.0	
Missing Cases[b]	586		
	7,827		

[a] Proposition codes to the left of the dash refer to independent variables and codes to the right of the dash refer to dependent variables. The first digit of each three-digit code refers to the actor type and the second two digits refer to the topic of inquiry. The codebook can be found in table 3.1.

[b] Of the 586 missing cases, 544 consist of independent variables that employed mixed topics of inquiry (see table 6.3). The 42 other missing cases consist of hypotheses that were tested by measures of association that did not range from 0.00 to |1.00|. Unlike later tests, however (see chapter 7), this test includes 107 hypotheses that are tested by only significance tests or passed a test by accepting the null hypothesis.

paradigm, inter-nation conflict-cooperation, was the most frequently employed dependent variable in research (60.5 percent of all dependent variables). Finally, it was found that the central proposition of the realist paradigm, relating national power to inter-nation conflict-cooperation, was the most frequently tested proposition in the field (41.7 percent of the 7,241 tested hypotheses). On the basis of these findings, it can be concluded that research in the field has been guided by the realist paradigm.

The findings of this chapter, when combined with the findings of the two preceding chapters, demonstrate that international relations inquiry has had an underlying coherence since the early fifties. The realist paradigm has been used by scholars to focus on certain phenomena and develop concepts and propositions about them. This theory construction, or paradigm articulation, has directed scholars to collect data on realist indicators. It has been shown in this chapter that the data collected in the field have been used primarily to test realist hypotheses. The tests of the three propositions on theory construction, data making, and research in the field have all been supported. Therefore, the claim that the realist paradigm has dominated international relations inquiry in the fifties and sixties has been given credence.

Chapter 7

Evaluation: The Adequacy of the Realist Paradigm

This book opened with the claims that the realist paradigm has dominated the field since the early fifties and that the realist paradigm has not been very effective in explaining behavior. Through a review of the literature and the use of quantitative techniques, it has been found that the realist paradigm has indeed been the major guiding force directing scholarly inquiry in each of the three major scientific activities of theory construction, data making, and research. These findings support the first claim and the interpretation of the field provided in chapter 2. The findings also lend credence to the general interpretation of all scientific work provided by Thomas Kuhn (1970a). However, the findings do not indicate whether the power of the realist paradigm to dominate the field has been beneficial for attaining the purpose of the field—the creation of knowledge. The second claim maintains that up to this time the realist paradigm has not been very beneficial, because it has failed to demonstrate any significant explanatory power. The present chapter will attempt to establish the validity of this claim.

The chapter is divided into five sections. The first specifies three criteria—accuracy, centrality, and scientific importance—that can be used to evaluate the adequacy of any paradigm. The second, third, and fourth sections operationally define each of the criteria respectively and apply them in an empirical "test" to determine the adequacy of the realist paradigm. The final section presents the conclusion and examines whether the claim that the realist paradigm has not been very effective in explaining behavior has been supported.

How to Evaluate Paradigms

The Criteria

In order to evaluate anything, it is necessary to specify the criteria that will be employed, justify their use, and indicate how they can be applied.[1] The major criterion that will be employed to evaluate paradigms is their ability to produce knowledge. This criterion is viewed as a *necessary condition* for an adequate paradigm. Its selection is justified

1. On the necessity of these three tasks see J. O. Urmson (1969:chaps. 8–10).

on the basis that the primary purpose of science is to produce knowledge. Other purposes of science, such as the improvement of human life, are seen as side benefits stemming from the acquisition of knowledge.

Once the production of knowledge has been selected as the major criterion, the next problem is to specify a set of criteria that can be used to determine whether or not a paradigm has produced any knowledge. It was seen in chapter 1 that whether a paradigm produced knowledge could be determined by examining the empirical content of its theories, that is, the number of hypotheses that have failed to be falsified. This criterion will be called the *criterion of accuracy*, since it reflects the ability of the paradigm to accurately predict behavior.

It was also seen in chapter 1 that the ability of a theory to produce hypotheses that fail to be falsified is only a minimum requirement. More important, a theory must fail to falsify hypotheses that are intended to test its central propositions, where centrality is defined as the level of generality, the scope, and the uniqueness of the proposition (see Stinchcombe 1968:17–22). The reason for this rule is that the central propositions form the heart of the theory, and if they are falsified, then any incidental propositions that fail to be falsified can be easily incorporated into a rival theory (if they are not already part of that rival theory). Applying this same logic to paradigms, it can be said that a paradigm's central propositions must fail to be falsified when tested. The latter principle will be called the *criterion of centrality*.

The criteria of accuracy and centrality provide two rules for determining whether a paradigm produces knowledge. Production of knowledge, however, is only a necessary condition for paradigm adequacy. The knowledge must also be of some value. A number of secondary criteria could be provided to assess the value of the produced knowledge, but there is not much consensus in the field over what those criteria might be. One major criterion that scholars agree on is that the knowledge should not be trivial. Recognizing that other secondary criteria can be employed, this analysis will only employ one, that the knowledge should be nonobvious to a large segment of scholars in the field. This criterion will be called the *criterion of scientific importance*.

A Framework for Evaluating Paradigms

In order to determine the extent to which the realist paradigm has satisfied the three criteria of paradigm adequacy, the following propositions will be tested:

4. The realist paradigm should tend to produce hypotheses that fail to be falsified.

5. The central propositions of the realist paradigm should tend to produce hypotheses that fail to be falsified.
6. Realist hypotheses that fail to be falsified should be of scientific importance.[2]

If the above propositions fail to be falsified, then it can be concluded that the realist paradigm has been an adequate guide to scientific international relations inquiry. If the above propositions are falsified, then the claim that the realist paradigm was not very effective in explaining behavior will be given credence. Before these propositions can be tested, it is necessary to specify what evidence will count as falsifying each of them. For example, proposition 4 states that the realist paradigm should produce hypotheses that fail to be falsified. As it stands, no decision-rule has been provided for determining how many hypotheses must be falsified before a paradigm can be declared to have inadequately satisfied the criterion of accuracy. If a "large" number of hypotheses were falsified, would this be a sufficient number to conclude that the realist paradigm had not satisfied the criterion of accuracy? Without a clearly established decision-rule to interpret the evidence, there is no way to answer this question.

The decision-rule that first comes to mind would be to employ a statistical significance level (such as .05). To insist that a paradigm in international relations produce a statistically significant number of "accurate" hypotheses, however, would be quite unfair, given the youthfulness of the discipline and the exploratory nature of much research. A fairer requirement might be one suggested by Lakatos (1970). He states that a theory's adequacy can be evaluated by comparing the empirical content of one theory with the empirical content of a rival theory (Lakatos 1970:116). Applying the same logic to paradigms, a decision-rule that would permit the three propositions to be tested would be to insist that the realist paradigm produce proportionally more knowledge than its rival paradigms. The problem with applying this rule is that research in rival paradigms such as Marxism, transnational relations, or issue

---

2. These propositions are numbered 4, 5, and 6 because they are the fourth, fifth, and sixth propositions tested in this analysis. A strong argument can be made that these three propositions provide a fair test for determining the adequacy of the realist paradigm. Proposition 4 applies the criterion of accuracy by maintaining that if realist hypotheses were consistently falsified it would make little sense to say that the paradigm was producing knowledge. Proposition 5 applies the criterion of centrality and provides a way to determine empirically if the most important part of the realist paradigm is accurate. Proposition 6 applies the criterion of scientific importance and provides a way to determine whether the knowledge produced by the paradigm is of any value.

politics has not been conducted in the field. The only alternative is to compare the performance of the realist paradigm with the nonrealist hypotheses that have been tested in the field (about 7 percent of all the hypotheses [see figure 6.3]). These nonrealist hypotheses share the common characteristic of "not being realist," but they do not share a well-defined rival paradigm. To expect such a "nonparadigm," which has so few tests, to produce proportionally more accurate findings than the realist paradigm is giving the latter more than the benefit of the doubt. Nevertheless, if the realist paradigm failed to pass this test, it would demonstrate that the realist paradigm was not adequate and suggest that even a simple rejection of one or more of the realist assumptions might provide a better guide to research. For these reasons, the decision-rule that proportionally more realist than nonrealist hypotheses should fail to be falsified or be of scientific importance will be employed.

The preceding decision-rule for testing the three propositions permits an empirical determination of the adequacy of the realist paradigm. However, all conclusions made on the basis of these tests must be tentative. The reason for this is that a number of ad hoc explanations could be offered to give a different interpretation to the test results. Therefore, after testing the three propositions, various ad hoc explanations will be reviewed in the concluding section.[3]

The Data

The sample consists of all correlational/explanatory articles listed in Jones and Singer, *Beyond Conjecture in International Politics*, that employ inductive statistics or measures of association to test hypotheses. A content analysis of the original articles produced a sample of 7,827 hypotheses. The following information was collected on these hypotheses: number of hypotheses tested in article; number of independent variables; actor, topic of inquiry, and paradigm of independent and dependent variables; name of independent and dependent variables; paradigm of hypothesis; statistics employed; significance level; strength of association. Reliability of the coded part of the data was established as .90. Since questions of data validity were discussed in chapter 6, there is no need to repeat the arguments here.

---

3. Of course there is a limit to the number of ad hoc explanations that can be introduced; otherwise a proposition becomes nonfalsifiable, since what counts as falsifying evidence is never specified. See Lakatos (1970:116–132); Hempel (1966:29).

The Criterion of Accuracy

Operationalization and Measurement

The criterion of accuracy maintains that in order to produce knowledge, a paradigm must produce hypotheses that fail to be falsified when tested. Two basic statistical approaches can be employed to determine when a hypothesis has failed to be falsified: significance tests (inductive statistics); and measures of association and related descriptive statistics (e.g., correlational analysis). However, when significance tests and measures of association are not used together, there is a problem in interpreting the results. First, significance tests tell only that there is a nonrandom relationship between variables; they do not describe the strength of the relationship. Without a measure of association, the scholar has no way of knowing how good the hypothesis would be as a guide to guessing the value of the dependent variable. Conversely, a measure of association without a significance test does not tell how generalizable a given hypothesis is to the population or to another sample. Without a significance test, the scholar only knows how good a guess can be made about one particular sample. It should be clear that the most information is provided by employing both types of analyses. When this is done, a hypothesis might be falsified either because it failed to be statistically significant or because it had a weak measure of association. Because of the latter requirement, falsification would not mean statistical falsification, that is, accepting the null hypothesis, but philosophical falsification, that is, rejecting a hypothesis as an adequate guide to knowledge. Since the use of these statistics provides the clearest rules for determining whether a hypothesis is falsified (philosophically), these rules will be employed to operationally define the criterion of accuracy. The accuracy of a paradigm, therefore, can be operationally stipulated as *the extent to which a paradigm produces hypotheses which, when tested by the use of inductive statistics and measures of association, are found to be statistically significant and have strong measures of association.*

Such an operational definition is valid for two reasons. First, inductive and descriptive statistics for testing hypotheses are widely used in the physical and social sciences; the practice is firmly grounded in mathematical theory. The requirement that both significance and strength of association should be examined is the traditional procedure accepted in social science.[4] Second, the operational definition could only be said to be invalid if it were maintained that hypotheses that were not tested by

4. Blalock (1960:chaps. 8 and 15, esp. pp. 225–228) provides a good discussion on this rule.

statistics were by definition inaccurate: This is not the case. The definition refers to only one of the ways hypotheses can be tested, and it can be interpreted as applying to only a sample of all tests. Furthermore, there appears to be no a priori reason to expect that such a sample should bias the results of the evaluation.

Now that the criterion of accuracy has been operationally defined, it is necessary to measure it. Measuring statistical significance is quite easy, since its use is based on the theory of probability (see Blalock 1960:chaps. 8 and 9). Within political science, the .05 level is usually taken as the dividing point between statistical significance and nonsignificance. Statistical significance can be measured by the following classification: greater than .05 is nonsignificant; .05 or less is statistically significant.

Measuring strength of association is more difficult for two reasons. First, unlike statistical significance, there is no firmly agreed upon rule on the cutoff point between strong and weak association. Second, it is difficult to compare different statistical measures. Both these problems can be solved by examining the purpose of statistical analysis and its nonmathematical rationale. Correlational analysis can be interpreted as a means of measuring how successful a person would be in guessing the value of one variable by knowing the value of another.[5] All measures of association use a scale, usually from 0.00 to |1.00|. A zero means that there is no association between the variables and attempts to guess the value of one variable on the basis of another would be very unsuccessful. A one, on the other hand, means that the association is perfect, and the attempt to guess the value of one variable on the basis of the value of another variable would almost always be successful. Between these two extremes, a measure of association provides an indicator of how successful guessing will be in a particular circumstance. The philosophical question that is of importance is how high a measure of association must be in order to accept a hypothesis as an adequate guide to knowledge, or how many unsuccessful guesses will be permitted before a hypothesis is rejected. No mathematical rule can make this decision. The individual scholar or community of scholars must establish a rule, indicate in what contexts it will be applied, and provide a rationale for acceptance of the rule.

The rules that have achieved the most consensus have been those used in the analysis of variance. In analysis of variance, the object of correlational analysis is to explain as much variance as possible, with the ultimate goal of explaining 100 percent. Since this is the object of research, a hypothesis is as useful as the percentage of variance it explains. This percentage of variance is usually spoken of in terms of deciles or

5. This guessing rationale is taken from Linton Freeman (1965:142ff.).

quartiles. For example, scholars speak of a hypothesis explaining less than 25 percent, 50 percent, or 75 percent of the variance. In each case, the lower part of the scale indicates that a hypothesis has not done very well; a hypothesis that explains 10 percent of the variance leaves 90 percent of it unexplained. This sort of hypothesis does not provide a very good guide to knowledge, and for this reason is often declared falsified. The cutoff point for falsification, however, is a matter of convention and could be raised or lowered depending on the state of research. In international relations research, 10 percent and 25 percent are often taken as cutoff points (e.g., Rummel 1968:202–213; Alger 1968:65). This rule, however, can only be applied to statistics that are interpretable in terms of variance (e.g., Pearson's r). What about other measures of association?

A similar argument can be made for all other measures of association that range from 0.00 to |1.00|. Measures of this type, such as Kendall's tau and Yule's Q, do not explain variance, but they do describe the strength of association. As such, they provide an estimate of how many successful and unsuccessful guesses a scholar can expect to make by using a particular hypothesis as a guide to prediction (see Freeman 1965:68–142). The stronger the measure of association, the fewer the unsuccessful guesses, and consequently the better the hypothesis. Thus, as with analysis of variance, the purpose of this type of statistical analysis is to produce hypotheses whose measures of association get as close to |1.00| as is possible; that is, to minimize the number of incorrect guesses. The question that remains unanswered is how many incorrect guesses will be permitted before a hypothesis is considered useless and is falsified. Again, there is no firm rule. It is clear, however, that a |.33| or a |.45| is weak and that a |.71| is much better. In this analysis, whatever magnitude is declared to be weak for a Pearson's r will also be declared weak for all other measures of association that range from 0.00 to |1.00|.

Although the problem of how to determine a cutoff point between strong and weak association has been resolved, the question of how to compare different statistical measures of association remains. The problem here is that a Pearson's r of .02 and a Kendall's tau of .02 are not mathematically equivalent. The problem is resolvable because, as indicated earlier, the decision to falsify or accept a hypothesis as an adequate guide to knowledge is not a mathematical decision. It is a philosophical decision based on a mathematical analysis of the data. On the nonmathematical level, a Pearson's r and a Kendall's tau of .02 are highly comparable. They are both "weak" associations. In terms of Freeman's (1965) guessing rationale they both indicate how successful a hypothesis has been in eliminating incorrect guesses. In this hypothetical case, neither one would be very successful. Thus, although the Pearson's r and Kendall's tau provide different mathematical information, the philosophical information they provide on the adequacy of a hypothesis as a guide to knowledge is the same—weak or not very good. Consequently, it would be perfectly legitimate to declare a hypothesis that had a Pearson's r or a Kendall's tau of .02 to be falsified.

On the basis of the preceding analysis, two indices—Predictive Power Index (PPI) A and B—were constructed to measure the accuracy of a hypothesis. These are reported in tables 7.1 and 7.2. In PPI (A) all statistically nonsignificant findings, no matter how high their measures of association, are placed in category 10 (i.e., very weak). Only those measures of association that were greater than |.33| and significant at the .05 level, or were greater than |.33| and were reported without a significance test are placed in the stronger categories of PPI (A). PPI (B) differs from PPI (A) only in that there are four categories in the scale. In this case nonsignificant findings are placed in category 25.

Whether Predictive Power Indices A and B provide a good or valid measure depends on the purpose for which they were created. In this

Table 7.1. Predictive Power Index A   PPI (A)

Description	Category	Significance	Range of measures
Very weak (inadequate hypothesis)	10	Not significant or not reported	0.00 to |.32|
	20	.05 or not reported	|.33| to |.45|
	30	.05 or not reported	|.46| to |.55|
	40	.05 or not reported	|.56| to |.63|
	50	.05 or not reported	|.64| to |.71|
	60	.05 or not reported	|.72| to |.77|
	70	.05 or not reported	|.78| to |.84|
Very strong (adequate hypothesis)	71+	.05 or not reported	|.85| to |1.00|

Table 7.2. Predictive Power Index B   PPI (B)

Description	Category	Significance	Range of measures
Very weak (inadequate hypothesis)	25	Not significant or not reported	0.00 to |.50|
	50	.05 or not reported	|.51| to |.71|
	75	.05 or not reported	|.72| to |.87|
Very strong (adequate hypothesis)	100	.05 or not reported	|.88| to |1.00|

analysis, the indices are being employed to interpret how effective an explanation the hypothesis provides. To say simply that a hypothesis has been "supported" or "not supported," as has been done in other analyses that review a large number of findings (see C. F. Hermann 1972b: Appendix), is to lose a tremendous amount of information and often not even provide a reliable measure, since the rules employed for determining "supported" are not specified. To repeat the actual findings, however, would not provide much interpretation and would be an exhausting process. Predictive Power Indices A and B try to strike a balance between providing too much or too little information, while at the same time providing a reliable measure.

Because of the scale's logic, it can only be applied to measures of association ranging from 0.00 to $|1.00|$. Measures that did not have this range were removed from the analysis.[6] Since these statistics consist of only 42 cases out of 7,827, it can be concluded that their removal does not substantially affect the findings reported in this study.[7]

Test Design

Proposition 4 maintained that if the realist paradigm were accurate, it would produce hypotheses that fail to be falsified. One of the best ways to test this proposition would be to employ Predictive Power Indices A and B to see whether realist or nonrealist hypotheses failed to be falsified more frequently. The test of such a hypothesis would provide evidence to determine how well the realist paradigm satisfied the criterion of accuracy in comparison to a nonrealist paradigm. Thus the hypothesis that can be used to test proposition 4 is:

4. Realist hypotheses should fail to be falsified more frequently than nonrealist hypotheses.

In order to test proposition 4, the 7,827 hypotheses that compose the test sample were coded as either realist or nonrealist according to the coding scheme outlined in chapter 3. The statistical significance and strength of association reported on each of the hypotheses were mea-

6. Hypotheses tested by Pearson's product moment correlation r, Spearman's rho, Partial Correlation r, Path coefficients, R^2 (path analysis), R^2 (regression), and standardized Regression Coefficients (Causal Modeling), account for over 90 percent of the cases in the sample. Hypotheses tested by Kendall's tau, Factor analysis loadings, Chi Square, Mann Whitney U Test, Yule's Q, and the Z test were included in the sample. Hypotheses tested by the Contingency coefficient C or the Phi coefficient were not included in the tests in this chapter.

7. In addition, 100 cases that were tested solely by significance tests, and all tests that sought to accept the null hypothesis (seven cases) were dropped.

sured on the two Predictive Power Indices. Since the two Predictive Power Indices did not produce substantially different findings, only the findings from PPI (B) will be reported in the main body of the analysis; the findings from PPI (A), which is a more refined measure, are briefly mentioned in the notes.

The Findings

The findings of the test of hypothesis 4 are reported in figure 7.1. It can be seen from this figure that 93.1 percent of the realist hypotheses were falsified, compared to 83.1 percent of the nonrealist hypotheses. This means that 93.1 percent of the realist hypotheses and 83.1 percent of the nonrealist hypotheses fell into the weak category of PPI (B); that is, they were statistically insignificant or had a measure of association of $|.50|$ or less.[8] Turning to the stronger categories in PPI (B), it can be seen that

Figure 7.1. Predictive Power of Realist Hypotheses (Hypothesis 4a)

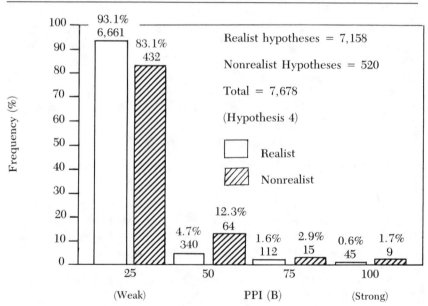

8. The findings on PPI (A) indicate that 80.2 percent of the realist hypotheses compared to 65.6 percent of the nonrealist hypotheses are statistically insignificant or have a measure of association of less than .33 (category 10); 90.7 percent of the realist hypotheses compared to 78.1 percent of the nonrealist hypotheses have a measure of association of less than .46 (categories 10 and 20).

only 2.2 percent of the realist hypotheses have a measure of association higher than $|.71|$ (categories 75 and 100) compared to 4.6 percent of the nonrealist hypotheses.

The test results of hypothesis 4 indicate that the realist paradigm has not been very successful in passing empirical tests. Although early success would not be expected, one would not expect about 90 percent of over 7,000 realist hypotheses to be falsified. Also, the fact that nonrealist hypotheses, which consist of simply rejecting the fundamental assumptions of realism, can more successfully pass empirical tests than the realist paradigm, which has been the object of much work, raises serious questions about the accuracy of the realist paradigm. In light of these findings, it can be said that proposition 4 has not been supported, and it can be tentatively concluded that the realist paradigm has not, up to this time, satisfied the criterion of accuracy.

The Criterion of Centrality

The criterion of centrality is based on the recognition that certain propositions in a paradigm are more important than others. They are more important either because the adherents of the paradigm claim that these propositions have greater theoretical explanatory power or because they are what distinguishes the paradigm from rival paradigms. Because these propositions form, in a sense, the heart of the paradigm, it is important that hypotheses testing these propositions should fail to be falsified. Unlike the criterion of accuracy, the criterion of centrality introduces a qualitative element in assessing paradigm adequacy. It does not treat every hypothesis as equal in importance, but establishes a category of hypotheses that are given more weight.

In this light, the criterion of centrality provides a test of the adequacy of the realist paradigm that is different from the test provided by the criterion of accuracy. Even though the tests applying the criterion of accuracy resulted in the tentative conclusion that the realist paradigm did not produce many accurate hypotheses, it could be argued on the basis of the criterion of centrality that it is not important if the noncentral realist propositions are found to be inaccurate if the central realist propositions are accurate. If the results of the tests of proposition 4 were due to a large number of noncentral realist hypotheses being falsified, this finding would not, given the criterion of centrality, be a sufficient basis for concluding that the realist paradigm is inadequate. That conclusion could only be made if the central propositions were found to be inaccurate. The tests of the criterion of centrality examine whether this is the case and thereby serve as a control on the validity of the test on the criterion of accuracy.

Operationalization and Measurement

Early in this chapter, *centrality* was defined as the level of generality, scope, and uniqueness of a proposition. The more universal the proposition, the greater its generality. For example, a proposition intended to hold for all nations during the last two hundred years is more general than a proposition intended to hold only for Latin American nations in the last twenty years. *Scope* refers to the variety of phenomena or behavior the proposition intends to explain. The greater the variety of phenomena a proposition intends to explain, the greater its scope. For example, a proposition that attempts to explain all kinds of inter-nation conflict-cooperation is obviously greater in scope than a proposition that attempts to explain only economic conflict-cooperation among nations. *Uniqueness* refers to whether rival theories contain the same proposition. Uniqueness is included because it is the criterion by which one theory or paradigm is distinguished from another. Unique propositions, no matter what their generality or scope, provide the reasons for selecting one theory or paradigm over a rival. These three definitions can be employed to operationally define the criterion of centrality as the failure to falsify hypotheses that: hold over long periods of time and a great deal of space; explain a variety of phenomena or behavior; and offer predictions that are not made by a rival paradigm(s).

One way of determining the importance or centrality of a hypothesis for a realist paradigm is to examine the relationships postulated among the most frequently used concepts in *Politics Among Nations*—balance of power, national power, and war.[9] Applying the operational criteria, albeit in a somewhat judgmental manner, it was found that propositions relating these concepts tended to be highly general, great in scope, and unique. They were general to the extent that they applied to all nations in the modern state system (i.e., since the Peace of Westphalia) (see Morgenthau 1960, 1973:8–10). They were great in scope in that the balance of power and national power were intended to explain not only war but all types of conflict-cooperation in the system (see Morgenthau 1960, 1973:27–28:chaps. 4 and 11). They were unique in that competing paradigms such as idealism, Marxism, transnational relations, and the issue politics paradigms did not offer them as explanations. In addition, these propositions are central to the paradigm in that, as was shown with the textual analysis presented in chapter 3, the relationship between national power and conflict-cooperation forms the key theoretical focus of *Politics Among Nations*. The notion of a balance of power can also be regarded as central because it sharpens the national power focus by describing the power relationship between two or more nations.

9. See chapter 3, pp. 32–33.

On the basis of this examination, it was decided that it would be valid to declare that the national power variables and alliance variables that were related to conflict-cooperation variables were indicators of central hypotheses in the realist paradigm. All other variable relationships were coded as noncentral. This nominal classification was used in the analysis as the first measure of the notion of centrality.

Two other measures of centrality were developed by assuming that any proposition that employed national power or inter-nation alliances as a predictor, or any proposition that tried to explain inter-nation conflict-cooperation, would be a central proposition in the realist paradigm. The rationale for this procedure was that, since these three concepts are the most frequently discussed and used concepts in the realist paradigm, any proposition using them in their respective roles as chief independent or dependent variables was more important to the paradigm than propositions not using them.

It should be evident that, despite any problems of measurement validity, the reliability of the measure provides some confidence in the results of the tests on centrality, because they are subject to additional and future tests.

Test Design

Proposition 5 maintained that if the realist paradigm satisfied the criterion of centrality, then its central propositions should produce hypotheses that fail to be falsified. The most obvious way to test this proposition would be to employ the measures of centrality and the Predictive Power Indices to see how many central realist hypotheses fail to be falsified in comparison to all other hypotheses, that is, noncentral realist hypotheses and nonrealist hypotheses. Since the central realist hypotheses were defined by the first measure of centrality as those hypotheses that relate national power or inter-nation alliances with inter-nation conflict-cooperation, the following hypothesis can be derived from proposition 5:

5a. Realist hypotheses that relate national power or inter-nation alliances with inter-nation conflict-cooperation should fail to be falsified more frequently than all other hypotheses—noncentral realist or nonrealist.

Two additional ways to test the criterion of centrality would be to examine whether the concepts the realist paradigm declares as theoretically powerful for explaining behavior do in fact successfully explain behavior and whether the realist paradigm has successfully explained those topics it set out to explain. It was established in chapter 3 that the concepts that play the largest role as predictors or independent variables in the realist paradigm were national power and inter-nation alliances. It was also established that the chief purpose of the realist paradigm was to explain inter-nation conflict-cooperation. Using the second and third measures of centrality, the following hypotheses can be derived from proposition 5:

5b. Hypotheses that employ national power or inter-nation alliances as independent variables should fail to be falsified more frequently than hypotheses that employ different independent variables.

5c. Hypotheses that employ inter-nation conflict-cooperation as a dependent variable should fail to be falsified more frequently than hypotheses that employ different dependent variables.

The three hypotheses that will be employed to determine how well the realist paradigm has satisfied the criterion of centrality provide a good test of the adequacy of the realist paradigm. These tests allow the realist paradigm to produce a large number of inaccurate hypotheses so long as its most central hypotheses fail to be falsified. Hypotheses 5a–5c provide evidence about how adequate the strategy of explaining inter-nation conflict-cooperation by national power or inter-nation alliances has been; how powerful national power and inter-nation alliances have been as predictors; and how successful the realist paradigm has been in achieving its own purpose—the explanation of inter-nation conflict-cooperation. These tests permit the power politics core of the realist paradigm to be examined.

The Findings

Hypothesis 5a predicted that realist hypotheses that related national power or inter-nation alliances with inter-nation conflict-cooperation should tend to fail to be falsified. Four hypotheses can be formed from relating these three concepts:

HY 1 National power *with* inter-nation conflict-cooperation
HY 2 Inter-nation conflict-cooperation *with* national power
HY 3 Inter-nation alliances *with* inter-nation conflict-cooperation
HY 4 Inter-nation conflict-cooperation *with* inter-nation alliances

In order to test hypothesis 5a, the preceding four hypotheses were selected from the data and compared to all the other hypotheses in the data.

The findings are reported in table 7.3, which employs PPI (A). From the table, it can be seen that HY 1, 2, and 3 account for 49.5 percent of all the hypotheses in the data, with HY 1, which was declared the most central in the realist paradigm, accounting for 39.0 percent of all the

Table 7.3. Performance of Central Realist Propositions (Hypothesis 5a)

	PPI (A)								Row total Total percentage	
	10	20	30	40	50	60	70	71+	(count)	(row percent)
Noncentral hypotheses	2,722 70.2	511 13.2	258 6.7	126 3.2	89 2.3	63 1.6	41 1.1	67 1.7	3,877	50.5
HY 1 (Nat. Pow. with Inter-Nat. Confl.-Coop.)	2,746 91.7	194 6.5	43 1.4	3 0.1	4 0.1	0 0.0	1 0.0	3 0.1	2,994	39.0
HY 2 (Inter-Nat. Confl.-Coop. with Nat. Pow.)	138 85.2	16 9.9	4 2.5	0 0.0	3 1.9	0 0.0	1 0.6	0 0.0	162	2.1
HY 3 (Inter-Nat. Alliances with Inter-Nat. Confl.-Coop.)	463 71.8	95 14.7	50 7.8	21 3.3	11 1.7	5 0.8	0 0.0	0 0.0	645	8.4
Column Total	6,069	816	355	150	107	68	43	70	7,678	
Total percentage	79.0	10.6	4.6	2.0	1.4	0.9	0.6	0.9	100.0	

NOTE: The number of cases differs from that in table 6.5 because independent variables with mixed topics of inquiry have been kept in the sample and cases employing statistical tests incompatible with PPI (A) have been dropped.

hypotheses tested.[10] It can be seen that HY 1 does very poorly, with 91.7 percent of its tests being statistically nonsignificant or having a measure of association of less than $|.33|$. If categories 10 and 20 are combined, then 98.2 percent of the hypotheses relating national power and inter-nation conflict-cooperation are falsified. Relating the concepts in the opposite manner (HY 2) does not help either, since 95.1 percent of these hypotheses are statistically nonsignificant or have a measure of association of less than $|.46|$. Relating inter-nation alliances with inter-nation conflict-cooperation (HY 3) does somewhat better in that only 71.8 percent of these hypotheses fall into category 10 and 86.5 percent in categories 10 and 20 combined. However, at the other end of the scale, none of HY 3's findings fall in the "strong" category of 70 and 71+. HY 2 produces one finding out of 162 in these categories, and HY 1 produces four out of 2,994.

These results are hardly encouraging for the realist paradigm. A comparison with the "other" hypotheses tested in the field shows that the three most central hypotheses of the realist paradigm do less well than the combined noncentral and nonrealist hypotheses. On the basis of this test, it can be tentatively concluded that hypothesis 5a has been falsified and that the realist paradigm has not been very successful in getting its central propositions to pass empirical tests.

Hypothesis 5b predicted that hypotheses that employ national power or inter-nation alliances as independent variables should fail to be falsified more frequently than hypotheses that employ different independent variables. This hypothesis examines how well specific concepts predict behavior, particularly how well the central realist (and power politics) concepts predict behavior. Hypothesis 5b was tested by ranking the various independent variables used in research according to their predictive power. Table 7.4 ranks the concepts according to the number of hypotheses that they produce in category 25 of PPI (B). It can be seen from table 7.4 that 94.1 percent of the hypotheses that employ national power and 93.2 percent of the hypotheses that employ inter-nation alliance as independent variables have been falsified. This means that hypotheses using these two variables tend to be statistically nonsignificant or have a measure of association less than $|.50|$. Only three concepts are weaker predictors. Six other concepts, four nonrealist and two realist, have over 85 percent of their hypotheses falling into the weak category. Of the remaining four concepts, all have less than 72 percent falling into the weak category. Of these concepts, three are nonrealist and one is realist. The findings from table 7.4 support two

10. No cases of HY 4 were found in the data. The main tests of this hypothesis come after 1970 (see O. R. Holsti, Hopmann, and Sullivan 1973).

Table 7.4. Rank Order of Realist and Nonrealist Independent Variables,
Percentage of Weak Findings (Hypothesis 5b)
N = 7,189

Concept	Rank	PPI (B) Category 25	Classifi- cation	Rank PPI (A) 10 and 20	
Nation (miscellaneous topics)[a]	1	100 %	Nr	1	(weak)
National isolationism	2	99.5	R	2	
Nations and other actors power	3	95.7	Nr	4	
NATIONAL POWER[t]	4	94.1	R	3	
INTER-NATION ALLIANCES[t]	5	93.2	R	5	
Nations and others decision makers perceptions	6	92.9	Nr	11	
Inter-nation conflict-cooperation	7	88.6	R	8	
Nation and supra- nationalism	8	87.9	R	10	
Nation and others non-war issues	9.5	87.5	Nr	6.5	
Nation and others (miscellaneous topics)[b]	9.5	87.5	Nr	6.5	
Nation and sociological characteristics	11	86.1	Nr	9	
Nation and others sociological characteristics	12	71.6	Nr	12	
Nation and others conflict-cooperation	13	70.0	Nr	13	
Inter-nation integration	14	57.9	R	14	
Nation and others alliances[c]	15	25.0	Nr	15	(strong)

R = Realist   [a]N = 2   [c]N = 4
Nr = Nonrealist   [b]N = 8   [t] = central concepts

conclusions: (1) the central realist (and power politics) concepts of national power and inter-nation alliances are poor predictors; and (2) the realist concept of inter-nation integration is one of the best predictors of all the concepts.[11]

Table 7.5 ranks the concepts according to their ability to produce strong measures of association (i.e., greater than $|.71|$). When the data are analyzed this way, some interesting results appear. First, seven concepts, six of them nonrealist, fail to produce any findings. The realist concepts of inter-nation alliances and national power still rank low (seventh and sixth from the top), with less than 2 percent of their findings in the strong categories of PPI (B). The nonrealist, sociological characteristics do rather well (3.0 percent and 14.9 percent, respectively). The nonrealist concept of conflict-cooperation also does well (12.0 percent). But by far the most powerful predictor is still the realist concept of integration (28.1 percent).

In light of the preceding tests of hypothesis 5b, the following conclusions can be tentatively made: (1) the central power politics concepts of the realist paradigm, national power and inter-nation alliances, are among the poorest predictors of behavior; (2) the strongest predictor is the realist concept of inter-nation integration, followed by the nonrealist concepts of sociological characteristics and conflict-cooperation; (3) a large number of realist and nonrealist concepts are poor predictors. Therefore, in terms of the criterion of centrality, hypothesis 5b has been falsified.

Hypothesis 5c predicted that hypotheses employing inter-nation conflict-cooperation as a dependent variable should fail to be falsified more frequently than hypotheses employing other dependent variables. This hypothesis examines how successful the realist paradigm has been in achieving its own purpose—the explanation of inter-nation conflict-cooperation. Hypothesis 5c was tested by ranking the various dependent variables used in research according to their predictive power.

Table 7.6 ranks the dependent variables from weak to strong by employing category 25 of PPI (B). It can be seen from this table that 95.4 percent of the hypotheses that attempt to explain inter-nation conflict-cooperation are falsified; that is, they either are statistically nonsignificant or have a measure of association of less than $|.50|$. Only two out of the ten other dependent variables are less successful. It is also evident

11. For a detailed assessment of specific topics and indicators within such broad topics as national power see Vasquez (1976b). When this is done, "military power and political status" have only 81.57 percent in category 25. These deal primarily with arms races and war. See below pp. 196–197. From a perspective of trying to discover what has been learned, that article elaborates on the many topics not treated here.

Table 7.5. Rank Order of Realist and Nonrealist Independent Variables, Percentage of Strong Findings (Hypothesis 5b)
N = 7,189

Concept	Rank	PPI (B) categories 75 and 100	Classifi- cation	Rank PPI (A) 10 and 20	Rank PPI (B) 25	
Nation (miscellaneous topics)[a]	12	0%	Nr	15	15	(weak)
Nations and other actors power	12	0	Nr	12	13	
Nation and others nonwar issues	12	0	Nr	9.5	6.5	
Nations and others (miscellaneous topics)[b]	12	0	Nr	9.5	6.5	
Nation and supranationalism	12	0	R	6	8	
Nations and others decision makers perceptions	12	0	Nr	5	10	
Nation and others alliances[c]	12	0	Nr	1	1	
National isolationism	8	0.5	R	15	14	
INTER-NATION ALLIANCES[t]	7	0.9	R	11	11	
NATIONAL POWER[t]	6	1.8	R	13	12	
Nation and sociological characteristics	5	3.0	Nr	7	5	
Inter-nation conflict-cooperation	4	5.6	R	8	9	
Nation and others conflict-cooperation	3	12.0	Nr	3	3	
Nation and others sociological characteristics	2	14.9	Nr	4	4	
Inter-nation integration	1	28.1	R	2	2	(strong)

R = Realist   [a]N = 2   [c]N = 4
Nr = Nonrealist   [b]N = 8   [t] = central concepts

that four nonrealist dependent variables and four realist dependent variables do better than inter-nation conflict-cooperation. Finally, on the basis of category 25 of PPI (B), it is clear that research has been most successful in predicting the nonrealist topic of issues and the nonrealist approach to supranationalism.

Table 7.6. Rank Order of Realist and Nonrealist Dependent Variables,
Percentage of Weak Findings (Hypothesis 5c)
N = 7,691

Concept	Rank	PPI (B) category 25	Classifi- cation	Rank PPI (A) 10 and 20	
Nation and sociological characteristics[a]	1	100 %	Nr	1	(weak)
Nation and supranationalism	2	96.2	R	2	
INTER-NATION CONFLICT-COOPERATION[t]	3	95.4	R	4	
Nation (miscellaneous topics)	4	94.3	Nr	3	
Inter-nation integration	5	86.8	R	9	
National isolationism	6	86.7	R	6	
Inter-nation alliances	7	84.9	R	5	
Nation and others conflict-cooperation	8.5	83.3	Nr	8	
National power	8.5	83.3	R	7	
National nonwar issues	10	78.9	Nr	11	
Nation and others supranationalism[b]	11	76.9	Nr	10	(strong)

R = Realist	[a]N = 1	[t] = central concept
Nr = Nonrealist	[b]N = 26	

Table 7.7 ranks the concepts according to how many hypotheses they have produced in categories 75 and 100 of PPI (B) (i.e., having a measure of association above $|.71|$). The realist dependent variables do significantly better than they did in table 7.6. The strongest concept, however, is the nonrealist concept of supranationalism; 11.5 percent of its hypotheses had a measure of association greater than $|.71|$. However, despite the generally better performance of the realist concepts, inter-nation conflict-cooperation—the central realist dependent variable—does not do very well; only 1.6 percent of its hypotheses have a measure of association greater than $|.71|$.

In light of the preceding tests of hypothesis 5c, the following conclusions can be tentatively made. First, most research has not been very successful in explaining behavior. Second, although most research efforts have tried to explain the central topic in the realist paradigm—

Table 7.7. Rank Order of Realist and Nonrealist Dependent Variables,
Percentage of Strong Findings (Hypothesis 5c)
N = 7,691

Concept	Rank	PPI (B) categories 75 and 100	Classifi- cation	Rank PPI (A) 10 and 20	Rank PPI (B) 25	
Nation and sociological characteristics[a]	10.5	0%	Nr	1	1	(weak)
Nation (miscellaneous topics)	10.5	0	Nr	3	4	
Nation and supranationalism	9	0.9	R	2	2	
National nonwar issues	8	1.4	Nr	11	9	
INTER-NATION CONFLICT-COOPERATION[t]	7	1.6	R	4	3	
Inter-nation integration	6	2.1	R	9	5	
National power	5	5.2	R	7	8	
Inter-nation alliances	4	5.4	R	5	7	
Nation and others conflict-cooperation	3	5.5	Nr	8	8	
National isolationism	2	7.1	R	6	6	
Nation and others supranationalism[b]	1	11.5	Nr	10	10	(strong)

R = Realist   [a]N = 1   [t] = central concept
Nr = Nonrealist   [b]N = 26

inter-nation conflict-cooperation—this effort has produced proportionally fewer findings than other efforts. This suggests that the realist paradigm has failed to conceptualize adequately the main dependent variable of the field. Third, the tests of hypothesis 5c showed that the most successful tests have been on attempts to predict the realist topics of national power, inter-nation alliances (the two main realist independent variables), national isolationism, and the nonrealist topics of conflict-cooperation and supranationalism. On the whole, then, the tests of hypothesis 5c have shown that although some realist concepts have been productive, the central realist concepts have not been very productive. Therefore, in terms of the criterion of centrality, hypothesis 5c has been falsified.

The three tests of proposition 5 are hardly encouraging for the realist paradigm. It has been found that the central realist hypotheses that relate national power or inter-nation alliances with inter-nation conflict-cooperation, employ national power or inter-nation alliances as predictors, or try to predict inter-nation conflict-cooperation have been consistently falsified. These findings indicate that the area of the realist paradigm that promised to be the most theoretically powerful, the central power politics framework, have been among the poorest performers in actually predicting behavior. It has been found that noncentral realist hypotheses and nonrealist hypotheses provide more adequate predictions of behavior, even though these hypotheses have not been as extensively elaborated and tested as the central realist hypotheses. In light of these findings, it can be said that proposition 5 has not been supported. Therefore, it can be tentatively concluded that the realist paradigm has not satisfied the criterion of centrality.

The Criterion of Scientific Importance

The tests of propositions 4 and 5 have attempted to examine how well the realist paradigm has satisfied the criteria of accuracy and centrality. These two criteria must be satisfied in order to declare a paradigm an adequate guide to knowledge. It was stated at the beginning of this chapter that if a paradigm satisfied these two necessary conditions, a number of secondary criteria could be applied to determine how valuable the knowledge was that the paradigm produced. It was also stated that only one secondary criterion would be employed in this analysis—the criterion of scientific importance. This criterion maintains that knowledge produced by the paradigm should not be trivial; that is, the produced knowledge should not be considered obvious or trivial to most scholars in the field. It might be thought that since the realist paradigm did so poorly in satisfying the criteria of accuracy and centrality, an attempt to apply the criterion of scientific importance is irrelevant. There is some validity to this argument, but the failure to apply this third criterion would result in not assessing the value of the few hypotheses in the field that have failed to be falsified. Therefore, it will be applied in this section.

Operationalization and Measurement

Because triviality is more subject to personal interpretation than other matters, the criterion of scientific importance is very difficult to operationalize and measure. Perhaps the best way to measure it would be to survey scholars and allow them to use their own criteria of triviality to code each hypothesis. Hypotheses that failed to be declared nontrivial by a large segment of the scholarly community could then be declared as "scientifically important." Such an effort would be expensive and would not deter readers from making their own "definitive" evaluation. Therefore, the author has simply coded the major findings as either trivial or nontrivial according to his own assessment of "importance." In order to provide the reader with some basis for determining how "biased" this "test" might be, the raw and coded data have been published in Vasquez (1974a:Appendix III).

Three types of trivial hypotheses were found in the data. The first type is a hypothesis that, even though it may be perceived as significant by the scholar testing it, is in fact highly descriptive and/or a familiar generalization made in newspapers or history texts. An example of this type is a hypothesis tested in an article by Chadwick Alger (1968) on the United Nations that finds that the percentage of the total UN budget a nation contributes is predicted by its GNP.

The second type is that which tends to correlate measures of the same concept, which hardly qualifies as scientifically important explanation. An example of this type are some of the hypotheses tested by Richard Chadwick (1969) in an article about the Inter-Nation Simulation. Although a number of scientifically important hypotheses are tested in that article, a large proportion of the ones that fail to be falsified really correlate different measures of the same concept. For example, Chadwick correlates threats with accusations and basic economic capability with quality of consumer goods in a nation.

A third type of trivial hypothesis is that which is highly idiographic and therefore of little importance in terms of building a general theory of international relations. Examples of this type are many of the hypotheses tested by Nils Gleditsch (1969) in an article about integration and airline networks. Typical of the hypotheses that failed to be falsified in that article was the hypothesis that correlated national population size with number of airline flights. While this finding may have policy implications, it does not seem to have much importance for building a general theory of international relations.

As indicated earlier, the notion of "failed to be falsified" is measured by using categories 75 and 100 of Predictive Power Index B, which means that any hypothesis not reported as statistically nonsignificant and has a measure of association of $|.72|$ or higher has failed to be falsified. It should be evident that, given the problems of operationalizing the criterion of scientific importance, the findings on this criterion are the most tentative of all those presented here. This situation is somewhat ameliorated by the fact that the findings on scientific importance are the least important for evaluating the adequacy of the realist paradigm.

Test Design

Proposition 6 maintained that if the realist paradigm satisfied the criterion of scientific importance, the hypotheses it produced that failed to be falsified should be important. Given the measurement problem with this criterion, the only hypothesis that will be tested is:

6. More realist than nonrealist hypotheses that fail to be falsified should be scientifically important.

In order to test hypothesis 6, it is necessary to employ a sample of hypotheses that have failed to be falsified in the field. The data used in the tests of propositions 1 and 2 consisted of all hypotheses that were tested in correlational/explanatory articles published from 1956 to 1970. Of these 7,827 hypotheses, only 7,691 could be used in all of the previous tests. Of these 7,691 hypotheses, only 181 have failed to be falsified (i.e., fell into categories 75 and 100 of PPI [B]). Of these, 157 were realist (2.2 percent of the 7,158 realist hypotheses tested), and 24 were nonrealist (4.6 percent of the 520 nonrealist hypotheses tested). In order to provide a data sample for the test of hypothesis 3, the 181 hypotheses were coded as either trivial or nontrivial. Because of the small number of cases for nonrealist hypotheses, the findings must be interpreted with caution.

The Findings

The performance of realist and nonrealist hypotheses, as evaluated by the criterion of scientific importance, is reported in figure 7.2. It can be seen from this figure that about two-thirds (69.5 percent) of the realist hypotheses were declared trivial, compared to about half (54.2 percent) of the nonrealist hypotheses. On the basis of this distribution it appears that the nonrealist hypotheses have performed slightly better. This finding suggests that accepting rather than rejecting realistic assumptions does not result in comparatively more scientifically important findings. However, before reaching this conclusion a more detailed review of the nontrivial findings is warranted.

Less than one-third (30.5 percent) of the 157 realist hypotheses that failed to be falsified were declared nontrivial. Most of these hypotheses attempted to explain three types of behavior—military expenditures, conflict, and UN voting.

The major findings on military expenditures are in an article on World War I by Robert North and Nazli Choucri (1968) and in the work of Paul Smoker (1964a; 1965b; 1966). North and Choucri (1968) fail to falsify seventeen of their hypotheses that attempt to explain in a nontrivial

Figure 7.2. The Scientific Importance of Realist Findings (Hypothesis 6)

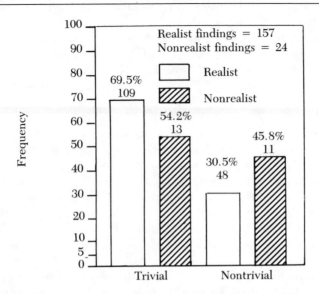

fashion the military budgets of the major powers in World War I. Smoker's work is concerned with testing and elaborating Lewis Richardson's model of arms races. He has been very successful in obtaining high correlations, but in order to do this it has been necessary, on occasion, for him to eliminate deviant cases.

The major findings on inter-nation conflict-cooperation come from four articles. The first is an article by Choucri and North (1969) on World War I. They use national attributes and levels of competition to predict the outbreak of violence. Of the many hypotheses they test, nine fail to be falsified. Additional major findings are two hypotheses that fail to be falsified in the J. D. Singer and Small (1966a) article on alliances. Singer and Small find a correlation between the number of times a nation was allied before a war and the number of battle deaths.

Another finding on conflict-cooperation is reported in an article by Maurice East and Philip Gregg (1967). By employing six independent variables, they can explain 81 percent of the variance for cooperation. However, when they use the same variables to try to explain conflict, they account for only 35 percent of the variance. The finding, then, is somewhat mixed, and the accuracy of the proposition from which it was drawn must be interpreted with caution. A third set of findings on conflict-cooperation deals with treaties between nations. Richard Chadwick (1969) uses economic variables to predict the number of economic, cultural, and military agreements a nation will sign.

Finally, an article by Midlarsky and Tanter (1967) on U.S. economic presence and internal conflict in Latin America contains two hypotheses that fail to be falsified. Both deal with the outbreak of revolution in non-democratic Latin American nations. Midlarsky and Tanter find a correlation of .85 between the per capita GNP of a nation and the number of revolutions it has, and a correlation of .73 between U.S. economic presence and the number of revolutions in a nation. As with the other research, a large number of their other hypotheses are falsified.

The third major area of significant findings for the realist paradigm is the attempt to explain UN votes. This research consists of two types. The first is concerned with uncovering what national attributes lead a nation to vote a particular way on a specific issue. Alker's (1964) research has been successful in producing findings in this area. He finds that various indicators of East-West alignment will predict voting patterns on East-West issues in the United Nations. He also discovers that communist nations do not support "supranationalism" votes in the UN. The work of Ellis and Salzberg (1965) reflects the second type of successful research in this area—the attempt to predict alignment patterns. Using a variety of indicators of dependence on the major Western powers—the United States, United Kingdom, France—as well as demographic and trade data, they are able to successfully predict African bloc adherence in the UN.

Although the findings of Alker and of Ellis and Salzberg have been declared nontrivial, they are really borderline cases. The studies have confirmed and made more precise some well-known "facts" familiar to any serious traditionalist scholar of the United Nations. Nevertheless, before their research, the hypotheses were never systematically tested.

It can be seen from figure 7.2 that almost half (45.8 percent) of the twenty-four nonrealist hypotheses that failed to be falsified were declared nontrivial. These hypotheses generally deal with individuals' attitudes toward international relations. Three of the findings come from O. R. Holsti's (1967) case study of John Foster Dulles. Holsti is somewhat successful in predicting the conditions under which Dulles would perceive Soviet policy as hostile. Six of the findings come from a study by Jerome Laulicht (1965a) on foreign policy attitudes of Canadian subnational groups and the general public. He is able to predict the attitudes of business, labor, and political elites as well as the voting public on coexistence-disarmament and internationalism. Another finding in this area is an extremely interesting one produced by Bruce Russett (1962a). He finds a correlation of .86 between a U.S. state involved in Anglo-American trade and the responsiveness of the state's congressmen to the United Kingdom on foreign policy questions. The final nonrealist hypothesis declared nontrivial deals with UN voting. Produced by Alker

(1964), it predicts UN votes on self-determination issues on the basis of membership in the "Old Europeans" group.[12]

The question is whether, in light of these findings, hypothesis 6 has been falsified. This is difficult to answer, because, on the one hand, some nontrivial knowledge has been gained about military expenditures, violence, and UN voting. On the other hand, it is quite sobering that of 7,827 hypotheses tested in the field, of which over 90 percent are realist, only 157 realist hypotheses failed to be falsified, and, of these, over two-thirds were trivial. This means that since 1956, only 48 realist hypotheses have produced findings of any major scientific importance. When the percentages of nontrivial findings for realist and nonrealist hypotheses are compared (see figure 7.2), it is clear that the nonrealist hypotheses have done proportionally better in satisfying the criterion of scientific importance. In other words, it cannot be claimed that, despite the poor performance of the realist paradigm on the first two criteria, its assumptions might be able to produce more important findings than a paradigm that rejected them. It can be tentatively concluded that proposition 6 has been falsified.

Conclusion and Implications

The three propositions tested in this chapter provide evidence for determining the adequacy of the realist paradigm. The tests of proposition 4 showed that on the whole the realist paradigm has not produced much knowledge. It also demonstrated that rejecting one or more of the realist assumptions produces proportionally more hypotheses that failed to be falsified. On the basis of the tests of proposition 4, it could be concluded that the realist paradigm has not satisfied the criterion of accuracy.

The tests of proposition 5 demonstrated that the central propositions of the realist paradigm were not as powerful in predicting behavior as they were theoretically expected to be. It was found that the central proposition of explaining inter-nation conflict-cooperation by using either the concepts of national power or inter-nation alliances was consistently falsified. Likewise, the central independent and dependent variables in the realist paradigm tended to rank lowest in terms of their power to successfully predict behavior. Finally, it was shown that certain noncentral realist and certain nonrealist concepts were more successful in predicting behavior than were the central realist concepts. Since the central realist propositions do not tend to produce hypotheses that

12. A propositional inventory of all the strong findings (and all the null findings) is provided in Vasquez (1976b:200–206).

fail to be falsified, it could be concluded that the realist paradigm has not satisfied the criterion of centrality.

The tests of proposition 6 demonstrated that the realist paradigm has not produced very many scientifically important findings. Although the important findings it has produced are interesting, it is quite striking to think that so much effort and time has produced so little. What is even more amazing is that research that rejected one or more realist assumptions produced proportionally more scientifically important findings. On the basis of the tests of proposition 6, it could be tentatively concluded that the realist paradigm has not satisfied the criterion of scientific importance.

The tests of the three propositions lead one to conclude that the realist paradigm has not been a very adequate guide to knowledge. The use of quantitative analysis to test aspects of the realist paradigm, which began in 1956 and was well underway by the mid-sixties, did not produce much knowledge by the seventies, although it commanded a great deal of effort. The field did not, as had been expected, move "beyond conjecture." The question that must be answered is why this is the case. This book suggests that the reason for this dismal performance is that the view of the world provided by the realist paradigm is incorrect. This explanation is certainly consistent with the evidence. However, a number of competing explanations, which on the surface also seem consistent with the evidence, can be offered. Before a final conclusion can be made, these ad hoc explanations must be scrutinized.

Six ad hoc explanations can be offered to account for the findings of the previous tests: (1) the findings are to be expected because of the youthfulness of the field; (2) the findings are due to the bivariate character of many of the hypotheses being tested, and as more complex relationships are tested the success rate of the realist paradigm will go up; (3) the findings might be due to the inaccuracy of one large article included in the sample;[13] (4) the findings are due to the particular statistics employed in the articles; (5) the findings show that quantitative analysis is inadequate, not that the realist paradigm is inadequate; (6) the findings are due to measurement error in the articles providing the sample.

Table 7.8 summarizes how these ad hoc explanations are assessed. Three, those that attributed the findings to the effects of the bivariate character of hypotheses, article size, and statistics employed, were tested and falsified. The ad hoc explanation that attributed the findings to

13. For example, one article by Rummel (1968) tested over 2,500 hypotheses. Since this analysis was repeated without the article and the results were substantially the same, the ad hoc explanation is not correct.

Table 7.8. Analysis of Ad Hoc Explanations

1. "Youth of the field"
   Correlation between year and PPI (B)
   Kendall's tau_c = 0.019
   Result: inconclusive

2. "Bivariate character of hypotheses"
   Correlation between number of independent variables and PPI (B)
   Kendall's tau_c = 0.041
   Result: falsified

3. "Size of article"
   Correlation between article size and PPI (B)
   Kendall's tau_c = -0.051
   Result: falsified

4. "Statistics employed"
   Correlation between statistic employed and PPI (B)
   Kendall's tau_c = 0.034
   Result: falsified

5. "Quantitative analysis inadequate"
   Untestable

6. "Measurement error"
   Untestable

the youthfulness of the field was also falsified, but because it could be argued that the entire pre-1970 period was youthful, the test was declared inconclusive. Two of the ad hoc explanations, the fifth and sixth, are untestable and must be assessed on the basis of their face validity.

The fifth ad hoc explanation suggests that the findings presented in this chapter do not show that the realist paradigm is inadequate but that quantitative analysis cannot be applied as a methodology for the study of the more interesting and important empirical questions in international relations. This is the position of the traditionalists and of Morgenthau himself.[14] The problems with this position are that it fails to explain why a "defective" method was more successful with nonrealist than realist hypotheses; it fails to account for the discovery of some nontrivial findings; and it sidesteps all the epistemological arguments made against the traditional method during the last decade and a half. This ad hoc explanation is therefore rejected.

The final ad hoc explanation maintains that the absence of major

14. Personal communication from Hans J. Morgenthau, March 13, 1973. See also Bull (1966).

findings in the field is due to measurement error in the original articles that reported the findings. This implies that as more accurate measures are developed more important findings will be produced. The problem with this explanation is that in conducting any quantitative research, a scholar does not know whether the findings are a result of the measurements and test design or because that is the way "reality" is structured. A valid test of this explanation would be logically impossible. The best that could be done would be to examine the measures and test designs employed in each article and make some assessment of their validity and reliability. The data to conduct such a test are not available and the adequacy of this explanation must therefore be left open to future analysis.

The above review of ad hoc explanations has eliminated four of them —the argument on the bivariate character of the hypotheses, the argument on the effect of articles, the argument on the effect of particular statistics, and the traditionalist argument on the inapplicability of quantitative analysis. The adequacy of two of the explanations, however, is still open to further analysis. The question that must now be addressed is: What can be concluded about the adequacy of the realist paradigm in light of the tests of propositions 4 through 6 and the two untested ad hoc explanations?

The findings presented in this chapter demonstrate that international relations inquiry has produced little knowledge. The findings in chapters 4 through 6 demonstrated that the realist paradigm has dominated the field since the early 1950s. This book maintains that there is a connection between the dominance of the realist paradigm in the field and the failure of the field to produce much knowledge. The evidence presented in this chapter does not falsify this claim, but lends it greater credence than the two ad hoc explanations, since it has passed a set of rigorous tests, but the ad hoc explanations have not.

It can therefore be concluded that while the present data analysis has not demonstrated beyond doubt that the realist paradigm is inadequate, it has raised the following questions about its adequacy. If the view of the world presented by the realist paradigm is correct or useful as a guide to understanding, why have so many hypotheses guided by this view been consistently falsified? If the view of the realist paradigm is correct, why have hypotheses that have rejected the view been falsified proportionally less often? If the view of the realist paradigm is correct, why have the central realist propositions, which have been extensively elaborated and tested, been consistently falsified? If the view of the realist paradigm is correct, why has the realist paradigm produced only 48 scientifically important findings out of 7,158 realist hypotheses that were tested from 1956 to 1970?

Evaluation of the Realist Paradigm

These questions must be answered. In Kuhn's terms, these questions pose an anomaly for the field. How the field deals with the anomaly depends on what individual scholars believe has caused the anomaly. The present chapter has gone about as far as possible in terms of delineating a "cause." Until there is more evidence, a definitive assessment of the adequacy of the realist paradigm cannot be made. The present analysis has served to raise as a serious question the possibility that the most fundamental assumptions of the field are incorrect.

The next chapter will try to answer these questions by taking a less synoptic view and a more in-depth approach toward research. This will provide another perspective on the question of measurement error, since a judgment on the validity of particular studies can be made. It will also provide additional evidence to examine the "youthfulness" explanation, by reviewing systematically the important research in the two subfields that have received the most attention in the past decade—foreign policy and the causes of war. When this is done, the conclusions reached in this chapter are given even further support.

Chapter 8

Theory and Research in the 1970s: The Emerging Anomalies

Introduction

The synoptic analysis presented in chapter 7 is not intended to supplant traditional literature reviews and assessments of research but to supplement them by providing a test design that will make claims about the adequacy of theory and paradigms subject to the principle of falsifiability. There are limitations to such an approach, however. As the two ad hoc explanations on measurement error and youthfulness of the field make clear, any body of evidence is subject to interpretation, even if only on the question of how much emphasis to put on the evidence. Rather than treating each finding equally, as the predictive power indices do, it might be argued that it would be more proper to place a different weight on research depending on the validity of its research design and the theoretical significance of its findings. After all, it might be argued that even in the physical sciences one or two important experiments, like the Michelson-Morley experiment or the investigations leading to the decoding of DNA, are much more important than the vast multitude of work published in a field. Although most of the flaws with which this potential criticism is concerned would be eliminated by the tests on the criterion of scientific importance, there is merit in systematically reviewing research to see if it is consistent with findings from a data-based and more synoptic approach. The present chapter will draw on the most important recent research on foreign policy and causes of war to assess the adequacy of the three fundamental assumptions of the realist paradigm.

Most of this research has already been reviewed in chapter 4 so in this chapter it is only necessary to integrate the relevant theories and findings required to assess the validity of the paradigm's fundamental assumptions. By reviewing research of the last ten years in terms of each assumption, it will be possible not only to assess potentially weak areas in each assumption but also to suggest how a new paradigm or different assumptions might correct these problems. The procedure for this review will be to treat the first and third assumptions in considerable detail. Since there is little work directly relevant to the second assumption, however, it will be assessed in light of the other two.

Once the research of the 1970s is reviewed, the most obvious conclusion to be drawn is that the ad hoc explanation on the youthfulness of the field has a great deal of merit. On the whole, the empirical research in the seventies has not only been more extensive, thorough, and sophisticated but has produced a number of important findings in the major subfields. These findings, once fully understood, belie some of the negative reviews of quantitative analysis that have grown in popularity in recent years (e.g., Waltz 1975:5–15). The explosion in quantitative research in the seventies, which uncovered some important nontrivial and nonobvious findings, suggests that the traditional argument against quantitative analysis was incorrect.

The ad hoc explanation on measurement error was probably only partially correct. More refined measures and sophisticated analysis of previously collected data did produce stronger findings (compare J. D. Singer and Small 1968 with Wallace 1973b and Bueno de Mesquita 1978). On the other hand, any measurement error produced by the data collection procedures was not so great as to require new data. Advancement has been attained by improving the analysis of existing data.

The existence of a body of strong findings does not change the assessment given in the last chapter on the adequacy of the realist paradigm; rather, it reinforces it, because now there are findings that would not be expected if the power politics explanations were accurate and the assumptions of the paradigm were valid. Of course, at this preliminary stage the research does not demonstrate conclusively the invalidity of the three assumptions, if indeed that were logically possible (since there can always be ad hoc explanations or theories to save the paradigm). The findings do, however, raise even more serious questions about the paradigm than the null findings in the sixties, and have already given rise to theories that deviate from the paradigm's assumptions.

The First Assumption

The first major assumption of the realist paradigm is that nation-states or their official decision makers are the most important actors in international politics. At the core of the realist paradigm, the power politics explanation makes the additional assumption that nation-state behavior can be explained and predicted on the basis of a rational-actor model. The accuracy and validity of this model has been seriously questioned by the findings of recent research in several of the subfields.

As might be expected, among the work that has undercut this model the most has been that associated with social and cognitive psychology. Experimental studies in this area have been employed to develop propositions on global political behavior in foreign policy making, deterrence and bargaining, and the causes of war. In each case, the belief that the nation-state can be understood as a rational actor or treated as a single collectivity for the purpose of analysis is called into serious question. The remainder of this section will examine the extent to which these two separate criticisms, rationality and treating states as a collectivity, are valid.

The work on foreign policy making relevant to this question can be divided into three areas: information processing; general decision making; and crisis decision making. The rational-actor model as employed by power politics theorists assumes that decision makers will behave in a similar fashion and will be affected not by personal or other idiosyncratic factors but only by the nature of the situation and the structure of the global environment (see Wolfers 1959). They then go on to argue that foreign policy can be deduced by seeing how any decision maker would pursue a nation's interest by acting on the basis of its selfish interest (see Morgenthau 1951).

Even though the rational-actor model employed by the power politics theorists is a more sophisticated and less stringent version of the rational decision-making model discussed in public administration,[1] it has been undercut by recent research in psychology. The first argument against the model is that individuals and groups generally do not make decisions in a rational manner, because they process information not on the basis of logical rules but on the basis of a set of psychological principles which do not necessarily correspond with logical reasoning (see Jervis 1976; Janis and Mann 1977). Generalizing from numerous studies in psychology and examining their plausibility to explain a number of diplomatic and historical events, Jervis (1976) argues that decision makers process information in terms of images they have developed of other actors and of the environment. These images are a product of past interactions and particularly of intense learning during traumatic experiences. These lessons of the past are often overgeneralized, producing inappropriate analogies (Jervis 1976:chap. 6; see also May 1973). New information that conforms to existing images tends to be emphasized, and information that is dissonant with the images is often not seen, ignored, or explained away (Jervis 1976:chaps. 5 and 7). Especially during crisis situations, overreliance on images and analogies to what worked in the past plays an important role in decision making (Jervis 1976:chap. 6; C. F. Hermann 1972a).

1. When assessing the rational-actor model, it is important that the specific version of this model used in power politics be analyzed. Otherwise there is a danger of criticizing a model that is an ideal type that no one really accepts as an accurate description or explanation of behavior.

These are strong tendencies, but this model does not mean that good decisions cannot be made or that the tendencies cannot be controlled. Jervis (1976:pp. 3–10, 165–172) relies on the example of scientific reasoning to show that such tendencies do not necessarily result in disastrous information processing. Nevertheless, it is clear that models of action, particularly foreign policy action, based on the assumption of selfish interest and/or calculation of costs and benefits, are too simplistic either as descriptions or predictions of behavior, and certainly as explanations. While the work of Jervis (1976) clearly undercuts the first assumption, it only raises serious questions and is not definitive because he provides mostly anecdotal and not replicable evidence for the countermodel. His most convincing evidence comes from experiments in another field (see also Janis and Mann 1977).

The second argument against the power politics version of the rational-actor model is that, since certain types of individuals and specific kinds of groups behave differently, it is incorrect to assume that they would all behave rationally. This means that a state's foreign policy cannot be deduced on the basis of a rational national-interest calculus, because personal and/or idiosyncratic factors affect individual behavior, and internal structural characteristics affect group decision making. There is some scientific evidence within the field relevant to this problem, consisting mostly of some experiments conducted with the Inter-Nation Simulation.

The findings from INS strongly support the claim that different individuals make different kinds of foreign policy. They show that persons who have a simple cognitive structure tend to be more aggressive (Driver 1965); persons who are more nationalistic or militaristic tend to escalate more quickly (Crow and Noel 1965:8, 20); and persons who are rigid tend to view the world in terms of good and evil (M. J. Shapiro 1966) (all cited in Guetzkow 1968:211–225; see also Guetzkow and Valadez 1981b).

The major reason this research has not received more attention within the discipline is the belief that real decision makers facing real situations would not behave in this manner. This objection has been handled in part by Margaret Hermann (1974), who compared personality and other individual characteristics of heads of state with the foreign policy of their nation-state. Although her sample was quite small, her evidence is very consistent with the claim that decision makers do not all behave the same way. She found that when heads of state are very nationalistic, have a simple cognitive structure, and do not have confidence in their ability to control events, their nation tends to be conflict-prone, to act unilaterally, and not to commit many resources (M. G. Hermann 1974:220–223). Evidence consistent with these findings is provided by Etheredge (1978), whose sample was larger.

It might be argued that such tendencies would be reduced in a group situation. Even though such a claim does not adequately account for M. G. Hermann's analysis, the research on this question suggests that this potential claim lacks merit and that the group structure itself introduces factors that make decision making deviate from directions that would be necessary for the power politics model to hold. One of the more popular propositions along these lines was the "groupthink" hypothesis offered by Janis (1972), which claimed that a group accentuates nonrational tendencies in the way it processes information (see also J. Thompson 1968; and Janis and Mann 1977). In a theoretical article, Charles Hermann (1978) stipulated the structural characteristics of a group that will encourage certain kinds of information processing and foreign policy behavior. A preliminary empirical test (M. G. Hermann, C. F. Hermann, and Dixon 1979) shows that there is an interaction effect between the structure of the group and the personal characteristics of decision makers and the foreign policy behavior of nation-states.

It must be emphasized that all these findings are preliminary and suggestive. They can all be criticized on methodological grounds, but as research continues the methodological objections are answered. To the extent the findings remain consistent in light of this further research, the more difficult it is to reject the findings for methodological reasons.

Studies of this kind have led some to try to explain or at least describe and predict foreign policy behavior by reconstructing the particular cognitive processes that specific decision makers might use in interpreting information and making a decision. The major work associated with this effort is the operational code approach of Alexander George (1969) and Ole Holsti (1970; 1976); the work on cognitive maps by Robert Axelrod (1976a; 1976b); the attempt of Bonham and Shapiro (1973; 1976) to simulate these cognitive processes with foreign policy data; and the cybernetic decision-making model of Steinbruner (1974), which attempts to combine some of the cognitive models with the bureaucratic models of Allison and Halperin (1972). Each of these related approaches suggests that foreign policy behavior can be described adequately and to a certain extent even predicted (see Bonham and Shapiro 1976) by using a cognitive approach. The more serious problem is how to convert this description into a theoretically significant explanation (O. R. Holsti 1976).

One way to do this is to ask new questions. For Holsti (1976:40–41), research topics on the decision maker as believer, perceiver, information processor, strategist, and learner now become pressing areas of inquiry. All this suggests that nation-labeling shorthands (like "England") that were adopted in the field can no longer be legitimately accepted. Instead, it appears necessary to start from the beginning. Fortunately, an extensive body of research in a sister discipline, psychology, provides a wealth of information and models that now have new relevance.

If these concerns were thought to affect decision making generally, their impact was seen as even greater under conditions of crisis. It was in the study of crises that the concerns with cognitive processes and group dynamics were first raised (R. C. Snyder and Paige 1958; Robinson and Snyder 1965; Pruitt 1965; Paige 1968; C. F. Hermann 1969a). Because of this initial concern, more research exists on crisis decision making than in any other area of foreign policy making. O. R. Holsti and George (1975) have reviewed the major research in this area in order to develop a theory of the effects of stress on decision making. They argued that, on the individual level, stress increases the effects of subjective appraisal, the reliance on cognitive as opposed to logical processes, and the impact of personality (O. R. Holsti and George 1975:302). The usual result is to produce a reduced attention span, greater cognitive rigidity, and a reduced time perspective (more concern with short-term than with long-term consequences). These factors tend to reduce receptivity to new information and tolerance for ambiguity, and to increase reliance on past experience and stereotyping (O. R. Holsti and George 1975:284). At the group level, high stress produces a smaller group and greater cohesion. These, in turn, generally restrict diversity of views and produce greater pressure for conformity, including putting the interest of the group before that of any particular member. While the latter may save the group from a deviating member, there is a danger of "groupthink."

At both the individual and group level, high stress tends to produce a decision-making process characterized by a restricted search for information, a reduced analysis and evaluation of alternative consequences, and a reduced choice of alternative policies (O. R. Holsti and George 1975: 284, 292). While such processes can increase the efficiency of decision making and reduce the impact of parochial interests (particularly of bureaucracies or of deviating individuals), the way in which information is processed does not conform to the assumption of the power politics explanation, which is that understanding reality is not a major obstacle once the role of power is appreciated. Instead, this research suggests that images arise in order to cope with information processing and that these images are subject to a number of perceptual distortions. Since these images can vary with different types of individuals, the foreign policy of a state cannot be deduced or explained by a rational-actor national interest perspective.

In addition to the work from psychology, the rational-actor model has also been criticized from a bureaucratic and organizational perspective. The bureaucratic view, as pointed out by Allison (1971) and Halperin (1974) (see also Allison and Halperin 1972), suggests that foreign policy is a product not of external politics but of internal political pressures and fights. This, of course, implies that personal, subnational, or organizational/bureaucratic interests, not solely the national interests, govern foreign policy making. In a further elaboration of organizational tendencies, Steinbruner (1974) treated foreign policy decision making as if it were a simple cybernetic system that responds to stimuli in terms of standard (almost programmed) operating procedures that permit little innovation or flexibility. Such a perspective obviously undercuts much of the power politics explanation; but, aside from several case studies (see Halperin and Kanter 1973), it is difficult to find a test that adequately measures the impact of bureaucratic and organizational factors.

The quantitative studies that come closest to fulfilling this requirement are those of Phillips and Crain (1974), Tanter (1974), and McCormick (1975). Each found that, except in a crisis situation, the foreign policy actions of states do not correlate as strongly with the actions others take toward them (reciprocity) as they do with their own previous actions. In other words, if one wants to know what the United States will do toward the USSR tomorrow, one should not look at what the USSR has done or is doing to the United States, but at what the United States did to the USSR yesterday. While such behavior could be seen as reflecting a basic rationale, it is also consistent with the view that foreign policy is a function of bureaucratic inertia and unchanging images.[2]

The best evidence that images play a predominant role in foreign policy making comes from the work on mirror images. While there have been a number of theoretical analyses on mirror images (White 1965; 1966; Bronfenbrenner 1961) as well as White's (1970) review of several cases, the best quantitative study is Gamson and Modigliani's (1971) study of the Cold War. They examine alternative belief systems (or explanations) of the Cold War, including the ones accepted by the respective official decision makers, and find that there is very little correspondence between the images each side has of the other and the way the other side behaves. On the other hand, self-images do account for one's own behavior. This means that each side refuses to accept the image that best predicts the other side's behavior. These findings support the mirror-image hypothesis and show that cognitive processes can have an impact not only on individual decisions but on the basic rationale and world view underlying a state's foreign policy.

The preceding evidence suggests that foreign policy is not based on a rational calculation of the national interest. Any alternative paradigm that sought to explain foreign policy would have to develop a set of concepts that would not only provide an accurate prediction of foreign

2. It should be pointed out, as O. R. Holsti and George (1975:295–300) have, that one of the "beneficial" effects of crisis is to eliminate or reduce this inertia. Unfortunately, stress has other "dysfunctional" effects.

policy output but a description of the role of cognitive and bureaucratic factors. One hopes that an explanation of these factors could be given in a theoretical manner that would reintroduce the effect of the foreign policies of other states. The major deficiency of the cognitive and bureaucratic approaches to date has been their failure to give a parsimonious explanation of when and why certain processes govern decision making. One way to do this would be to supplement a rational cost-benefit calculus with psychological decision-making calculi and then explain under what conditions decision makers or groups are likely to employ each calculus.

If these criticisms of the power politics explanation of foreign policy making are correct, then the errors made at this level of analysis must inevitably affect the predictions realists make about inter-state interactions. Again, the empirical evidence is only preliminary and limited, but there is enough to suggest that rational-actor models cannot account for behavior in the two circumstances in which realist explanations would be expected to be most applicable—crisis interactions and the onset of war. In both cases, serious questions have been raised about the validity of a rational-actor model.

If adherents to the realist paradigm have claimed anything for their paradigm, it has been its ability to explain the struggle for power. The failure to account for this behavior is a serious anomaly requiring explanation. The scientific study of inter-state interactions during crises is just beginning, with the major studies being those of McClelland (1961; 1968; 1972a); O. R. Young (1968); Azar (1972); and G. H. Snyder and Diesing (1977). Of these, only the last is directly relevant to the rational-actor model. An examination of three models—a rational maximizing utility model; a bounded rationality model (similar to Simon's [1957] model); and a bureaucratic model—resulted in Diesing's (G. H. Snyder and Diesing 1977:chap. 5) conclusion that the assumptions for the use of a rational cost-benefit analysis are rarely met and, more important, that actors do not exhibit the kinds of bargaining behavior that would be expected if this model were adequate. Glenn Snyder (G. H. Snyder and Diesing 1977:348, 407–408) dissented from this conclusion, arguing that the evidence is not as clear or as damaging as Diesing maintained. Both agreed, however, that the bounded rationality model, which includes elements drawn from cognitive psychology, provided a better fit for decision making. They suggested that this model was an ideal type and that the bureaucratic model supplemented it. They also suggested when and why deviations would be likely to occur (G. H. Snyder and Diesing 1977:405–407). In particular, the combination of bounded rationality and bureaucracy was seen as the best explanation of how inter-state interactions change each state's behavior.

Equally interesting and relevant is their analysis of information processing and decision makers' definitions of the situation. Their examination of cases led both Snyder and Diesing to reject rational utility models employed in a game-theoretic analysis of crisis bargaining in favor of a model that took into account differing perceptions and misunderstandings. Unlike a power politics perspective, their model did not assume that the power structure will be accurately perceived and/or make behavior conform to certain patterns. Of critical importance for Snyder and Diesing were decision makers' images and whether they were "hardliners" or "soft-liners." This dichotomy, although somewhat simple, makes the analysis much more theoretical and less descriptive than the work on operational codes and cognitive maps in the foreign policy subfield. Snyder and Diesing's analysis fits in nicely with the work on mirror images, brings in important political variables, and gives a role to the kind of bureaucratic and domestic political in-fighting that Neustadt (1970) discussed. Their analysis suggests that the decision process that produces strategies is not a function of the kinds of power calculations that Morgenthau and other realists talked about.

Even more damaging to the first assumption of the realist paradigm has been the empirical analysis of deterrence theory and coercive bargaining. This has been more damaging because deterrence theory is an elaboration of the realist paradigm and does not rely solely on the power politics framework; for it to fail indicates the need for more radical changes. The comparative case studies of George and Smoke (1974), the earlier analyses of Rapoport (1964) and Russett (1963b), as well as the studies of Morgan (1977) and Jack Snyder (1978), all undermined the empirical accuracy of most of the propositions on deterrence and compellence. The primary criticism of the work of Kahn, Schelling, and others was that decision makers (even when advised by the strategic experts) do not think in the rational terms the theory says they should and do not engage in the predicted kinds of behavior. In addition, the behavior they do engage in has consequences that are not anticipated by the theory (see George and Smoke 1974; Russett 1963b). If this theory cannot account for American behavior, one cannot help but doubt its relevance for decision makers who have a different culture, history, language, and ideology.

The evidence on deterrence theory is building slowly, and it all suggests the same conclusion—that images and perceptions are much more critical than rational calculations. Snyder and Diesing showed that this is the case with game theory in particular, demonstrating that utility-maximizing approaches to game theory simply do not account for crisis behavior as well as other models do. They found that contending actors often had different perceptions of the situation, and they used this insight to expand and enrich the conventional typology of games (zero-sum, Prisoner's Dilemma, Chicken) into such games as Bully, Big Bully, Protector, Deadlock, Called Bluff, Protector, and Critical Risk (G. H. Snyder and Diesing 1977:chap. 2). Again, while the evidence is not complete, the direction of the findings is consistent with what was found in the last chapter. As the assumptions of rationality are abandoned, explanations of behavior are bound to be more accurate. In addition, this research suggests the kinds of variables and research topics that might be necessary to develop a more complete and adequate paradigm.

Some of the research on the causes of war also undercuts the rationality assumption. For power politics theorists, war should not be a product of misperception, and yet there is now some strong evidence from the 1914 studies and from the theoretical work of Ralph White (1966; 1970; see also Stoessinger 1961; 1971; Heradstveit 1979) to suggest that misperception plays an important role in the onset of war. War is not the rational or Machiavellian calculation and test of strength that many realists implied. Many wars start by reaching a point of no return beyond which all are helpless (Russett 1962b). Elements of anger, frustration, and hostility (O. R. Holsti, North, and Brody 1968; O. R. Holsti 1972), perhaps fueled by status inconsistency (Wallace 1973a), create a hostile spiral that results in war (see J. D. Singer 1958). Wars like this become wars that everyone wants and at the same time nobody wants.

The cognitive and psychological aspects of the onset of war have clearly been underemphasized by the realist paradigm generally and by power politics explanations specifically. To claim, however, that all wars are avoidable if cooler heads prevail, or if decision makers perceive their true interests and each other's motives accurately, is to go to the opposite extreme and make the same kind of idealist errors that led to the realist reaction in the first place. The recent research on war and misperception, when combined with earlier realist insights on the importance of conflict of interest, suggests that hard-line and soft-line views are both too simplistic. On a more theoretical level, any alternative paradigm will need at minimum a typology of wars that can adequately distinguish wars that result from misperception from those that do not, and a theory that can explain why each type is different and the conditions under which each is likely to occur. The research on misperception and war points to a deficiency in the realist paradigm and in the rational-actor model, but it fails to deal with the realist critique of soft-line foreign policy. Any successful competitor of the realist paradigm must fill that gap and develop a theory of war broader than the one on misperception.

After the criticism of the rational-actor model, the two other major areas of the first assumption of the realist paradigm that have been criticized are the notion that nation-states are unitary actors and the idea that non–state actors are relatively unimportant. The idea of the nation-state as a unitary actor is sometimes referred to as the *billiard ball model*, or *black-boxing international politics* (Burton et al. 1974:6). Clearly, the research of G. H. Snyder and Diesing (1977) and of Jervis (1976), as well as the theoretical work of Allison (1971) and Halperin (1974), raises serious questions about treating decision making in a state as if the state were a single collectivity. Nation-states may not have a single interest or a single coherent policy developed by a cohesive group; instead, the foreign policy of a state may very well reflect internal political outcomes. In light of the research mentioned here, it cannot be automatically assumed that the state is a unitary actor; rather, this must be investigated empirically to determine which states can be treated in a billiard ball fashion and whether they can be treated that way in all issue areas.

The problem with treating the nation-state as a unitary actor is primarily conceptual. Is it, for example, better to treat Chile as a single nation-state with a government and foreign policy, or as a set of competing and conflicting groups fighting over who should control the economic resources and the governmental apparatus of the state? In the latter conception, the nation-state is not even seen as an entity, but as the territorial location of the battle and as a set of political institutions which, if controlled by one of the groups, gives that group additional resources and weapons. In such a conceptualization, the real groups or entities in politics might be seen as classes (see Wallerstein 1976) or transnational coalitions among groups (see Galtung 1971; Kaiser 1971). In this perspective, the concepts of penetration and imperialism would be used to determine the real coalitions in the world. To a certain extent, the realist proscription against interference in the internal politics of another nation-state has made it tardy in recognizing the extent to which penetration and transnational coalitions have played an important role in world politics.

Questions such as these have led to a greater focus on the non–state actors that were playing an important political role. The role of multinational corporations, either as mechanisms of technology transfer or as agents of neo-colonialism, was investigated by a number of scholars, all of whom agreed that these entities could not be seen as handmaidens of nation-states (although there was less agreement about whether they were handmaidens of a particular class). The role of corporations in controlling oil and in the production of food on the global level and the role of the International Monetary Fund and the International Bank for Reconstruction and Development in controlling states' economies has also pointed out the limited view presented by a so-called state-centric perspective. Finally, the de-emphasis on intergovernmental organizations in the realist paradigm has been seen as hiding their current and potential role in creating global regulations (Keohane and Nye 1974; 1977).

Unfortunately, most of this work has either been conceptual or has consisted of case studies. A better way of testing each perspective is needed. To a certain extent, this is provided by Mansbach, Ferguson, and Lampert (1976), whose quantitative examination of the role of non–state actors permits the evidence to falsify their claims. They find that non–state actors play an important role in understanding conflict and that their influence varies according to the region and issue area. In addition, their data suggest that the unitary model of behavior may not be as useful a model as looking at specific intragovernmental actors (see Mansbach et al. 1976:chap. 11).

The work on transnational relations, non–state actors, and neo-colonialism has made a strong case against the conceptualization of the world along state-centric lines. How devasting this is for the realist paradigm is an open question. It is clear that a truly transnational society has not emerged and does not seem likely to do so in the near future. Since this is the case, it is then a relatively simple matter for adherents of the realist paradigm to include those non–state actors that are important without changing very much in their analysis. Since the realist paradigm never totally ignored non–state actors, the criticism posed by a transnational perspective can be interpreted as one of emphasis. Indeed, one could argue that the realist concern with sovereignty is simply an idealist, legalistic vestige and that a true analysis of power would certainly look at penetration. In all these ways, the transnational criticism is considerably less radical than is often implied.

The review of the first assumption suggests that it is an inadequate guide to inquiry because the behavior of nation-states cannot be explained solely by the power realities of world politics. This is because individual decision makers will differ, and the ability of governments to act in a unitary fashion will vary. Recent research has delineated the pitfalls of trying to deduce the foreign policy of a state by using a rational-actor model. In addition, the bureaucratic politics perspective has caused questions to be raised about the potency of external factors on the foreign policy of a state in noncrisis situations. Finally, the presence of non–state actors and the role they play in penetration has raised questions about the fundamental conception provided by the paradigm's state-centric emphasis.

The Third Assumption

The third assumption of the realist paradigm maintains that international politics is a struggle for power and peace. This is a picture of the world, and as such it is very difficult to determine whether this picture, as opposed to some other picture, is a useful guide to inquiry. The analysis in the previous chapter raised serious questions about the picture by examining its research output; this section will examine it more directly by asking whether this picture of the world has produced explanations that provide a complete and accurate understanding of global behavior.

The major claim that can be made against the third assumption, particularly in its classic power politics format, is that *realpolitik* explanations do not provide a theory of world politics, but merely an image that decision makers can have of the world. Power politics is not so much an explanation as a description of one type of behavior found in the global political system. If this is correct, then power politics behavior itself must be explained; it does not explain.

As an image of the world employed by policy makers, power politics promotes certain kinds of behavior and often leads to self-fulfilling prophecies. An adequate theory of world politics would seek to discover when policy makers adopt a power politics image of the world, what kinds of behavior this image fosters, and when such behavior results in war. If this approach is correct, then it should be possible to find non–power politics behavior and to develop a theory of what conditions promote power politics and non–power politics behavior, and how a system or issue area characterized by one mode of behavior might be transformed to the other. Such an approach would provide an authentic alternative to the realist paradigm because it would not only explain everything the realist paradigm purported to explain but would also discover and explain a vast area of behavior that the realist paradigm purportedly ignored.

How does one tell if this second approach is more adequate? There are two possible tests. The first is to see if power politics behavior is just one kind of behavior in the world, and the second is to see if the realist paradigm's explanations of power politics behavior are adequate. The first test can be reduced to the claim that power politics behavior is historically contingent and confined to certain issue areas, and that an examination of other historical periods or issue areas will not reveal any power politics behavior. Power politics behavior can be defined as perceptions of insecurity (the security dilemma); struggles for power; the use of Machiavellian stratagems; the presence of coercion; attempts to balance power; and the use of war to settle disputes. In certain historical eras, particularly during the twentieth century periods associated with World War I, World War II, and the Cold War, this kind of behavior proliferated. In other periods, 1816–1870 and most of the Middle Ages, for example, this sort of behavior did not predominate. Even in times when it did, power politics tended to be characteristic mainly of big power diplomacy on certain issues. For other aspects of world politics, like the spread of imperialism, the anticolonial struggles, and the emergence of neo-colonialism, power politics did not provide an appropriate explanation or image. From this perspective, the realists' main error has been to confuse certain periods of history with all of history, and certain issues with the entire population of issues. As Jervis (1976:chap. 6) would claim, the traumatic lessons learned from the past were overgeneralized.

While there has been little historical research on this question (see Luard 1976, for an exception), there has been an increasing realization that the coming of détente and the ending of the Cold War inaugurated a period of superpower relations that may not be fully apprehended through a power politics prism (see McClelland 1977). When this phenomenon is coupled with some of the major economic transformations occurring along North-South lines, many scholars have seen national security issues and their power politics prone behavior being replaced by other issues (see Morse 1976; and Keohane and Nye 1977).

The analysis of issue areas suggests to some that power politics behavior is confined to territorial and military issues and does not reflect behavior in other issue areas (particularly economic questions, but also other transnational areas that need regulation—e.g., food, the sea, the environment, air travel, etc.). Handelman et al. (1973), Coplin (1974: chap. 13), Kihl (1971), Hopkins and Puchala (1978), and Vasquez (1974b) have given credence to this view, and a data-based study of issue areas by O'Leary (1976) shows that behavior does vary by issue area. This suggests that a period that appears power politics prone is probably dominated by certain kinds of issues or some other issue characteristic (see Dean and Vasquez 1976:18–28). An issue politics paradigm could provide a very attractive alternative to the realist paradigm in that it provides a broader perspective that explains both power politics and non–power politics behavior and the relationship between the two. Before such a paradigm can be taken seriously, however, it requires a real theory, not just a framework, and some supporting evidence. By the end of the 1970s, unfortunately, neither was forthcoming.[3] These criticisms of the realist paradigm raise conceptual problems that the paradigm's adherents must address and that may with further work provide important anomalies.

3. This author has over the years attempted to develop elements of an issue theory of politics (see Vasquez 1974b; Dean and Vasquez 1976; Vasquez 1976a). A theory of world politics that is based on an issue politics paradigm and that is as complete and as policy relevant as the power politics explanations of the realist paradigm is now in the process of being completed; see Mansbach and Vasquez (1981b).

Since research on issues and on non–power politics behavior is still limited, greater reliance must be put on a second test: Does power politics explain what it purports to explain best? A review of the research of the 1970s is more satisfying than the review of the research of the 1960s; now that there are stronger findings, a better assessment of this question can be made. The answer seems to be that the realist paradigm has produced some findings, but that on the whole it has failed to account for a great deal of behavior it would have been expected to predict. Furthermore, the areas in which it has successfully generated predictions have been better predicted by non–power politics propositions.

The assessment will focus on the area that has been the major concern of the realist paradigm—the analysis of conflict struggles and of the onset of war. In both these areas, the failures and successes of the realist paradigm, particularly the central part of it, power politics, will be reviewed. Next, findings from non–power politics explanations, which might serve as possible anomalies for the paradigm, will be reviewed.

As mentioned earlier, the power politics approach has prided itself on its ability to explain and guide the struggle for power. Several of the strategies it prescribes have been tested by Russell Leng (1980) to see if following those strategies produces the predicted consequences. He then tested a counterrealist model. His analysis produced mixed results. On the one hand, he found, as realists would predict, that threats are somewhat more successful than promises in getting adversaries to do what one wants, and that, as negative inducements increase, the probability of compliance increases. He also found, however, as the counterrealist model he tested predicted, that when controlling for the power of the contending parties, defiance, not compliance, was the consequence of threats, and at times this defiance in the face of threats can lead to a cycle of interaction that produces war. These latter findings, although only preliminary because of the sample size, suggest that a power politics strategy will not work with actors that are relatively equal in power, and that to take a consistently hard line often results in war.

Similar kinds of lock-in, no-escape spirals were found by G. H. Snyder and Diesing (1977:chap. 2). They found that pure hard-line strategies are not always successful and do not always avoid war. Their empirical investigation of successful strategies shows that there is a need to combine coercion, persuasion, and accommodation with trust and face-saving techniques (Snyder and Diesing 1977:chap. 3). Other empirical studies have produced findings consistent with these (see George, Hall, and Simons 1971; O. R. Young 1968:chap. 9; McClelland 1972a).

A related weakness within the realist paradigm is its relative inability to offer detailed strategic guidance when compared to the more social psychological orientation reflected in Morton Deutsch (1973) or in Rubin and Brown (1975). Whereas social psychological models have been developed and tested and can explain and apprehend different stages of the bargaining process, realism seems to flounder and rely on insight and the "art" of diplomacy. In this sense, the realist paradigm has failed to provide much understanding of the dynamics of bargaining, even though specific findings may sometimes be consistent with its propositions.

The inability to understand the dynamics of interaction is best reflected in the inability of power politics explanations to account for why and when the struggle for power approaches or degenerates into a state of war. J. D. Singer (1980:xxiv–xxvi) and his associates in the Correlates of War project stipulate the following temporal stages in a conflict system: (1) a rivalry between states in which each party is salient to the other and they both have an above average conflict pattern; (2) a "disputatiousness" stage in which behavior is designed to thwart or punish the other side; (3) the escalation of one serious dispute to war. The realist paradigm relies on several power explanations to explain the transition from each stage, and recent research in the field raises questions about the validity of these explanations and whether they are more useful than other approaches.

Among the strongest findings associated with the realist paradigm are those on the magnitude and severity of war. Michael Haas (1970; 1974:chap. 10) found that different types of systems (bipolarity, multipolarity) have different kinds of wars, with bipolar systems having infrequent but severe wars and multipolar systems having frequent but less severe wars. Wallace (1973b) found that severe wars are most apt to occur when there is very high polarity (many actors and few alliances) and very low polarity (few actors and many alliances). He interprets this finding to mean that when there are no alliances the weak fall victim to the strong, and when there are many alliances, intense rivalry and preparation for war develop. Similarly, Bueno de Mesquita (1978) found that, for the twentieth century, increasing tightness (more alliance bonds) is associated with longer wars.

Less clear-cut are the relationships between alliances and the presence or absence of war. J. D. Singer and Small (1968) did not find any relationship between the number of wars and the number of alliance bonds in the system. Reanalyzing this data, Ostrom and Hoole (1978) found that within the first three years after alliances are made, there is a significant positive relationship with the onset of war; four to twelve years after they are made there is a negative relationship; and after twelve years there is no relationship. This very descriptive statistical analysis suggests that alliances do not prevent war but are indicators of preparation for war. Bueno de Mesquita (1978) found little relationship between the type of alliance system and the occurrence of war; but he did find that increasing systemic tightness in the twentieth century does lead to war, whereas declining tightness (fewer alliance bonds) does not. All these suggest that the balance of power and alliance aggregation generally do not prevent war, but are preparations for war. This conclusion is given further support by an examination of the balance of power during its heyday, 1870–1881 by Rosecrance et al. (1974), who found that there was no relationship between the balance of power and conflict.

The studies on polarity and on the balance of power pose anomalies for the realist paradigm, or at least that aspect of it that places emphasis on alliances as a way toward peace. In the mid-sixties, many scholars debated whether a bipolar or multipolar system would produce peace. If the realist paradigm were an adequate guide to inquiry, at least one side would have been expected to be correct. Instead, both were wrong. The only major difference is whether one will pay the Grim Reaper all at once with a few severe wars, or on the installment plan with many wars.

It is now clear that alliances do not produce peace but lead to war. Alliance making is an indicator that there is a danger of war in the near future (less than four years). This means that the attempt to balance power is itself part of the very behavior that leads to war. This conclusion supports the earlier claim that power politics is an image of the world that encourages behavior that helps bring about war. Since it is now known that alliances, no matter what their form, do not bring about peace, the theoretically interesting question is what causes actors to seek alliances. This question begins to push beyond the parameters of the third assumption.

Although the findings on alliances are not very promising for the realist paradigm, some will point out that many realists, for example Morgenthau (1960, 1973:chap. 14), were among the first to delineate the problems in using the balance of power as a peace mechanism. For them, not alliances but the actual distribution of power is critical. Here, as J. D. Singer, Bremer, and Stuckey (1972) make clear, there are two contradictory propositions in the realist tradition. One maintains that power parity prevents war, because no side will initiate a war unless it is sure of winning. The other maintains that preponderance of power prevents war, because no side will initiate war unless it has a chance of winning. The findings produced in this study are among the most impressive for the realist paradigm and power politics. Singer, Bremer, and Stuckey found a strong relationship between parity of power and peace for the nineteenth century, but a moderate relationship between preponderance and peace in the twentieth century. This is an important finding, indicating that power politics explanations can produce strong correlations, but at the same time it poses something of an anomaly, because there is no theoretical reason (and the one offered by Singer et al. appears very weak) for why one relationship should hold in one century and the opposite should hold in the next.

In related studies, Bremer (1980) and Ferris (1973) added evidence that power politics behavior itself leads to war. Bremer (1980:68–82) found that the more powerful states are, the more involved they become in wars. He concluded that this does not lend much credence to the often expressed view that strength is the best insurance against war. Ferris (1973:115–116) found that changes in the distribution of power in the system are related to the amount of war in the system. This means that changes in power are apt to set off a security dilemma and interstate rivalry. This interpretation is supported by Ferris's second and third findings, which maintain that the greater the disparity of power between states, or the greater the change in capability, the greater the probability that states will become involved in intense conflicts. While aspects of these findings lend some credence to power politics explanations, they also provide descriptions of power politics behavior that, if put in a broader theoretical perspective, could support an alternative to the realist paradigm.

The broader perspective, for which there is evidence, is the status explanation of conflict and war. Following Galtung (1964c), Michael Wallace (1972) has elaborated a status-inconsistency model that can incorporate many of the findings that support the realist paradigm into a nonrealist model with greater explanatory power. Before constructing this model, Wallace (1970; 1973a) attempted a direct comparison between status inconsistency explanations and distribution of power explanations and found the former more able to pass empirical tests. He then developed a path model which remains the most complete model of the onset of war to date. Wallace (1972) found that changes in the capability of states lead to status inconsistency. A system that is high in status inconsistency tends to promote alliance aggregation, which in turn tends to encourage arms races, which have a very strong correlation with war. This path to war, then, exemplifies a power politics syndrome and supports the claim that such behavior ends in war. Its opposite, the path to peace, occurs when status inconsistency in the system is low. This is positively correlated with the number (and presumably the effectiveness) of IGOs, which are negatively correlated with arms races. The last path provides evidence that can be used to suggest that war is a way of making decisions, and that if certain images associated with power politics can be avoided, then alternative modes of decision making may work. Such an interpretation would place global decision making and the resolution of issues at the heart of analysis and see the struggle for power as a means to an end rather than the end itself.

Wallace's model is consistent with the findings of Choucri and North (1975), who maintained that war occurs because an increase in population, a need for resources, and technology encourage nations to expand abroad. This leads to an intersection of interests, which leads to a conflict of interests. With these come perceptions of threats, which are dealt with by increased military expenditures, alliances, and arms races. Under these conditions, crises tend to proliferate, and, because of the likelihood of misperception and a hostile spiral, one crisis is apt to be unsuccessfully managed and to result in war. In the period after 1870, that crisis occurred in 1914. Choucri and North's model is different from Wallace's in that it specifies more clearly the sources of status inconsistency, and in doing so relies on aspects of a Marxist analysis.

The findings on the causes of war, which is what the realist paradigm purported to explain and understand so much better than the idealist paradigm, appear in light of the preceding findings to pose an anomaly for the realist paradigm. Concepts such as the balance of power and national power have not resulted in propositions that have passed empirical tests in an unambiguous manner. In addition, other models, especially those associated with status, have provided better empirical results and a broader theoretical explanation, which supports the claim made here that power politics is a type of behavior that precedes war and is not an explanation of it. Further evidence for this view is provided by a status model of foreign policy behavior developed by Rummel (1972a).

Rummel (1972a) has produced two pieces of evidence that undercut the third assumption of the realist paradigm. The first is that status-field theory can produce very high correlations, indeed some of the strongest published in the 1970s, when used to predict general foreign policy behavior. The second is that as long as foreign policy behavior is treated as a unidimensional struggle characterized by conflict-cooperation, efforts to predict behavior will not be very successful. This is because conflict and cooperation are separate and uncorrelated dimensions, which means that the same variables cannot predict both. In a factor analysis of American foreign policy behavior, Rummel (1972a) found that it could be classified in six patterns: deterrence, Cold War, negative sanctions, foreign aid, Western European (type) cooperation, and Anglo-American (type) cooperation. Most of these patterns were predicted by looking at the attribute distances between the United States and the target state. Rummel's theory suggests that status-related explanations could provide a basis for explaining not only war but more general foreign policy behavior. It also provides critical evidence to show that inter-nation interactions should not be characterized along a simple conflict-cooperation dimension. This supports the contention that different issue areas encourage different behavior.

Toward a New Paradigm

What is significant about the preceding findings is not any single definitive finding (each individual piece of research could be challenged or explained away), but the consistent pattern that appears to be emerging from the research. As the field truly begins to progress, propositions based on realist assumptions do not do as well as those that reject realist assumptions. This conclusion holds for both the first assumption and the third, and for studies dealing with both foreign policy and the causes of war. Specific research findings have been produced that would not have been expected if power politics explanations were accurate, and realist assumptions seem to ignore certain phenomena or ways of perceiving these phenomena that have later led to important theoretical explanations and accurate predictions. While there is no need at this point to decide whether the realist paradigm should be rejected, it can be concluded that the research of the seventies has called that paradigm into question, that the paradigm has still failed to satisfy the criteria of accuracy and centrality, and that it has satisfied the criterion of scientific importance less well than status, social psychological, or cognitive psychological explanations of global behavior.

In light of this conclusion, a few words can be said about the realist paradigm's second assumption. The studies based on status and psychological models challenge this assumption by showing that a theory based at the individual or group level can account for behavior at the global level. This finding is emerging in a number of the social sciences, which suggests that there will not be a single theory of economics, politics, sociology, psychology, and world politics, but a single theory for each topic that cuts across these fields. Thus, one might expect a single theory of perception, of information processing, of decision making, of interaction, of conflict, and of violence. Each of these theories could then be adapted to fit the peculiar circumstances of a specific discipline, much as theories of mechanics are adapted to take cognizance of climatic and atmospheric conditions. This suggests that international relations inquiry should become more interdisciplinary than it has been and that it should incorporate more general political science theory and research. In particular, it should take a more general definition of politics, perhaps David Easton's (1965b:50) "authoritative allocation of values," and help develop a general theory of how collectivities allocate values authoritatively under different conditions—with legitimate governments, with no government, etc. Now that the possibility has arisen that international politics is not necessarily a struggle for power and peace, a more general definition of politics may lead to a more correct view of the world that international relations scholars are trying to study.

If the analysis presented in this chapter and chapter 7 is correct, the most pressing task for the field is to develop an alternative paradigm. When the findings on status explanations are coupled with social psychological models, the elements of a potentially powerful nonrealist paradigm begin to take shape. While a detailed exposition of those elements is beyond the scope of this book, the general outlines can be suggested, and the major problems that a new paradigm must deal with can be delineated.

Attempting to create a new paradigm is no mean task, and the best way to begin is with a new definition of politics. A juxtaposition of Easton's (1965b:50) authoritative allocation of values with Morgenthau's (1948) struggle for power would probably lead to a number of insights. In particular, it would have the effect of putting issues at the center of any inquiry, thereby making power politics behavior and the kinds of issues associated with it but one aspect, albeit a very important one, of a general theory of world politics.

The next task would be to reconceptualize the major dependent variables in the field. Rummel (1972a) has already demonstrated empirically that the concept of conflict-cooperation does not provide a useful guide for predicting foreign policy behavior because these are two separate dimensions. This means that different models of each must be developed, and it suggests that the dynamics of conflict may be different from the dynamics of cooperation. Since this suggestion is not entirely incongruent with certain social psychological models (see M. Deutsch 1973), the latter might be helpful. In a similar vein, some of the findings on war, for example those on misperception and war, suggest that more attention to developing a theoretically based typology of wars might help produce stronger findings. Finally, much of the behavioral work in foreign policy has been confined to explaining conflict-cooperation or participation and has gone far astray from analyzing the substantive content that is usually referred to when speaking of the foreign policy of a nation. There is a pressing need to return to that original topic of inquiry.

The issue politics paradigm advocated by Coplin and O'Leary (1971; see also Coplin, O'Leary, and Mills 1972; Handelman et al. 1973) provides an alternative picture of the world that could aid in reconceptualizing each of the major dependent variables. For them, politics consists of raising and resolving issues. This means that the purpose of politics is to get a desired authoritative allocation of values for the issues that are considered the most salient. With this assumption, the struggle for power is only one aspect of behavior and a means to a greater end. If scholars took this assumption, the first thing they would want to explain about foreign policy is an actor's issue position on each issue on the global agenda. Next, they would want to explain the interactions actors take to get their issue position accepted. Interaction can involve conflict and cooperation, which might be distinguished along three lines: (1) differences (or agreement) in issue position; (2) the exchange of positive or negative acts as a way of changing the other side's issue position; and (3) the development of attitudes of friendship or hostility. Finally, scholars would want to know how an issue would be resolved, and how the values represented by that issue would be authoritatively allocated. There would be a need to develop a typology of allocation mechanisms, of which war would be one type.[4]

It should be clear from the literature review in this chapter and in chapter 4 that the explanation of each of the preceding topics will have to incorporate the findings on perception and information processing from cognitive and social psychology with the findings on the effect of status differences and inconsistency on foreign policy interactions and the onset of war. The development of such models and theories will be an immense task, but with more and more evidence emerging from empirical studies, as well as existing findings in related disciplines, the effort could take on the classic characteristics of a puzzle-solving activity. Before this can be done, a more adequate conceptual framework and set of assumptions about the world must be developed.

The Future of the Scientific Study of International Relations

The findings presented in this chapter and in chapter 7 present an anomaly for the field. The anomaly is that the extensive hypothesis testing that has been going on in the field has not produced many strong findings supporting the realist paradigm. This book claims that the reason there have been so few findings is that the realist paradigm is an inadequate guide to inquiry. Others, of course, will not be so quick to accept this conclusion. Nor should they be, since evidence is still coming in. Those who would reject the conclusion would turn to the two untested ad hoc explanations to support their position—youthfulness of the field and measurement error. Each of these explanations implies a different research strategy that scholars might use to deal with the anomaly. A review of these strategies will provide some guidance as to

4. Mid-range theories for each of these topics have been developed in Mansbach and Vasquez (1981b).

how scholarship in the field might proceed until the evidence on the realist paradigm becomes more definitive.

The ad hoc explanations that account for the absence of much produced knowledge in the field by attributing it to either the youthfulness of the field or measurement error imply that the anomaly is only temporary. These two explanations suggest that as more research is conducted, measurement will improve and the amount of produced knowledge will increase. The explanations imply that there is nothing seriously wrong with the realist paradigm. The strategy these explanations recommend to scholars is the continuation of research on realist hypotheses and the development of more sophisticated measures of realist concepts. Adopting this strategy has the advantage of allowing scholars to build on the extensive work already done. But the strategy has the disadvantage of not really permitting the two explanations to be falsified. For example, if continued research produces results, then it could be concluded that the explanations were correct. If continued research does not produce any results, however, it could always be argued that better measures or more time are needed. At some point the possibility must be faced that the paradigm, not the research, is inaccurate. Adherents to this position, therefore, must explain the emergence of new anomalies in the research conducted in the 1970s.

This book attributes the absence of many findings in the field to the dominance of an inadequate paradigm—that is, the realist paradigm. It assumes that although there may be some measurement error in research, the primary problem lies not in the research methodology of the field but in the incorrectness of the hypotheses that are being tested. Until a paradigm is found that shows promise of adequately explaining behavior, there will be no major progress in research. This implies that the realist paradigm must be rejected as the dominant paradigm in the field. Since the realist paradigm is not likely to be rejected in the absence of a better paradigm, the strategy that this explanation suggests is to have more paradigm diversity in the field.

Given these various explanations, what would be a good strategy for scholars in the field to adopt in order to increase the amount of knowledge produced in the field? One way of deciding on a strategy would be to adopt a procedure offered by Braybrooke and Lindblom (1963). They suggest that when knowledge of "causes" is limited, as they are in this case, decisions should be incremental (Braybrooke and Lindblom 1963:61–79). If this rule were used here, there would be no need to choose between the prescriptions offered by the various explanations. Aspects of both prescriptions could be followed and their consequences observed to see if they were aiding the field in producing knowledge.

What would such an incrementalist strategy look like? First, under this strategy the realist paradigm would not be rejected, nor would research on it cease. A number of large data projects in the field are producing new realist indicators. The rest of this decade will probably be needed to analyze this data fully. It would be foolish not to conduct this research given the tremendous amount of time and money already devoted to the projects. An evaluation of this research will provide further evidence on the adequacy of the realist paradigm. If at the end of this research not many findings are produced, then the realist paradigm could be rejected.

Second, given the absence of many findings to date, no new projects guided by the realist paradigm should be permitted to occupy a large amount of the intellectual energy and financial resources of the field. Rather, more attention should be devoted to developing new paradigms; articulating and elaborating already existing paradigms, such as Marxism, issue politics and transnational relations; and collecting data and conducting research on hypotheses derived from these new paradigms. This has already begun as the field enters the 1980s, which is good, because until such work is conducted, the adequacy of rival paradigms cannot be evaluated. Unless such work is encouraged and financed, adherents of the realist paradigm can always claim that, despite its poor performance, there is no rival available to replace the realist paradigm.

This incrementalist strategy has two advantages. First, if followed it would provide data to test the various explanations of the anomaly. Following the strategy would, in a sense, be a quasi-experiment. Further evidence would be provided on the fruitfulness of additional research on the realist paradigm and the adequacy of rival paradigms. Second, given the limited knowledge of the "causes" of the anomaly, the strategy would minimize costs by not acting on the basis of one explanation. If one explanation, for example, the argument on the youthfulness of the field, were accepted and turned out to be incorrect, then tremendous resources would have been wasted. By acting on the basis of both explanations, high risks are avoided.

It should be clear from the above strategy that periodic and systematic evaluation of research in the field is needed. Without evaluation it cannot be known how useful various research approaches are. The present analysis has attempted to demonstrate how quantitative analysis can be used to conduct such evaluations. In a field with few findings, there will always be questions about the utility of various paradigms. If the framework developed in this analysis allows these questions to be asked systematically and answered on the basis of evidence, it will have served its purpose.

References

Abolfathi, F. (1980) "Threat, public opinion, and military spending in the United States, 1980–1990," pp. 83–133 in P. J. McGowan and C. W. Kegley (eds.), Threats, Weapons, and Foreign Policy. Sage International Yearbook of Foreign Policy Studies, Vol. 5. Beverly Hills, Calif.: Sage Publications.

Abolfathi, F., J. J. Hayes, and R. Hayes (1979) "Trends in United States response to international crises: Policy implications for the 1980's," pp. 57–85 in C. W. Kegley and P. J. McGowan (eds.), Sage International Yearbook of Foreign Policy Studies, Vol. 4. Beverly Hills, Calif.: Sage Publications.

Abravanel, M., and B. Hughes (1975) "Public attitudes and foreign policy behavior in western democracies," pp. 46–73 in W. Chittick (ed.), The Analysis of Foreign Policy Outputs. Columbus, Ohio: Charles E. Merrill.

Agee, P. (1975) Inside the Company: A CIA Diary. Harmondsworth, England: Penguin.

Alcock, N. (1972) The War Disease. Oakville, Ontario: CPRI Press.

Alcock, N., and G. Kohler (1979) "Structural violence at the world level: Diachronic findings." Journal of Peace Research 16:255–262.

Alcock, N., and K. Lowe (1969) "The Vietnam war as a Richardson process." Journal of Peace Research 6:105–112.

Alcock, N., and A. G. Newcombe (1970) "The perception of national power." Journal of Conflict Resolution 14:335–343.

Alger, C. (1961) "Non-resolution consequences of the U.N. and their effect on international conflict." Journal of Conflict Resolution 5:128–145.

——— (1963) "Use of the inter-nation simulation in undergraduate teaching," pp. 150–189 in H. Guetzkow et al. Simulation in International Relations. Englewood Cliffs, N.J.: Prentice-Hall.

——— (1965) "Personal contact in intergovernmental organizations," pp. 523–547 in H. C. Kelman (ed.), International Behavior: A Social Psychological Analysis. New York: Holt, Rinehart and Winston.

——— (1966) "Interaction and negotiation in a committee of the United Nations General Assembly." Peace Research Society (International) Papers 5:141–159.

——— (1968) "Interaction in a committee of the U.N. General Assembly," pp. 51–84 in J. D. Singer (ed.), Quantitative International Politics. New York: The Free Press.

References

———— (1970) "Research on research: A decade of quantitative and field research on international organizations." International Organization 24:414–450.

Alger, C., and S. Brams (1967) "Patterns of representation in national capitals and intergovernmental organizations." World Politics 19:646–663.

Alker, H. R., Jr. (1964) "Dimensions of conflict in the general assembly." American Political Science Review 58:642–657.

———— (1965a) Mathematics and Politics. New York: Macmillan.

———— (1965b) "Supranationalism in the United Nations." Peace Research Society (International) Papers 3:197–212.

———— (1966) "The long road to international theory: Problems of statistical nonadditivity." World Politics 18:623–655.

———— (1971) "Research paradigms and mathematical politics." Paper presented at the 1971 IPSA Roundtable on "Quantitative Methods and Political Substance: Toward Better Research Strategies," Mannheim, Germany.

Alker, H. R., and P. F. Bock (1972) "Propositions about international relations," pp. 385–490 in J. Robinson (ed.), Political Science Annual, Vol. 3. Indianapolis: Bobbs-Merrill.

Alker, H. R., and D. Puchala (1968) "Trends in economic partnership: The North Atlantic Area, 1928–1963," pp. 287–316 in J. D. Singer (ed.), Quantitative International Politics. New York: The Free Press.

Alker, H. R., and B. M. Russett (1965) World Politics in the General Assembly. New Haven, Conn.: Yale University Press.

Allison, G. (1969) "Conceptual models and the Cuban missile crisis." American Political Science Review 63:689–718.

———— (1971) Essence of Decision: Explaining the Cuban Missile Crisis. Boston: Little, Brown.

Allison, G., and M. Halperin (1972) "Bureaucratic politics: A paradigm and some policy implications." World Politics 24(Supplement): 40–89.

Almond, G. A. (1950) The American People and Foreign Policy. New York: Harcourt, Brace and World.

———— (1960) "Introduction: A functional approach to comparative politics," pp. 3–65 in G. Almond and J. S. Coleman (eds.), The Politics of the Developing Areas. Princeton, N.J.: Princeton University Press.

Andriole, S. J., J. Wilkenfeld, and G. W. Hopple (1975) "A framework for the comparative analysis of foreign policy behavior." International Studies Quarterly 19:160–198.

Andriole, S. J., and R. A. Young (1977) "Toward the development of an integrated crisis warning system." International Studies Quarterly 21:107–150.

Angell, R. C. (1965) "An analysis of trends in international organizations." Peace Research Society (International) Papers 3:185–195.

———— (1967) "The growth of transnational participation." Journal of Social Issues 23:108–129.

———— (1969) Peace on the March: Transnational Participation. New York: Van Nostrand.

Armor, D., J. Giacquinta, R. McIntosh, and D. Russell (1967) "Professors' attitudes toward the Vietnam war." Public Opinion Quarterly 31:159–175.

Aron, R. (1955) The Century of Total War. Boston: Beacon Press.

———— (1966) Peace and War. New York: Doubleday.

Ashby, W. R. (1952) Design for a Brain. New York: John Wiley.

Ashley, R. K. (1976) "Noticing pre-paradigmatic progress," pp. 150–158 in J. Rosenau (ed.), In Search of Global Patterns. New York: The Free Press.

Austin, J. L. (1962) How to Do Things with Words. New York: Oxford University Press.

Axelrod, R. (ed.) (1976a) Structure of Decision. Princeton, N.J.: Princeton University Press.

———— (1976b) "Decision for neo–imperialism: The deliberations of the British eastern committee in 1918," pp. 77–95 in R. Axelrod (ed.), Structure of Decision. Princeton, N.J.: Princeton University Press.

Ayer, A. J. (1946) Language, Truth, and Logic. London: Victor Gollancz.

Azar, E. (1970) "Analysis of International Events." Peace Research Reviews 4:1–113.

———— (1972) "Conflict escalation and conflict reduction in an international crisis: Suez, 1956." Journal of Conflict Resolution 16:183–201.

———— (1980) "The conflict and peace data bank (COPDAB) project." Journal of Conflict Resolution 24:143–152.

Azar, E., and J. D. Ben-Dak (eds.) (1975) Theory and Practice of Events Research. London: Gordon and Breach.

Azar, E., and T. Havener (1976) "Discontinuities of the symbolic environment: A problem in scaling events." International Interactions 2:231–246.

Baldwin, D. A. (1974) "The power of positive sanctions." World Politics 24:19–38.

Ball, M. (1951) "Bloc voting in the general assembly." International Organization 5:3–31.

Banks, A. S. (1971) Cross-Polity—Series Data. Cambridge, Mass.: MIT Press.

———— (1973) Cross-National Data Analysis. Syracuse, N.Y.: Syracuse University International Relations Program.

Banks, A. S., and R. B. Textor (1963) A Cross-Polity Survey. Cambridge, Mass.: MIT Press.

References

Baran, P. A., and P. M. Sweezy (1968) Monopoly Capital: An Essay on the American Economic and Social Order. New York: Monthly Review Press.

Barkun, M. (1968) Law Without Sanction. New Haven, Conn.: Yale University Press.

Barrera, M., and E. B. Haas (1969) "The operationalization of some variables related to regional integration: A research note." International Organization 23:150–160.

Barringer, R. (1972) War: Patterns of Conflict. Cambridge, Mass.: MIT Press.

Bartos, O. J. (1974) Process and Outcome of Negotiations. New York: Columbia University Press.

Bauer, R. A., I. S. Pool, and L. A. Dexter (1963) American Business and Public Policy: The Politics of Foreign Trade. Chicago: Aldine-Atherton.

Beal, R. S. (1976) "A contra-Kuhnian view of the discipline's growth," pp. 158–161 in J. Rosenau (ed.), In Search of Global Patterns. New York: The Free Press.

Beard, C. A. (1934) The Idea of the National Interest. New York: Macmillan.

Beitz, C. (1980) Political Theory and International Relations. Princeton, N.J.: Princeton University Press.

Bell, R., D. V. Edwards, and R. Wagner (eds.) (1969) Political Power: A Reader in Theory and Research. New York: The Free Press.

Bell, W. (1960) "Images of the United States and the Soviet Union held by Jamaican elite groups." World Politics 12:225–248.

Beres, L. R. (1980) Apocalypse: Nuclear Catastrophe in World Politics. Chicago: University of Chicago Press.

Bernstein, R. A., and P. Weldon (1968) "A structural approach to the analysis of international relations." Journal of Conflict Resolution 12:159–181.

Bertalanffy, L. (1956) "General systems theory." General Systems 1:1–10.

Bertelsen, J. (1976) "The Palestinian Arabs: A non-state nation systems analysis." Sage Professional Papers in International Studies 02–043. Beverly Hills, Calif.: Sage Publications.

Bingham, J. (1961) Courage to Change: An Introduction to the Life and Thought of Reinhold Niebuhr. New York: Scribner's.

Blachowicz, J. A. (1971) "Systems theory and evolutionary models of the development of sciences." Philosophy of Science 38:178–199.

Blainey, G. (1973) The Causes of War. New York: The Free Press.

Blalock, H. M., Jr. (1960) Social Statistics. New York: McGraw-Hill.

——— (1968a) "The measurement problem: A gap between the language of theory and research," pp. 5–27 in H. M. Blalock and A. B. Blalock (eds.), Methodology in Social Research. New York: McGraw-Hill.

———— (1968b) "Theory building and causal inferences," pp. 155–198 in H. M. Blalock and A. B. Blalock (eds.), Methodology in Social Research. New York: McGraw-Hill.

———— (1969) Theory Construction: From Verbal to Mathematical Formulations. Englewood Cliffs, N.J.: Prentice-Hall.

Blechman, B. M. (1972) "Impact of Israeli reprisals on behavior of the bordering Arab nations directed at Israel." Journal of Conflict Resolution 16:155–182.

———— (1980) "Do negotiated arms limitations have a future?" Foreign Affairs 59:102–126.

Blechman, B. M., and S. S. Kaplan (1978) Force without War. Washington, D.C.: Brookings Institution.

Bloomfield, L. P. (1960) The United Nations and U.S. Foreign Policy. Boston: Little, Brown.

Bloomfield, L. P., and A. C. Leiss (1969) Controlling Small Wars: A Strategy for the 1970's. New York: Knopf.

Bobrow, D. B., S. Chan, and J. A. Kringen (1977) "Understanding how others treat crises." International Studies Quarterly 21:199–224.

———— (1979) Understanding Foreign Policy Decisions: The Chinese Case. New York: The Free Press.

Bonham, G. M., and M. J. Shapiro (1973) "Simulation in the development of a theory of foreign policy decision-making," pp. 55–71 in P. J. McGowan (ed.), Sage International Yearbook of Foreign Policy Studies, Vol. 1. Beverly Hills, Calif.: Sage Publications.

———— (1976) "Explanation of the Unexpected: the Syrian intervention in Jordan in 1970," pp. 113–141 in R. Axelrod (ed.), Structure of Decision. Princeton, N.J.: Princeton University Press.

Bonham, G. M., M. J. Shapiro, and T. L. Trumble (1979) "The October War." International Studies Quarterly 23:3–44.

Borgese, E. M. (1968) The Ocean Regime. Santa Barbara, Calif.: Center for the Study of Democratic Institutions.

Boulding, E. (1964) "The content of international studies in college: A review." Journal of Conflict Resolution 8:60–69.

Boulding, K. (1956) The Image: Knowledge in Life and Society. Ann Arbor: University of Michigan Press.

———— (1959) "National images and international systems." Journal of Conflict Resolution 3:120–131.

———— (1961) "Political implications of general systems research." General Systems Yearbook 6:1–7.

———— (1962) Conflict and Defense: A General Theory. New York: Harper & Row.

References

Boynton, G. R. (1976) "Cumulativeness in international relations," pp. 145–150 in J. N. Rosenau (ed.), In Search of Global Patterns. New York: The Free Press.

Brady, L. P. (1975) "Explaining foreign policy behavior using transitory qualities of situations." Paper presented at annual meeting of the American Political Science Association, San Francisco.

——— (1978) "The situation and foreign policy," pp. 173–191 in M. East, S. A. Salmore, and C. F. Hermann (eds.), Why Nations Act. Beverly Hills, Calif.: Sage Publications.

Brams, S. (1966a) "Transaction flows in the international system." American Political Science Review 60:880–898.

——— (1966b) "Trade in the North Atlantic area: An approach to the analysis of transformation in a system." Peace Research Society (International) Papers 6:143–164.

——— (1968) "A note on the cosmopolitanism of world regions." Journal of Peace Research 5:87–95.

——— (1969a) "The search for structural order in the international system: Some models and preliminary results." International Studies Quarterly 13:254–280.

——— (1969b) "The structure of influence relationships in the international system," pp. 583–599 in J. N. Rosenau (ed.), International Politics and Foreign Policy, rev. ed. New York: The Free Press.

Brams, S., and M. K. O'Leary (1970) "An axiomatic model of voting bodies." American Political Science Review 64:449–470.

Braybrooke, D., and C. E. Lindblom (1963) A Strategy of Decision: Policy Evaluation as a Social Process. New York: The Free Press.

Braybrooke, D., and A. Rosenberg (1972) "Comment: Getting the war news straight: The actual situation in the philosophy of science." American Political Science Review 66:818–826.

Brecher, M. (1974) "Inputs and decisions for war and peace: The Israel experience." International Studies Quarterly 18:131–177.

——— (1975) Decision in Israel's Foreign Policy. London: Oxford University Press.

——— (1977) "Toward a theory of international crisis behavior." International Studies Quarterly 21:39–75.

Brecher, M., B. Steinberg, and J. Stein (1969) "A framework for research on foreign policy behavior." Journal of Conflict Resolution 13:75–101.

Bremer, S. A. (1977) Simulated Worlds. Princeton, N.J.: Princeton University Press.

——— (1980) "National capabilities and war proneness," pp. 57–82 in J. D. Singer (ed.), The Correlates of War II. New York: The Free Press.

References

Bremer, S. A., J. D. Singer, and U. Luterbacher (1973) "The population density and war proneness of European nations, 1916–1965." Comparative Political Studies 6:329–349.

Brewer, T. L. (1973) "Issue and context variation in foreign policy." The Journal of Conflict Resolution 17:89–115.

Brickman, P., P. Shaver, and P. Archibald (1968) "American tactics and American goals in Vietnam as perceived by social scientists." Peace Research Society (International) Papers 10:79–104.

Brodie, B. (1945) "The atomic bomb and American security," Memorandum No. 18, Yale Institute of International Studies.

———— (1959) "The anatomy of deterrence." World Politics 11:173–191.

———— (1966) Escalation and the Nuclear Option. Princeton, N.J.: Princeton University Press.

———— (1973) War and Politics. New York: Macmillan.

Brody, R. A. (1963) "Some systemic effects of the spread of nuclear weapons technology: A study through simulation of a multi-nuclear future." Journal of Conflict Resolution 7:663–753.

———— (1972) "Problems in the measurement and analysis of international events," pp. 45–58 in E. Azar, R. A. Brody, and C. A. McClelland (eds.), International Events Interaction Analysis: Some Research Considerations. Sage Professional Papers in International Studies, 02–001. Beverly Hills, Calif.: Sage Publications.

Bronfenbrenner, U. (1961) "The mirror image in Soviet-American relations. Journal of Social Issues 27:46–51.

Brown, B. R. (1977) "Face-saving and face-restoration in negotiating," pp. 275–299 in D. Druckman (ed.), Negotiations. Beverly Hills, Calif.: Sage Publications.

Brown, R. (1963) Explanation in Social Science. Chicago: Aldine.

Bryce, J. (1922) International Relations. New York: Macmillan.

Buchan, A. (ed.) (1966) A World of Nuclear Powers? Englewood Cliffs, N.J.: Prentice-Hall.

Bueno de Mesquita, B. (1975) "Measuring systemic polarity." Journal of Conflict Resolution 19:197–216.

———— (1978) "Systemic polarization and the occurrence and duration of war." Journal of Conflict Resolution 22:241–267.

Bull, H. (1969) "International theory: The case for a classical approach." World Politics 18:361–377; reprinted, pp. 20–38, in K. Knorr and J. N. Rosenau (eds.), Contending Approaches to International Politics. Princeton, N.J.: Princeton University Press.

———— (1972) "The theory of international politics, 1919–1969," pp. 30–56 in B. Porter (ed.), The Aberystwyth Papers: International Politics 1919–1969. London: Oxford University Press.

———— (1977) The Anarchical Society. New York: Columbia University Press.

References

Burgess, P. M. (1970) "Nation-typing for foreign policy analysis: A partitioning procedure for constructing typologies," pp. 3–66 in E. Fedder (ed.), Methodological Concerns in International Studies. St. Louis: University of Missouri Center for International Studies.

Burgess, P. M., and J. E. Harf (1975) Global Analysis: A Data Scheme and Deck for Univariate and Bivariate Analysis. New York: Consortium for International Studies Education of the International Studies Association.

Burgess, P. M., and R. W. Lawton (1972) Indicators of International Behavior: An Assessment of Events Data Research. Sage Professional Paper in International Studies, 02–010. Beverly Hills, Calif.: Sage Publications.

Burns, A. L. (1957) "From balance to deterrence: A theoretical analysis." World Politics 9:494–529.

———— (1961) "Prospects for a general theory of international relations," pp. 25–45 in K. Knorr and S. Verba (eds.), The International System. Princeton, N.J.: Princeton University Press.

———— (1968a) "Quantitative approaches to international politics," pp. 171–201 in M. Kaplan (ed.), New Approaches to International Relations. New York: St. Martin's Press.

———— (1968b) Of Powers and Their Politics: A Critique of Theoretical Approaches. Englewood Cliffs, N.J.: Prentice-Hall.

———— (1972) "Scientific and strategic-political theories of international politics," pp. 56–85 in B. Porter (ed.), The Aberystwth Papers: International Politics 1919–1969. London: Oxford University Press.

Burrowes, R. (1974) "Mirror, mirror, on the wall . . .: A comparison of event data sources," pp. 383–406 in J. N. Rosenau (ed.), Comparing Foreign Policies. New York: Halsted/John Wiley.

Burrowes, R., and B. Spector (1973) "The strength and direction of relationships between domestic and external conflict and cooperation: Syria, 1961–67," pp. 294–321 in J. Wilkenfeld (ed.), Conflict Behavior and Linkage Politics. New York: David McKay.

Burstein, P., and W. Freudenburg (1976) "Ending the Vietnam war: The impact of war costs, public opinion, and anti-war demonstration on Senate voting on Vietnam war bills." Paper presented to annual meeting of the American Political Science Association, Chicago.

Burt, R. (1978) "The scope and limits of SALT." Foreign Affairs 56: 756–760.

Burton, J. W. (1967) International Relations: A General Theory. Cambridge: Cambridge University Press.

———— (1968) Systems, States, Diplomacy, and Rules. Cambridge: Cambridge University Press.

———— (1969) Conflict and Communication. New York: The Free Press.

———— (1972) World Society. Cambridge: Cambridge University Press.

Burton, J. W., A. Groom, C. Mitchell, and A. De Reuck (1974) The Study of World Society: A London Perspective. Pittsburgh: International Studies Association.

Butterfield, H. (1953) Christianity, Diplomacy and War. London: Epworth Press.

Butterfield, H., and M. Wight (eds.) (1966) Diplomatic Investigations. Cambridge, Mass.: Harvard University Press.

Butterworth, R. L. (1976) Managing Interstate Conflict: Data with Synopses. Pittsburgh: University Center of International Studies, University of Pittsburgh.

———— (1978) "Do conflict managers matter?" International Studies Quarterly 22:195–214.

CACI (1975) Crisis Inventory. Arlington, Va.: CACI, Inc., Final Technical Report.

Callahan, P., L. Brady, and M. Hermann (eds.) (1982) Describing Foreign Policy Behavior. Beverly Hills, Calif.: Sage Publications.

Campbell, J., and L. Cain (1965) "Public opinion and the outbreak of war." Journal of Conflict Resolution 9:318–328.

Cannizzo, C. A. (1980) "The costs of combat: Death, duration, and defeat," pp. 233–257 in J. D. Singer (ed.), The Correlates of War: II. New York: The Free Press.

Caplow, T., and K. Finsterbusch (1968) "France and other countries: A study of international interaction." Journal of Conflict Resolution 12:1–15.

Caporaso, J. A. (1978) "Dependence, dependency, and power in the global system: A structural and behavioral analysis." International Organization 32:13–43.

Caporaso, J. A., and M. D. Ward (1979) "The United States in an interdependent world: The emergence of economic power," pp. 139–169 in C. W. Kegley and P. J. McGowan (eds.), Challenges to America. Sage International Yearbook of Foreign Policy Studies, Vol. 4. Beverly Hills, Calif.: Sage Publications.

Cardoso, F. H., and E. Faletto (1979) Dependency and Development in Latin America. Berkeley and Los Angeles, Calif.: University of California Press.

Carnap, R. (1952) The Continuum of Inductive Methods. Chicago: University of Chicago Press.

———— (1962) The Logical Foundations of Probability. Chicago: University of Chicago Press.

Carr, E. H. (1939, 1964) The Twenty Years' Crisis: An Introduction to the Study of International Relations. New York: Harper & Row.

———— (1947) The Soviet Impact on the Western World. New York: Macmillan.

―――― (1951) The Bolshevik Revolution. New York: Macmillan.

Caspary, W. R. (1970) "The mood theory: A study of public opinion and foreign policy." American Political Science Review 64:536–547.

Cattell, R. (1949) "The dimension of culture patterns by factorization of national characters." Journal of Abnormal and Social Psychology 44:443–469.

Chadwick, R. N. (1969) "An inductive empirical analysis of intra- and international behavior, aimed at a partial extension of inter-nation simulation theory." Journal of Peace Research 6:193–214.

Chan, S. (1978) "Chinese conflict calculus and behavior: Assessment from a perspective of conflict management." World Politics 30:391–410.

―――― (1979) "Rationality, bureaucratic politics and belief system: Explaining the Chinese policy debate, 1964–66." Journal of Peace Research 16:333–348.

Chan, S., J. A. Kringen, and D. B. Bobrow (1979) "A Chinese view of the international system," pp. 271–289 in J. D. Singer and M. D. Wallace (eds.), To Augur Well. Beverly Hills, Calif.: Sage Publications.

Chase-Dunn, C. (1978) "Core-periphery relations: The effects of core competition," pp. 156–176 in B. W. Kaplan (ed.), Social Change in the Capitalist World Economy. Political Economy of the World-System Annuals, Vol. 1. Beverly Hills, Calif.: Sage Publications.

Cheever, D. (1949) "The role of the U.N. in the conduct of United States foreign policy." World Politics 2:390–405.

Cherryholmes, C. (1966) "Some current research on effectiveness of educational simulations: Implications for alternative strategies." American Behavioral Scientist 10:4–8.

Chi, H. (1968) "The Chinese warlord system as an international system," pp. 403–425 in M. Kaplan (ed.), New Approaches to International Relations. New York: St. Martin's Press.

Choi, C. Y. (1977) "The contemporary foreign behavior of the United States and Soviet Union: An application of status-field theory," pp. 403–464 in R. Rummel (ed.), Field Theory Evolving. Beverly Hills, Calif.: Sage Publications.

Choucri, N. (1969a) "The perceptual base of non-alignment." Journal of Conflict Resolution 13:57–74.

―――― (1969b) "The non-alignment of Afro-Asian states: Policy, perception, and behavior." Canadian Journal of Political Science 2:1–17.

―――― (1972) "In search of peace systems: Scandinavia and the Netherlands; 1870–1970," pp. 239–299 in B. M. Russett (ed.), Peace, War, and Numbers. Beverly Hills, Calif.: Sage Publications.

―――― (1974) Population Dynamics and International Violence: Propositions, Insights, and Evidence. Lexington, Mass.: D. C. Heath.

Choucri, N., and R. North (1969) "The determinants of international violence." Peace Research Society (International) Papers 12:33–63.

——— (1975) Nations in Conflict: National Growth and International Violence. San Francisco: Freeman.

Cimbala, S. J. (1969) "Foreign policy as an issue area: A roll call analysis." American Political Science Review 63:148–156.

Clark, G., and L. Sohn (1958) World Peace Through World Law. Cambridge, Mass.: Harvard University Press.

Clark, J., M. O'Leary, and E. Wittkopf (1971) "National attributes associated with dimensions of support of the United Nations." International Organization 25:1–25.

Claude, I. L. (1956, 1964) Swords into Plowshares. New York: Random House.

——— (1962) Power and International Relations. New York: Random House.

Cobb, R., and C. Elder, (1970) International Community: A Regional and Global Study. New York: Holt, Rinehart and Winston.

Cobb, S. A. (1969) "Defense spending and foreign policy in the House of Representatives." Journal of Conflict Resolution 13:358–369.

Coddington, A. (1965) "Policies advocated in conflict situations by British newspapers." Journal of Peace Research 2:398–404.

——— (1968) Theories of the Bargaining Process. Chicago: Aldine.

Cohen, B. C. (1957) The Political Process and Foreign Policy: The Making of the Japanese Peace Settlement. Princeton, N.J.: Princeton University Press.

——— (1963) The Press and Foreign Policy. Princeton, N.J.: Princeton University Press.

——— (1967) "Mass communication and foreign policy," pp. 195–212 in J. Rosenau (ed.), Domestic Sources of Foreign Policy. New York: The Free Press.

——— (1973) The Public's Impact on Foreign Policy. Boston: Little, Brown.

Cohen, S., H. C. Kelman, F. Miller, and B. Smith (1977) "Evolving intergroup techniques for conflict resolution: An Israeli-Palestinian pilot workshop." Journal of Social Issues 33:165–190.

Collingwood, R. G. (1940) An Essay on Metaphysics. Oxford: Clarendon Press.

Collins, B. E., and H. Guetzkow (1964) A Social Psychology of Group Processes for Decision-Making. New York: John Wiley.

Coplin, W. D. (1964) "The image of power politics: A cognitive approach to the study of international politics." Ph.D. Dissertation, American University.

References

——— (1965) "International law and assumptions about the state system." World Politics 17:615–635.

——— (1966a) The Functions of International Law. Chicago: Rand McNally.

——— (1966b) "Inter-nation simulation and contemporary theories of international relations." American Political Science Review 9:562–578.

——— (1968) "The world court in the international bargaining process," pp. 317–333 in R. W. Gregg and M. Barkun (eds.), The United Nations System and its Functions. Princeton, N.J.: Van Nostrand.

——— (1970) "Current studies of the functions of international law: Assessments and suggestions," pp. 149–208 in J. A. Robinson (ed.), Political Science Annual, Vol. 2. Indianapolis: Bobbs-Merrill.

——— (1971) Introduction to International Politics. Chicago: Markham.

——— (1974) Introduction to International Politics. 2nd ed. Chicago: Rand McNally.

——— (1980) Introduction to International Politics. 3rd ed. Englewood Cliffs, N.J.: Prentice-Hall.

Coplin, W. D., S. Mills, and M. K. O'Leary (1973) "The PRINCE concepts and the study of foreign policy," pp. 73–103 in P. J. McGowan (ed.), Sage International Yearbook of Foreign Policy Studies, Vol. 1. Beverly Hills, Calif.: Sage Publications.

Coplin, W. D., and M. K. O'Leary (1971) "A simulation model for the analysis and explanation of international interactions." Paper presented to the annual meeting of the International Studies Association, San Juan, Puerto Rico.

Coplin, W. D., and J. M. Rochester (1972) "The Permanent Court of International Justice, the International Court of Justice, the League of Nations, and the United Nations: A comparative empirical survey." American Political Science Review 66:529–550.

Copson, W. (1973) "Foreign policy conflict among African states, 1964–1969," pp. 189–217 in P. J. McGowan (ed.), Sage International Yearbook of Foreign Policy Studies, Vol. 1. Beverly Hills, Calif.: Sage Publications.

Corning, P. A. (1973) "Human violence: Some causes and implications," pp. 119–151 in C. R. Beitz and T. Herman (eds.), Peace and War. San Francisco: Freeman.

Cox, R. W., H. K. Jacobson, et al. (1973) The Anatomy of Influence: Decision-Making in International Organization. New Haven, Conn.: Yale University Press.

Crow, W. J. (1963) "A study of strategic doctrines using the Inter-Nation Simulation." Journal of Conflict Resolution 7:580–589.

References

Crow, W. J., and R. C. Noel (1965) "The valid use of simulation results." La Jolla, Calif.: Western Behavioral Sciences Institute.

Dahl, R. (1963) Who Governs: Democracy and Power in an American City. New Haven, Conn.: Yale University Press.

Davidson, R. H., D. M. Kovenock, and M. K. O'Leary (1966) Congress in Crisis: Politics and Congressional Reform. Belmont, Calif: Wadsworth.

Dean, P. D., and J. A. Vasquez (1976) "From power politics to issue politics: Bipolarity and multipolarity in light of a new paradigm." Western Political Quarterly 29:2–28.

Denton, F. H. (1966) "Some regularities in international conflict, 1820–1949." Background 9:283–296.

Denton, F. H., and W. Phillips (1968) "Some patterns in the history of violence." Journal of Conflict Resolution 12:182–195.

deRivera, J. H. (1968) The Psychological Dimension of Foreign Policy. Columbus, Ohio: Charles E. Merrill.

Destler, I. M. (1972) Presidents, Bureaucrats and Foreign Policy. Princeton, N.J.: Princeton University Press.

Deutsch, K. W. (1953) Nationalism and Social Communication. Cambridge, Mass.: MIT Press.

——— (1954) Political Community at the International Level: Problems of Definition and Measurement. Garden City, N.Y.: Doubleday.

——— (1956) "Shifts in the balance of communication flows: A problem of measurement in international relations." Public Opinion Quarterly 20:143–160.

——— (1964a) "Communication theory and political integration," pp. 46–74 in P. Jacob and J. Toscano (eds.), The Integration of Political Communities. Philadelphia: Lippincott.

——— (1964b) The Nerves of Government. New York: The Free Press.

——— (1964c) "Transaction flows as indicators of political cohesion," pp. 75–119 in P. Jacob and J. Toscano (eds.), The Integration of Political Communities. Philadelphia: Lippincott.

——— (1966) "Integration and arms control in the European political environment: A summary report." American Political Science Review, 60:354–365.

——— (1968) The Analysis of International Relations. Englewood Cliffs, N.J.: Prentice-Hall.

——— (1980) "An interim summary and evaluation," pp. 287–295 in J. D. Singer (ed.), The Correlates of War: II. New York: The Free Press.

Deutsch, K. W., S. Burrell, R. Kann, M. Lee, M. Lichterman, R. Lindgren, F. Lowenheim, and R. Van Wagenen (1957) Political

Community and the North Atlantic Area. Princeton, N.J.: Princeton University Press.

Deutsch, K. W., and A. Eckstein (1961) "National industrialization and the declining share of the international economic sector." World Politics 13:267–299.

Deutsch, K. W., and R. Savage (1960) "A statistical model of gross analysis of transaction flows." Econometrika 28:551–572.

Deutsch, K. W., and D. Senghaas (1973) "The steps to war: A survey of system levels, decision stages, and research results," pp. 275–329 in P. J. McGowan (ed.), Sage International Yearbook of Foreign Policy Studies, Vol. 1. Beverly Hills, Calif.: Sage Publications.

Deutsch, K. W., and J. D. Singer (1964) "Multipolar power systems and international stability." World Politics 16:390–406.

Deutsch, M. (1958) "Trust and Suspicion." Journal of Conflict Resolution 2:265–279.

——— (1973) The Resolution of Conflict. New Haven, Conn.: Yale University Press.

Deutsch, M., and R. M. Krauss (1962) "Studies of interpersonal bargaining." Journal of Conflict Resolution 6:52–76.

deVisscher, C. (1957) Theory and Reality in Public International Law. Princeton, N.J.: Princeton University Press.

Donelan, M. D., and M. J. Grieve (1973) International Disputes: Case Histories 1945–1970. New York: St. Martin's Press.

Doob, L. W. (1970) Resolving Conflict in Africa: The Fermeda Workshop. New Haven, Conn.: Yale University Press.

Doran, C. (1971) The Politics of Assimilation. Baltimore: Johns Hopkins University Press.

Doran, C., R. Pendley, and G. Antunes (1973) "A test of cross-national event reliability." International Studies Quarterly 12:175–203.

Dougherty, J., and R. Pfaltzgraff, Jr. (1971) Contending Theories of International Relations. Philadelphia: Lippincott.

Downs, A. (1966) Inside Bureaucracy. Boston: Little, Brown.

Driver, M. J. (1965) "A cognitive structure analysis of aggression, stress, and personality in an Inter-Nation Simulation." Lafayette, Ind.: Purdue University.

——— (1977) "Individual differences as determinants of aggression in the Inter-Nation Simulation," pp. 335–344 in M. Hermann (ed.), A Psychological Examination of Political Leaders. New York: The Free Press.

Druckman, D. (1968) "Ethnocentrism in the Inter-Nation Simulation." Journal of Conflict Resolution 12:45–68.

——— (1977a) (ed.) Negotiations. Beverly Hills, Calif.: Sage Publications.

———— (1977b) "Social-psychological approaches to the study of negotiation," pp. 15–44 in D. Druckman (ed.), Negotiations. Beverly Hills, Calif.: Sage Publications.

———— (1977c) "The person, role and situation in international negotiations," pp. 406–456 in M. Hermann (ed.), A Psychological Examination of Political Leaders. New York: The Free Press.

Druckman, D., A. A. Benton, F. Ali, and J. S. Bagur (1976) "Cultural differences in bargaining behavior: India, Argentina, and the United States." Journal of Conflict Resolution 20:413–452.

Dunn, F. S. (1948) "The scope of international relations." World Politics 1:140–151.

———— (1949) "The present course of international relations research." World Politics 2:80–95.

———— (1950) War and the Minds of Men. New York: Harper.

East, M. (1972) "Status discrepancy and violence in the international system: An empirical analysis," pp. 299–319 in J. N. Rosenau, V. Davis, and M. East (eds.), The Analysis of International Politics. New York: The Free Press.

———— (1975) "Explaining foreign policy behavior using national attributes." Paper presented to the annual meeting of the American Political Science Association, San Francisco.

———— (1978) "National attributes and foreign policy," pp. 123–143 in M. East, S. A. Salmore, and C. F. Hermann (eds.), Why Nations Act. Beverly Hills, Calif.: Sage Publications.

East, M., and P. Gregg (1967) "Factors influencing cooperation and conflict in the international system." International Studies Quarterly 11:244–269.

East, M., and C. F. Hermann (1974) "Do nation-types account for foreign policy behavior?," pp. 269–303 in J. Rosenau (ed.), Comparing Foreign Policies. New York: Halsted/John Wiley.

East, M., S. A. Salmore, and C. F. Hermann (1978) (eds.) Why Nations Act: Theoretical Perspectives for Comparative Foreign Policy Studies. Beverly Hills, Calif.: Sage Publications.

Easton, D. (1965a) A Systems Analysis of Political Life. New York: John Wiley.

———— (1965b) A Framework for Political Analysis. Englewood Cliffs, N.J.: Prentice-Hall.

Eckhardt, W. (1965) "War propaganda, welfare values, and political ideologies." Journal of Conflict Resolution 9:345–358.

Eckhardt, W., and R. White (1967) "A test of the mirror-image hypothesis: Kennedy and Khrushchev." Journal of Conflict Resolution 11:325–332.

Ellis, W., and J. Salzberg (1965) "Africa and the U.N.: A statistical note." American Behavioral Scientist 8:30–32.

References

Ellsberg, D. (1959) "The theory and practice of blackmail." Public lecture at Lowell Institute, Boston.

Elrod, R. B. (1976) "The Concert of Europe: A fresh look at an international system." World Politics 28:159–174.

Esser, J. K., and S. S. Komorita (1975) "Reciprocity and concession making in bargaining." Journal of Personality and Social Psychology 31:864–872.

Etheredge, L. S. (1978) A World of Men: The Private Sources of American Foreign Policy. Cambridge, Mass.: MIT Press.

Etzioni, A. (1962) "The dialectics of supranational unification." American Political Science Review 56:927–955.

——— (1963) "The epigenesis of communities at the international level." American Journal of Sociology 68:407–421.

——— (1965) Political Unification. New York: Holt, Rinehart and Winston.

——— (1967) "The Kennedy experiment." Western Political Quarterly 20:361–380.

Falk, R. A. (1971) This Endangered Planet. New York: Random House.

——— (1975) A Study of Future Worlds. New York: The Free Press.

Feld, W. J. (1972) Non-Governmental Forces and World Politics: A Study of Business, Labor and Political Groups. New York: Praeger.

——— (1979) International Relations: A Transnational Approach. Sherman Oaks, Calif.: Alfred.

Feldstein, H. S. (1967) "A study of transaction and political integration: Transnational labour flow within the European economic community." Journal of Common Market Studies 6:24–55.

Ferris, W. (1973) The Power Capabilities of Nation-States. Lexington, Mass.: D. C. Heath.

Feyerabend, P. K. (1976) "On the critique of scientific reason," pp. 109–143 in R. S. Cohen et al. (eds.), Boston Studies in the Philosophy of Science, Vol. 39. Dordrecht, Holland: D. Reidel.

Fink, C. F. (1965) "More calculations about deterrence." Journal of Conflict Resolution 9:54–66.

Finnegan, R. B. (1970) "Patterns of influence in international relations research." Journal of International and Comparative Studies 3:84–106.

——— (1972a) "The field of international relations: The view from within." Towson State Journal of International Affairs 7:1–24.

——— (1972b) "International relations: The disputed search for method." Review of Politics 34:40–66.

Fisher, W. E. (1969) "An analysis of the Deutsch social-causal paradigm of political integration." International Organization 23:254–290.

Fleming, D. F. (1961) The Cold War and Its Origins, 1917–1960. Garden City, N.Y.: Doubleday.

Fleming, W. G. (1969) "Sub-Saharan Africa: Case studies of international attitudes and transactions of Ghana and Uganda," pp. 94–161 in J. N. Rosenau (ed.), Linkage Politics. New York: The Free Press.

Fox, W. T. R. (1949) "Interwar international relations research: The American experience." World Politics 2:67–80.

――――― (1968) The American study of International Relations. Columbia, S.C.: Institute of International Studies.

Fox, W. T. R., and A. B. Fox (1961) "The teaching of international relations in the United States." World Politics 13:339–359.

Franck, T. M., and E. Weisband (1979) Foreign Policy by Congress. New York: Oxford University Press.

Frank, A. G. (1969) Capitalism and Underdevelopment in Latin America. New York: Monthly Review Press.

Franke, W. (1968) "The Italian city-state system as an international system," pp. 426–458 in M. Kaplan (ed.), New Approaches to International Relations. New York: St. Martin's Press.

Frankel, J. (1963) The Making of Foreign Policy: An Analysis of Decision-Making. New York: Oxford University Press.

――――― (1970) National Interest. New York: Praeger.

Freeman, L. (1965) Elementary Applied Statistics. New York: John Wiley.

Frohock, F. (1974) Normative Political Theory. Englewood Cliffs, N.J.: Prentice-Hall.

Gaddis, J. L. (1972) The United States and the Origins of the Cold War, 1941–1947. New York: Columbia University Press.

Galtung, J. (1964a) "An editorial." Journal of Peace Research 1:1–4.

――――― (1964b) "Summit meetings and international relations." Journal of Peace Research 1:36–54.

――――― (1964c) "A structural theory of aggression." Journal of Peace Research 1:95–119.

――――― (1966) "East-West interaction patterns." Journal of Peace Research 3:146–277.

――――― (1971) "A structural theory of imperialism." Journal of Peace Research 8:81–119.

――――― (1980) The True Worlds: A Transnational Perspective. New York: The Free Press.

Galtung, J., and T. Hoivik (1971) "Structural and direct violence." Journal of Peace Research 8:73–76.

Galtung, J., and M. Ruge (1965a) "Patterns of diplomacy." Journal of Peace Research 2:101–135.

――――― (1965b) "The structure of foreign news." Journal of Peace Research 2:64–91.

Gamson, W., and A. Modigliani (1965) "Soviet responses to Western foreign policy." Peace Research Society (International) Papers 3:47–78.

References

———— (1968) "Some aspects of Soviet-Western conflict." Peace Research Society (International) Papers 9:9–24.

———— (1971) Untangling the Cold War. Boston: Little, Brown.

Garnham, D. (1976) "Power parity and lethal international violence, 1969–1973." Journal of Conflict Resolution 20:379–394.

Garson, G. D. (1971, 1976) Handbook of Political Science Methods. 1st and 2nd eds. Boston: Holbrook Press.

George, A. L. (1969) "The operational code: A neglected approach to the study of political leaders and decision-making." International Studies Quarterly 13:190–222.

———— (1972) "The case for multiple advocacy in making foreign policy." American Political Science Review 66:751–785.

———— (1974) "Adaptation to stress in political decision-making: The individual, small group, and organizational contexts," pp. 167–245 in G. V. Coelho, D. A. Hamburg, and J. E. Adams (eds.), Coping and Adaptation. New York: Basic Books.

George, A. L., and J. George (1956) Woodrow Wilson and Colonel House. New York: Dover.

George, A. L., D. Hall, and W. Simons (1971) The Limits of Coercive Diplomacy. Boston: Little, Brown.

George, A. L., and R. Smoke (1974) Deterrence in American Foreign Policy: Theory and Practice. New York: Columbia University Press.

Gillespie, J. V., and D. A. Zinnes (eds.) (1976) Mathematical Models of International Relations. New York: Praeger.

Gillespie, J. V., D. Zinnes, P. A. Schrodt, and G. S. Tahim (1980) "Sensitivity analysis of an armaments race model," pp. 275–301 in P. J. McGowan and C. W. Kegley (eds.), Threats, Weapons, and Foreign Policy. Sage International Yearbook of Foreign Policy Studies, Vol. 5. Beverly Hills, Calif.: Sage Publications.

Gillespie, J. V., D. Zinnes, P. A. Schrodt, G. S. Tahim, and R. M. Rubison (1977) "An optimal control model of arms races." American Political Science Review 71:226–244.

Gleditsch, N. (1967) "Trends in world airline patterns." Journal of Peace Research 4:366–408.

———— (1969) "The international airline network: A test of the Zipf and Stouffer hypotheses." Peace Research Society (International) Papers 11:123–153.

Gochman, C. S. (1975) "Status, conflict and war: The major powers, 1820–1970." Ph.D. dissertation, University of Michigan.

———— (1976) "Studies of international violence: Five easy pieces?" Journal of Conflict Resolution 20:539–560.

———— (1980) "Status, capabilities, and major power conflict," pp. 83–123 in J. David Singer (ed.), The Correlates of War: II. New York: The Free Press.

References

Gochman, C. S., and J. L. Ray (1979) "Structural disparities in Latin America and Eastern Europe, 1950–1970." Journal of Peace Research 16:231–254.

Graber, D. A. (1969) "Perceptions of Middle East conflict in the U.N., 1953–1965." Journal of Conflict Resolution 13:454–484.

Gray, C. S., and K. Payne (1980) "Under the nuclear gun: Victory is possible." Foreign Policy 39:14–27.

Green, P. (1966) Deadly Logic: The Theory of Nuclear Deterrence. Columbus, Ohio: Ohio State University Press.

Greenstein, F. I., and N. W. Polsby (eds.) (1975) International Politics, Handbook of Political Science, Vol. 8. Reading, Mass.: Addison-Wesley.

Gregg, R. (1965) "The Latin American bloc in United Nations elections." Southwestern Social Science Quarterly 46:146–154.

Guetzkow, H. (1950) "Long range research in international relations." American Perspective 4:421–440. Reprinted in pp. 53–59 J. N. Rosenau (ed.), International Politics and Foreign Policy. New York: The Free Press.

——— (1959) "A use of simulation in the study of inter-nation relations." Behavioral Science 4:183–191.

——— (1963a) "A use of simulation in the study of inter-nation relations," pp. 82–94 in H. Guetzkow (ed.), Simulation in Social Science: Readings. Englewood Cliffs, N.J.: Prentice-Hall.

——— (1963b) "Structured programs and their relations to free activity within the Inter-Nation Simulation," pp. 103–149 in H. Guetzkow et al., Simulation in International Relations: Development for Research and Teaching. Englewood Cliffs, N.J.: Prentice-Hall.

——— (1968) "Some correspondences between simulations and realities in international relations," pp. 202–269 in M. Kaplan (ed.), New Approaches to International Relations. New York: St. Martin's Press.

——— (1976) "An incomplete history of fifteen short years in simulating international processes," pp. 247–258 in F. Hoole and D. Zinnes (eds.), Quantitative International Politics. New York: Praeger.

Guetzkow, H., C. F. Alger, R. A. Brody, R. C. Noel, and R. C. Snyder (1963) Simulation in International Relations: Developments for Research and Teaching. Englewood Cliffs, N.J.: Prentice-Hall.

Guetzkow, H., and W. L. Hollist (1976) "Some instructive experiences gained in simulating international processes, 1957–1972," pp. 328–346 in F. Hoole and D. Zinnes (eds.), Quantitative International Politics. New York: Praeger.

Guetzkow, H., and J. Valadez (eds.) (1981a) Simulated International Processes. Beverly Hills, Calif.: Sage Publications.

References

——— (1981b) "International relations theory: Contributions of simulated international processes," pp. 197–252 in H. Guetzkow and J. Valadez (eds.), Simulated International Processes. Beverly Hills, Calif.: Sage Publications.

Gulick, E. V. (1955) Europe's Classical Balance of Power. Ithaca, N.Y.: Cornell University Press.

Haas, E. B. (1953) "The balance of power: prescription, concept, or propaganda?" World Politics 5:442–477.

——— (1956) "Regionalism, functionalism, and universal international organization." World Politics 8:238–263.

——— (1958a) The Uniting of Europe. Stanford, Calif.: Stanford University Press.

——— (1958b) "The challenge of regionalism." International Organization 12:440–458.

——— (1960) Consensus Formation in the Council of Europe. Berkeley, Calif.: University of California Press.

——— (1961) "International integration: The European and the universal process." International Organization 15:366–392.

——— (1962) "System and process in the International Labor Organization: A statistical afterthought." World Politics 14:339–352.

——— (1964) Beyond the Nation-State: Functionalism and International Organization. Stanford, Calif.: Stanford University Press.

——— (1967) "*The Uniting of Europe* and the uniting of Latin America." Journal of Common Market Studies 5:315–343.

——— (1975) "Is there a hole in the whole? Knowledge, technology, interdependence and the construction of international regimes." International Organization 29:827–876.

Haas, E. B., R. Butterworth, and J. Nye (1972) Conflict Management by International Organizations. Morristown, N.J.: General Learning Press.

Haas, E. B., and P. Schmitter (1964) "Economics and differential patterns of political integration: Projections about unity in Latin America." International Organization 18:705–737.

Haas, M. (1965) "Societal approaches to the study of war." Journal of Peace Research 2:307–323.

——— (1968) "Social change and national aggressiveness, 1900–1960," pp. 215–244 in J. D. Singer (ed.), Quantitative International Politics. New York: The Free Press.

——— (1969) "Communication factors in decision making." Peace Research Society (International) Papers 12:65–86.

——— (1970) "International subsystems: Stability and polarity." American Political Science Review 64:98–123.

——— (1974) International Conflict. Indianapolis: Bobbs-Merrill.

Hahn, W., and J. Neff (eds.) (1960) American Strategy for the Nuclear Age. Garden City, N.Y.: Anchor-Doubleday.

Halperin, M. H. (1972) "The decision to deploy the ABM." World Politics 25:62–95.

——— (1974) Bureaucratic Politics and Foreign Policy. Washington, D.C.: Brookings Institution.

Halperin, M. H., and A. Kanter (eds.) (1973) Readings in American Foreign Policy: A Bureaucratic Perspective. Boston: Little, Brown.

Hammond, P. Y. (1965) "Foreign policy making and administrative politics." World Politics 17:657–671.

Hamner, W. C., and G. A. Yukl (1977) "The effectiveness of different offer strategies in bargaining," pp. 137–160 in D. Druckman (ed.), Negotiations. Beverly Hills, Calif.: Sage Publications.

Handelman, J., J. A. Vasquez, M. K. O'Leary, and W. D. Coplin (1973) "Color it Morgenthau: A data-based assessment of quantitative international relations." Presented at the annual meeting of the International Studies Association, New York.

Hanrieder, W. F. (1965) "The international system: Bipolar or multi-bloc?" Journal of Conflict Resolution 9:299–308.

Hanson, N. (1965) Patterns of Discovery. Cambridge: Cambridge University Press.

Harsanyi, J. C. (1961) "On the rationality postulates underlying the theory of cooperative games." Journal of Conflict Resolution 5:179–196.

Hart, J. (1976) "Comparative cognition: Politics of international control of the oceans," pp. 180–217 in R. Axelrod (ed.), Structure of Decision. Princeton, N.J.: Princeton University Press.

Hartmann, F. H. (1957, 1978) The Relations of Nations. New York: Macmillan.

Harvard University Computation Laboratory (1955) Tables of the Cumulative Binomial Probability Distribution. Cambridge, Mass.: Harvard University.

Hazlewood, L., J. J. Hayes, and J. R. Brownell (1977) "Planning for problems in crisis management." International Studies Quarterly 21:75–105.

Healy, B., and A. Stein (1973) "The balance of power in international history: Theory and reality." Journal of Conflict Resolution 17:33–62.

Hempel, C. G. (1952) Fundamentals of Concept Formation in Empirical Science. Chicago: University of Chicago Press.

——— (1966) Philosophy of Natural Science. Englewood Cliffs, N.J.: Prentice-Hall.

——— (1968) "Explanation in science and history," pp. 54–79 in P. H.

Nidditch (ed.), The Philosophy of Science. New York: Oxford University Press.

Henehan, M. T. (1981) "A data-based evaluation of issue typologies in the comparative study of foreign policy." Paper presented to the annual meeting of the International Studies Association.

Hensley, T. (1968) "National bias and the International Court of Justice." Midwest Journal of Political Science 12:568–586.

Heradstveit, D. (1979) The Arab-Israeli Conflict: Psychological Obstacles to Peace. Oslo, Norway: Universitetsforlaget.

Hermann, C. F. (1967) "Validation problems in games and simulations with special reference to models of international politics." Behavioral Science 12:216–231.

——— (1969a) Crises in Foreign Policy. Indianapolis: Bobbs-Merrill.

——— (1969b) "International crisis as a situational variable," pp. 409–421 in J. Rosenau (ed.), International Politics and Foreign Policy. 2nd ed. New York: The Free Press.

——— (1971) "What is a foreign policy event?," pp. 295–321 in W. Hanrieder (ed.), Comparative Foreign Policy. New York: David McKay.

——— (1972a) "Threat, time, and surprise: A simulation of international crisis," pp. 187–216 in C. F. Hermann (ed.), International Crises. New York: The Free Press.

——— (ed.) (1972b) International Crises: Insights from Behavioral Research. New York: The Free Press.

——— (1972c) "Policy classification: A key to the comparative study of foreign policy," pp. 58–79 in J. N. Rosenau, V. Davis, and M. East (eds.), The Analysis of International Politics. New York: The Free Press.

——— (1978) "Decision structure and process influences on foreign policy," pp. 69–102 in M. East, S. A. Salmore, and C. F. Hermann (eds.), Why Nations Act. Beverly Hills, Calif.: Sage Publications.

——— (1979) "Why new foreign policy challenges might not be met: Constraints on detecting problems and setting agendas," pp. 269–306 in C. W. Kegley and P. J. McGowan (eds.), Challenges to America. Sage International Yearbook of Foreign Policy Studies, Vol. 4. Beverly Hills, Calif.: Sage Publications.

Hermann, C. F., and L. P. Brady (1972) "Alternative models of international crisis behavior," pp. 281–320 in C. F. Hermann (ed.), International Crises: Insights from Behavioral Research. New York: The Free Press.

Hermann, C. F., M. East, M. G. Hermann, B. Salmore, and S. Salmore (1973) Creon: A Foreign Events Data Set. Sage Professional Papers in International Studies, 02–024. Beverly Hills, Calif.: Sage Publications.

Hermann, C. F., and M. G. Hermann (1967) "An attempt to simulate the outbreak of World War I." American Political Science Review 61: 400–416.

——— (1979) "Summary of the external components in the CREON project's conceptual framework for explaining foreign policy behavior." Paper presented at the annual meeting of the Northeastern Political Science Association, Newark, New Jersey.

Hermann, C. F., M. G. Hermann, and R. A. Cantor (1974) "Counter-attack or delay: Characteristics influencing decision-makers' responses to the simulation of an unidentified attack." Journal of Conflict Resolution 18:75–106.

Hermann, M. G. (1974) "Leader personality and foreign policy behavior," pp. 201–234 in J. N. Rosenau (ed.), Comparing Foreign Policies. New York: Halsted/John Wiley.

——— (1976) "When leader personality will affect foreign policy: Some propositions," pp. 326–333 in J. N. Rosenau (ed.), In Search of Global Patterns. New York: The Free Press.

——— (1978) "Effects of personal characteristics of personal leaders on foreign policy," pp. 49–68 in M. East, S. A. Salmore, and C. F. Hermann (eds.), Why Nations Act. Beverly Hills, Calif.: Sage Publications.

——— (1980) "Explaining foreign policy behavior using the personal characteristics of political leaders." International Studies Quarterly 24:7–46.

Hermann, M. G., C. F. Hermann, and W. J. Dixon (1979) "Decision structures and personal characteristics in comparative foreign policy." Paper presented at the annual meeting of the Midwest Political Science Association, Chicago.

Hermann, M. G., and N. Kogan (1977) "Effects of negotiators' personalities on negotiating behavior," pp. 247–275 in D. Druckman (ed.), Negotiations. Beverly Hills, Calif.: Sage Publications.

Herz, J. (1942) "Power politics and world organization." American Political Science Review 36:1039–1052.

——— (1950) "Idealist internationalism and the security dilemma." World Politics 2:157–180.

——— (1951) Political Realism and Political Idealism. Chicago: University of Chicago Press.

——— (1957) "The Rise and demise of the territorial state." World Politics 9:473–493.

——— (1959) International Politics in the Atomic Age. New York: Columbia University Press.

References

———— (1968) "The territorial state revisited: Reflections on the future of the nation-state." Polity 1:11–34.

———— (1971) "Relevancies and irrelevancies in the study of international relations." Polity 4:25–47.

Hilton, G. (1973) "A Review of the Dimensionality of Nations Project." Sage Professional Paper in International Studies, 02–015. Beverly Hills, Calif.: Sage Publications.

Hobson, J. A. (1902 [1938]) Imperialism: A Study. London: George Allen and Unwin.

Hoffman, F. (1967) "The functions of economic sanctions." Journal of Peace Research 4:140–160.

Hoffmann, S. (1959) "Long road to international relations theory." World Politics 11:346–378.

———— (ed.) (1960) Contemporary Theory in International Relations. Englewood Cliffs, N.J.: Prentice-Hall.

Hoggard, G. (1972) "An analysis of the 'real' data: Reflections on the uses and validity of international interaction data." Paper presented at the annual meeting of the International Studies Association, Dallas.

———— (1974) "Differential source coverage in foreign policy analysis," pp. 353–381 in J. N. Rosenau (ed.), Comparing Foreign Policies. New York: Halsted/John Wiley.

Hoivik, T. (1971) "Social inequality—the main issues." Journal of Peace Research 8:119–142.

Hollist, W. L. (1977) "An analysis of arms processes in the United States and the Soviet Union." International Studies Quarterly 21: 503–528.

Holsti, K. J. (1966) "Resolving international conflict: A taxonomy of behavior and some figures on procedure." Journal of Conflict Resolution 10:272–296.

———— (1972) International Politics: A Framework for Analysis. Englewood Cliffs, N.J.: Prentice-Hall.

Holsti, O. R. (1962) "The belief system and national images: A case study." Journal of Conflict Resolution 3:244–252.

———— (1965a) "The 1914 case." American Political Science Review 59:365–378.

———— (1965b) "Perceptions of time, perceptions of alternatives, and patterns of communication as factors in crisis decision-making." Peace Research Society (International) Papers 3:79–120.

———— (1965c) "East-West conflict and Sino-Soviet relations." Journal of Applied Behavioral Science 1:115–130.

———— (1966) "External conflict and internal consensus: The Sino-Soviet case," pp. 343–358 in P. Stone et al. (eds.), General Inquirer. Cambridge, Mass.: MIT Press.

References

———— (1967) "Cognitive dynamics and images of the enemy: Dulles and Russia," pp. 25–96 in D. Findlay, O. R. Holsti, and R. Fagen (eds.), Enemies in Politics. Chicago: Rand McNally.

———— (1969) Content Analysis for the Social Sciences and Humanities. Reading, Mass.: Addison-Wesley.

———— (1970) "The 'operational code' approach to the study of political leaders: John Foster Dulles' philosophical and instrumental beliefs." Canadian Journal of Political Science 3:123–157.

———— (1972) Crisis Escalation War. Montreal: McGill–Queens University Press.

———— (1976) "Foreign policy formation viewed cognitively," pp. 18–54 in R. Axelrod (ed.), Structure of Decision. Princeton, N.J.: Princeton University Press.

Holsti, O. R., R. Brody, and R. North (1965) "Measuring affect and action in international reaction models: Empirical materials from the 1962 Cuban crisis." Peace Research Society (International) Papers 2:170–190.

Holsti, O. R., and A. L. George (1975) "The effects of stress on the performance of foreign policy-makers," pp. 255–319 in Political Science Annual, Vol. 6. Indianapolis: Bobbs-Merrill.

Holsti, O. R., P. T. Hopmann, and J. D. Sullivan (1973) Unity and Disintegration in International Alliances: Comparative Studies. New York: John Wiley.

Holsti, O. R., R. North, and R. Brody (1968) "Perception and action in the 1914 crisis," pp. 123–158 in J. D. Singer (ed.), Quantitative International Politics. New York: The Free Press.

Holsti, O. R., and J. N. Rosenau (1979a) "America's foreign policy agenda: the post-Vietnam beliefs of American leaders," pp. 231–268 in C. Kegley and P. McGowan (eds.), Challenges to America. Sage International Yearbook of Foreign Policy Studies, Vol. 4. Beverly Hills, Calif.: Sage Publications.

———— (1979b) "Vietnam, consensus, and the belief systems of American leaders." World Politics 32:1–56.

Holsti, O. R., and J. D. Sullivan (1969) "National-international linkages: France and China as non-conforming alliance members," pp. 147–195 in J. N. Rosenau (ed.), Linkage Politics. New York: The Free Press.

Holt, R. T., and J. E. Turner (1971) "Competing paradigms in comparative politics," pp. 23–27 in R. Holt and J. E. Turner (eds.), Methodology of Comparative Research. New York: The Free Press.

Hopkins, R., and R. Mansbach (1973) Structure and Process in International Politics. New York: Harper & Row.

Hopkins, R., and D. J. Puchala (eds.) (1978) The Global Political Economy of Food. Special ed. of International Organization 32:1.

References

Hopmann, P. T. (1967) "International conflict and cohesion in the communist system." International Studies Quarterly 11:212–236.

———— (1972) "Internal and external influences on bargaining in arms control negotiations: The partial test ban," pp. 213–239 in B. M. Russett (ed.), Peace, War, and Numbers. Beverly Hills, Calif.: Sage Publications.

———— (1974) "Bargaining in arms control negotiations: The Seabeds Denuclearization Treaty." International Organization 28:313–348.

———— (1978) "Asymmetrical bargaining in the Conference on Security and Cooperation in Europe." International Organization 32:141–177.

Hopmann, P. T., and T. King (1976) "Interactions and perceptions in the test ban negotiations." International Studies Quarterly 20:105–143.

Hopple, G., P. Rossa, and J. Wilkenfeld (1980) "Threat and foreign policy: The overt behavior of states in conflict," pp. 19–53 in P. J. McGowan and C. W. Kegley (eds.), Threats, Weapons, and Foreign Policy. Sage International Yearbook of Foreign Policy Studies, Vol. 5. Beverly Hills, Calif.: Sage Publications.

Horvath, W. J. (1968) "A statistical model for the duration of wars and strikes." Behavioral Science 13:18–28.

Horvath, W. J., and C. Foster, (1963) "Stochastic models of war alliances." Journal of Conflict Resolution 7:110–116.

Hosoya, C. (1968) "Miscalculations in deterrent policy: Japanese-U.S. relations, 1938–1941." Journal of Peace Research 5:97–115.

Hovet, T. (1960) Bloc Politics in the U.N. Cambridge, Mass.: Harvard University Press.

Hudson, M. (1977) Arab Politics: The Search for Legitimacy. New Haven: Yale University Press.

Huntington, S. P. (1961) The Common Defense: Strategic Problems in National Politics. New York: Columbia University Press.

Ikle, F. C. (1964) How Nations Negotiate. New York: Praeger.

———— (1971) Every War Must End. New York: Columbia University Press.

Ikle, F. C., and N. Leites (1962) "Political negotiation as a process of modifying utilities." Journal of Conflict Resolution 6:19–28.

Inglehart, R. (1967) "An end to European integration." American Political Science Review 61:91–105.

Jacob, P., and J. Toscano (eds.) (1964) The Integration of Political Communities. Philadelphia: Lippincott.

Jacobsen, K. (1969) "Sponsorship in the U.N." Journal of Peace Research 6:235–256.

Jacobson, H. K. (1979) Networks of Interdependence: International Organizations and the Global Political System. New York: Knopf.

Janis, I. L. (1972) Victims of Groupthink. Boston: Houghton Mifflin.

References

Janis, I. L., and L. Mann (1977) Decision Making. New York: The Free Press.

Jensen, L. (1963) "Soviet-American bargaining behavior in the postwar disarmament negotiations." Journal of Conflict Resolution 7:522–541.

——— (1965) "Military capabilities and bargaining behavior." Journal of Conflict Resolution 9:155–163.

——— (1966) "American foreign policy elites and the prediction of international events." Peace Research Society (International) Papers 5:199–209.

——— (1968) "Approach-avoidance bargaining in the test-ban negotiations." International Studies Quarterly 12:152–160.

——— (1969) "Postwar democratic politics: National international linkages in the defense policy of the defeated states," pp. 304–323 in J. N. Rosenau (ed.), Linkage Politics. New York: The Free Press.

Jervis, R. (1970) The Logic of Images in International Relations. Princeton, N.J.: Princeton University Press.

——— (1976) Perception and Misperception in International Politics. Princeton, N.J.: Princeton University Press.

——— (1979) "Deterrence theory revisited." World Politics 31:289–324.

Jessup, P. (1956) Transnational Law. New Haven, Conn.: Yale University Press.

Jones, S., and J. D. Singer (1972) Beyond Conjecture in International Politics: Abstracts of Data-based Research. Itasca, Ill.: F. E. Peacock.

Kahn, H. (1960) On Thermonuclear War. Princeton, N.J.: Princeton University Press.

——— (1962) Thinking About the Unthinkable. New York: Horizon.

——— (1968) On Escalation: Metaphors and Scenarios, rev. ed. Baltimore: Penguin.

Kaiser, K. (1971) "Transnational politics: Toward a theory of multinational politics." International Organization 25:790–818.

Kaplan, M. (1957) System and Process in International Politics. New York: John Wiley.

——— (1966) "The new great debate: Traditionalism vs. science in international relations." World Politics 19:1–20, reprinted pp. 36–61 in K. Knorr and J. N. Rosenau (eds.), Contending Approaches to International Politics. Princeton, N.J.: Princeton University Press, 1969.

——— (1967) "Systems theory," pp. 150–163 in J. C. Charlesworth (ed.), Contemporary Political Analysis. New York: The Free Press.

——— (ed.) (1968) New Approaches to International Relations. New York: St. Martin's Press.

Kaplan, M., A. L. Burns, and R. E. Quandt (1960) "Theoretical analysis of the 'balance of power.'" Behavioral Science 5:240–252.

Kato, M. (1968) "A model of U.S. foreign aid allocation: An application of a rational decision-making scheme," in J. Mueller (ed.), Approaches to Measurement in International Relations. New York: Appleton-Century-Crofts.

Katz, P. (1972) Psyop Automated Management Information Systems PAMIS Foreign Media Analysis File. Kensington, Md.: American Institutes for Research.

Katz, P., M. M. Lent, and E. J. Novotny (1973) Survey of Chinese News Media Content in 1972: A Quantitative Analysis. Kensington, Md.: American Institute for Research.

Kaufman, R. R., H. I. Chernotsky, and D. S. Geller (1975) "A preliminary test of the theory of dependency." Comparative Politics 7:303–330.

Kaufmann, W. W. (1964) The McNamara Strategy. New York: Harper & Row.

Kay, A. (1969) "The impact of African states on the United Nations." International Organization 23:20–47.

Kean, J., and P. J. McGowan (1973) "National attributes and foreign policy participation: A path analysis," pp. 219–251 in P. J. McGowan (ed.), Sage International Yearbook of Foreign Policy Studies, Vol. 1. Beverly Hills, Calif.: Sage Publications.

Kecskemeti, P. (1958) Strategic Surrender: The Politics of Victory and Defeat. Stanford, Calif.: Stanford University Press.

Kegley, C. W. (1973) "A General Empirical Typology of Foreign Policy Behavior." Sage Professional Papers in International Studies, 02–014. Beverly Hills, Calif.: Sage Publications.

Kegley, C. W., G. Raymond, and R. Skinner (1980) "A comparative analysis of nuclear armament," pp. 231–255 in P. J. McGowan and C. W. Kegley (eds.), Threats, Weapons, and Foreign Policy. Sage International Yearbook of Foreign Policy Studies, Vol. 5. Beverly Hills, Calif.: Sage Publications.

Kegley, C. W., S. A. Salmore, and D. J. Rosen (1974) "Convergences in the measurement of interstate behavior," pp. 309–339 in P. J. McGowan (ed.), Sage International Yearbook of Foreign Policy Studies, Vol. 2. Beverly Hills, Calif.: Sage Publications.

Kegley, C. W., and R. J. Skinner (1976) "The case-for-analysis problem," pp. 303–318 in J. N. Rosenau (ed.), In Search of Global Patterns. New York: The Free Press.

Kegley, C. W., and E. Wittkopf (1979) American Foreign Policy: Pattern and Process. New York: St. Martin's Press.

Kelman, H. C. (ed.) (1965) International Behavior: A Social-Psychological Analysis. New York: Holt, Rinehart and Winston.

Kelsen, H. (1942) Law and Peace in International Relations. Cambridge, Mass.: Harvard University Press.

———— (1950) The Law of the United Nations. New York: Praeger.

———— (1952) Principles of International Law. New York: Rinehart.

Kennan, G. F. ("X") (1947) "The sources of Soviet conduct." Foreign Affairs 25:566–582.

———— (1952) American Diplomacy, 1900–1950. New York: Mentor.

———— (1966) Realities of American Foreign Policy. New York: Norton.

Keohane, R. O., (1969) "Who cares about the General Assembly?" International Organization 23:141–149.

Keohane, R. O., and J. Nye, Jr. (eds.) (1971, 1972) Transnational Relations and World Politics. Cambridge, Mass.: Harvard University Press.

———— (1974) "Transgovernmental Relations and International Organizations." World Politics 27:39–62.

———— (1977) Power and Interdependence: World Politics in Transition. Boston: Little, Brown.

Kihl, Y. W. (1971) Conflict Issues and International Civil Aviation Decisions: Three Cases. Graduate School of International Studies, University of Denver. Monograph Series in World Affairs 8/1.

Kirk, G. (1947) The Study of International Relations in American Colleges and Universities. New York: Council on Foreign Relations.

Kissinger, H. A. (1957a) Nuclear Weapons and Foreign Policy. New York: Harper.

———— (1957b) A World Restored. Boston: Houghton Mifflin.

———— (1961) The Necessity for Choice. New York: Harper.

———— (1966) "Domestic structure and foreign policy." Daedalus 95: 503–529.

Klingberg, F. L. (1952) "The historical alternation of moods in American foreign policy." World Politics 4:239–273.

———— (1966) "Predicting the termination of war: Battle casualties and population losses." Journal of Conflict Resolution 10:129–171.

———— (1970) "Historical periods, trends, and cycles in international relations." Journal of Conflict Resolution 14:505–511.

———— (1979) "Cyclical trends in American foreign policy moods and their policy implications," pp. 37–55 in C. W. Kegley and P. J. McGowan (eds.), Challenges to America. Sage International Yearbook of Foreign Policy Studies, Vol. 4. Beverly Hills, Calif.: Sage Publications.

Knorr, K. (1956) The War Potential of Nations. Princeton, N.J.: Princeton University Press.

———— (1970) Military Power and Potential. Lexington, Mass.: Lexington Books.

Knorr, K., and T. Read (1952) (eds.) Limited Strategic War: Essays on Nuclear Strategy. New York: Praeger.

Knorr, K., and J. N. Rosenau (1969a) "Tradition and science in the study of international politics," pp. 3–19 in K. Knorr and J. N. Rosenau (eds.), Contending Approaches to International Politics. Princeton, N.J.: Princeton University Press.

———— (eds.) (1969b) Contending Approaches to International Politics. Princeton, N.J.: Princeton University Press.

Koertge, N. (1978) "Towards a new theory of scientific inquiry," pp. 253–278 in G. Radnitzky and G. Anderson (eds.), Progress and Rationality in Science. Dordrecht, Holland: D. Reidel.

Kolko, G. (1968) The Politics of War: The World and U.S. Foreign Policy, 1943–45. New York: Random House.

———— (1969) The Roots of American Foreign Policy: An Analysis of Power and Purpose. Boston: Beacon Press.

Kolko, J., and G. Kolko (1972) The Limits of Power: The World and U.S. Foreign Policy, 1945–1954. New York: Harper & Row.

Kothari, R. (1975) Footsteps into the Future. New York: The Free Press.

Kuhn, T. S. (1957) The Copernican Revolution. Cambridge, Mass.: Harvard University Press.

———— (1962, 1970a) The Structure of Scientific Revolutions. 1st and expanded ed. Chicago: University of Chicago Press.

———— (1970b) "Reflections on my critics," pp. 231–278 in I. Lakatos and A. Musgrave (eds.), Criticism and the Growths of Knowledge. Cambridge: Cambridge University Press.

———— (1971) "Second thoughts on paradigms," pp. 459–517 in F. Suppe (ed.), The Structure of Scientific Theories. Urbana, Ill.: University of Illinois Press.

———— (1977) The Essential Tension. Chicago: University of Chicago Press.

LaFeber, W. (1967) America, Russia, and the Cold War, 1945–1967. New York: John Wiley.

Lakatos, I. (1970) "Falsification and the methodology of scientific research programmes," pp. 91–196 in I. Lakatos and A. Musgrave (eds.), Criticism and the Growth of Knowledge. Cambridge: Cambridge University Press.

Lakatos, I., and A. Musgrave (eds.) (1970) Criticism and the Growth of Knowledge. Cambridge: Cambridge University Press.

Lall, A. (1966) Modern International Negotiations. New York: Columbia University Press.

Lamb, C., and B. M. Russett (1969) "Politics in the emerging regions." Peace Research Society (International) Papers 12:1–31.

Lampert, D. E. (1975) "The developmental basis of nonstate behavior: Nonstate actors and regional political development in Western Europe and Latin America." Ph.D. dissertation, Rutgers University.

References

Lampert, D. E., L. Falkowski, and R. Mansbach (1978) "Is there an international system?" International Studies Quarterly 22:143–166.

Lancaster, F. W. (1916) Aircraft in Warfare: The Dawn of the Fifth Arm. London: Constable.

Lasswell, H. D. (1930) Psychopathology and Politics. Chicago: University of Chicago Press.

———— (1948) Power and Personality. New York: Norton.

Laulicht, J. (1965a) "An analysis of Canadian foreign policy attitudes." Peace Research Society (International) Papers 3:121–136.

———— (1965b) "Public opinion and foreign policy decisions." Journal of Peace Research 2:147–160.

Lauren, P. G. (1972) "Ultimata and coercive diplomacy." International Studies Quarterly 16:131–166.

Leites, N. (1951) The Operational Code of the Politburo. New York: McGraw-Hill.

———— (1953) A Study of Bolshevism. Glencoe, Ill.: The Free Press.

Leng, R. J. (1980) "Influence strategies and interstate conflict," pp. 125–157 in J. D. Singer (ed.), Correlates of War: II. New York: The Free Press.

Leng, R. J., and R. A. Goodsell (1974) "Behavioral indicators of war proneness in bilateral conflicts," pp. 191–226 in P. J. McGowan (ed.), Sage International Yearbook of Foreign Policy Studies, Vol. 2. Beverly Hills, Calif.: Sage Publications.

Leng, R. J., and H. B. Wheeler (1979) "Influence strategies, success, and war." Journal of Conflict Resolution 23:655–684.

Lenin, V. I. (1914 [1967]) The War and Russian Social Democracy in Selected Works, Vol. 1. New York: International Publishers.

———— (1917 [1967]) Imperialism: The Highest Stage of Capitalism in Selected Works, Vol. 1. New York: International Publishers.

Lerner, D., and M. N. Kramer (1963) "French elite perspectives on the United Nations." International Organization 17:54–75.

Levy, A. (1977) "Coder's manual for identifying serious inter-nation disputes, 1816–1965." Correlates of War Project, Ann Arbor, Michigan (internal memo).

Levy, M. J., Jr. (1969) "'Does it matter if he's naked?' bawled the child," pp. 87–109 in K. Knorr and J. N. Rosenau (eds.), Contending Approaches to International Politics. Princeton, N.J.: Princeton University Press.

Licklider, R. (1971) The Private Nuclear Strategists. Columbus, Ohio: Ohio State University Press.

Lijphart, A. (1963) "The analysis of bloc voting in the general assembly: A critique and a proposal." American Political Science Review 57: 902–917.

References

——— (1964) "Tourist traffic and integration potential." Journal of Common Market Studies 3:251–262.

——— (1974) "The structure of the theoretical revolution in international relations." International Studies Quarterly 18:41–74.

Lindberg, L. N. (1963) The Political Dynamics of European Economic Integration. Stanford, Calif.: Stanford University Press.

Lindberg, L. N., and S. Scheingold (1970) Europe's Would-Be Policy: Patterns of Change in the European Community. Englewood Cliffs, N.J.: Prentice-Hall.

——— (eds.) (1971) Regional Integration: Theory and Research. Cambridge, Mass.: Harvard University Press.

Lindblom, C. (1959) "The science of muddling through." Public Administration Review 19:79–88.

Linkskold, S., D. McElwain, and M. Wanner (1977) "Cooperation and the use of coercion by groups and individuals." Journal of Conflict Resolution 21:531–549.

Lippmann, W. (1922) Public Opinion. New York: Macmillan.

Liska, G. (1957) International Equilibrium: A Theoretical Essay on the Politics and Organization of Security. Cambridge, Mass.: Harvard University Press.

——— (1962) Nations in Alliance: The Limits of Interdependence. Baltimore: Johns Hopkins University Press.

Liske, C. (1975) "Changing patterns of partisanship in senate voting on defense and foreign policy, 1946–1969," pp. 135–176 in P. J. McGowan (ed.), Sage International Yearbook of Foreign Policy Studies, Vol. 3. Beverly Hills, Calif.: Sage Publications.

Lodal, J. M. (1978–1979) "SALT II and American Security." Foreign Affairs 57:245–268.

Logue, J. J. (ed.) (1972) The Fate of the Oceans. Villanova, Pa.: Villanova University Press.

Lowi, T. J. (1964) "American business, public policy, case studies and political theory." World Politics 26:677–715.

——— (1967) "Making democracy safe for the world: National politics and foreign policy," pp. 295–331 in J. N. Rosenau (ed.), Domestic Sources of Foreign Policy. New York: The Free Press.

Luard, E. (1976) Types of International Society. New York: The Free Press.

Luce, R. D., and H. Raiffa (1957) Games and Decisions. New York: John Wiley.

Lynch, C. (1980) "Bibliography of recent comparative foreign policy studies, 1975–1979," pp. 313–319 in P. J. McGowan and C. W. Kegley (eds.), Threats, Weapons, and Foreign Policy. Sage International Yearbook of Foreign Policy Studies, Vol. 5. Beverly Hills, Calif.: Sage Publications.

References

McClelland, C. A. (1961) "The acute international crisis." World Politics 14:182–204.

——— (1964) "Action structures and communication in two international crises: Quemoy and Berlin." Background 7:201–215.

——— (1965) "A system theory and human conflict," pp. 250–273 in E. McNeil (ed.), The Nature of Human Conflict. Englewood Cliffs, N.J.: Prentice-Hall.

——— (1966) Theory and the International System. New York: Macmillan.

——— (1967) "The World/Interaction Survey: A research project on theory and measurement of international interaction and transaction." University of Southern California (mimeographed).

——— (1968) "Access to Berlin: The quantity and variety of events, 1948–1963," pp. 159–187 in J. D. Singer (ed.), Quantitative International Politics. New York: The Free Press.

——— (1970) "International interaction analysis in the predictive mode." University of Southern California (mimeographed).

——— (1972a) "The beginning, duration, and abatement of international crises: Comparisons in two conflict arenas," pp. 83–111 in C. F. Hermann (ed.), International Crises. New York: The Free Press.

——— (1972b) "Some effects on theory from the international event analysis movement," pp. 15–43 in E. Azar, R. Brody, and C. A. McClelland (eds.), International Events Interaction Analysis: Some Research Considerations. Sage Professional Papers in International Studies, 02–001. Beverly Hills, Calif.: Sage Publications.

——— (1976) "An inside appraisal of the world event interaction survey," pp. 105–110 in J. N. Rosenau (ed.), In Search of Global Patterns. New York: The Free Press.

——— (1977) "The anticipation of international crises." International Studies Quarterly 21:15–38.

McClelland, C. A., and G. Hoggard (1969) "Conflict patterns in the interactions among nations," pp. 711–724 in J. N. Rosenau (ed.) International Politics and Foreign Politics. New York: The Free Press.

McCormick, J. (1975) "Evaluating models of crisis behavior: Some evidence from the Middle East." International Studies Quarterly 19: 17–45.

McDougal, M. S., and F. Felsciano (1961) Law and Minimum World Public Order. New Haven, Conn.: Yale University Press.

McDougal, M. S., and H. D. Lasswell (1959) "The identification and appraisal of diverse systems of public order." American Journal of International Law 53:1–29.

McDougal, M. S., H. D. Lasswell, and I. A. Vlasic (1963) Law and Public Order in Space. New Haven, Conn.: Yale University Press.

References

McGowan, P. J. (1968) "Africa and non-alignment." International Studies Quarterly 12:262–295.

———— (1969) "The pattern of african diplomacy: A quantitative comparison." Journal of Asian and African Studies 4:202–221.

———— (1974a) "A Bayesian approach to the problem of events data validity," pp. 407–433 in J. N. Rosenau (ed.), Comparing Foreign Policies. New York: Halsted/John Wiley.

———— (1974b) "Adaptive foreign policy behavior: An empirical approach," pp. 45–54 in J. N. Rosenau (ed.), Comparing Foreign Policies. New York: Halsted/John Wiley.

McGowan, P. J., and K. Gottwald (1975) "Small state foreign policies." International Studies Quarterly 19:469–500.

McGowan, P. J., and T. H. Johnson (1979) "The AFRICA Project and the comparative study of African foreign policy," pp. 190–241 in M. W. Delaney (ed.), Aspects of International Relations in Africa. Bloomington, Ind.: African Studies Program, Indiana University.

McGowan, P. J., and M. K. O'Leary (1971) Comparative Foreign Policy Analysis Materials. Chicago: Markham.

McGowan, P. J., and H. B. Shapiro (1974) The Comparative Study of Foreign Policy: An Inventory of Scientific Findings. Beverly Hills, Calif.: Sage Publications.

McGowan, P. J., and D. Smith (1978) "Economic dependency in black Africa: An analysis of competing theories." International Organization 32:179–235.

McLellan, D. (1971) "The 'operational code' approach to the study of political leaders: Dean Acheson's philosophical and instrumental beliefs." Canadian Journal of Political Science 4:52–75.

McNamara, R. S. (1968) The Essence of Security. New York: Harper & Row.

McNeil, E. B. (1962) "Waging experimental war: A review of Sherif et al. Intergroup conflict and cooperation: The Robbers Cave experiment." Journal of Conflict Resolution 2:77–81.

Macridis, R. (1958, 1962, 1967) Foreign Policy in World Politics. 1st, 2nd, and 3rd eds. Englewood Cliffs, N.J.: Prentice-Hall.

Maddox, R. J. (1973) The New Left and the Origins of the Cold War. Princeton, N.J.: Princeton University Press.

Magdoff, H. (1969) The Age of Imperialism. New York: Monthly Review Press.

Mahoney, R., and R. Clayberg (1980) "Images and threats: Soviet perceptions of international crises, 1946–1975," pp. 55–81 in P. J. McGowan and C. W. Kegley (eds.), Threats, Weapons, and Foreign Policy. Sage International Yearbook of Foreign Policy Studies, Vol. 5. Beverly Hills, Calif.: Sage Publications.

References

Mahoney, R. B., Jr. (1976) "American political-military operations and the structure of the international system, 1946–1975." Paper presented to the annual meeting of the Section on Military Studies of the International Studies Association, Ohio State University.

Mandel, E. (1969) Marxist Economic Theory. New York: Monthly Review Press.

Manno, C. S. (1966) "Majority decision and minority response in the U.N. General Assembly." Journal of Conflict Resolution 10:1–20.

Mansbach, R., Y. Ferguson, and D. Lampert (1976) The Web of World Politics. Englewood Cliffs, N.J.: Prentice-Hall.

Mansbach, R., and J. A. Vasquez (1981a) "The effect of actor and issue classifications on the analysis of global conflict-cooperation." Journal of Politics 43:861–875.

———— (1981b) In Search of Theory: A New Paradigm for Global Politics. New York: Columbia University Press.

March, J. (1966) "The power of power," pp. 34–70 in D. Easton (ed.), Varieties of Political Theory. Englewood Cliffs, N.J.: Prentice-Hall.

Marcuse, H. (1964) One Dimensional Man. Boston, Mass.: Beacon Press.

Masakatsu, K. (1969) "A model of U.S. and foreign allocation: An application of a rational decision-making scheme," pp. 198–215 in J. Mueller (ed.), Approaches to Measurement in International Relations. New York: Appleton-Century-Crofts.

Masterman, M. (1970) "The nature of a paradigm," pp. 59–89 in I. Lakatos and A. Musgrave (eds.), Criticism and the Growth of Knowledge. Cambridge: Cambridge University Press.

May, E. (1973) "Lessons" of the Past: The Use and Misuse of History in American Foreign Policy. New York: Oxford University Press.

Mazrui, A. (1976) A World Federation of Cultures: An African Perspective. New York: The Free Press.

Mendlovitz, S. H. (ed.) (1977) On the Creation of a Just World Order. New York: The Free Press.

Merritt, R. (1966) Symbols of American Community: 1735–1775. New Haven, Conn.: Yale University Press.

Meyer, D. B. (1960) The Protestant Search for Political Realism 1919–1941. Berkeley and Los Angeles: University of California Press.

Meyers, B. (1966) "African voting in the U.N. General Assembly." Journal of Modern African Studies 4:213–227.

Michalak, S. J. (1979) "Theoretical perspectives for understanding international interdependence." World Politics 32:136–150.

Midlarsky, M. (1975) On War. New York: The Free Press.

Midlarsky, M., and R. Tanter (1967) "Toward a theory of political instability in Latin America." Journal of Peace Research 4:209–227.

References

Milbrath, L. (1967) "Interest groups and foreign policy," pp. 231–251 in J. N. Rosenau (ed.), Domestic Sources of Foreign Policy. New York: The Free Press.

Milburn, T. W. (1959) "What constitutes effective deterrence?" The Journal of Conflict Resolution 3:138–145.

——— (1969) "Intellectual history of a research project," pp. 263–283 in D. G. Pruitt and R. C. Snyder (eds.), Theory and Research on the Causes of War. Englewood Cliffs, N.J.: Prentice-Hall.

——— (1972) "The management of crises," pp. 259–277 in C. F. Hermann (ed.), International Crises. New York: The Free Press.

Miller, W. E. (1967) "Voting and foreign policy," pp. 213–230 in J. N. Rosenau (ed.), Domestic Sources of Foreign Policy. New York: The Free Press.

Miller, W. E., and D. Stokes (1963) "Constituency influence in congress." American Political Science Review 57:45–56.

Milstein, J. S. (1972) "American and Soviet influence, balance of power, and Arab-Israeli violence," pp. 139–164 in B. M. Russett (ed.), Peace, War, and Numbers. Beverly Hills, Calif.: Sage Publications.

Milstein, J. S., and W. Mitchell (1968) "Dynamics of the Vietnam conflict: A quantitative analysis and predictive computer simulation." Peace Research Society (International) Papers 10:163–213.

——— (1969) "Computer simulation of international processes: The Vietnam War and the pre-World War I naval race." Peace Research Society (International) Papers 12:117–136.

Mitchell, E. J. (1968) "Inequality and insurgency: A statistical study of South Vietnam." World Politics 20:421–438.

Mitrany, D. (1943 [1966]) A Working Peace System. Chicago: Quadrangle Books.

Modelski, G. (1961) "Agraria, and industria," pp. 118–143 in K. Knorr and S. Verba (eds.), The International System. Princeton, N.J.: Princeton University Press.

——— (1970) "Simulations, realities and international relations theory." Simulations and Games 1:111–134.

Modigliani, A. (1972) "Hawks and doves, isolationism and political distrust: An analysis of public opinion on military policy." American Political Science Review 56:960–978.

Moe, R. C., and S. C. Teel (1970) "Congress as policy maker: A necessary reappraisal." Political Science Quarterly 85:463–467.

Moll, K. D., and G. M. Luebbert (1980) "Arms race and military expenditure models." Journal of Conflict Resolution 24:153–185.

Moore, D. W. (1974a) "Governmental and societal influences on foreign policy in open and closed nations," pp. 171–199 in J. N. Rosenau (ed.), Comparing Foreign Policies. New York: Halsted/John Wiley.

―――― (1974b) "National attributes and nation typologies: A look at the Rosenau genotypes," pp. 251–267 in J. N. Rosenau (ed.), Comparing Foreign Policies. New Yor : Halsted/John Wiley.

Moos, M., and T. I. Cook (1954) Power through Purpose: The Realism of Idealism as a Basis for Foreign Policy. Baltimore: Johns Hopkins University Press.

Morgan, P. (1977) Deterrence. Beverly Hills, Calif.: Sage Publications.

Morgenthau, H. J. (1946) Scientific Man vs. Power Politics. Chicago: University of Chicago Press.

―――― (1948, 1954, 1960, 1967, 1973, 1975) Politics Among Nations: The Struggle for Power and Peace. 1st, 2nd, 3rd, 4th, and 5th, and 5th rev. eds. New York: Knopf.

―――― (1951) In Defense of the National Interest. New York: Knopf.

―――― (1952) "Another great debate: The national interest of the United States." American Political Science Review 46:961–988.

―――― (1955) "Reflections on the state of political science." Review of Politics 17:431–460.

―――― (1958) Dilemmas of Politics. Chicago: University of Chicago Press.

―――― (1962) "A political theory of foreign aid." American Political Science Review 56:301–309.

―――― (1965a) Vietnam and the United States. Washington, D.C.: Public Affairs Press.

―――― (1965b) "International relations, 1960–1964." Annals of the American Academy of Political and Social Science 370:163–171.

―――― (1967) "Common-sense and theories of international relations." Journal of International Affairs 21:207–214.

―――― (1969) A New Foreign Policy for the United States. New York: Praeger.

―――― (1970) Truth and Power: Essays of a Decade, 1960–70. New York: Praeger.

Morgenthau, H. J., and K. W. Thompson (eds.) (1950) Principles and Problems of International Politics. New York: Knopf.

Morse, E. L. (1976) Modernization and the Transformation of International Relations. New York: The Free Press.

Moses, L. E., R. A. Brody, O. R. Holsti, J. B. Kadane, and J. S. Milstein (1967) "Scaling data on inter-nation action." Science 156 (26 May):3778.

Moskos, C., and W. Bell (1964) "Emergent Caribbean nations face the outside world." Social Problems 12:24–41.

Mueller, J. E. (ed.) (1969) Approaches to Measurement in International Relations: A Non-Evangelical Survey. New York: Appleton-Century-Crofts.

———— (1971) "Trends in popular support for the wars in Korea and Vietnam." American Political Science Review 65:358–375.

———— (1976) "War, presidents, and public opinion," pp. 111–113 in J. N. Rosenau (ed.), In Search of Global Patterns. New York: The Free Press.

Musgrave, A. (1976) "Method or Madness?" pp. 457–491 in R. Cohen et al. (eds.), Boston Studies in the Philosophy of Science, Vol. 39. Dordrecht, Holland: D. Reidel.

———— (1978) "Evidential support, falsification, heuristics, and anarchism," pp. 181–201 in G. Radnitzky and G. Anderson (eds.), Progress and Rationality in Science. Dordrecht, Holland: D. Reidel.

Nagel, E. (1961) The Structure of Science. New York: Harcourt, Brace and World.

Namenworth, Z., and T. L. Brewer (1966) "Elite editorial comment on the European and Atlantic communities in four continents," pp. 401–427 in P. Stone et al. (eds.), General Inquirer. Cambridge, Mass.: MIT Press.

Naroll, R. (1968) "Imperial cycles and world order." Peace Research Society (International) Papers 7:83–102.

Naroll, R., V. L. Bullough, and F. Naroll (1974) Military Deterrence in History. A Pilot Cross-Historical Survey. Albany, N.Y.: State University of New York Press.

Nash, J. F. (1950) "The bargaining problem." Econometrica 18:155–162.

Neumann, J. von, and O. Morgenstern (1944) Theory of Games and Economic Behavior. Princeton, N.J.: Princeton University Press.

Neustadt, R. E. (1960) Presidential Power. New York: John Wiley.

———— (1970) Alliance Politics. New York: Columbia University Press.

Nicolson, H. (1939a) Diplomacy. London: Oxford University Press.

———— (1939b) The Congress of Vienna. New York: Harcourt.

Niebuhr, R. (1940) Christianity and Power Politics. New York: Scribner's.

———— (1941) "The illusion of world government." Foreign Affairs 27:379–388.

———— (1946) "The myth of world government." The Nation 162:312–314.

———— (1952) The Moral Implications of Loyalty to the United Nations. New Haven, Conn.: Edward W. Hazen Foundation.

———— (1953) Christian Realism and Political Problems. New York: Scribner's.

———— (1965) Man's Nature and His Communities. New York: Scribner's.

Noel, R. C. (1963) "Inter-nation simulation participant's manual," pp.

43–69 in H. Guetzkow et al., Simulation in International Relations. Englewood Cliffs, N.J.: Prentice-Hall.

North, R. C. (1963) "International relations: Putting the pieces together." Background 7:119–130.

——— (1976) "The Stanford studies in international conflict and integration," pp. 349–353 in F. Hoole and D. Zinnes (eds.), Quantitative International Politics: An Appraisal. New York: Praeger.

North, R. C., and N. Choucri (1968) "Background conditions to the outbreak of the First World War." Peace Research Society (International) Papers 9:125–137.

North, R. C., O. R. Holsti, and N. Choucri (1976) "A reevaluation of the substantive contribution of the Stanford studies in conflict and integration," pp. 435–459 in F. Hoole and D. Zinnes (eds.), Quantitative International Politics: An Appraisal. New York: Praeger.

Northedge, F. S. (1968, 1974) The Foreign Policies of the Powers. New York: Praeger.

Northedge, F. S., and M. D. Donelan (1971) International Disputes: The Political Aspects. New York: St. Martin's Press.

Nye, J. S., Jr. (ed.) (1968) International Regionalism: Readings. Boston: Little, Brown.

——— (1971) Peace in Parts: Integration and Conflict in Regional Organization. Boston: Little, Brown.

Ohlstrom, B. (1966) "Information and propaganda." Journal of Peace Research 1:75–88.

O'Leary, M. K. (1969) "Linkages between domestic and international politics in underdeveloped nations," pp. 324–346 in J. N. Rosenau (ed.), Linkage Politics. New York: The Free Press.

——— (1974) "Foreign policy and bureaucratic adaptation," pp. 55–70 in J. N. Rosenau (ed.), Comparing Foreign Policies. New York: Halsted/John Wiley.

——— (1976) "The role of issues," pp. 318–325 in J. N. Rosenau (ed.), In Search of Global Patterns. New York: The Free Press.

Olsen, L. J., and I. M. Jarvad (1970) "The Vietnam conference papers, a case study of a failure of peace research." Peace Research Society (International) Papers 14:155–170.

Olson, R. S. (1979) "Economic coercion in world politics." World Politics 31:471–494.

Olson, W. C. (1972) "The growth of a discipline," pp. 1–29 in B. Porter (ed.), The Aberystwyth Papers: International Politics 1919–1969. London: Oxford University Press.

Organski, A. F. K. (1958, 1968) World Politics. 1st and 2nd eds. New York: Knopf.

References

Organski, A. F. K., and J. Kugler (1977) "The cost of major wars: The Phoenix factor." American Political Science Review 71:1347–1366.

———— (1978) "Davids and Goliaths: Predicting the outcomes of international wars." Comparative Political Studies 11:141–180.

Organski, A. F. K., and K. Organski (1961) Population and World Power. New York: Knopf.

Osgood, C. E. (1959) "Suggestions for winning the real war with communism." Journal of Conflict Resolution 3:295–325.

———— (1962) Alternative to War or Surrender. Urbana, Ill.: University of Illinois Press.

Osgood, R. (1953) Ideals and Self-Interest in America's Foreign Relations. Chicago: University of Chicago Press.

———— (1957) Limited War: The Challenge to American Strategy. Chicago: University of Chicago Press.

Ostrom, C. W. (1977) "Evaluating alternative decision-making models: An empirical test between an arms race model and an organizational politics model." Journal of Conflict Resolution 21:235–266.

———— (1978) "A reactive linkage model of the U.S. defense expenditure policymaking process." American Political Science Review 72:941–973.

Ostrom, C. W., and F. Hoole (1978) "Alliances and war revisited: A research note." International Studies Quarterly 22:215–236.

Page, B. I., and R. A. Brody (1972) "Policy voting and the electoral process: The Vietnam war issue." American Political Science Review 66:979–995.

Paige, G. (1968) The Korean Decision: June 24–30, 1950. New York: The Free Press.

———— (1972) "Comparative case analysis of crisis decisions: Korea and Cuba," pp. 41–55 in C. F. Hermann (ed.), International Crises: Insights from Behavioral Research. New York: The Free Press.

Parenti, M. (ed.) (1971) Trends and Tragedies in American Foreign Policy. Boston: Little, Brown.

Parsons, T. (1961) "An outline of the social system," pp. 30–79 in T. Parsons, E. Shils, K. Naegele, and J. Pitts (eds.), Theories of Society. New York: The Free Press.

Patchen, M. (1970) "Models of cooperation and conflict: A critical review." Journal of Conflict Resolution 14:389–408.

Peterson, S. (1975) "Research on research: Events data studies, 1961–1972," pp. 263–309 in P. J. McGowan (ed.), Sage International Yearbook of Foreign Policy Studies, Vol. 3. Beverly Hills, Calif./London: Sage Publications.

Phillips, W. R. (1973) "The conflict environment of nations: A study of conflict inputs to nations in 1963," pp. 124–148 in J. Wilkenfeld (ed.), Conflict Behavior and Linkage Politics. New York: David McKay.

———— (1978) "Prior behavior as an explanation of foreign policy," pp. 161–172 in M. East, S. A. Salmore, and C. F. Hermann (eds.), Why Nations Act. Beverly Hills, Calif.: Sage Publications.

Phillips, W. R., and R. C. Crain (1974) "Dynamic foreign policy interactions: Reciprocity and uncertainty in foreign policy," pp. 227–266 in P. McGowan (ed.), Sage International Yearbook of Foreign Policy Studies, Vol. 2. Beverly Hills, Calif.: Sage Publications.

Phillips, W. R., and R. V. Rimkunas (1979) "A cross-agency comparison of U.S. crisis perception," pp. 237–270 in J. D. Singer and M. D. Wallace (eds.), To Augur Well. Beverly Hills, Calif.: Sage Publications.

Pipes, R. (1981) U.S.–Soviet Relations in the Era of Detente. Boulder, Colo.: Westview.

Plano, J. C., and R. Riggs (1967) Forging World Order. New York: Macmillan.

Platig, E. R. (1967) International Relations Research: Problems of Evaluation and Advancement. Santa Barbara, Calif.: Clio Press.

Pomper, G. M. (1972) "From confusion to clarity: Issues and American voters, 1956–1968." American Political Science Review 66:415–428.

Pool, I., and A. Kessler (1965) "The kaiser, the tsar, and the computer." American Behavioral Scientist 8:31–38.

Popper, K. (1935, 1959) Logik der Forschung: The Logic of Scientific Discovery. London: Hutchinson.

———— (1970) "Normal science and its dangers," pp. 51–58 in I. Lakatos and A. Musgrave (eds.), Criticism and the Growth of Knowledge. Cambridge: Cambridge University Press.

Porter, B. (ed.) (1972) The Aberystwyth Papers: International Politics 1919–1969. London: Oxford University Press.

Powell, C. A., D. Andrus, W. A. Fowler, and K. Knight (1974) "Determinants of foreign policy behavior: A causal modeling approach," pp. 151–170 in J. N. Rosenau (ed.), Comparing Foreign Policies. New York: Halsted/John Wiley.

Pruitt, D. G. (1962) "An analysis of responsiveness between nations." Journal of Conflict Resolution 6:5–18.

———— (1965) "Definition of the situation as a determinant of international action," pp. 343–432 in H. C. Kelman (ed.), International Behavior: A Social Psychological Analysis. New York: Holt, Rinehart and Winston.

Pruitt, D. G., and S. A. Lewis (1977) "The psychology of integrative bargaining," pp. 161–192 in D. Druckman (ed.), Negotiations. Beverly Hills, Calif.: Sage Publications.

References

Puchala, D., and S. Fagen (1974) "International politics in the 1970's: The search for a perspective." International Organization 28:247–266.

Quandt, R. E. (1961) "On the use of game models in theories of international relations," pp. 69–76 in K. Knorr and S. Verba (eds.), The International System: Theoretical Essays. Princeton, N.J.: Princeton University Press.

Quester, G. (1966) Deterrence Before Hiroshima. New York: John Wiley.

——— (1972) "Some conceptual problems in nuclear proliferation." American Political Science Review 66:490–497.

Rapoport, A. (1957) "Lewis F. Richardson's mathematical theory of war." Journal of Conflict Resolution 1:249–299.

——— (1960) Fights, Games and Debates. Ann Arbor, Mich.: University of Michigan Press.

——— (1964) Strategy and Conscience. New York: Schocken Books.

Rapoport, A., and A. M. Chammah (1965) Prisoner's Dilemma. Ann Arbor, Mich.: University of Michigan Press.

Raser, J. R. (1965) "Learning and affect in international politics." Journal of Peace Research 2:216–226.

Raser, J. R., and W. Crow (1963) Capacity to Delay Response: Explication of a Deterrence Concept and Plan for Research Using the Inter-Nation Simulation. La Jolla, Calif.: Western Behavioral Science Institute.

——— (1969) "A simulation study of deterrence theories," pp. 136–149 in D. G. Pruitt and R. C. Snyder (eds.), Theory and Research on the Causes of War. Englewood Cliffs, N.J.: Prentice-Hall.

Rattinger, H. (1976) "From war to war: Arms races in the Middle East." International Studies Quarterly 20:501–531.

Ray, J. L. (1974) "Status inconsistency and war involvement among European states, 1816–1970." Ph.D. dissertation, University of Michigan.

——— (1978) "Status inconsistency and aggressive war involvement in Europe, 1816–1970." Paper presented to the annual convention of the International Studies Association, Washington, D.C.

——— (1980) "The measurement of system structure," pp. 36–54 in J. D. Singer (ed.), The Correlates of War: II. New York: The Free Press.

Ray, J. L., and J. D. Singer (1973) "Measuring the concentration of power in the international system." Sociological Methods and Research 1:403–437.

Ray, J. L., and T. Webster (1978) "Dependency and economic growth in Latin America." International Studies Quarterly 22:409–434.

Reinken, D. L. (1968) "Computer explorations of the 'balance of power':

A project report," pp. 459–481 in M. Kaplan (ed.), New Approaches to International Relations. New York: St. Martin's Press.

Reinton, P. O. (1967) "International structure and international integration: The case of Latin America." Journal of Peace Research 4:334–365.

Rhee, S. W. (1977a) "Communist China's foreign behavior: An application of field theory model II," pp. 315–369 in R. J. Rummel (ed.), Field Theory Evolving. Beverly Hills, Calif.: Sage Publications.

———— (1977b) "China's cooperation, conflict and interaction behavior viewed from Rummel's field theoretic perspective," pp. 371–401 in R. J. Rummel (ed.), Field Theory Evolving. Beverly Hills, Calif.: Sage Publications.

Richardson, L. W. (1960a) Arms and Insecurity. Chicago: Quadrangle Books.

———— (1960b) Statistics of Deadly Quarrels. Chicago: Quadrangle Books.

Rieselbach, L. N. (1960a) "The basis of isolationist behavior." Public Opinion Quarterly 24:645–657.

———— (1960b) "Quantitative techniques for studying voting behavior in the U.N. General Assembly." International Organization 14:291–306.

———— (1964) "The demography of the congressional vote on foreign aid, 1939–1958." American Political Science Review 88:577–588.

Riggs, F. W. (1957) "Agraria and industria: Toward a typology of comparative administration," pp. 23–116 in W. J. Siffin (ed.), Toward the Comparative Study of Public Administration. Bloomington, Ind.: Indiana University Press.

———— (1961) "International relations as a prismatic system," pp. 144–181 in K. Knorr and S. Verba (eds.), The International System. Princeton, N.J.: Princeton University Press.

Riggs, R. (1958) Politics in the U.N. Urbana, Ill.: University of Illinois Press.

Riggs, R., M. Heinz, B. Hughes, and T. Volgy (1970) "Behavioralism in the study of the United Nations." World Politics 22:197–236.

Riker, W. (1962) The Theory of Political Coalitions. New Haven, Conn.: Yale University Press.

———— (1964) "Some ambiguities in the notion of power." American Political Science Review 58:341–349.

Robinson, J. A. (1962) Congress and Foreign Policy Making. New York: Dorsey Press.

Robinson, J. A., L. Anderson, M. G. Hermann, and R. C. Snyder (1966) "Teaching with the Inter-Nation Simulation and case studies." American Political Science Review 60:53–65.

References

Robinson, J. A., and R. C. Snyder (1965) "Decision-making in international politics," pp. 435–463 in H. Kelman (ed.), International Behavior: A Social Psychological Analysis. New York: Holt, Rinehart and Winston.

Robinson, T. W. (1967) "A national interest analysis of Sino-Soviet relations." International Studies Quarterly II:135–175.

Rogow, A. (1963) James Forrestal: A Study of Personality, Politics, and Policy. New York: Macmillan.

Rosecrance, R. (1963) Action and Reaction in World Politics. Boston: Little, Brown.

———— (1966) "Bipolarity, multipolarity and the future." Journal of Conflict Resolution 10:314–327.

———— (1973) International Relations: Peace or War? New York: McGraw-Hill.

Rosecrance, R., A. Alexandroff, B. Healy, and A. Stein (1974) "Power, balance of power, and status in nineteenth century international relations." Sage Professional Papers in International Studies, 02–029. Beverly Hills, Calif.: Sage Publications.

Rosecrance, R., and A. Stein (1973) "Interdependence: Myth or reality?" World Politics 26:1–27.

Rosen, S. (1972) "War power and the willingness to suffer," pp. 167–184 in B. M. Russett (ed.), Peace, War, and Numbers. Beverly Hills, Calif.: Sage Publications.

———— (1973) (ed.) Testing the Theory of the Military-Industrial Complex. Lexington, Mass.: Lexington Books.

———— (1977) "A stable system of mutual nuclear deterrence in the Arab-Israeli conflict." American Political Science Review 71:1367–1383.

Rosen, S., and J. R. Kurth (eds.) (1974) Testing Theories of Economic Imperialism. Lexington, Mass.: Lexington Books.

Rosenau, J. N. (1961a) Public Opinion and Foreign Policy. New York: Random House.

———— (1961b, 1969a) (ed.) International Politics and Foreign Policy. 1st and revised eds. New York: The Free Press.

———— (1962) "Consensus-building in the American national community: Some hypotheses and some supporting data." Journal of Politics 24: 639–661.

———— (1966) "Pre-theories and theories of foreign policy," pp. 27–93 in R. B. Farrell (ed.), Approaches to Comparative and International Politics. Evanston, Ill.: Northwestern University Press.

———— (1967a) "The premises and promises of decision-making analysis," pp. 189–211 in J. Charlesworth (ed.), Contemporary Political Analysis. New York: The Free Press.

———— (1967b) "Foreign policy as an issue-area," pp. 11–50 in J. N. Rosenau (ed.), Domestic Sources of Foreign Policy. New York: The Free Press.

———— (1968a) "The national interest," pp. 34–40 in International Encyclopedia of the Social Sciences, Vol. 11. New York: Crowell-Collier.

———— (1968b) The Scientific Study of Foreign Policy. New York: The Free Press.

———— (1968c) "Private preferences and political responsibilities: The relative potency of individual and role variables in the behavior of U.S. senators," pp. 17–50 in J. D. Singer (ed.), Quantitative International Politics. New York: The Free Press.

———— (1969b) (ed.) "Toward the study of national-international linkages," pp. 44–63 in J. N. Rosenau (ed.), Linkage Politics. New York: The Free Press.

———— (1970) The Adaptation of National Societies. New York: McCaleb-Seiler.

———— (1971) "Comparative foreign policy—fad, fantasy, or field," pp. 67–94 in J. N. Rosenau (ed.), Scientific Study of Foreign Policy. New York: The Free Press.

———— (1972) "Adaptive polities in an interdependent world." Orbis 16:153–171.

———— (1973) "Theorizing across systems: Linkage politics revisited," pp. 25–56 in J. Wilkenfeld (ed.), Conflict Behavior and Linkage Politics. New York: David McKay.

———— (1981) The Study of Global Interdependence. New York: Nichols.

———— (1981) The Study of Political Adaptation. New York: Nichols.

Rosenau, J. N., P. M. Burgess, and C. F. Hermann (1973) "The adaptation of foreign policy research: A case study of an anti–case study project." International Studies Quarterly 17:119–144.

Rosenau, J. N., and G. D. Hoggard (1974) "Foreign policy behavior in dyadic relationships: Testing a pre-theoretical extension," pp. 117–149 in J. N. Rosenau (ed.), Comparing Foreign Policies. New York: Halsted/John Wiley.

Rosenau, J. N., and G. H. Ramsey (1975) "External and internal typologies of foreign policy behavior: Testing the stability of an intriguing set of findings," pp. 245–262 in P. J. McGowan (ed.), Sage International Yearbook of foreign policy studies, Vol. 3. Beverly Hills, Calif.: Sage Publications.

Rosenberg, M. J. (1967) "Attitude change and foreign policy in the cold war era," pp. 111–159 in J. N. Rosenau (ed.), Domestic Sources of Foreign Policy. New York: The Free Press.

Rourke, F. E. (1969) Bureaucracy, Politics, and Public Policy. Boston: Little, Brown.

References

Rowe, E. T. (1964) "The emerging anti-colonial consensus in the U.N." Journal of Conflict Resolution 8:209–230.

———— (1969) "Changing patterns in the voting success of member states in the U.N. General Assembly, 1945–1966." International Organization 23:231–253.

———— (1971) "The U.S., the U.N. and the Cold War." International Organization 25:59–78.

———— (1974) "Aid and coups d'etat." International Studies Quarterly 18:239–255.

Rubin, J., and B. R. Brown (1975) The Social Psychology of Bargaining and Negotiation. New York: Academic Press.

Rudner, R. S. (1972) "Comment: On evolving standard views in philosophy of science." American Political Science Review 66:827–845.

Ruge, M. (1964) "Technical assistance and parliamentary debates." Journal of Peace Research 2:77–94.

Ruggie, J. G. (1975) "International responses to technology: Concepts and trends." International Organization 29:557–583.

Ruggie, J. G., and E. B. Haas (eds.) (1975) International responses to technology. Special ed. of International Organization 29.

Rummel, R. J. (1963) "Dimensions of conflict behavior within and between nations." General Systems Yearbook 8:1–50.

———— (1964) "Testing some possible predictors of conflict behavior within and between nations." Peace Research Society (International) Papers 1:79–111.

———— (1966a) "A social field theory of foreign conflict behavior." Peace Research Society (International) Papers 4:131–150.

———— (1966b) "Some dimensions in the foreign behavior of nations." Journal of Peace Research 3:201–224.

———— (1967a) "Dimensions of dyadic war, 1820–1952." Journal of Conflict Resolution 11:176–184.

———— (1967b) "Some attributes and behavioral patterns of nations." Journal of Peace Research 2:196–206.

———— (1968) "The relationship between national attributes and foreign conflict behavior," pp. 187–214 in J. D. Singer (ed.), Quantitative International Politics. New York: The Free Press.

———— (1969) "Indicators of cross-national and international patterns." American Political Science Review 63:127–147.

———— (1971, 1977a) "A status-field theory of international relations," pp. 199–255 in R. J. Rummel (ed.), Field Theory Evolving. Beverly Hills, Calif.: Sage Publications.

———— (1972a) "U.S. foreign relations: Conflict, cooperation, and attribute distances," pp. 71–114 in B. M. Russett (ed.), Peace, War, and Numbers. Beverly Hills, Calif.: Sage Publications.

——— (1972b) The Dimensions of Nations. Beverly Hills, Calif.: Sage Publications.

——— (1976a) "The roots of faith," pp. 10–30 in J. N. Rosenau (ed.), In Search of Global Patterns. New York: The Free Press.

——— (1976b) Peace Endangered: The Reality of Détente. Beverly Hills, Calif.: Sage Publications.

——— (1976c) The Conflict Helix. Understanding Conflict and War, Vol. 2. Beverly Hills, Calif.: Sage Publications.

——— (1977a) Field Theory Evolving. Beverly Hills, Calif.: Sage Publications.

——— (1977b) Conflict in Perspective. Understanding Conflict and War, Vol. 3. Beverly Hills, Calif.: Sage Publications.

——— (1979) War, Power, Peace. Understanding Conflict and War, Vol. 4. Beverly Hills, Calif.: Sage Publications.

Russett, B. M. (1962a) "International communication and legislative behavior: The senate and the house of commons." Journal of Conflict Resolution 6:291–307.

——— (1962b) "Cause, surprise and no escape." Journal of Politics 24:3–22.

——— (1963a) Community and Contention: Britain and America in the Twentieth Century. Cambridge, Mass.: MIT Press.

——— (1963b) "The calculus of deterrence." Journal of Conflict Resolution 7:97–109.

——— (1964) "Measures of Military Effort." American Behavioral Scientist 7:26–29.

——— (1966) "Discovering voting groups in the U.N." American Political Science Review 60:327–339.

——— (1967a) International Regions and the International System. Chicago: Rand McNally.

——— (1967b) "Pearl Harbor: Deterrence theory and decision theory." Journal of Peace Research 2: 89–105.

——— (1968a) "Delineating international regions," pp. 317–352 in J. D. Singer (ed.), Quantitative International Politics. New York: The Free Press.

——— (1968b) "Components of an operational theory of international alliance formation." Journal of Conflict Resolution 12:285–301.

——— (1968c) "Is there a long-run trend toward concentration in the international system?" Comparative Political Studies 1:103–122.

——— (1968d) "Regional trading patterns, 1938–1963." International Studies Quarterly 12:360–379.

——— (1969) "The young science of international politics." World Politics 22:87–94.

——— (1970a) "Methodological and theoretical schools in international relations," pp. 87–106 in N. D. Palmer (ed.), A Design for International Relations Research: Scope, Theory, Methods and Relevance. Philadelphia: American Academy of Political and Social Sciences.

—— (1970b) What Price Vigilance? New Haven, Conn.: Yale University Press.

—— (1971) "An empirical typology of international military alliances." Midwest Journal of Political Science 15:262–289.

—— (1972) "The revolt of the masses: Public opinion on military expenditures," pp. 299–319 in B. M. Russett (ed.), Peace, War, and Numbers. Beverly Hills, Calif.: Sage Publications.

—— (1973) "New editors for an 'old' journal." Journal of Conflict Resolution 17:3–6.

—— (1976a) "Apologia pro vita sua," pp. 31–37 in J. N. Rosenau (ed.), In Search of Global Patterns. New York: The Free Press.

—— (1976b) "Evaluating the evaluations," pp. v–x in F. W. Hoole and D. A. Zinnes (eds.), Quantitative International Politics: An Appraisal. New York: Praeger.

Russett, B. M., and H. R. Alker, Jr., K. W. Deutsch, and H. D. Lasswell (1964) World Handbook of Political and Social Indicators. New Haven, Conn.: Yale University Press.

Russett, B. M., and E. C. Hanson (1975) Interest and Ideology. San Francisco: W. H. Freeman.

Russett, B. M., and C. Lamb (1969) "Global patterns of diplomatic exchange, 1963–64." Journal of Peace Research 1:37–55.

Russett, B. M., and R. J. Monsen (1975) "Bureaucracy and polyarchy as predictors of performance: A cross-national examination." Comparative Political Studies 8:5–31.

Russo, A. J. (1972) "Economic and social correlates of government control in South Vietnam," pp. 314–324 in I. Feierabend, R. Feierabend, and T. Gurr (eds.), Anger, Violence and Politics: Theories and Research. Englewood Cliffs, N.J.: Prentice-Hall.

Sabrosky, A. N. (1975) "From Bosnia to Sarajero." Journal of Conflict Resolution 9:3–24.

—— (1980) "Interstate alliances: Their reliability and the expansion of war," pp. 161–198 in J. D. Singer (ed.), Correlates of War: II. New York: The Free Press.

Sallagar, F. (1975) The Road to Total War. New York: Van Nostrand Reinhold.

Salmore, B. G., and S. A. Salmore (1975) "Regime constraints and foreign policy behavior." Paper presented at the annual meeting of the American Political Science Association, San Francisco.

Salmore, S. A. (1972) "National attributes and foreign policy: A multivariate analysis." Ph.D. dissertation, Princeton University.

References

Salmore, S. A., and C. F. Hermann (1969) "The effect of size, development, and accountability on foreign policy." Peace Research Society (International) Papers 14:15–30.

Salmore, S. A., M. G. Hermann, C. F. Hermann, and B. Salmore (1978) "Conclusion: Toward integrating the perspectives," pp. 191–209 in M. East, S. A. Salmore, and C. F. Hermann (eds.), Why Nations Act. Beverly Hills, Calif.: Sage Publications.

Salmore, S. A., and D. Munton (1974) "An empirically based typology of foreign policy behaviors," pp. 329–352 in J. N. Rosenau (ed.), Comparing Foreign Policies. New York: Halsted/John Wiley.

Sawyer, J. (1967) "Dimensions of nations: Size, wealth, and politics." American Journal of Sociology 73:145–172.

Sawyer, J., and H. Guetzkow (1965) "Bargaining and negotiation in international relations," pp. 460–520 in H. C. Kelman (ed.), International Behavior: A Social-Psychological Analysis. New York: Holt, Rinehart and Winston.

Scheffler, I. (1967) Science and Subjectivity. Indianapolis: Bobbs-Merrill.

Schelling, T. C. (1960) The Strategy of Conflict. New York: Oxford University Press.

——— (1966) Arms and Influence. New Haven, Conn.: Yale University Press.

Schelling, T. C., and M. H. Halperin (1961) Strategy and Arms Control. New York: Twentieth Century Fund.

Schmitter, P. C. (1969a) "Further notes on operationalizing some variables related to regional integration." International Organization 23:327–336.

——— (1969b) "Three neo-functional hypotheses about international integration." International Organization 23:161–166.

——— (1970) "A revised theory of regional integration." International Organization 24:836–869.

Schuman, F. (1933) International Politics. New York: McGraw-Hill.

Schwarzenberger, G. (1941) Power Politics. New York: Praeger.

——— (1962) The Frontiers of International Law. London: Stevens.

Schwerin, E. W. (1977) "U.S. foreign relations for 1963," pp. 301–314 in R. J. Rummel (ed.), Field Theory Evolving. Beverly Hills, Calif.: Sage Publications.

Scott, A. M. (1965) The Revolution in Statecraft: Informal Penetration. New York: Random House.

Selsam, H., and H. Martel (eds.) (1963) Reader in Marxist Philosophy. New York: International Publishers.

Sewell, J. P. (1966) Functionalism and World Politics. Princeton, N.J.: Princeton University Press.

References

Shapere, D. (1964) "The structure of scientific revolutions." Philosophical Review 73:383–394.

———— (1971) "The paradigm concept." Science 172:706–709.

Shapiro, M. J. (1966) "Cognitive rigidity and perceptual orientations in an inter-nation simulation." Evanston, Ill.: Northwestern University (mimeographed).

Shapiro, M. J., and G. M. Bonham (1973) "Cognitive process and foreign policy decision-making." International Studies Quarterly 17:147–174.

Shimony, A. (1976) "Comments on two epistemological theses of Thomas Kuhn," pp. 569–588 in R. S. Cohen et al. (eds.), Boston Studies in Philosophy of Science, Vol. 39. Dordrecht, Holland: D. Reidel.

Shubik, M. (1959) Strategy and Market Structure. New York: John Wiley.

———— (1967) "The uses of game theory," pp. 239–272 in J. C. Charlesworth (ed.), Contemporary Political Analysis. New York: The Free Press.

Sigal, L. V. (1979) "Rethinking the unthinkable." Foreign Policy 34: 35–51.

Sigler, J. H. (1969) "News flow in the North African international subsystem." International Studies Quarterly 13:381–397.

———— (1972a) "Reliability problems in the measurement of international events in the elite press," pp. 9–30 in J. H. Sigler, J. O. Field, and M. L. Adelman (eds.), Applications of Event Data Analysis. Sage Professional Paper in International Studies, 02–002. Beverly Hills, Calif.: Sage Publications.

———— (1972b) "Cooperation and conflict in the United States-Soviet-Chinese relations, 1966–1971." Peace Research Society (International) Papers 19:107–128.

Simon, H. (1957) Administrative Behavior. 2nd ed. New York: Macmillan.

Singer, J. D. (1958) "Threat-perception and the armament-tension dilemma." Journal of Conflict Resolution 2:90–105.

———— (1960) "Theorizing about theory in international politics." Journal of Conflict Resolution 4:431–442.

———— (1961) "The level of analysis problem in international relations," pp. 72–92 in K. Knorr and S. Verba (eds.), The International System: Theoretical Essays. Princeton, N.J.: Princeton University Press.

———— (1963) "Inter-nation influence: a formal model." American Political Science Review 57:420–430.

———— (1964) "Soviet and American foreign policy attitudes: a content analysis of elite articulations." Journal of Conflict Resolution 8:424–485.

———— (1965) "Data-making in international relations." Behavioral Science 10:68–80.

———— (1966a) "National alliance commitments and war involvement, 1815–1945." Peace Research Society (International) Papers 5:109–140.

———— (1966b) "The behavioral science approach to international relations: Payoff and prospects." SAIS Review 10:12–20.

———— (ed.) (1968a) Quantitative International Politics. New York: The Free Press.

———— (1968b) "Alliance aggregation and the onset of war, 1815–1945," pp. 245–286 in J. D. Singer (ed.), Quantitative International Politics. New York: The Free Press.

———— (1969a) "Formal alliances, 1816–1965: An extension of the basic data." Journal of Peace Research 3:257–282.

———— (1969b) "The incompleat theorist: Insight without evidence," pp. 62–86 in K. Knorr and J. N. Rosenau (eds.), Contending Approaches to International Relations. Princeton, N.J.: Princeton University Press.

———— (1970) "From a 'a study of war' to peace research: Some criteria and strategies." Journal of Conflict Resolution 14:527–542.

———— (1972) The Scientific Study of Politics: An Approach to Foreign Policy Analysis. Morristown, N.J.: General Learning Press.

———— (1976) "The correlates of war project: Continuity, diversity, and convergence," pp. 21–42 in F. Hoole and D. Zinnes (eds.), Quantitative International Politics. New York: Praeger.

———— (1979a) "The management of serious international disputes: Historical patterns since the Congress of Vienna." Paper presented to the 11th World Congress of the International Political Science Association, Moscow.

———— (ed.) (1979b) The Correlates of War: I. New York: The Free Press.

———— (ed.) (1980) The Correlates of War: II. New York: The Free Press.

Singer, J. D., S. Bremer, and J. Stuckey (1972) "Capability distribution, uncertainty, and major power war, 1820–1965," pp. 19–48 in B. M. Russett (ed.) Peace, War, and Numbers. Beverly Hills, Calif.: Sage Publications.

Singer, J. D., and M. Small (1966a) "National alliance commitments and war involvement, 1815–1945." Peace Research Society (International) Papers 5:109–140.

———— (1966b) "The composition and status ordering of the international system, 1815–1940." World Politics 18:236–282.

———— (1968) "Alliance aggregation and the onset of war, 1815–1945," pp. 247–286 in J. D. Singer (ed.), Quantitative International Politics. New York: The Free Press.

References

———— (1972) The Wages of War, 1816–1965: A Statistical Handbook. New York: John Wiley.

Singer, J. D., and M. Wallace (1970) "Intergovernmental organization and the preservation of peace, 1816–1965: Some bivariate relationships." International Organization 24:520–547.

Singer, M. R. (1972) Weak States in a World of Power. New York: The Free Press.

Singer, M. R., and B. Sensenig III (1963) "Elections within the United Nations." International Organization 17:901–925.

Siverson, R. M. (1973) "Role and perception in international crisis: The cases of Israeli and Egyptian decision makers in national capitals and the United Nations." International Organization 27:329–346.

Siverson, R. M., and J. King (1979) "Alliances and the expansion of war," pp. 37–50 in J. D. Singer and M. D. Wallace (eds.), To Augur Well. Beverly Hills, Calif.: Sage Publications.

Small M., and J. D. Singer (1969) "Formal alliances, 1815–1965: An extension of the basic data." Journal of Peace Research 6:257–282.

———— (1973) "Diplomatic importance of states, 1816–1970: an extension and refinement of the indicator." World Politics 25:579–599.

———— (1976) "The war proneness of democratic regimes." Jerusalem Journal of International Relations 1:49–69.

———— (1979) "Conflict in the international system, 1816–1977: Historical trends and polity futures," pp. 89–115 in C. K. Kegley and P. J. McGowan (eds.), Challenges to America. Sage International Yearbook of Foreign Policy Studies, Vol. 4. Beverly Hills, Calif.: Sage Publications.

Small, M. et al. (forthcoming) The Strength of Nations: Comparative Capabilities Since Waterloo.

Smith, B. L. R. (1966) The RAND Corporation: Case Study of a Non-Profit Research Institute. Cambridge, Mass.: Harvard University Press.

Smith, R. (1969) "On the structure of foreign news: Comparison of the New York Times and the Indian White Papers." Journal of Peace Research 1:23–36.

Smoke, R. (1977) War: Controlling Escalation. Cambridge, Mass.: Harvard University Press.

Smoker, P. L. (1963) "A mathematical study of the present arms race." General Systems Yearbook 8:51–59.

———— (1964a) "Fear in the arms race: A mathematical study." Journal of Peace Research 1:55–64.

———— (1964b) "Sino-Indian relations: A study in trade, communication and defense." Journal of Peace Research 2:65–76.

———— (1965a) "A preliminary empirical study of an international integrative subsystem." International Associations 1:638–646.

References

———— (1965b) "Trade, defense, and the Richardson theory of arms races." Journal of Peace Research 2:161–176.

———— (1966) "The arms race: A wave model." Peace Research Society (International) Papers 4:151–192.

———— (1967) "Nation-state escalation and international integration." Journal of Peace Research 1:61–75.

———— (1969) "A time series analysis of Sino-Indian relations." Journal of Conflict Resolution 13:172–191.

———— (1972) "International processes simulations: A description," pp. 315–365 in J. A. Laponce and P. L. Smoker (eds.), Experimentation and Simulation in Political Science. Toronto: University of Toronto Press.

Snyder, G. H. (1961) Deterrence and Defense: Toward a Theory of National Security. Princeton, N.J.: Princeton University Press.

———— (1965) "The balance of power and the power of terror," pp. 184–201 in P. Seabury (ed.), The Balance of Power. San Francisco: Chandler.

———— (1972) "Crisis bargaining," pp. 217–256 in C. F. Hermann (ed.), International Crises: Insights from Behavioral Research. New York: The Free Press.

Snyder, G. H., and P. Diesing (1977) Conflict Among Nations: Bargaining, Decision Making, and System Structure. Princeton, N.J.: Princeton University Press.

Snyder, J. (1978) "Rationality at the brink: The role of cognitive processes in failures of deterrence." World Politics 30:345–365.

Snyder, R. C., H. Bruck, and B. Sapin (1954) Decision-Making as an Approach to Study of International Politics. Princeton, N.J.: Foreign Policy Analysis Project, Princeton University.

———— (eds.) (1962) Foreign Policy Decision-Making. New York: The Free Press.

Snyder, R. C., and G. Paige (1958) "The United States decision to resist aggression in Korea: The application of an analytic scheme." Administrative Science Quarterly 3:342–378.

Spanier, J. (1960, 1977) American Foreign Policy Since World War II. 1st and 7th eds. New York: Praeger.

———— (1972) Games Nations Play. New York: Praeger.

Sprout, H., and M. Sprout (1951) Foundations of National Power. Princeton, N.J.: D. Van Nostrand.

———— (1971) Toward a Politics of the Planet Earth. New York: Van Nostrand Reinhold.

Spykman, N. (1942) America's Strategy in World Politics: The United States and the Balance of Power. New York: Harcourt, Brace and World.

References

Starr, H. (1972) War Coalitions: The Distribution of Payoffs and Losses. Lexington, Mass.: Lexington Books.

———— (1974) "The quantitative international relations scholar as surfer: Riding the 'fourth' wave." Journal of Conflict Resolution 18:336–368.

Stassen, G. H. (1972) "Individual preference versus role-constraint in policy making: Senatorial responses to Secretaries Acheson and Dulles." World Politics 27:96–119.

Stein, A. S. (1980) The Nation at War. Baltimore: Johns Hopkins University Press.

Steinbruner, J. D. (1974) The Cybernetic Theory of Decision. Princeton, N.J.: Princeton University Press.

Stephens, J. (1973) "The Kuhnian paradigm and political inquiry: An appraisal." American Journal of Political Science 17:467–488.

Stinchcombe, A. (1968) Constructing Social Theories. New York: Harcourt, Brace and World.

Stockholm International Peace Research Institute (SIPRI) (1968/69) Stockholm International Peace Research Institute Yearbook of World Armaments and Disarmament. New York: Humanities Press.

Stoessinger, J. G. (1961, 1975) The Might of Nations. 1st and 5th eds. New York: Random House.

———— (1965) The United Nations and the Superpowers. New York: Random House.

———— (1971) Nations in Darkness: China, Russia, and America. New York: Random House.

———— (1978) Why Nations Go to War. New York: St. Martin's Press.

Stohl, M. (1975) "War and domestic political violence: The case of the United States, 1890–1970." Journal of Conflict Resolution 19:379–416.

Sullivan, J. D. (1972) "Cooperating to conflict: Sources of informal alignments," pp. 115–138 in B. M. Russett (ed.), Peace, War, and Numbers. Beverly Hills, Calif.: Sage Publications.

Sullivan, M. P. (1972) "Symbolic involvement as a correlate of escalation: The Vietnam case," pp. 185–213 in B. M. Russett (ed.), Peace, War, and Numbers. Beverly Hills, Calif.: Sage Publications.

———— (1976) International Relations: Theories and Evidence. Englewood Cliffs, N.J.: Prentice-Hall.

———— (1978) "Competing frameworks and the study of contemporary international politics." Journal of International Studies (Millennium) 7:93–110.

———— (1979a) "Foreign policy articulations and U.S. conflict behavior," pp. 215–235 in J. D. Singer and M. D. Wallace (eds.), To Augur Well. Beverly Hills, Calif.: Sage Publications.

———— (1979b) "Transnationalism, power politics, and the realities of the present system." Paper prepared for the Western Political Science Association annual meeting, Portland, Oregon.

Taagepera, R. (1968) "Growth curves of empires." General Systems Yearbook 13:171–175.

Tanter, R. (1966) "Dimensions of nations, 1958–60." Journal of Conflict Resolution 10:41–64.

——— (1974) Modelling and Managing International Conflicts. Beverly Hills, Calif.: Sage Publications.

Tarski, A. (1949) "The semantic conception of truth," pp. 52–84 in H. Feigl and W. Sellars (eds.), Readings in Philosophical Analysis. New York: Appleton-Century-Crofts.

Taylor, C. L., and M. Hudson (1972) World Handbook of Political and Social Indicators. 2nd ed. New Haven, Conn.: Yale University Press.

Taylor, T. (1978a) "Power politics," pp. 122–140 in T. Taylor (ed.), Approaches and Theory in International Relations. London: Longman.

——— (ed.) (1978b) Approaches and Theory in International Relations. London: Longman.

Tedeschi, J. T., and T. V. Bonoma (1977) "Measures of last resort: Coercion and aggression in bargaining," pp. 213–246 in D. Druckman (ed.), Negotiations. Beverly Hills, Calif.: Sage Publications.

Teune, H., and S. Synnestvedt (1965) "Measuring international alignment." Orbis 9:171–189.

Thompson, J. (1968) "How could Vietnam happen? An autopsy." Atlantic Monthly, April 1968, pp. 47–53.

Thompson, K. W. (1952) "The study of international politics: A survey of trends and developments." Review of Politics 14:433–443.

——— (1960) Political Realism and the Crisis of World Politics: An American Approach to Foreign Policy. Princeton, N.J.: Princeton University Press.

Thompson, W. R., R. D. Duval, and A. Dia (1979) "Wars, alliances, and military expenditures." Journal of Conflict Resolution 23:629–654.

Thompson, W. R., and G. Modelski (1976) "Global conflict intensity and great power summitry behavior." Journal of Conflict Resolution 21: 339–376.

Thorndike, T. (1978) "The revolutionary approach: The Marxist perspective," pp. 54–99 in T. Taylor (ed.), Approaches and Theory in International Relations. London: Longman.

Thorson, S. J. (1974) "National political adaptation," pp. 71–114 in J. N. Rosenau (ed.), Comparing Foreign Policies. New York: Halsted/John Wiley.

——— (1976) "The inter-nation simulation project: A methodological appraisal," pp. 284–327 in F. Hoole and D. Zinnes (eds.), Quantitative International Politics. New York: Praeger.

References

Tornebohm, H. (1976) "Inquiring systems and paradigms," pp. 635–654 in R. S. Cohen et al. (eds.), Boston Studies in Philosophy of Science, Vol. 39. Dordrecht, Holland: D. Reidel.

Toulmin, S. (1950) The Place of Reason in Ethics. Cambridge: Cambridge University Press.

——— (1953) Philosophy of Science: An Introduction. New York: Harper & Row.

——— (1967) "Conceptual revolutions in science," pp.331–347 in R. S. Cohen and M. W. Wartofsky (eds.), Boston Studies in Philosophy of Science, Vol. 3. Dordrecht, Holland: D. Reidel.

——— (1970) "Does the distinction between normal and revolutionary science hold water?," pp. 39–47 in I. Lakatos and A. Musgrave (eds.), Criticism and the Growth of Knowledge. Cambridge: Cambridge University Press.

——— (1972) Human Understanding, Vol. 1. Princeton, N.J.: Princeton University Press.

——— (1976) "History, praxis and the 'Third World'," pp. 655–675 in R. S. Cohen, et al. (eds.), Boston Studies in Philosophy of Science, Vol. 39. Dordrecht, Holland: D. Reidel.

Tucker, R. W. (1952) "Professor Morgenthau's theory of political realism." American Political Review 46:214–224.

——— (1958) "The study of international politics." World Politics 10:639–647.

——— (1968) Nation or Empire. Baltimore: Johns Hopkins University Press.

Turner, G. B., and R. D. Challener (eds.) (1960) National Security in the Nuclear Age: Basic Facts and Theories. New York: Praeger.

Urmson, J. O. (1968) The Emotive Theory of Ethics. New York: Oxford University Press.

Vasquez, J. A. (1974a) "The power of paradigms: An empirical evaluation of international relations inquiry." Ph.D. dissertation, Syracuse University.

——— (1974b) "Alternative perspectives on the U.N. conference on the human environment," pp. 60–83 in J. Handelman, H. B. Shapiro, and J. A. Vasquez, Introductory Case Studies for International Relations: Vietnam, the Middle East and the Environmental Crisis. Chicago: Rand McNally.

——— (1976a) "A learning theory of the American anti-Vietnam War movement." Journal of Peace Research 13:299–314.

——— (1976b) "Statistical findings in international politics." International Studies Quarterly 20:171–218.

Verba, S. (1961) "Assumptions of rationality and non-rationality in models of the international system," pp. 93–117 in K. Knorr and S. Verba (eds.), The International System: Theoretical Essays. Princeton, N.J.: Princeton University Press.

Vincent, J. (1968) "National attributes as predictors of delegate attitudes at the United Nations." American Political Science Review 62:916–931.

——— (1969) "The convergence of voting and attitude patterns at the United Nations." Journal of Politics 31:952–983..

——— (1971) "Predicting voting patterns in the general assembly." American Political Science Review 65:471–498.

——— (1972) "An application of attribute theory to general assembly voting patterns, and some implications." International Organization 26:551–583.

Voevodsky, J. (1969) "Quantitative behavior of warring nations." Journal of Psychology 72:269–292.

Wallace, M. (1970) "Status inconsistency, vertical mobility, and international war, 1825–1964." Ph.D. dissertation, University of Michigan.

——— (1971) "Power, status and international war." Journal of Peace Research 8:23–36.

——— (1972) "Status, formal organization, and arms levels as factors leading to the onset of war, 1820–1964," pp. 49–71 in B. M. Russett (ed.), Peace, War, and Numbers. Beverly Hills, Calif.: Sage Publications.

——— (1973a) War and Rank Among Nations. Lexington, Mass.: D. C. Heath.

——— (1973b) "Alliance polarization, cross-cutting, and international war, 1815–1964." Journal of Conflict Resolution 17:575–604.

——— (1975) "Clusters of nations in the global system, 1865–1964." International Studies Quarterly 19:67–110.

——— (1979a) "Arms races and escalation: Some new evidence." Journal of Conflict Resolution 23:3–16.

——— (1979b) "Early warning indicators from the Correlates of War project," pp. 17–35 in J. D. Singer and M. Wallace (eds.), To Augur Well. Beverly Hills, Calif.: Sage Publications.

——— (1980) "Accounting for superpower arms spending," pp. 259–273 in P. J. McGowan and C. W. Kegley (eds.), Threats, Weapons, and Foreign Policy. Sage International Yearbook in Foreign Policy Studies, Vol. 5. Beverly Hills, Calif.: Sage Publications.

——— (1981) "Old nails in new coffins: The para bellum hypothesis revisited." Journal of Peace Research 18:91–96.

Wallace, M., and J. D. Singer (1970) "Inter-governmental organization in the global system, 1816–1964: A quantitative description." International Organization 24:239–287.

Wallace, M., and J. M. Wilson (1978) "Non-linear arms race models." Journal of Peace Research 15:175–192.

Wallensteen, P. (1968) "Characteristics of economic sanctions." Journal of Peace Research 3:248–267.

——— (1973) Structure and War. Stockholm: Raben and Sjogren.

Walleri, R. D. (1978) "The political economy literature on North-South relations: Alternative approaches and empirical evidence." International Studies Quarterly 22:587–624.

Wallerstein, I. (1974) "The rise and future demise of the world capitalist system." Comparative Studies in Society and History 14:390.

——— (1976) The Modern World System. New York: Academic Press.

Waltz, K. N. (1959) Man, the State, and War. New York: Columbia University Press.

——— (1964) "The stability of a bipolar world." Daedalus 93:982–907.

——— (1967) Foreign Policy and Democratic Politics. Boston: Little, Brown.

——— (1975) "Theory of international relations," pp. 1–85 in F. I. Greenstein and N. W. Polsby (eds.), International Politics, Handbook of Political Science, Vol. 8. Reading, Mass.: Addison-Wesley.

Waskow, A. J. (1964) "New roads to a world without war." Yale Review 54:85–111.

Watkins, J. (1970) "Against normal science," pp. 25–37 in I. Lakatos and A. Musgrave (eds.), Criticism and the Growth of Knowledge. Cambridge: Cambridge University Press.

Weede, E. (1976) "Overwhelming preponderance as a pacifying condition among contiguous Asian dyads, 1950–1969." Journal of Conflict Resolution 20:395–411.

——— (1980) "Arms races and escalation: Some persisting doubts." Journal of Conflict Resolution 24:285–287.

Weigert, K., and R. Riggs (1969) "Africa and United Nations elections: an aggregate data analysis." International Organization 23:1–19.

Weiss, H. K. (1963) "Stochastic models for the duration and magnitude of a 'deadly quarrel.'" Operations Research 11:101–121.

Weissberg, R. (1969) "Nationalism, integration, and French and German elites." International Organization 23:337–347.

Wheeler, H. (1980) "Postwar industrial growth," pp. 258–284 in J. D. Singer (ed.), The Correlates of War: II. New York: The Free Press.

White, R. K. (1949) "Hitler, Roosevelt, and the nature of war propaganda." Journal of Abnormal and Social Psychology 44:157–175.

——— (1965) Images in the Context of International Conflict: Soviet Perceptions of the U.S. and U.S.S.R.," pp. 236–276 in H. C. Kelman (ed.), International Behavior. New York: Holt, Rinehart and Winston.

References

———— (1966) "Misperception and the Vietnam War." Journal of Social Issues 22:1–164.

———— (1970) Nobody Wanted War. Garden City, N.Y.: Doubleday.

———— (1977) "Misperception in the Arab-Israeli conflict." Journal of Social Issues 33:190–222.

Wiegele, T. C. (1973) "Decision-making in an international crisis." International Studies Quarterly 17:295–335.

———— (1978) "The psychophysiology of elite stress in five international crises." International Studies Quarterly 22:467–511.

Wiener, N. (1954) The Human Use of Human Beings. Boston: Houghton Mifflin.

Wight, M. (1946) Power Politics. "Looking Forward" Pamphlet No. 8. London: Royal Institute of International Affairs.

———— (1966) "Why is there no international theory?" in H. Butterfield and M. Wight (eds.), Diplomatic Investigations. Cambridge, Mass.: Harvard University Press.

Wilkenfeld, J. (1968) "Domestic and foreign conflict behavior of nations." Journal of Peace Research 1:56–69.

———— (1975) "A time-series perspective on conflict behavior in the Middle East," pp. 177–212 in P. J. McGowan (ed.), Sage International Yearbook of Foreign Policy Studies, Vol. 3. Beverly Hills, Calif.: Sage Publications.

Wilkenfeld, J., G. W. Hopple, and P. J. Rossa (1979) "Sociopolitical indicators of conflict and cooperation," pp. 109–151 in J. D. Singer and M. Wallace (eds.), To Augur Well. Beverly Hills, Calif.: Sage Publications.

Wilkenfeld, J., G. W. Hopple, P. J. Rossa, and S. J. Andriole (1980) Foreign Policy Behavior. Beverly Hills, Calif.: Sage Publications.

Willetts, P. (1972) "Cluster-bloc analysis and statistical inference." American Political Science Review 66:569–582.

Williams, L. P. (1970) "Normal science, scientific revolutions and the history of science," pp. 49–50 in I. Lakatos and A. Musgrave (eds.), Criticism and the Growth of Knowledge. Cambridge: Cambridge University Press.

Williams, W. A. (1959) The Tragedy of American Diplomacy. New York: Delta.

Wilson, J. (1956) Language and the Pursuit of Truth. Cambridge: Cambridge University Press.

Wittman, D. (1979) "How a war ends." Journal of Conflict Resolution 23:743–763.

Wohlstetter, A. (1959) "The Delicate Balance of Terror." Foreign Affairs 38:211–234.

Wolfers, A. (1949) "Statesmanship and moral choice." World Politics 1:175–195.

——— (1951) "The pole of power and the pole of indifference." World Politics 4:39–63.

——— (1952) "National security as an ambiguous symbol." Political Science Quarterly 67:481–502.

——— (1959) "The actors in international politics," pp. 83–106 in W. T. R. Fox (ed.), Theoretical Aspects of International Relations. South Bend, Ind.: University of Notre Dame Press.

——— (1962) Discord and Collaboration. Baltimore: Johns Hopkins University Press.

Wolin, S. T. (1968) "Paradigms and political theories," pp. 125–152 in P. King and B. C. Parekh (eds.), Politics and Experience. Cambridge: Cambridge University Press.

Worrall, J. (1978) "The ways in which the methodology of scientific research programmes improves on Popper's methodology," pp. 45–70 in G. Radnitzky and G. Andersson (eds.), Progress and Rationality in Science. Dordrecht, Holland: D. Reidel.

Wright, Q. (1942, 1965a) A Study of War. 1st and 2nd eds. Chicago: University of Chicago Press.

——— (1955) The Study of International Relations. New York: Appleton-Century-Crofts.

——— (1965b) "The escalation of international conflicts." Journal of Conflict Resolution 9:434–449.

Wright, Q., and C. J. Nelson (1939) "American attitudes toward Japan and China, 1937–38." Public Opinion Quarterly 3:46–62.

Yamamoto, Y., and S. Bremer (1980) "Wider wars and restless nights: Major power intervention in ongoing war," pp. 199–229 in J. D. Singer (ed.), The Correlates of War: II. New York: The Free Press.

Yeselson, A., and A. Gaglione (1977) A Dangerous Place: The United Nations as a Weapon in World Politics. New York: Grossman.

Young, O. R. (1967) The Intermediaries: Third Parties in International Crises. Princeton, N.J.: Princeton University Press.

——— (1968) The Politics of Force. Princeton, N.J.: Princeton University Press.

——— (1969) "Professor Russett: Industrious tailor to a naked emperor." World Politics 21:486–511.

——— (1972) "The actors in world politics," pp. 125–144 in J. N. Rosenau, V. Davis, and M. East (eds.), The Analysis of International Politics. New York: The Free Press.

Young, R. (1977) "Perspectives on international crisis." International Studies Quarterly 21:5–14.

References

Zaninovich, G. (1962) "Pattern analysis of variables within the international system: The Sino-Soviet example." Journal of Conflict Resolution 6:253–268.

Zartman, I. W. (1977) "Negotiation as a joint decision-making process." Journal of Conflict Resolution 21:619–638.

Zimmerman, W. (1973) "Issue area and foreign policy process: A research note in search of a general theory." American Political Science Review 67:1204–1212.

Zimmern, A. (1936) The League of Nations and the Rule of Law. London: Macmillan.

——— (1939) (ed.) University Teaching of International Relations. Paris: International Institute of Intellectual Co-operation, League of Nations.

Zinn, H. (1971) The Politics of History. Boston: Beacon Press.

Zinnes, D. (1966) "A comparison of hostile state behavior in simulate and historical data." World Politics 18:474–502.

——— (1967) "An analytical study of the balance of power theories." Journal of Peace Research 3:270–288.

——— (1968) "Expression and perception of hostility in pre-war crisis: 1914," pp. 85–119 in J. D. Singer (ed.), Quantitative International Politics. New York: The Free Press.

——— (1970) "Coalition theories and the balance of power," pp. 351–368 in S. Groennings, E. Kelley, and M. Leiserson (eds.), The Study of Coalition Behavior: Theoretical Perspectives and Cases from Four Countries. New York: Holt, Rinehart and Winston.

——— (1976) Contemporary Research in International Relations. New York: The Free Press.

Zinnes, D., R. C. North, and H. E. Koch (1961) "Capability, threat and the outbreak of war," pp. 469–482 in J. N. Rosenau (ed.), International Politics and Foreign Policy. New York: The Free Press.

Zinnes, D., J. Zinnes, and R. McClure (1972) "Hostility in diplomatic communication: A study of the 1914 crisis," pp. 139–162 in C. F. Hermann (ed.), International Crises. New York: The Free Press.

Name Index

Name Index

Name Index

Finnegan, R. B., 21 n, 26, 42–45
Finsterbusch, K., 163
Fisher, W. E., 163
Fleming, D. F., 122
Fleming, W. G., 163
Foltz, W., 106
Foster, C., 163
Fox, W. T. R., 14–16, 18, 43
Franck, T. M., 79
Frank, A. G., 122–125
Franke, W., 83
Frankel, J., 53
Freeman, L., 178 n, 179
Freudenburg, W., 79, 97
Frohock, F., 9 n

Gaddis, J. L., 122
Gaglione, A., 112
Galtung, J., 55, 57–58, 60, 84, 95, 108, 113, 123–125, 129, 163–164, 214, 221
Gamson, W., 52, 74, 139 n, 150, 164, 210
Garnham, D., 90–91
Garson, G. D., 123
Geller, D. S., 125, 154
George, A. L., 70, 72–74, 103–105, 208–210, 212, 218
George, J., 73
Gillespie, J. V., 108–109
Gleditsch, N., 164, 195
Gochman, C. S., 91 n, 92–93, 125, 148, 152, 154
Goodsell, R. A., 93, 108, 152
Graber, D. A., 163
Gray, C. S., 100
Green, P., 106 n
Gregg, P., 164, 197
Gregg, R., 164
Grieve, M. J., 96
Guetzkow, H., 20 n, 21 n, 43, 52, 56, 67–68, 73, 107, 138, 207
Gulick, E. V., 81

Haas, E. B., 43, 81, 111–113, 115–117, 152, 163
Haas, M., 21 n, 69, 87, 164, 219
Hahn, W., 123
Hall, D., 103, 218
Halperin, M. H., 76–77, 100, 208–210, 214
Hammond, P. Y., 76

Hamner, W. C., 107
Handelman, J., 3, 60, 118 n, 120, 129, 217, 224
Hanrieder, W. F., 86
Hanson, N., 28, 125
Harf, J. E., 146
Harsanyi, J. C., 100, 107
Hartmann, F. H., 56, 80
Havener, T., 139 n
Hayes, J. J., 72, 108, 153
Hayes, R., 108, 153
Hazlewood, L., 72, 108, 153
Healy, B., 82, 220
Hempel, C. G., 9 n, 121, 176 n
Henehan, M. T., 151
Hensley, T., 114
Heradstveit, D., 75, 213
Hermann, C. F., 56, 62–64, 67–72, 76–77, 100, 139 n, 142, 146–149, 151, 181, 206, 208–209
Hermann, M. G., 63–64, 67–68, 71, 100, 107, 146, 148–149, 151, 207–208
Herz, J., 43, 50, 55, 81, 98, 110
Hilton, G., 138
Hobson, J. A., 122
Hoffman, F., 164
Hoffmann, S., 17, 43–44, 46 n
Hoggard, G., 61–62, 139, 163
Hoivik, T., 124
Hollist, W. L., 68, 108
Holsti, K. J., 56, 164
Holsti, O. R., 72–74, 77–78, 82, 139 n, 141, 163–164, 188 n, 198, 208–210, 213
Hoole, F., 87, 90, 219
Hopkins, R., 55–56, 84, 120, 217
Hopmann, P. T., 82, 108, 164, 188 n
Hopple, G., 77, 139 n, 155
Horvath, W. J., 163
Hosoya, C., 102
Hovet, T., 112
Hudson, M., 138
Hughes, B., 79, 110
Huntington, S. P., 79

Ikle, F. C., 97, 107
Inglehart, R., 116

Jacobsen, K., 163
Jacobson, H. K., 111–112
Janis, I. L., 206–208

Name Index

Name Index

McElwain, D., 107
McGowan, P. J., 53, 62, 125, 139 n, 150, 154, 164
Mackinder, H., 55
McLellan, D., 74
McNamara, R. S., 99
McNeil, E. B., 107
Macridis, R., 52
Maddox, R. J., 122
Magdoff, H., 60, 122
Mahan, A., 55
Mahoney, R. B., 153
Mandel, E., 122
Mann, L., 70, 206–208
Manno, C. S., 163
Mansbach, R., 55–56, 75, 84, 120, 129, 151, 215, 217, 225 n
Mao Zedong, 35
Marcuse, H., 35, 122
Martel, H., 122
Marx, K., 35
Masterman, M., 1, 3–5, 18
May, E., 75, 206
Mazrui, A., 84, 113
Mendlovitz, S. H., 84, 113
Merritt, R., 116
Meyer, D. B., 17 n
Meyers, B., 163
Michalak, S. J., 118
Midlarsky, M., 92, 164, 198
Milbrath, L., 78
Milburn, T. W., 72, 98 n, 99
Mill, J. S., 10
Miller, W. E., 78
Mills, S., 53–54, 56, 120–121, 224
Milstein, J. S., 77, 139 n, 151, 164
Mitchell, E. J., 99
Mitchell, W., 164
Mitrany, D., 15, 34, 115
Modelski, G., 84, 108
Modigliani, A., 52, 74, 97, 139 n, 150, 164, 210
Moe, R. C., 79
Moll, K. D., 154
Monsen, R. J., 93
Moon, P. T., 15
Moore, D. W., 61
Morgan, P., 102, 212
Morgenstern, O., 100
Morgenthau, H. J., xii, 13 n, 15 n, 21 n, 66, 201; his research program, 19, 22, 31–35, 137, 184; his role in

the field, 16–19, 22–23, 26, 39, 41–64, 71, 80–81, 88–89, 104, 107, 109, 111–113, 115, 127, 137–138; his theory, 17–18, 26–33, 35–36, 39, 48–50, 54–59, 78, 80, 88, 109, 111, 115, 120, 123 n, 184, 206, 220, 224
Morse, E. L., 55, 84, 119, 217
Moses, L. E., 139 n
Moskos, C., 164
Mueller, J. E., 79, 97
Munton, D., 139 n
Musgrave, A., 10, 11 n

Namenworth, Z., 163
Naroll, F., 91 n
Naroll, R., 91 n, 163
Nash, J. F., 100
Neff, J., 123
Nelson, C. J., 163
Neumann, J. von, 100
Neustadt, R. E., 76
Newcombe, A. G., 56
Newton, I., 6 n, 7
Nicolson, H., 16, 107
Niebuhr, R., 16, 39, 43, 49, 109–110, 115–116
Noel, R. C., 56, 68, 207
Noel-Baker, P., 15
North, R. C., 55–56, 72–73, 77, 81, 93, 97, 141, 163–164, 196–197, 213, 222
Northedge, F. S., 52, 96
Novotny, E. J., 149 n
Nye, J. S., Jr., 3, 60, 84, 111–113, 116–119, 122, 125, 130, 152, 215, 217

Ohlstrom, B., 164
O'Leary, M. K., 3, 53–54, 56, 60, 112, 118 n, 120–121, 129–130, 151, 164, 217, 224
Olsen, L. J., 113, 124
Olson, R. S., 108
Olson, W. C., 13 n, 15, 16, 17, 26 n
Organski, A. F. K., 39, 55–56, 80–81, 97
Organski, K., 39, 55
Osgood, C. E., 53, 75, 100, 106
Osgood, R., 49, 99
Ostrom, C. W., 87, 90, 108, 219

Name Index

Page, B. I., 79
Paige, G., 64, 66, 69–70, 72, 77, 209
Parenti, M., 51, 125
Parsons, T., 83
Patchen, M., 107
Payne, K., 100
Pendley, R., 139 n, 150
Peterson, S., 139 n
Pfaltzgraff, R., 14 n, 16 n, 17, 22, 26 n, 83, 98 n
Phillips, W. R., 76–77, 153, 163, 210
Pipes, R., 100
Plano, J. C., 111
Platig, E. R., 17, 18
Pomper, G. M., 78
Pool, I., 78
Popper, K., 9–11, 28, 157
Porter, B., 13
Potter, P., 15
Powell, C. A., 62
Pruitt, D. G., 52, 70, 75, 107, 209
Ptolemy, 7
Puchala, D., 119, 163, 217

Quandt, R. E., 83, 101
Quester, G., 100, 102

Raiffa, H., 100
Ramsey, G. H., 61
Rapoport, A., 100, 105–107, 128, 212
Raser, J. R., 67, 107
Rattinger, H., 108
Ray, J. L., 92, 125, 140, 146, 154
Raymond, G., 100
Read, T., 99
Reinken, D. L., 83
Reinton, P. O., 164
Rhee, S. W., 85
Richardson, L. W., 5 n, 21 n, 89, 96, 108, 133–136, 139–140, 144, 155, 197
Rieselbach, L. N., 112, 163–164
Riggs, F. W., 83
Riggs, R., 110–112, 164
Riker, W., 82, 101
Rimkunas, R. V., 153
Robinson, J. A., 67 n, 70, 79, 209
Robinson, T. W., 18
Rochester, J. M., 114
Rogow, A., 73
Rosecrance, R., 83, 86–87, 100, 125, 220

Rosen, D. J., 139 n
Rosen, S., 96, 100, 125
Rosenau, J. N., 20–22, 43–44, 46 n, 53–54, 56–57, 59–64, 66, 68, 71, 78–79, 119, 125, 129, 146–148, 163
Rosenberg, A., 9
Rosenberg, M. J., 52, 74–75
Rossa, P., 77, 139 n, 155
Rourke, F. E., 76
Rowe, E. T., 112, 141, 163
Rubin, J., 107, 219
Ruge, M., 163–164
Ruggie, J. G., 113
Rummel, R. J., 55–59, 61, 85–86, 93–96, 100, 129, 138, 141, 151, 163–164, 179, 200 n, 222, 224
Russett, B. M., 6 n, 21 n, 37 n, 43, 48, 78, 82, 93, 102–104, 112, 116, 125, 137, 138 n, 139 n, 141, 154, 163–164, 198, 212–213
Russo, A. J., 99

Sabrosky, A. N., 82, 93
Sallagar, F., 100
Salmore, B. G., 63, 71, 146, 148–149, 151
Salmore, S. A., 62–64, 71, 139 n, 146–149, 151
Salzberg, J., 164, 198
Sapin, B., 44–46, 59, 64, 66
Savage, R., 115
Sawyer, J., 56, 107, 138, 163
Scheffler, I., 10 n, 11
Scheingold, S., 116
Schelling, T. C., 43–45, 98, 100–104, 106, 212
Schmitter, P. C., 116, 163
Schuman, F., 16, 17 n, 39, 56
Schwarzenberger, G., 16, 113
Schwerin, E. W., 85
Scott, A. M., 60
Selsam, H., 122
Sensenig, B., 164
Sewell, J. P., 115
Shapere, D., 3, 8, 10 n, 24, 39
Shapiro, M. J., 68, 74–75, 207–208
Shaver, P., 164
Shimony, A., 10 n
Shotwell, J. T., 15
Shubik, M., 100
Sigal, L. V., 100
Sigler, J. H., 139 n, 163

Name Index

Subject Index

Subject Index

Functionalism, 34, 53, 83, 114–115, 123

Game theory, 35, 39, 64, 83, 98, 100–108, 127, 212

Geographic factors in world politics, 15, 32, 55, 119, 152

Government, 27, 46, 224

Hard–liners, 212–213, 218

Harmony of interest, 14, 18

History, 14, 19, 28, 50, 75, 81, 83–84, 88, 110–111, 124 n, 133, 146, 152–153, 206, 212, 216–217; revisionist (U.S.), 51, 122–123

Homogeneity, 61–62, 94

Hostility, 69, 72, 94, 96, 213, 218, 222, 225

Idealism, 13–19, 23, 33, 49, 51, 60, 78, 84, 88, 106, 109–112, 115, 117–118, 128, 135, 136 n, 213, 215

Idealist paradigm, 13–18, 23, 34, 46, 80, 88, 113–114, 128–130, 133, 222

Ideology, 48, 51, 84, 98, 101, 108, 122–125, 127–129, 153, 212; dangers of, in the field, 104, 123 n, 124 n, 127–129

Images. See Perception

Imperialism, 32, 58, 122–125, 154, 215, 217

Individual characteristics, 107, 146, 150–151; and effect on foreign policy, 59, 61, 63, 68–69, 75, 206–210, 215

Induction, 10, 57–58, 130, 152

Information processing, 69–70, 75, 206, 208, 212, 225

Institutionalization, 14–15, 23, 84–85, 114

Integration, 19, 31, 33, 110, 114–118, 129, 147, 168, 169, 171, 189, 191–193, 195

Interactions, 71, 85, 88, 141, 146, 150–151, 211, 219, 223, 225

Interdependence, 55, 102, 118–119, 121, 125, 154

Interdisciplinary approaches to international relations, 15, 75, 84, 99, 107, 135, 223

Internal conflict, 57, 77, 138, 198

International law, 14–16, 19, 130, 135, 215; as a subfield, 112–114

International organization, 15–16, 18–19, 31, 45, 84–85, 92, 118, 129, 140, 147–148, 168, 171, 214; as a subfield, 110–112

International politics, change in, 54, 82–83, 88, 99, 101, 119, 121, 217

International regimes, 113, 215, 217

International relations inquiry: change in, 13–23, 33, 38–40, 47–131; definitions of, 14–15, 18, 24, 28, 29 n; future of, 225–227; goals of, 14–16, 18, 23, 47, 72, 88, 122; history of, 13–23, 132–141; most influential works in, 16–17, 42–47; scientific approach to, 16, 19–23, 225–227

Inter-Nation Simulation (INS). See Simulated International Processes (SIP)

Inter-University Comparative Foreign Policy project, 56

Invisible colleges, 5 n–6 n, 48

Isolationism, 31–32, 49, 78, 147, 168, 169, 171, 189, 191–192

Issue area, 34, 55, 59–61, 71, 75, 78, 86–87, 117–118, 120–121, 147, 149, 151, 198, 214–218, 223

Issue politics paradigm, 60, 86–87, 117, 120–121, 125, 142, 155–156, 175–176, 217–218, 223–225, 227

Issue position, 31, 33, 53–54, 225

Issues, 147, 168, 171, 189, 191–193, 217–218, 222–225

Issue salience, 31, 34, 150

Knowledge, 4–5, 15, 85, 89, 107, 157; production of, 9–12, 173–181, 183, 193–194, 199–202, 226–227

League of Nations, 14, 18, 31, 80, 114, 128

Learning theory, 75, 107, 208

Legitimacy, 27, 112, 224

Limited war, 96, 99, 101

Linkages, 119

McCarthy era, 51, 123

Marxism, 16, 35, 117, 122–123, 128, 143, 154–156, 175, 227

Marxist paradigm, 35, 51, 58, 60, 93, 97, 113, 122–125, 156, 222, 227